OXFORD MEDIEVAL TEXTS

General Editors

J. W. BINNS   D. D'AVRAY
M. S. KEMPSHALL   R. C. LOVE

THE LETTERS OF ADAM MARSH

THE LETTERS OF ADAM MARSH

VOLUME TWO

EDITED AND TRANSLATED BY
C. H. LAWRENCE

CLARENDON PRESS · OXFORD

OXFORD

UNIVERSITY PRESS

Great Clarendon Street, Oxford OX2 6DP

Oxford University Press is a department of the University of Oxford.
It furthers the University's objective of excellence in research, scholarship,
and education by publishing worldwide in

Oxford New York

Auckland Cape Town Dar es Salaam Hong Kong Karachi
Kuala Lumpur Madrid Melbourne Mexico City Nairobi
New Delhi Shanghai Taipei Toronto

With offices in

Argentina Austria Brazil Chile Czech Republic France Greece
Guatemala Hungary Italy Japan Poland Portugal Singapore
South Korea Switzerland Thailand Turkey Ukraine Vietnam

Oxford is a registered trade mark of Oxford University Press
in the UK and in certain other countries

Published in the United States
by Oxford University Press Inc., New York

British Library Cataloguing in Publication Data

Data available

Library of Congress Cataloging in Publication Data

Data available

Typeset by Anne Joshua, Oxford
Printed in Great Britain
on acid-free paper by
MPG Books Group, Bodmin and King's Lynn

ISBN 978-0-19-957584-8

3 5 7 9 10 8 6 4 2

ACKNOWLEDGEMENTS

In preparing this successor to the first volume of Adam's letters, my debts to other scholars have increased in number and degree. In the first place, I want to record my deep gratitude to the editors of the series, Professor David d'Avray, Dr J. W. Binns, Dr Rosalind Love, and Dr Matthew Kempshall, who have continued with inexhaustible patience to read my texts and translations both in typescript and proof. They have saved me from several mistakes and their comments and suggestions have been invaluable. I am much indebted to Dr Patricia Neuton, who took great pains to advise on the ambiguities of Brother Adam's Anglo-Norman postscript to Queen Eleanor; also to Dr Michael Robson, OFM, who kindly supplied me with notes about some of his Franciscan brethern of the thirteenth century. I should also like to express my gratitude to my old friend Professor Donald Logan for his continuing encouragement over the years, not least for the characteristic generosity with which, at an earlier stage of the project, he made me a present of his own volume of Brewer's edition of the letters in the Rolls Series. Margaret Du Boulay kindly helped with the index. Finally I want to record my thanks to Dr Bonnie Blackburn, who copy-edited my texts with meticulous care and scholarly acumen.

CONTENTS

ABBREVIATIONS   ix

THE LETTERS   291

INDEX OF QUOTATIONS AND ALLUSIONS   649

INDEX   654

ABBREVIATIONS

AFH	*Archivum Franciscanum Historicum*
AHDL	*Archives d'histoire doctrinale et littéraire du Moyen Age*
ALKG	*Archiv für Litteratur und Kirchengeschichte des Mittelalters*, ed. H. Denifle and F. Ehrle, 6 vols. (Berlin and Freiburg, 1885–92)
Ann. Mon.	*Annales Monastici*, ed. H. R. Luard, 4 vols. (RS, 1864–9)
Berger	*Les Registres d'Innocent IV*, ed. E. Berger (École française de Rome, 1884–1921)
BHL	*Bibliotheca Hagiographica Latina*, 2 vols. (Société des Bollandistes; Brussels, 1898–1901)
BL	British Library
BLR	*Bodleian Library Record*
Book of Fees	*The Book of Fees, commonly called Testa de Nevill*, 3 vols. (HMSO, 1920–31)
BRUO	A. B. Emden, *A Biographical Register of the University of Oxford to AD 1500*, 3 vols. (Oxford, 1957–9)
CChaR	*Calendar of Charter Rolls* (HMSO)
CCR	*Calendar of Close Rolls* (HMSO)
Chron. Maj.	*Mathaei Parisiensis Chronica Majora*, ed. H. R. Luard, 7 vols. (RS, 1872–9)
CLibR	*Calendar of Liberate Rolls* (HMSO)
Councils & Synods	*Councils and Synods with other Documents Relating to the English Church*, ii, ed. F. M. Powicke and C. R. Cheney (Oxford, 1964)
CPL	*Calendar of Papal Letters Relating to Great Britain and Ireland, 1198–1302*, ed. W. H. Bliss (HMSO, 1898)
CPR	*Calendar of Patent Rolls* (HMSO)
CSEL	*Corpus Scriptorum Ecclesiasticorum Latinorum*
Curia Regis Rolls	*Curia Regis Rolls, 1243–45* (HMSO, 1922–)

CYS	Canterbury and York Society
Eccleston	*Fratris Thomae vulgo dicti de Eccleston de Adventu Fratrum Minorum in Angliam*, ed. A. G. Little (2nd edn., Manchester, 1951)
EHR	*English Historical Review*
Fasti	*Fasti Ecclesiae Anglicane 1066–1300*, i (St Paul's London); iii (Diocese of Lincoln), ed. D. E. Greenway (London 1968, 1977)
Grosseteste Epistolae	*Roberti Grosseteste Episcopi Lincolniensis Epistolae*, ed. H. R. Luard (RS, 1861)
HUO	*History of the University of Oxford*, i: *The Early Schools*, ed. J. I. Catto (Oxford, 1984)
JEH	*Journal of Ecclesiastical History*
MGH SS	Monumenta Germaniae Historica Scriptores
MOFPH	Monumenta Ordinis Fratrum Praedicatorum Historica
ODNB	*Oxford Dictionary of National Biography*
OHS	Oxford Historical Society
PL	*Patrologiae cursus completus, Series Latina*, ed. J. P. Migne, 221 vols. (Paris, 1844–64)
PRS	Pipe Roll Society
RAL	*Registrum Antiquissimum of the Cathedral Church of Lincoln*, ed. C. W. Foster and K. Major (Lincoln Record Society, 1931–50)
Rotuli Grosseteste	*Rotuli Roberti Grosseteste Episcopi Lincolniensis*, ed. F. N. Davis (CYS, 1913)
Rotuli Gravesend	*Rotuli Ricardi Gravesend Diocesis Lincolniensis*, ed. F. N. Davis (CYS, 1924)
RS	Rolls Series of Chronicles of Great Britain and Ireland (HMSO)
RTAM	*Recherches de théologie ancienne et médiévale*
Salimbene	*Cronica Fratris Salimbene de Adam*, ed. O. Holder-Egger (MGH SS, 1913)
SAUO	*Statuta Antiqua Universitatis Oxoniensis*, ed. Strickland Gibson (Oxford, 1931)
Sbaralea	*Bullarium Franciscanum*, ed. J. H. Sbaralea (Rome, 1759)
Trivet, Annales	*Nicholai Trivet Annales*, ed. T. Hog (London, 1845)

THE LETTERS OF
ADAM MARSH

110

To John Mansel, provost of Beverley

f. 50ᵛ Venerabili uiro, domino Iohanni preposito Beuerlac'[1] Frater Ada, rectitudinis consilium et premium uirtutis.

Piget nimiis grandium negotiorum importunitatibus causarum exilium humiles deprecatus ingerere, sed timorata pietas et propinquitas cognata hoc attemptare compulit, cuius fiduciam uestre serenitatis prestitit inolita benignitas. Proinde pro Thoma de Marisco,[2] michi secundum carnem propinquo et, ut reor, de sua salute sollicito, clementie uestre supplico circumspectioni, obsecrans attentius ut eidem secundum sue necessitatis exigentiam uobis uiua uoce, si placet, exponendam, desiderati effectus fauorabile presidium exhibere uelitis.

Valeat magnificentie uestre desiderabilis incolumitas in Christo, etc.

111

To Jerome de Chauston

Venerabili uiro, domino Ieronimo de Cauxstun Frater Ada, gratiam in presenti et gloriam in futuro.

Licet multiplicatis intercessionum uicibus occupationum uestrarum non irrationabiliter uerear inferre fastidium, tamen propter indubitata frequentium experimentorum argumenta fiduciam interpellandi michi prestitit uestre sedulitatis amicitia. Quocirca pro Thoma de Marisco, michi secundum lineam consanguinitatis coniuncto, uestre discretionis rogo suauitatem quatenus eidem in negotio suo, uiua uoce, si placet, exponendo, salutare presidium uelitis impendere.

Valeat benignitatis uestre dilectio in Christo, etc.

---

110 [1] Mansel, the king's minister, a noted pluralist, was made provost of Beverley in 1247 and held the office until his death in 1265: R. C. Stacey in *ODNB*. Cf. Letters 75 and n. and 129.

To John Mansel, provost of Beverley

Brother Adam to the venerable lord John, provost of Beverley,[1] righteous counsel and the reward of virtue.

I am ashamed to intrude upon the pressing demands of great business with humble requests for lowly cases, but timid piety and a close bond of kinship have compelled me to undertake this venture, with a confidence inspired by your customary kindness. I therefore beg of your kindness and prudence on behalf of Thomas Marsh,[2] a relative of mine by blood, who is, as I think, concerned for his salvation, with a pressing request that you would favour him with your help to gain the outcome he desires in accordance with his need, which he will, if you please, explain to you by word of mouth.

Wishing your magnificence the health you desire, in Christ, etc.

111

To Jerome de Chauston

Brother Adam to the venerable lord Jerome de Chauston, grace in the present life and glory in the life to come.

Although I am fearful, not without reason, of wearying you in your employment by multiplying the times I appeal to you, yet the frequent experience of your unwavering friendship gives me confidence to make an appeal. So I am asking your wise and gentle self on behalf of Thomas Marsh, a blood-relative of mine, with a request that you would grant him your effective help in his business which he will, if you please, explain to you by word of mouth.

Farewell kind and dear friend in Christ, etc.

[2] Thomas Marsh, Adam's cousin or nephew, was entrusted by him with several missions to prelates; cf. Letters 12, 95, 111, 231.

112

To Master Reginald of Bath

Viro uenerabili magistro Reginaldo de Bathonia[1] Frater Ada, salutem et sincerum debite deuotionis affectum.

Cum, sicut intellexi, magister Robertus de Northum[2] iterum ad litis certamen inter uos et ipsum pridem habitum iam redierit et, ut dicit, iudices sui ad grauamen uestrum in tantum processerint, quod sententiam excommunicationis in uos, quod absit, decreuerint fore promulgandam, cupiens, sicut dignum est, per omnia paci uestre iuxta modulum meum consulere pariter et honori, presentem discretioni uestre litteram destinare curaui, suadens in Domino, ut considerantes exitum et importunitates memorate cause, per deliberatam maturioris consilii circumspectionem, si sic uobis uisum fuerit, studeatis dampnis dissensionum per amicabilem occurrere compositionem.

113

To Thomas of Anstan

Honorabili uiro, domino Thomae de Anesti Frater Ada, salutem et post pacem temporis beatam gloriam eternitatis.

Eximia lati cordis munificentia, quam apud prouisiuam uestre pietatis industriam frequens fame clarioris assertio multiplici commendat experientia, non tam fiduciam interpellandi prebuit quam ademit impetrandi diffidentiam. Eapropter pro magistro Willielmo de Standun,[1] uiro cui et honesta conuersatio, et ingenium docile, et prouecta scientia, et eloquium conueniens, commendationem afferre perhibentur, quem ad eruditionem impendendam litterarum liberalium ab annis tenerioribus uestro fretum patrocinio promouit propitia diuinitas, presentem liberalitati uestre petitionem destinare studui, rogans attentius quatinus eidem importuna rei familiaris tenuitate laboranti, ut nouerit et uoluerit, ob uberiorem fauoris superni retributionem uestra subuenire uelit beneuolentia.

---

112   [1] Cf. Letter 29 and n. 1.
    [2] To distinguish from M. Robert of Norton, who was Fellow of Merton College and Dean of Arches in 1324: *BRUO* ii. 1375.

112

To Master Reginald of Bath

Brother Adam to the venerable Master Reginald of Bath,[1] greetings
and sincere and devoted affection.

I understand that Master Robert of Norton[2] a short time ago
renewed the litigation earlier undertaken between you and him and
that, as he says, his judges have proceeded so far to your disadvantage
that they have decreed that a sentence of excommunication is to be
published against you, which heavens forbid. Desiring, as I should, in
everything according to my limited ability to promote your peace and
likewise your honour, I have made it my concern to send you this
letter, to urge you in the Lord, in view of the troublesome outcome of
this case, that you would, after more mature consultation, if so it
seems good to you, make an amicable settlement to obviate the
damage of dissension.

113

To Thomas of Anstan

Brother Adam to the honourable lord Thomas of Anston, greetings
and after peace in time the blessed glory of eternity.

The conspicuous munificence of your generous heart, experience
of which together with your goodness and considerate kindness has
gained you a shining reputation, not only gives me confidence to
appeal to you; it has also removed my diffidence in making a request.
So I am eagerly directing this petition to your generous person on
behalf of Master William of Standon,[1] a man recommended by his
upright life, his talent for study, his progress in learning, and his apt
discourse, who was impelled from his youth to take up the study of
liberal letters, depending with divine favour upon your patronage. It
is my earnest request that you would be kind enough to give him
assistance as he toils, in accordance with your known wishes, under
the disadvantage of meagre family resources, this to bring you a richer
reward of heavenly favour.

113   [1] Otherwise obscure, but believed by Emden to be an Oxford master: *BRUO* iii.
1757.

Quo fiat ut quod in agro*a* fecundiori benedictione seminaueritis, cum habundantiori frugum incremento, ad salutarem multorum refectionem, feliciter metere ualeatis. Denique quis unquam explicare ualebit in hiis que nunc agi conspiciuntur nouissimorum dierum temporibus periculosissimis horrenda spectacula cunctis mortalibus, uidelicet profanas pestes demonialium nequitiarum dira rabie sacratissimum Saluatoris sanctuarium et uiolenter irrumpentes*b* et irrepentes fraudulenter et blandienter inuadentes et infestantes peruicaciter?

Illos loquor, qui usquequaquam, pro nefas, et arrogare dignitatem pastorum, et latronum immanitatem exercere non uerentur in animas, canine uoracitatis impudentiam assiduis urgendo direptionibus; contra quos licet obstinatam perdite reprobationis arrogantiam nequaquam terreat, tamen tonat illud interminationis prophetice tonitruum: 'Ve pastoribus Israel, qui pascebant semetipsos! Nonne greges pascuntur a pastoribus? Lac comedebatis, et lanis operiebamini; quod crassum est occidebatis; gregem autem meum non pascebatis. Quod infirmum fuit non consolidastis, et quod egrotum non sanastis; quod fractum est non alligastis, et quod abiectum est non reduxistis, et quod perierat non quesistis; sed cum austeritate imperabatis eis et cum potentia. Et disperse sunt oues, eo quod non esset pastor; et facte sunt in deuorationem omnis bestie agri, et disperse sunt.'[2]

f. 51 Hec sunt certe, mi pater desideratissime, quibus plectendis in presentiarum cernimus omnes, plus in rerum euentibus | quam oraculis prophetarum, formidandi examinis tribunalis sententiam, et super prelatos, et super clerum, et super principes, et super populum dignissima districtione deseuire, non destituram procul dubio quousque compleuerit illud quod alibi contra indomitabilem prelationis usurpate malignitatem ait Michas iii, 'Nonne Dominus in medio nostrum? Non uenient super nos mala. Propter hoc, causa uestri, Sion quasi ager arabitur, et Ierusalem quasi aceruus lapidum erit, et mons templi in excelsa siluarum.'[3] Quid ergo? In tantis ecclesiastice dissipationis execrationibus profecto restat hoc solum immense perditionis remedium, ut uos et uestri complices, quibus est salutaris zeli scientia clarior saluandis animabus, et per sanctum contemplande ueritatis otium, et per pium impendende caritatis officium, tanto uigilantius insistatis, quanto pertinacius illis perdendis

---

113 *a* aggere *MS.*   *b* erumpentes *MS.*

[2] Ezek. 34: 2–5.   [3] Mic. 3: 11–12.

May you by this be able to reap in happiness a more abundant harvest from the blessing you have sown in a more fertile field, for the feeding and salvation of many. In the end, who can explain the things now seen to be happening in these most dangerous days, sights fearful to all mortal men, that is, the impious pests of diabolical wickedness who with madness and violence break into the holy sanctuary of the Saviour, creeping into it by fraud, assailing it with flattery and persistently troubling it?

I am speaking of those who all the time have no fear, for shame, in appropriating to themselves the dignity of pastors and perpetrating monstrous robbery of souls, plundering them remorselessly like hungry dogs. Although it in no way frightens them in their obstinate arrogance and damned wickedness, that sentence of the prophet sounds with a voice of thunder: 'Woe to the shepherds of Israel that fed themselves! Should not the flocks be fed by the shepherds? You ate the milk and you clothed yourselves with the wool, and you killed that which was fat, but my flock you did not feed. The weak you have not strengthened, and that which was sick you have not healed; that which was broken you have not bound up, and that which was driven away you have not brought again; neither have you sought that which was lost; but you ruled over them with rigour and with a high hand; and my sheep were scattered because there was no shepherd, and they became the prey of all the beasts of the field and were scattered.'[2]

This is surely the punishment, my dear father, that we all now observe is to be inflicted, more by the outcome of events than by the oracles of the prophets—the judgement of the dread tribunal coming with fitting severity upon both prelates and clergy, upon both princes and people, which undoubtedly will not cease until that which Micah says in another place shall be fulfilled against the unrestrainable and malicious usurpation of prelacy: 'Is not the Lord in the midst of us? No evil shall come upon us. Therefore, because of you Sion shall be ploughed as a field and Jerusalem shall be as a heap of stones and the mountain of the temple as the high places in the forest.'[3] What then? In the face of such curses upon the destruction of the Church, the only remedy against immense ruin is for you and your associates, who possess a clearer knowledge and zeal for the salvation of souls, all the more to persevere in vigilance, both by making opportunity for the contemplation of truth and by the pious duty of bestowing charity, and to be the more watchful of

passim inuigilant, qui nec Dominum timent nec homines reuerentur; sed cum horrendissima diuine maiestatis blasphemia, ⟨et⟩ cum dampnatissimo humane saluationis detrimento inhiare non desistunt. Valeat paternitatis uestre desiderabilis incolumitas in Christo semper et beatissima Virgine. Licet in hac parte foret opus sermo longus et interpretabilis, compescui calamum, sciens quod ad animam mistici eloquii non ignaram, et ex euangelica sanctione persuasam diuinitus, qualiacunque uerba facio saltem occasionem ⟨sunt⟩ prestitura sapienti.

114

To Robert of Esthall

Amicissimo patri, domino Roberto de Estal'[1] Frater Ada, salutem et post laboriosum cursum temporis gloriosum brauium eternitatis.

In angustia cordis et angustia temporis, pro angusto negotio angustam litteram latiori liberalitatis uestre sedulitati[a] scribere me compulit compassionis anxietas. Rogo igitur quatinus ob contemplationem superpii Saluatoris, Philippo Pathy, multimodis dire uexationis uiolentiis pregrauato, apud malleum uniuerse patrie Petrum de Esrigge, tam facinoribus quam flagitiis Deo detestandum et hominibus execrandum, secundum quod lingue loquuntur omnium, consilii salutaris et efficacis adiutorii fauorem beneuolum impertiri non ducatis indignum.

Ecce coram suauissima uestre discretionis industria plurimum uereor inclito comiti Cornubie[2] nisi immanitatibus dicti scelerati curet maturius adhibere remedium. Coegit me inusitate malitie efferatior atrocitas et feditas contagiosior stilum acuere contra nepharium.

Valeat uestre dilectionis ueneranda pietas in Christo Iesu semper et beatissima Virgine.

---

114   [a] sedulitatis *MS*.

those damned creatures who neither fear the Lord nor honour man, but ceaselessly stand with their mouths open, blaspheming the divine Majesty, with damnable harm to human salvation.

Wishing you health, dear father, ever in Christ and the Blessed Virgin. Although this subject needs a long and more analytical discourse, I have restrained my pen, knowing that to a soul not unacquainted with mystical language and divinely convinced by the law of the Gospel, any words I write will at least offer an opportunity to a wise man.

114

To Robert of Esthall

Brother Adam to my most dear father, lord Robert of Esthall,[1] greetings, and after the toil of life in time the glorious prize of eternity.

At a distressful time, I have been driven by compassion and anxiety to write you a distressed letter about a distressful business with an appeal to your persistent generosity. My request is that out of regard for our most blessed Saviour you would condescend to grant your kind favour, salutary advice, and effective help to Philip Pathy, who is heavily burdened and harassed by many forms of violence at the hands of Peter de Esrigge, the hammer of the whole country, who, as everyone says, is made abominable to God and man by his shameful misdeeds and crimes.

You see, to confide in your discretion, I very much fear the intervention of the noble earl of Cornwall,[2] unless you take care to apply an early remedy for the monstrous deeds of this criminal. His extraordinarily malicious insolence and contagious filthiness have forced me to sharpen my pen against the wretched man.

Farewell to your beloved and good self, ever in Christ and the Blessed Virgin.

114 [1] On Robert of Esthall see Letter 27 n. 6.
      [2] On Richard of Cornwall see letter 30 n. 6 and *passim*.

115

To Master Eustace of Lynn

Honorabili uiro, magistro Eustacio de Len[1] Frater Ada, facere
iudicium et diligere misericordiam, et solicitum ambulare cum
Domino Deo Dei Filio.

Ad magistri Roberti de Abendun', quondam rectoris ecclesie de
Risberg',[2] per sanctum Eadmundum[3] in eadem beneficiati piam
recordationem, nec non ad supplicem instantiam uirorum uenerabil-
ium executorum testamenti eiusdem magistri Roberti, prouide disertitudinis uestre pietati presentem consensi dirigere petitionem,
humili quantum ualeo rogans attentione, quatinus de consueta
serene circumspectionis beneuolentia, ob contemplationem Illius
qui ait, 'Mortuo ne prohibeas gratiam; nec desis plorantibus in
consolatione';[4] prudenti uiro, magistro Petro de Wyleby,[5] qui hactenus per dies plurimos officium eruditionis impendende in iure
canonico studens Oxonie conuenienti sustinuit uigilantia, pro expe-
dienda testamenti memorati executione, uestram adeunti presentiam,
quatinus nec ueritas offenditur nec deseritur misericordia, in nunc
dicto gratiose pietatis negotio, patrocinii prouisiui fauorem beneuolum exhibere non ducatis indignum.

Valeat serenitatis uestre sospes incolumitas in Christo semper et
beatissima Virgine.

116

To Master Ralph of Sempringham

(1251)

Honorabili uiro magistro Radulfo de Simplingham,[1] Frater Ada,
Spiritum Sanctum infallabilis consilii et fortitudinis inuincibilis.

Cum legissem diligentius et plenius intellexissem circumspectum
littere uestre tenorem, sollicitus timor mentem anxiam admodum
occupauit, pro eo quod desideratissimam uniuersitatis emulande

---

115 [1] Eustace of Lynn, Official of the Archbishop of Canterbury; see Letter 26 n. 6; cf.
Letters 34, 56 and n., 93.
  [2] Robert of Abingdon, brother of Archbishop Edmund, died 1243 or 1244: Lawrence, *St
Edmund of Abingdon*, pp. 144–6.

115

To Master Eustace of Lynn

Brother Adam to the honourable Master Eustace of Lynn,[1] do justice, love mercy, and walk carefully with the Lord, the Son of God.

I have agreed to address this petition to your wise and eloquent person out of pious recollection of Master Robert of Abingdon,[2] formerly rector of the church of Risborough, a benefice granted him by St Edmund,[3] and also at the pressing request of the venerable executors of the said Master Robert's will. It comes with a humble and earnest request that, with your customary prudence and kindness, out of regard for Him who says 'restrain not grace from the dead; be not wanting in comforting them that weep',[4] you would be so good as to accord your kind favour and patronage to the prudent Master Peter de Wileby,[5] who as a scholar at Oxford has for many days until now discharged the office of teaching canon law with suitable care, and who is approaching you to expedite the execution of Master Robert's will, so far as this pious business does not involve any deviation from truth or abandonment of mercy.

Wishing your serenity safety and health ever in Christ and the Blessed Virgin.

116

To Master Ralph of Sempringham

(1251)

Brother Adam to the honourable Master Ralph of Sempringham,[1] the Holy Spirit of unerring counsel and invincible strength.

When I had read and more fully understood the tenor of your discreet letter, my mind was seized with anxiety with the thought that the most desirable peace of the distinguished university is in fearful

---

[3] St Edmund of Abingdon, Archbishop of Canterbury 1233–40; canonized 1246.
[4] Ecclus. 7: 37–8.
[5] Master Peter de Wileby witnessed a conveyance in Oxford in 1246–7: *BRUO* iii. 2047.

116   [1] On Master Ralph, chancellor of Oxford, see Letter 16 and n. *BRUO* iii. 169.

tranquillitatem formidando subito concussionis periculo subiacere
consideraui. Hoc autem in imminenti causarum grandium discrimine
uidetur esse consultum, ut prouisiua uestre discretionis industria,
cum uenerando cetu sapientum uobis iugiter, ⟨qui⟩ in hiis quibus
honori diuino seruitur et prospicitur saluti ecclesiastice assistere
dignoscuntur,ᵃ dissensionum fomitem reprimere et procurare quie-
tudinem studentium non desistat, sub pia beneuole longanimitatis
expectatione, quousque per clementem superbenigni Saluatoris dispensationem, quod propitia diuinitate fiet, sine more dispendio
imperetur uentis conspirationum et mari perturbationis,² et fiat
tranquillitas magna scolarium.

Ceterum scripsi litteram porrigendam decano Oxoniensi, suadens
eidem et supplicans, ut propter pauescenda turbaminum imminentium discrimina executioni supersedeat sibi a magistro R⟨oberto⟩ de
Sancta Agatha³ demandate, nichilominus per litteram aliam signans et
supplicans memorato magistro Roberto, ut perpensis tantorum
discriminum circumstantiis maturum rebus periculosis remedium
incunctanter curet adhibere.

Apud uenerandum quoque patrem, dominum Lincolniensem,
prout facto opus fuerit modicitatis mee, partes interponere propo-
nerem, prout diuinitus concedetur, ut per propensiorem sue provi-
sionis diligentiam, optato fine, cuncta celitus conquiescant. In
benefico uestri gratia acto magistriᵇ S. de Londino, Domino propitio,
uobis usquequaque seruabitur indempnitas.

Valeat uestre pietatis incolumitas in Christo semper et beatissima
Virgine.

117

To Robert of Esthall

Amantissimo in Christo patri, domino Roberto de Esthall¹ Frater
Ada, datum optimum gratie et glorie donum perfectum.ᵃ

Licet immeritam mee modicitatis tenuitatem reuocauerit faciei
uerecundia, tamen fiduciam cordis animauit ad interpellandum
probata dilectionis uestre liberalitas. Proinde sedulam serenitatis
uestre munificentiam suppliciore deuote affectionis interuentu
precor obnixius, ob Ipsius contemplationem qui tam celebra legis

116 ᵃ dinoscuntur MS.   ᵇ magistro MS.

117 ᵃ The words of greeting are followed in the MS by the words Faciei uerecundiam, quam
ab interpellando reuocat, which the copyist has deleted by writing uacat above them.

danger of a sudden upheaval. In a case of great and immediate danger the best course seems to be for your wise and perceptive self, together with the venerable congregation of wise men, who are known to support you in matters serving the honour of God and procuring the safety of the Church, to continue without ceasing to suppress the flames of dissension and to work to quieten the students; this in the hope that goodwill and patience will triumph until, through the merciful dispensation of our Saviour, which, God willing, will be forthcoming without delay, the winds of conspiracy and the sea of disturbance may be commanded to cease[2] and a great peace may come upon the scholars.

But I have written a letter to hand to the dean of Oxford, to persuade him and beg him, in view of our fear of imminent disturbance, to postpone execution of the sentence required of him by Master Robert of St Agatha.[3] None the less I have sent a signal to Master Robert by another letter and begged him not to hesitate in providing a wise settlement for these dangerous matters, having regard to the great dangers of the situation.

I have also made a proposal to our venerable father, the lord of Lincoln, so far as there is need of my humble self, to intervene between the parties, God willing, so that through his wise provision the end may be achieved and, with heaven's help, everything may end in peaceful agreement. Thanks to you, by the kind action of Master S. of London, you will, by the Lord's favour, be wholly secured against damage.

Wishing you health and security ever in Christ and the Blessed Virgin.

117

To Robert of Esthall

Brother Adam to my dear father in Christ, lord Robert of Esthall,[1] the best gift of grace and the perfect gift of glory.

Although shame makes my undeserving self reluctant to appeal to you, nevertheless, proof of your generosity and love gives me confidence to do so. Therefore I humbly beg your munificence to be so good as to procure through some household messenger of your

---

[2] The language recalls Christ's stilling of the storm; cf. Luke 8: 23–4.
[3] Master Robert of St Agatha; see Letter 22 n. 1.

117   [1] For Esthall, canon of Lincoln, see Letter 27 n. 6; cf. Letter 106.

sue iussione commendauit, specialissimo michi in Christo magistro Iohanni de Londin',[2] iuxta cogentem necessitatis sue requisitionem, quatenus et pietati consulitur et prospicitur honestati, per aliquem de familiaribus beneuolentie uestre nuntiis optatam benigne subuentionis gratiam, si tamen a uestro hoc non dissideat beneplacito, ut ualueritis, uideritis, uolueritis procurare non ducatis indignum. Si effectum petitionis difficultatis[b] obsistentia non excludit, memoratus magister Iohannes uiua uoce quod petitur discretioni uestre plenius insinuabit.

Concedat uobis, oro, Dei uirtus, Dei sapientia, Dei sanctificatio, f. 51ᵛ uigorem strenuum, sensum industrium, | zelum saluificum in uerbis uite,[3] in exemplis uite, in sacramentis uite, ad honorem Altissimi, ad coronam uestri, ad profectum populi felici sollicitudinis celice uigilantia.

118

To Master John de Stokes

(c. 1250)

Magistro Iohanni de Stokes[1] Frater Ada, uite gratiam et patrie gloriam.

Si quid iuxta quod presumitur in commisso uisitationis officio ecclesie Dei reformande, non tam canonice traditioni quam sanctioni euangelice, uos et collega uester, uir commendabilis, studiosa incesseritis uigilantia, ut libet latius lingue loquantur, occurrit diuinus apostolus sui silens erudiendo, michi autem inquiens, 'Pro minimo est ut a uobis iudicer, aut ab humano die; sed neque meipsum iudico'.[2] Est nempe qui queret ante iudicet.

Verumptamen audiamus Scripturam uniuersis mortalibus clamantem: 'Quis gloriabitur mundum se habere cor?'[a][3] Et iterum, 'Omnes iustitie nostre',[4] etc. Propter quod, 'beatus', inquit, 'qui semper pauidus est'.[5] Et iterum, 'Verebar omnia opera mea, sciens quod non parceres delinquenti. Si autem lotus fuero aquis niuis, tamen sordibus',[6] etc. Quid ergo? An non longanimiter sustinebimus

---

[b] difficultatia MS.

118 [a] se habere cor: added in the margin by a corrector of the same period.

---

[2] Master John of Londiniis was party to a peace settlement between Northerners and Southerners at Oxford in 1274: BRUO ii. 1157. Possibly he was the Master John of London praised by Bacon for his grasp of mathematics: Opera Rogerii Baconis hactenus inedita, ed. J. S. Brewer (RS 1859), pp. 34–5.

goodwill your kind assistance for Master John of London,[2] a particular friend of mine in Christ, according to his need, inasmuch as it is consonant with goodness and honesty, so far as you can, think fit, and wish, out of regard for Him who famously commanded such acts. If this request is not debarred by difficulties, the said Master John will indicate to you by word of mouth what is requested.

I beg that the power of God, the wisdom of God, and the sanctifying spirit of God may grant you strength and energy, wisdom, and a saving zeal for the words of life,[3] in the examples of your life, and for the sacraments of life, to the glory of the Most High, to be your crown, to the advancement of the people through your heavenly care and vigilance.

118

To Master John de Stokes

(c.1250)

Brother Adam to Master John de Stokes,[1] a life of grace and the glory of our heavenly homeland.

If you and your admirable colleague have made any progress, as is presumed, in your vigilant discharge of the duty of visitation that you have been assigned, for the reform of the Church of God, in accordance with canon law and the decrees of the Gospel—it is a pleasure to speak more widely—the divine apostle meets you with his words, tacitly instructing himself, but saying to me 'to me it is a very small thing to be judged by you or by man's day. But neither do I judge my own self.'[2] Truly there is One who inquires before judging.

Yet let us hear Scripture calling to all mortal men: 'Who boasts that he has a pure heart?'[3] And again, 'All our righteousness', etc.[4] On this account, 'Blessed', he says, 'is he who is always fearful',[5] and again, 'I feared all my works, knowing that thou wouldst not spare the offender; if I have washed with snow, yet in filth', etc.[6] What then?

---

[3] A favoured expression of Adam's to mean 'preaching'.

118 [1] Master John de Stokes witnessed acts as a member of Grosseteste's familia from 1241 to 1249: Major, 'The familia of Grosseteste', p. 238.

[2] 1 Cor. 4: 3.   [3] Prov. 20: 9.
[4] Cf. Isa. 64: 6.   [5] Prov. 28: 14.
[6] Job 9: 28, 30.

arguentes quantumcunque nobis conscii non fuerimus, cum constat quod ob id iustificati non simus apud Eum de quo scriptum est 'Celi non sunt mundi in conspectu eius, et in angelis suis reperit Ipse prauitatem?'[7]

Ad id quod epistole inseruistis de conciliandis cordibus personarum insignium, uidelicet uestrorum[b] magistrorum Symonis de Valentia[8] et Roberti de Marisco,[9] a quibus in pacifico pastionis moderamine tanta pendet salus animarum, totis exilitatis mee uiribus, preter saluificam emulationem pacis reficiende in uiris ecclesiasticis, me[c] compellit apud unumquemque uestrum singularis amicitie necessitudo. Ceterum prudentie serpentine columbina simplicitas,[10] qua spirituali legum eternarum cogentia rectores celicos pollere precipit saluandis animabus Auctor animarum, 'qui amat animas',[11] licet nonnumquam foueat dissensiones sine odio, et interdum dispensata[d] suauium litigiorum certamina exercere cognoscatur, non controuersiis instaurandis sed concordiis; semper tamen satagat discreta pietas ut sic ueritas cara defendatur, ne offendatur uera caritas.

Proinde consultum esse uidetur, ut nullatenus uestre discretionis epistolam epistole magistri Symonis responsiuam, certe secundum planum sui uehementiores ultricium obiurgationum acrimonias preferentem, una cum sua uobis transmissa, sicut cogitastis, eidem remittatis,[e] non uosmetipsos defendentes, carissime,[f] sed amabili[g] amoris benigni sine felle seuitiam responsione molliori, secundum sapientie documentum, in unanimen amicitie profectum conuertentes. Vix istud tantillum qualitercunque inter innumeras lacerantium occupationum pressuras scripto uestro rescribere ualui.

Valeat etc.

119

To Bartholomew, rector of Reedwell

Dilecto amico in Christo domino Bartolomeo, rectori ecclesie de Raddewelle,[1] Frater Ada, salutem et sincerum debite dilectionis affectum.

Vobis innatam rogo benignitatem ut magistro S. Gyen,[2] quondam doctori uestro, super debito quo eidem tenemini, uidelicet xl

---

[b] uestrorum: uestri et *MS.*   [c] me: *MS adds* mei.   [d] dispensatam *MS.*
[e] remittere *MS.*   [f] carissimi *MS.*   [g] amabilem *MS.*

Shall we not put up patiently with those who accuse us, in so far as we are not aware of guilt, since it is established that on account of this are we not justified by Him of whom it is written 'The heavens are not pure in his sight and in his angels he discovers wickedness'?[7]

As to what you included in your letter about winning the hearts of distinguished people, that is, of your masters Symon of Valence[8] and Robert Marsh,[9] on whose quiet pastoral governance the salvation of souls so much depends, I am driven with all my poor strength by an urge to restore peace among churchmen, and also by the compulsion of a special friendship with each one of you. But the creator of souls and lover of souls commands heaven's rectors by the force of eternal law to display the wisdom of a serpent and the simplicity of a dove[10] for the salvation of souls; though He sometimes encourages disagreements without rancour, and is known to allow contests and sweet disputes, not to engender conflict but to establish concord; but discriminating goodness is ever active for the protection of beloved truth in such a way that true charity suffers no harm.

So it seems advisable in no way to send your letter in reply to Symon's, sharper in its acerbity than his and rebuking him by way of revenge, as you thought, together with the letter he sent you, but to send one not in self-defence, beloved, but a kind one, devoid of gall, as wisdom instructs, with a gentle reply turning rage into agreement and friendship. I have scarcely been able to write this little note in answer to your letter, being under the pressure of numberless distracting affairs. Farewell, etc.

119

To Bartholomew, rector of Reedwell

Brother Adam to our dear friend in Christ, Sir Bartholomew de Raddenwelle,[1] greetings and sincere affection and devotion.

I ask you, out of your natural kindness, to be so good as to satisfy without delay Master St Germans,[2] your former teacher, by settling

[7] Job 15: 15 and 4: 18.
[8] Master Symon was evidently a faculty member of Oxford when Adam supported his request for a loan from the university chest; cf. Letter 127; *BRUO* iii. 1940.
[9] For Robert Marsh see Letter 33 n. 1 and Introduction, p. xix.
[10] Cf. Matt. 10: 16. [11] Wisd. 11: 27.

119 [1] Possibly Reedwell, Scotland. [2] Cf. Letter 101.

solidorum sterlingorum, satisfacere curetis sine more dispendio, secundum quod diuine legis cogit auctoritas et honestas requirit ingenuitatis uestre, scientes quod prefate pecunie dilata solutio iam a multis diebus modicitati mee roborem intulit pariter et angustiam. Valeat fidei uestre uigilantia in Christo semper et beatissima Virgine.

Propter formidandum summi iudicis examen aduertat indolis uestre laudabilis industria quod, secundum immutabiles diuinorum eloquiorum sententias, rectoribus animarum consultum nullatenus esse poterit, nisi pascendis gregibus dominicis per uerbum sancte predicationis, per exemplum sancte conuersationis, per affectum pie deprecationis, in carnis maceratione, in cordis compunctione, in sacramentorum dispensatione, sine quibus in die reddende rationis eterne iudicii condempnatio non euaditur. Aut curis^a quas dampnabiliter usurparunt, ⟨uel⟩ uiris facturis fructus earum, aut nesciunt aut nolunt, ut oportet, inuigilare, nec propter effrenatam bonorum ecclesiasticorum peruasionem omnibus seculis horrendum stupende proditionis piaculum admittunt.^{b}

In eternum ualeat, etc.

120

To John of Crakehall

Viro uenerabili, domino Iohanni de Crakhal',[1] Frater Ada, augmentum gratie et glorie plenitudinem.

Cum sicut melius nouit uestra discretio, Willielmus, germanus meus, balliuus de Bugeden'[2] frequenter ualetudinum pregrauetur molestiis, propter quod ad ministerium domini episcopi de cetero, sicut oportet, nequaquam uideatur ydoneus, uestram rogo serenitatem ut apud dictum dominum satagere uelitis, quod ipsum sine more dispendio licentiare dignetur redire ad propria, et domui sue, sicut Domino dabit, disponere.

Valeat uestre circumspectionis industria in Christo semper, etc.

119　　^{a} curas *MS*.　　^{b} admittant *MS*.

the debt of 40 shillings sterling that you owe him, as divine law and your honour require. You know, your delay in paying the money now many days overdue has already caused shame and discomfort to my poor self.

May your faith and vigilance ever flourish in Christ and the Blessed Virgin.

In your admirably conscientious character, in view of the fearful last Judgement, you should be aware that, in accord with the changeless decrees of God's words, there can be no advice to rectors of souls except to devote themselves to feeding the Lord's flocks by holy preaching, by the example of a holy life, by devotion to holy prayer, by castigation of the flesh, by heartfelt compunction, and by dispensing the sacraments. Without these, they will not escape eternal condemnation on the day when account must be rendered. Either they do not know the pastoral office they have damnably usurped or are unwilling to watch over it as they ought, or over the men who are to harvest the fruits of it; nor do they offer any propitiation for their shocking betrayal, the most ghastly invasion of ecclesiastical goods ever to be seen.

Farewell for ever, etc.

120

To John of Crakehall

Brother Adam to the venerable Sir John of Crakehall,[1] an increase of grace and the fullness of glory.

As you well know, William, my brother, the bailiff of Buckden,[2] is seriously afflicted with ill health so that it seems he is no longer fit for the service of the lord bishop as required. I therefore ask you if you would be good enough to make earnest representations to the lord bishop to permit him without delay to return home and set his property in order, as the Lord shall grant.

May your wisdom ever flourish in Christ, etc.

---

120 [1] John of Crakehall; see Letter 21 n. 1.

[2] Buckden (Huntingdon), an episcopal manor and a favourite residence of Grosseteste. On William the bailiff see Introduction, p. xix.

121

To John Crakehall, steward of the bishop of Lincoln

(1249–50)

Predilecto sibi in Christo domino Iohanni, domini Lyncolniensis
senescallo, Frater Ada salutem in Domino.

Pro caro michi Iohanne, preposito de Bugeden,[1] uobis innate
supplico benignitati, quatenus eundem in suarum necessitatum
articulis et clementer audire et dirigere misericorditer non ducatis
indignum, quoad fieri poterit rationabiliter, prouidentes intuitu
Domini ut nec per simplicitatem fides ipsius denigretur aut rei
familiaris incurrat detrimentum.

Valeat pietatis uestre suauitas in Christo semper et beatissima
Virgine.

122

To John of Crakehall

Amicissimo sibi in Christo domino Iohanni de Crakhal', domini
Lyncolniensis senescallo, Frater Ada, salutem et obsequialem
deuote modicitatis affectionem.

Rogeri Cuchur, sicut credo, iuuenis bone spei supplicationi
consentiens, presentem litteram uestre scripsi dilectioni, rogans, si
placet, ut eidem iam a sue lesionis discrimine per Dei gratiam
liberato, sicut noueritis et uolueritis, fauoris beneuoli gratiam dignemini impertiri.

Valeat serenitatis uestre pietas in Christo, etc.

123

To Peter of Stamford

Dilectissimo patri in Christo domino Petro de Stanford, custodi
Hospitalis de Lutrewrth,[1] Frater Ada salutem, et spiritum consilii
cum spiritu fortitudinis.

---

121   [1] John succeeded William Marsh as bailiff c.1249; cf. Letter 120. Crakehall

121

To John Crakehall, steward of the bishop of Lincoln

(1249–50)

Brother Adam to his dear lord in Christ, John, steward of the lord bishop of Lincoln, greetings in the Lord.

I beg you of your kindness to be so good as to graciously hear my dear John, the bailiff of Buckden,[1] and direct him with compassion, as far as can be reasonably done out of respect for the Lord, to prevent his trust being abused through his simplicity or his domestic property being harmed.

Farewell, gentle friend, ever in Christ and the Blessed Virgin.

122

To John of Crakehall

Brother Adam to his dear friend in Christ Sir John of Crakehall, steward of the lord bishop of Lincoln, greetings and devoted duty and affection.

Acceding to the supplication of Roger Cuchur, a young man I believe to be of good promise, I have written you this letter with a request that you would, if you please, grant him your grace and favour. As you know and would wish, he is now by the grace of God out of danger from his injury.

Farewell your serenity in Christ, etc.

123

To Peter of Stamford

Brother Adam to our very dear father in Christ, Sir Peter of Stamford, warden of Lutterworth Hospital,[1] greetings and a spirit of counsel and a spirit of fortitude.

apparently relinquished the stewardship on accompanying Grosseteste to the papal Curia in 1250.

123   [1] Peter of Stamford; see Letter 65 n. 1.

Mitto uobis litteras nobilis uiri domini Galfridi Dispensatoris[2] domino Lyncolniensi deferendas, per quas dictus dominus Galfridus personam uestram presentat dicto domino Lyncolniensi ad ecclesiam de Soleby.[3] Proinde propter gloriam diuini nominis, propter honorem beate Virginis, propter animarum salutem, propter beatitudinis coronam, uos moneo, uos rogo, uos inuito, ut sine more dispendio f. 52 cum dictis litteris | uestre presentationis accedatis ad memoratum patrem dominum Lyncolniensem, onus prefati regiminis diuinitate propitia suscepturi. Noueritis quoque quod huc accedit consilium amantissimi patris, fratris Iohannis de Stanford.[4] Nequaquam conatus sum insistere suasoriis, credens quod pie menti persuadeat efficaciter in causa pietatis pius Dei Filius.

Valeat uestre dilectionis pietas in Christo semper et beatissima Virgine. Mitto uobis litteras domino Lyncolniensi per uos porrigendas.

124

To Aymer de Valence (Lusignan)

(1249)

Illustri uiro, domino Aimaro,[1] fratri domini regis, Frater Ada salutem, et post transitum temporalium mansionem eternorum.

Licet modicitatem meam et tenuitas meritorum meorum et uestre serenitatis excellentia calamum herere compulerit, tamen et cause magnitudo et concepta fiducia, quominus presentem petitionem uobis inolite scriberem benignitati, deuoti ⟨serui⟩ uestri mentem quiescere non permisit.

Proinde cum uenerandi patris domini Aniani,[2] quem pontificali dignum infula celebris fama denuntiat, apostolice sedis auctoritas uelud sanctionibus consonam euangelicis confirmauerit electionem, beneuolentie uestre supplico sedulitati, rogans humiliter quatinus ob honoris diuini et ecclesiastice salutis contemplationem, apud regie dominationis clementiam, secundum quod rerum requirit urgentia, presens pietatis negotium uestre uelit claritatis industria, adhibitis opportunitatum circumstantiis, in Domino promouere.

[2] Geoffrey Despencer; see Letter 65 n. 2.
[3] Sulby (Northamptonshire). The date of his institution is not recorded.
[4] Brother John of Stamford was present at Lyons in 1245 during the Council; was custodian of Oxford in 1253; and succeeded Peter of Tewkesbury as provincial minister of

I am sending you the letters to take to the lord bishop of Lincoln by which the noble lord Geoffrey Despenser[2] presents you to the bishop for institution to the church of Sulby.[3] For the glory of the divine name, the honour of the Blessed Virgin, the salvation of souls, and for a crown of beatitude, I admonish you, I ask you, and I invite you to proceed without delay to our father the bishop with these letters of presentation, ready to undertake the burden of the said rectorship with the help of God. You should also know that this is with the advice of our beloved father, Brother John of Stamford.[4] I have in no way attempted to insist by persuasion, in the belief that in a righteous cause a righteous mind is effectively persuaded by the righteous Son of God.

Farewell, beloved, ever in Christ and the Blessed Virgin. I am sending you letters for delivery to the lord bishop of Lincoln.

124

To Aymer de Valence (Lusignan)

(1249)

Brother Adam to the illustrious lord Aymer,[1] brother of the lord king, greetings, and after the passing of things temporal a dwelling place in eternity.

Although my poor merits and your excellency's rank made my humble self hesitant to take up my pen, the great importance of the case and a sense of trust allowed the mind of your devoted servant no rest without my writing to make this request of your kindness.

As his abundant renown declares the venerable father Anian to be worthy of episcopal distinction, and his election has been confirmed by the Apostolic See as being in accord with the decrees of the Gospel,[2] I humbly beg you, for the honour of God and the safety of the Church, to move the clemency of the lord king, as opportunity arises, to act in this sacred matter as the urgency of the situation requires.

England in 1258: Eccleston, pp. 11, 64 and n., 97, 101; Little, *The Greyfriars in Oxford*, pp. 128, 138. Cf. Letters 168, 176, 211.

124 [1] Aymer de Valence (Lusignan), half-brother of Henry III, took up residence in England in 1247. Under pressure from the king, he was elected bishop of Winchester on 4 Nov. 1250; cf. Letters 4, 17, 57 n. 1, 60, 68.

[2] Anian I (Einion)'s election to the see of St Asaph's was contested by the king, but a papal mandate to the archbishop to confirm the election was issued by Innocent IV on 20 Feb. 1248: Berger, i. 555. He was consecrated bishop in Nov. 1249.

Concedat uobis, oro, in hiis et in cunctis reuerendum Dei sanctuarium contingentibus, per timorem sanctum quod prudenter discernitis, geritis fortiter, temperanter cohibetis, iusteque distribuitis, ad illum finem perseueranter dirigere, ubi erit Deus omnia in omnibus, eternitate certa et pace perfecta in Christo,[3] etc.

125

To William of Hemingborough

(1249–50)

Predilecto amico, domino Willielmo de Hemingeb'[1] Frater Ada.

Cursorem domini Cantuariensis, presentis cartule portitorem, qui michi destinatas memorati domini et domine regine litteras detulit, quem et ego cum eorundem litteris et meis ministro[2] nostro destinatis, ad dictum ministrum transmitto. Peto, si placet, sicut competenter uideritis hospitio colligi faciatis.

Valete semper in Christo. Salutetis obsequio mei, rogo, dominum senescallum[3] cum gratiarum actionibus. Iterum ualeat, etc.

126

To Master Henry of Anjou

Magistro Henrico de Andegauia Frater Ada, felices salutarium uotorum successus.

Cum dominus Iohannes de Pescham[1] scolaris, quem et honestior conuersatio et litteratura prouectior commendabiliter illustrant, celesti succensus desiderio nuper Fratrum Minorum religiosam institutionem intrauerit, ad instantiam karissimi nepotis uestri H., cuius adholescentiam innocentialem ingenium docile et laudabile studium, mos placidus et leta spes, ex diuinitatis gratia reddunt acceptam, circumspecte discretionis uestre serenitati litteram presentem

---

[3] Augustine, *De civitate Dei*, xix. 20; *CSEL* xl, ii. 407.

125 [1] William of Hemingborough was a member of Grosseteste's *familia*. As such he witnessed letters of institution between 1242 and 1249. In 1250–1 he was appointed a canon with the prebend of Bishop Norton: Major, 'The familia of Grosseteste', p. 230.
[2] William of Nottingham, provincial of the English Friars Minor 1240–54.
[3] John of Crakehall, Grosseteste's steward 1235–50.

I pray the Lord may grant that in these matters and in everything relating to the venerable sanctuary of God you may, through holy fear, direct what you discern with prudence, perform with resolution, constrain with moderation, and distribute with justice, to that end where God will be all in all, in sure eternity and perfect peace, in Christ, etc.[3]

125

To William of Hemingborough

(1249–50)

Brother Adam to his very dear friend Sir William of Hemingborough.[1]

The courier of the lord archbishop of Canterbury has brought letters addressed to me from the archbishop and from the lady queen, and I am sending him on to our minister[2] with their letters and with letters of my own directed to the minister. I ask you, if you regard it as appropriate, to be so kind as to arrange for him to be placed in a guest-house.

Farewell ever in Christ. Please convey my greetings and obedience to the lord steward.[3] Again, farewell.

126

To Master Henry of Anjou

Brother Adam to Master Henry of Anjou, a happy outcome to your holy desires.

Since Sir John of Pecham,[1] a scholar noteworthy for his upright life and advanced learning, has recently been fired by heavenly desire to enter the religious institute of the Friars Minor, I have consented to send your serene and wise lordship this letter at the request of your dear nephew H., whose teachable talent and admirable zeal for learning, peaceful conduct, and joyful hope by the grace of God

---

126 [1] John Pecham studied Arts at Paris, but completed the course for the magistracy at Oxford *c*.1252; joined the Friars Minor at Oxford, possibly under Adam's influence; incepted as doctor of theology at Paris; and was archbishop of Canterbury 1279–92: D. L. Douie, *Archbishop Pecham* (Oxford, 1952); *BRUO* iii. 1445–7.

destinare consensi, rogans attentius quatinus sine more dispendio insinuare curetis, quem censueritis in officio eruditionis impendende memorato H. nepoti uestro, loco predicti Iohannis, quondam instructoris eiusdem, substituendum. Suggessit autem michi predictus H., nepos uester, de quodam P. scolare Oxoniensi ad hanc sollicitudinem satis ydoneo, quod etiam alias ex testimonii credibilis audiui assertione.
Valeat uestre sinceritatis, etc.

127

To Master Robert of St Agatha

Honorabili uiro magistro Roberto de Sancta Agatha[1] Frater Ada, sincerum debite deuotionis affectum.

Tanto fiducialius liberalem sedulitatis uestre beneuolentiam interpello, licet modicitatis mee hoc merita non requirant, quanto presertim in causis fauorabilibus uestre disertitudinis affectio suauior michi displicendi diffidentiam ingerit et administrat confidentiam impetrandi. Quocirca pro uenerabili patre magistro Symone de Valentinis[2] uestre circumspectionis inolite benignitati affectuose supplico, rogans obnixius quatinus eidem iuxta presentem necessitatis sue cogentiam, de prouisiua consuete pietatis industria, efficacem consultioris auxilii subuentionem exhibere non ducatis indignum; pro eo quod ea que petuntur, si fuerint impensa, remunerationem ampliorem a diuinitate promerentur, et is pro quo petitur titulis dignioribus gratie multiplicioris diuinitus insignitur.

Lator presentium uobis, si placet, uiua uoce negotii tenorem plenius exponet, quod non immerito tamquam proprium amplecti compellor in Domino. Hoc est autem quod expediri satagitur: uidelicet ut mutuum .xl. librarum per discretionis uestre diligentiam concedatur memorato magistro Symoni de pecunia uniuersitatis Oxoniensis deposita ex munere caritatiuo magistri Willielmo de Dunelm',[3] cuius in Christo pia est recordatio, sub forma certe cautionis quam competere censueritis. Ut autem amplius liqueat quod in hac parte desiderat prefatus magister Symon et nonnulli

---

127   [1] Robert of St Agatha; see Letter 22 n. 1; *BRUO* iii. 1623.
   [2] Simon of Valence; see *BRUO* iii. 1940. Adam's warm support for his request suggests that he was a Master of Arts, seeking finance to pursue the study of theology; see n. 3 below.
   [3] William of Durham, a former regent in theology at Paris, died in 1249, bequeathing

make his innocent youth acceptable. This is to request that you would
be so good as to suggest without delay whom you consider should be
substituted for the task of educating your nephew H. in place of the
said John, who was his former teacher. Your nephew H. has made me
a suggestion regarding one P., a scholar of Oxford who would be quite
suitable for this charge; and I have heard this also from trustworthy
statements elsewhere.

Farewell, sincerely, etc.

127

To Master Robert of St Agatha

Brother Adam to the honourable Master Robert of St Agatha,[1]
sincere affection and devotion.

I am appealing to your kindness and generosity, though I do not
deserve it, with all the more confidence as your gentle concern,
especially in deserving cases, assures me that I shall not displease
you and gives me confidence to make such an appeal. So with
affection I am supplicating your native kindness and foresight on
behalf of the venerable father and master Simon of Valence,[2] with a
request that with your usual goodness and considerate kindness you
would not disdain to grant him your effective assistance and advice
in his present need. I ask this because God promises a more
abundant reward to those who respond to a request with gifts,
and because the person for whom the request is made is marked out
by God as a worthy recipient of manifold grace.

The bearer of this letter will, if you please, explain to you more
fully by word of mouth the nature of the business. It is a deserving
case, which I feel obliged in the Lord to embrace as my own. What we
are actively seeking to procure is this: that through your discreet
intervention a loan of 40 pounds should be granted to the said Master
Simon, under a fixed security that you consider appropriate, from the
money of the University of Oxford that was deposited as a charitable
gift by Master William of Durham[3] of pious memory in Christ. In
order to clarify further what Master Simon and his friends in Christ

310 marks to the University of Oxford to be invested to support ten masters of arts studying
theology: *BRUO* i. 612. On loan chests of the university see T. H. Aston and Rosamund
Faith in *HUO* i. 274–82. An early statute laid down that custodians of the chests were to be
elected by congregation: *SAUO*, pp. 71–2.

amicorum ipsius in Domino, mitto uobis presentibus inclusam litteram, quam michi pro dicto negotio, si fieri potest, expediendo quidam uir magnus michi ⟨misit⟩ in spirituali dilectione coniunctus. Valeat uestre dilectionis, etc.

128

To Master Robert of St Agatha

(1251–5)

Honorabili uiro magistro Roberto de Sancta Agatha[1] Frater Ada, uie gratiam et gloriam patrie.

Benefice fidelis amicitie liberalitati, quam apud sinceritatem uestram erga meam exilitatem certis multiplicium argumentorum indiciis benignius affici frequentius experior, oro, satisfaciat munificentie celestis superbeneuola retributio. Ad instantiam supplicem magistri Walteri Gyffard,[2] uiri, ut reor, discretioni uestre non incogniti, presentem prudentie uestre consensi dirigere petitionem, rogans affectuose quatinus eidem in negotio suo uobis, ut intellexi, per ipsius litteram plenius exponendo, quatenus nec offenditur ueritas nec iustitia deseritur sed et honori prospicitur et consulitur utilitati, petitam fauoris beneuoli gratiam impertiri non ducatis indignum.

Valeat dilectionis uestre benigna suauitas in Christo, etc.

129

To John Mansel, provost of Beverley

(1248)

Honorabili uiro, domino Iohanni Mansell, preposito Beuerlac',[1] Frater Ada salutem, et post pacem temporis gloriam eternitatis.

Etsi inter tam uaria aulici laboris negotia claram uestre serenitatis industriam uigilante uigilantia desudare considerem, tamen expedite[a] circumspectionis inolita benignitas apud uestram spectabiliter residens

---

129   [a] expedire MS.

128   [1] See Letter 22 n. 1.
   [2] Walter Giffard was regent master in arts at Oxford by 1251 when he and his brother Godfrey received a royal gift from Henry III on their inception: CCR 1247–51, p. 459. He

desire, I am enclosing with this a letter, sent me by a great man to whom I am bound by a bond of spiritual love, in order to speed the said business if it can be done.

Farewell, dear friend, etc.

128

To Master Robert of St Agatha

(1251–5)

Brother Adam to the honourable Master Robert of St Agatha,[1] grace on your journey and glory in your homeland.

I have experienced many sure indications of your benevolent and loyal friendship towards my wretched self, for which I pray you may receive an abundant heavenly reward. I have agreed to send you this request at the supplication of Master Walter Giffard,[2] a man not unknown, I think, to your prudent self, with an affectionate request that you would bestow on him the grace of your kind favour in his business, to be more fully explained to you, as I understand, by his own letter; this is so far as there may be nothing contrary to truth or justice, but rather the advancement of his honour and usefulness.

Wishing you, my dear and kind friend, health in Christ, etc.

129

To John Mansel, provost of Beverley

(1248)

Brother Adam to the honourable lord John Mansel, provost of Beverley,[1] greetings, and after the peace of time the glory of eternity.

Although I considered how your serene lordship toils with vigilance and application over such a variety of business at court, nevertheless your eminence's natural kindness that remains conspicuously unimpaired and your prompt wisdom encouraged my

was elected bishop of Bath and Wells in 1264 and was translated to the archbishopric of York in 1265: *BRUO* ii. 762–3.

129 [1] On Mansel see Letter 110 n. 1.

eminentiam, herentem calamum ad presentem petitiunculam animauit. Igitur pro domino Petro de Kyllum,[2] latore presentium, quem ad
regimen ecclesie Beate Virginis Oxoniensis de uestre pietatis, ut reor,
assensu, regalis excellentia ob Saluatoris contemplationem saluandis
f. 52ᵛ animabus presentare curauit, | uestram humiliter rogo clementiam
quatinus dictum rectorem, ad presentiam domini regis accedentem,
fauorabiliter suscipere et consultius expedire, si uestro sederit beneplacito, non ducatis indignum.

Dirigat, oro, desideratissime strenuitatis uestre et ingenium precipuum et facundum eloquium auctor uite, per uiam que ducit ad
uitam, ut in omnibus et recte discernatis, et geratis fortiter, et
cohibeatis temperanter, et iuste distribuatis, omnem uiuendi ordinem
ad illum finem referentes ubi est Deus omnia in omnibus, eternitate
certa et pace perfecta.[3] In Christo, etc.

130

To John of Crakehall

Amantissimo sibi in Christo Iohanni de Crakhal',[1] domini Lyncolniensis senescallo, Frater Ada, gratiam in presenti et gloriam in
futuro.

Liceat improbum uideri ualeat animum emulatione iusta preditum
ad exhibendam iustitiam interpellare, tamen karus michi in Christo
Warnerius, uinitor municipalis Oxoniensis, per suam obtinuit impro-
bitatem ut presentem petitionem uestre dirigerem serenitati, per
quam uestram rogo discretionem quatinus de consueta rectitudinis
beneuolentia iugiter gerente promptitudinem, ut quod iustum est
iuste exequamini, uelitis dicto Warnerio fauorabile patrocinium
impendere tam efficaciter quam misericorditer, ut que sua sunt sibi
restituantur a quibusdam*a* in manerio de Thame' degentibus, quibus,
ut asserit, dudum mutui prestitit beneficium.

Valete, ut supra.

130 *a* quibus *MS.*

---

[2] Kyllum was presented by the crown to St Mary's, Oxford, on 26 Nov. 1248: *CPR*
1247–58, p. 33. Cf. Letter 10.

hesitant pen to submit this little petition. I am making this request on behalf of Sir Peter Kyllum,[2] bearer of this letter, whom the king's excellence has presented, I think with your agreement, to the rectory of the church of the Blessed Virgin at Oxford, out of regard for our Saviour and the salvation of souls. I ask you to receive the said rector with favour and, if you please, to look after him with all consideration, when he comes to the presence of the lord king.

I pray that the author of life may direct your outstanding genius, enviable energy, and fluent speech by the road that leads to life, that in all things you may judge rightly, act with vigour, constrain with moderation, and distribute with justice, referring every rule of life to that end where God is all in all in sure eternity and perfect peace.[3] In Christ, etc.

130

To John of Crakehall

Brother Adam to his very dear lord in Christ John of Crakehall,[1] steward of the lord bishop of Lincoln, grace in the present and glory in the life to come.

It may seem monstrous to importune the spirit of a man conspicuously endowed with a zeal for justice to ask him to render someone his just rights; however, my beloved in Christ Warner, the town vintner of Oxford, has obtained by his importunate persistence that I should send your serenity this request, asking you, with your customary kindness and rectitude, always prompt to execute justice, to grant the said Warner your favour and support, combining mercy with efficacy, so that he may receive restitution of his own property from certain persons dwelling on the manor of Thame, to whom, as he asserts, he some time ago granted the favour of a loan.

Farewell, as above.

---

[3] Cf. Augustine, *De civitate Dei*, xix. 20; CSEL xl, ii. 407; one of Adam's favoured valedictions.

130 [1] For Crakehall see Letter 21 n. 1.

131

To Master Hugh de Mortimer

Honorabili uiro, domino Cantuariensi officiali, magistro Hugoni de Mortuo Mari,[1] Frater Ada, post felicem cursum temporis beatum brauium eternitatis.

Tanto fiducialius ad prouisiuum disertitudinis uestre patrocinium in necessariis considerationis pie negotiis recurritur, quanto apud sinceritatem uestram emulatio iusta serenum ingenium specialius insignire dinoscitur. Eapropter pro muliere paupere de Rading', nomine Mylisand, quam, ut dicitur, in cause matrimonialis pia prosecutione iniurie multiplices fallacium diffugiorum perperam pregrauarunt, beneuolam auctoritatis uestre discretionem attentius obsecro, quatinus eidem secundum salutarem necessitatis sue requisitionem, quatenus nec detrahitur misericordie nec ueritati obuenitur, ob Saluatoris intuitum, subuentum pietatis efficacia maturiori exhibere non ducatis indignum.

Valeat saluifica strenuitatis uestre sospitas ad salutaria dispensationis ecclesiastice moderamina in Christo semper et beatissima Virgine.

132

To Master Simon de Walton

Honorabili uiro, magistro Simon de Waletun'[1] Frater Ada, gratie uiam et gloriam patrie.

Licet modicitatem meam ab interpellando ⟨tenuitas meritorum⟩[a] reuocauerit, eandem ⟨probata dilectionis uestre liberalitas⟩[b] ad interpellandum animauit. Quocirca pro dilecto michi in Christo Iohanne, latore presentium, liberali pietatis uestre discretioni affectuose supplico, rogans obnixius quatinus eidem in urgentiori necessitatis negotio optatum propensioris gratie subsidium, quatenus et adheretur misericordie et ueritati obtemperatur, ob contemplationem Saluatoris benignius exhibere non ducatis indignum.

Valeat serenitatis uestre integra sospitas in Christo, etc.

---

132 [a] *Suggested by the editor to replace an evident lacuna in the text.*   [b] *Supplied by editor as for (a) above.*

131

To Master Hugh de Mortimer

Brother Adam to the honourable Master Hugh de Mortimer,[1] Official to the lord of Canterbury, after a happy career in time the blessed prize of eternity.

The knowledge that your lucid intelligence is especially distinguished by your zeal for justice gives one all the more confidence in appealing to your discerning patronage in cases of need where piety is concerned. For this reason I entreat the kind assistance of your office for a poor woman of Reading named Melisande, who in prosecuting her matrimonial case is said to be suffering many and various wrongs through fraudulent evasions. I ask you, out of regard for our Saviour, to be so kind as to give her your early and efficacious help in response to her reasonable request and her need, so long as it involves nothing contrary to mercy or truth.

Wishing you health and energy for your safe management of the affairs of the Church, ever in Christ and the Blessed Virgin.

132

To Master Simon de Walton

Brother Adam to the honourable Master Simon of Walton,[1] grace on your journey and glory in your homeland.

Although my lack of merit discouraged my poor self from appealing to you, the proven generosity of your love has encouraged me to do so. I am therefore affectionately begging you, out of your goodness and generosity, on behalf of John, my beloved in Christ, the bearer of this letter, with a pressing request that you would be kind enough to grant him the assistance of your favour in his business of which he has pressing need, out of regard for our Saviour, so long as there is no abandonment of mercy or truth.

Wishing your serenity all health in Christ, etc.

131 [1] Hugh de Mortimer appears as Official of Archbishop Boniface on 6 Feb. 1248: *CPR 1247–58*, p. 8; he was still acting in that capacity on 26 July 1256: ibid. p. 489.

132 [1] Simon of Walton was a king's clerk who served several times as a justice in eyre between 1246 and and 1252; he was bishop of Norwich 1257–66: *BRUO* iii. 1975–6.

133

To Simon de Montfort, earl of Leicester

(1249–51)

f. 53 Illustri domino Simoni comiti Leycestriensi Frater Ada, salutem in mundi Saluatore.

Quoniam occurrit opportunitas interuenientis, uidelicet Petri de Pontissara, fidelis*a* uestri, quod uoce nequeo hoc ago littera, scilicet desiderate dominationi uestre modicitatem meam presentem exhibeo.

Quoniam 'immittit angelus Domini in circuitu timentium eum et eripiet eos',[1] indubitanter spero quod timoratam uestre pietatis animam et inter hostilitatum discrimina et inter molimina proditionum et ultra inter ancipites seculi uacillantis euentus, Illius conseruabit clementia de quo scriptum est, 'Rex, qui sedet in solio iudicii, dissipat omne malum intuitu suo';[2] si tamen, sicut insinuaui, ex diuini nominis timore sancto, qui permanet in eternum, indefessa sollicitudine satagatis, ut sit et in persona uestra et in militibus uestris et in seruientibus uestris, et in uniuersis regimen uestrum contingentibus, ad Dominum pia deuotio, ad homines fedus inuiolatum, inuicem fides uel amicitia, sigillatim honesta conuersatio, ad beneuolos socialis concordia, ad discolos rationabilis controuersia, ad universos caritas intemerata. Talibus enim hostiis promeretur Deus. Quod 'si Deus pro nobis quis contra nos?'[3]

Recolamus indesinenter uigilantissimam Dei dispensationem circa diuinum prophetam Helyseum, cui, quia timorem Dei non deseruit, ipsum ab hominum timore eripiens superna protectio, cum armatorum contra inermem conspirasset seuitia, castrorum celestium igneas acies numerosius ad subueniendum destinauit.[4]

Breuiauit epistolam breuitas temporis. Nuper scripsit uobis dominus Lyncolniensis. Scripsi etiam et ego. Studeat, oro, uestre discretionis diligentia cum effectu diuine uoluntati, secundum quod littere preferunt, incunctanter adhibere consensum. Molestum est quod postquam recepi litteram uestram dudum confectam, super desiderabili status uestri prosperitate, quem conseruet sempiterna miseratio, certitudinem nullam audiui.

133   *a* fidens *MS.*

133

To Simon de Montfort, earl of Leicester

(1249–51)

Brother Adam to the illustrious lord Simon, earl of Leicester, greetings in the Saviour of the world.

As there is an opportunity of communication between us, in the form of your faithful servant Peter of Pontoise, I am doing by letter what I cannot do orally, that is making my humble self present to your lordship as I desire.

Because 'the angel of the Lord encamps round about them that fear him and shall deliver them',[1] I have a sure hope that in the midst of conflict and danger, the contrivances of treachery and the uncertainties of a shifting world, your anxious and devout soul will be preserved by the mercy of Him of whom it is written 'The king that sitteth on the throne of judgement, scattereth away all evil with his look';[2] so long as you strive, as I have assumed you do, with unwearying effort, out of a holy fear of the divine name which endures for ever, to maintain your pious devotion to the Lord, both in yourself and your soldiers and in your servants, and in everything pertaining to your governance; maintaining unbroken covenants with men, amd trust and friendship between one another, individually living an upright life, offering a peaceful alliance to those of good will, to the rebellious reasonable opposition, to all an inviolate charity. For by such offerings is God's favour won. 'If God be for us, who is against us?'[3]

We constantly recall God's watchful care of the holy prophet Elisha: because he did not abandon his fear of God, heaven delivered him from the fear of men when an armed conspiracy had risen against him, unarmed as he was, and repeatedly sent him fiery reinforcements.[4]

Shortage of time has shortened my letter. The lord bishop of Lincoln wrote to you recently; and I also wrote. Strive diligently and efficaciously, I pray you, unhesitatingly to carry out the divine will, as it is set before you by our letters. It troubles me that since receiving your letter, which was written some time ago, I have had no reliable news of your desired welfare. May the everlasting pity of God keep you.

133   [1] Ps. 33: 8.   [2] Prov. 20: 8.
      [3] Rom. 8: 31.   [4] Possibly the reference is to 4 Kgs. (2 Kgs.) 1: 9–12.

Valeat, oro, uestre serenitatis secundum hominem utrumque incolumitas in Christo semper et beatissima Virgine.

134

To Simon de Montfort, earl of Leicester

(October 1251)

Illustri uiro, domino Simoni comiti Leycestriensi, Frater Ada, salutem et spiritum salutaris consilii cum spiritu inuicte fortitudinis. In festo Sancti Dyonisii[1] putabat se comitissa lectum puerperii conscensuram, quamuis non sicut coniiciebat dies pariendi aduenisset.[2] Cumque loqueretur michi domina super hiis que et uestri et sui tam salutem perhennem quam statum temporalem contingunt, et inter alia michi innotuisset quod uicarium cancellarii Sarisbiriensis, curandis animabus ecclesie de Hodiham[3] obligatum, uobiscum duxissetis Vasconiam, miratus sum quamplurimum pro eo quod cum periculo manifesto tam innumerabilis populi uel ad tempus uiduare consensistis dictam ecclesiam dicto uicario, per immutabilem Dei legem ad continuam residentiam pro salute iugiter operanda constricto, et etiam pro eo quod hominem, de cuius affectione uel industria uel conuersatione uobis nec per sufficiens testimonium nec per experientiam probabilem facta est presumptio rationabilis; et*a* insuper pro eo quod homini incognito et domino suo, quasi rem magnam ob contemplationem uestri fecerint, uestram in posterum excellentiam constituere uoluistis obnoxiam.

Quid plura? Non mediocriter anxiatus animus meus de hiis cogitat. Quid etenim claram pie mentis circumspectionem obtenebrauerit ignoro in re tam euidentis erroris. Auget autem dolorem ⟨quod⟩, prout audio, quasdam habetis ineptias, quibus in hac parte factum non immerito reprobandum putatis*b* posse defensari.*c* Parcat eis, oro, Dominus, qui illas cordi beneuolo persuadere curauerunt.

Reuelet uobis oculos celestis illuminatio ad considerandam diuine uoluntatis ueritatem, ne presentis seculi fallaciis seducti, quod absit,

---

134 *a* est *MS.*   *b* petatis *MS.*   *c* defensare *MS.*

---

134 [1] 9 Oct.
[2] The expected birth was that of the Montforts' fifth son, Richard. Adam's report of his conversation with the Countess Eleanor, which he sends to Montfort in Gascony, indicates that she was then at Kenilworth; but Letter 30 tells us that Eleanor accompanied Simon

I pray your serenity may enjoy health and safety in both your interior and your exterior life, ever in Christ and the Blessed Virgin.

134

To Simon de Montfort, earl of Leicester

(October 1251)

Brother Adam to the illustrious lord Simon, earl of Leicester, greetings and a spirit of wise counsel with a spirit of unvanquished resolution.

On the feast of St Denis[1] the countess conjectured that she was going into labour,[2] although the day of birth had not arrived as she supposed. When her ladyship was speaking to me about matters relating to both your eternal salvation and hers and your temporal situation, she mentioned to me, among other things, that you had taken with you to Gascony the vicar of the chancellor of Salisbury, who is bound to the cure of souls at the church of Odiham.[3] I was very much surprised by the fact that you had, with obvious danger to so many people, agreed to deprive that church even for a time of its said vicar, who is bound by the immutable law of God to continuous residence for the continual work of salvation, and by the fact that you had agreed to take up a man of whose affection, application, and manner of life you had no reasonable assurance either from adequate testimony or from proven experience; and also by the fact that your excellency was willing to place yourself under a future obligation to an unknown man and his lord, as if they had done you some great service out of their regard for you.

What more can I say? I am not a little disturbed to think of this. I do not know what obscured the clarity and prudence of your pious mind to cause such an error. It makes me more sorry that you have, as I hear, some absurd arguments by which you think it possible to defend an act which deserves to be condemned. I pray the Lord may forgive those who took pains to persuade your kind heart of these arguments.

May a heavenly illumination enlighten you to contemplate the true will of God, that you be not seduced, which God forbid, by the

back to Gascony in mid-June 1252, following his trial *coram rege*. It therefore appears that the childbirth that was expected early in October must have been in 1251 while Simon was in Gascony.   [3] Odiham (Hampshire).

cum cecis ducibus ceci in foueam corruatis.[4] Propter Dei honorem,
propter uestri salutem, propter ecclesie necessitatem, studeat, obsecro, deinceps uestra pia discretio presentem corrigere transgressionem, remittendo ad oues proprias suum pastorem pro quibus apud
formidandum iudicem suam animam defixit, et in similibus de cetero
constantius, cautius et salubrius, propter benedictum Dei Filium,
negotiari.

Sit benedictio superne dispensationi, quamuis non cessent obstetricationes[d] malignantium et insidiantium molimina, fiduciam conceperunt amici uestri in Christo, quod susceptum onus[5] per Ipsius
adiutorium magnifice, sapienter et utiliter, quamuis non sine laboriosi
sudoris grauamine, supportabitis.

135
To Simon de Montfort, earl of Leicester

Illustri uiro, domino Simoni comiti Leycestriensi, Frater Ada.

O benignissime comes, quantam puritatem, quantam claritatem,
quantam sanctitatem a diuina retributione in regno Dei percipietis,
pro eo quod ad ecclesiam Dei purgandam, illuminandam et sancti-
ficandam, tam felici sollicitudine per ydoneum regimen indefesse
satagitis. Quid enim umquam Dei Filio cogitari poterit tam gratiose
complacitum quam ut saluandis animabus iugiter inuigiletur, pro
quibus Ipse pii cruoris effusione sub tantis agoniis rubricare uoluit
salutifere crucis patibulum?

Quid proderit paci ciuium prospicere et pacem domesticorum non
custodire? Attendamus quia 'melior est patiens uiro forti; et qui
dominatur animo ⟨suo⟩ expugnatore urbium'.[1] Miror ni prudentie
uestre subtilitas aduertat quid per hunc intendo sermonem.

Valeat uestre serenitatis eminentia, etc. Rescribat michi, si placet,
exquisite de omnibus que rescribenda iudicaueritis, uestrum super eis
insinuando sensum pariter et beneplacitum.

---

[d] obstetricationes *a curious expression in this context; perhaps it could be rendered*
'brainchildren', or possibly 'entanglements'.

deceits of the present age and with blind leaders fall blindly into the ditch.[4] For the honour of God, for your own salvation and the needs of the Church, I beg your lordship to correct this transgression and send back their pastor to his own sheep, for whom he has pledged his soul to the dread judge, and in similar cases to act for the future with more steadiness, greater care, and more salutary judgement, for the sake of the blessed Son of God.

Blessed be the dispensation of heaven, although there be no end to the contrivances of the malicious and the efforts of the cunning, your friends in Christ have concluded with confidence that you will, through His help, support the burden you have undertaken[5] magnificently, wisely and usefully, though not without heavy sweat and toil.

135

To Simon de Montfort, earl of Leicester

Brother Adam to the illustrious lord Simon, earl of Leicester.

O most kind earl, what shining purity, glory, and holiness will be your divine reward in the kingdom of God because you toil tirelessly and with such happiness and solicitude to purify, illuminate, and sanctify the Church of God through appropriate governance. For whatever can be thought so pleasing to the Son of God as perpetual vigilance for the salvation of souls, for whom He wished to redden the saving gibbet of the cross by pouring out his blood in so much agony?

What will be the use of providing for the peace of your citizens and not maintaining peace in your household? Let us keep in mind that 'the patient man is better than the valiant; and he that ruleth his spirit, than he that taketh cities'.[1] I shall be surprised if your prudence and subtlety fail to grasp my meaning.

Farewell your eminence, etc. Write back to me, if you please, in detail about everything you judge worthwhile, indicating your mind and good pleasure regarding everything.

---

[4] Cf. Matt. 15: 14.
[5] i.e. the royal commission to the governor of Gascony; cf. Letters 30 n. 8 and 133.

135   [1] Prov. 16: 32.

136

To Simon de Montfort, earl of Leicester

(?1252, post June)

Illustri domino comiti Leycestriensi Frater Ada salutem.

Desiderabilis status uestri incolumitas, quam ex tenore littere michi transmisse perpendere potui, sit diuino nomini benedictio, cordi meo letas ingessit gratiarum actiones. De reditu uestro tamen tam festino non modicam concepi admirationem, licet nouerim quod ipsum requisierit causarum grandium urgens consideratio. Igitur 'uiriliter agite, et mens uestra confortetur in Domino',[1] de quo sperandum indubitanter ⟨est⟩, quod per ipsius clementissimam dispensationem qui non despicit presumentes de se, quantumcumque uideantur insperati euentus sanos salutarium propositorum conceptus retardare ipsos, propter sui nominis honorem et salutem Ipsi fideliter obsequentium, ad laudabilem supra quam optari ualeat consummationem perducere dignabitur.

Etsi multiplex experientia tenuem prestet fiduciam ad habenda super negotiis de quibus scripsistis circumspecta, secundum quod res requirunt consilia, diuinitate tamen | propitia, in cuius manu corda sunt regum,[2] diffidendum nullatenus est, quominus 'humiliati sub potenti manu Dei, omnem sollicitudinem nostram in Ipsum proiiciamus, quoniam Ipsi est cura de nobis',[3] quod iustum est iuste persequendo, ambiguos actionum nostrarum exitus ad certum finem diuine uoluntatis dirigamus.

Valeat serenissima nobilitas uestra. Valeat et illustris comitissa. Valeant et carissima pignore uestra.[4] Valeant et omnia dignam dominationem uestra contingentia, in Christo semper et beatissima Virgine.

f. 53ᵛ

---

136 [1] Cf. Ps. 26: 14.   [2] Cf. Prov. 21: 1.   [3] 1 Pet. 5: 6–7.
    [4] i.e. his sons, whom Montfort placed in Grosseteste's household for their education. Adam's valediction needs to be seen in connection with Letter 30, in which he reports to

136

To Simon de Montfort, earl of Leicester

(?1252, post June)

Brother Adam to the illustrious lord, the earl of Leicester, greetings.

I give joyful and heartfelt thanks for your safety, of which I have been able to gather news from the letters sent me. Blessed be the name of God for it. I was, however, not a little astonished at the haste of your return, though I knew that it was required by an urgent consideration of great questions. So 'do manfully, and thy mind shall be strengthened in the Lord'.[1] Of Him we must hope without doubting that through his most merciful dispensation, He who does not despise those who trust in Him, may deign—however much well-conceived plans seem to be set back by unexpected events—to bring them to a glorious completion beyond anything we could have desired, for the honour of his name and the salvation of those who faithfully serve Him.

Although much experience gives one slender hope that the needful wise counsels will prevail as the matter demands in the business about which you wrote, still, with the favour of God, in whose hands are the hearts of kings,[2] we must on no account lose faith, so that 'humbling ourselves under the mighty hand of God, we may cast all our care upon Him, for He hath care of us';[3] and pursuing justice by means that are just, we may direct our actions with the uncertainty of their outcome to a sure end which is the will of God.

Farewell, your serene lordship. Farewell to your illustrious countess, and farewell to your dearest pledges;[4] and may all things touching your lordship prosper, ever in Christ and the Blessed Virgin.

Grosseteste that the earl, accompanied by his countess and children, had returned to Gascony on 13 June 1252, following his trial before the king.

137

To Simon de Montfort, earl of Leicester

Illustri uiro, comiti Leycestriensi, Frater Ada. Si tota mentis fiducia pergamus in Illum, qui uenientes ad se non eiicit foras,[1] nec unquam deserit de sua misericordia presumentes, licet labores nostri optatum non sortiantur effectum, Deo melius aliquid prouidente semper omnibus qui colunt Ipsum, uigiles actuum nostrorum sollicitudines ad salutatiorem exitum perducentur. Quamobrem si quod intendimus proueniat, bene quidem; sin autem, certissime speremus longe desiderabiliora quam conceperimus. Per omnia sit diuino nomini superexaltata benedictio; perhenniter quoque obseruetur et Filio Dei fides inuiolata et legitimum fedus filiis hominum.

Immodica uisa est littera serenitatis uestre michi nuper transmissa ⟨circa⟩ illam quam, nec immerito fateor, erga nobilitatem uestram inter mortales specialem concepi affectionem, quasi in hiis quecunque uestre scripsi discretioni, super quam conueniret claros excellentie uestre titulos expresserim. Super quo cor meum hactenus non reprehendit, cum in hoc, ut reor, nec ab exemplis recesserim sapientum, nec rationis obuenerim exigentiis. Certum etenim est quod, licet ignobilis anime stultitia et suis honoribus eleuetur in superbiam et suis laudibus deiiciatur ad ignauiam, tamen illustris anime sapientia et ex illis ad humilitatem inclinatur et ex istis ad uirtutem animatur. Propter hoc, mi desideratissime comes, in hac parte nec uirorum[a] timeo discrimen nec meam accusationem, sperans quod ex hoc diuinitatis clementia et uobis et michi pariter fiet in sapientiam.

Quanto magis precipitem ruentis mundi processum conspicio, tanto districtius formidandas diuinorum iudiciorum sententias indubitanter aduerto uniuersis quos bestialis uesania[b] infatuauit. Sed quid? In hoc tantummodo consultum erit electis ut Saluatoris sui iussionibus obtemperent ubi, cum horrendas seculi ruinas premisisset, subiungit 'Hiis autem fieri incipientibus, respicite, et leuate capita uestra, quoniam appropinquat redemptio uestra'.[2]

Protractiorem epistolam temporis excludit angustia.

---

137 [a] uirium *MS*   [b] *after* uesania *MS adds* non, *seemingly contrary to the sense of the passage.*

137

To Simon de Montfort, earl of Leicester

Brother Adam to the illustrious earl of Leicester.

If we turn with total trust to Him who does not cast out those who come to Him[1] nor ever deserts those who have confidence in his mercy, although our labours do not produce the effect we desire, God always provides something better for those who worship Him, and the acts on which we have expended so much anxiety will be brought to a healthier outcome. For this reason, if what we strive for prospers, well and good; but if not, let us surely expect far more desirable things than we had thought of. Above all, let us in everything bless the name of God, forever maintain our faith in the Son of God undiminished, and keep lawful covenants with the sons of men.

You overreacted in the letter which your serenity recently sent me with respect to that special affection which, and not without reason, I confess I expressed for your lordship above all mortal men, as if, in whatever things I addressed to your discernment, I exaggerated beyond what was seemly your lordship's titles to glory. In this my heart does not so far rebuke me, since in this I have not, as I think, departed from the examples of the wise nor acted contrary to the demands of reason. For it is certain that, although an ignoble and foolish soul is both puffed up by honours and made slothful by praise, a wise and illustrious soul is disposed to humility by the former and stimulated to virtue by the latter. In this respect, my dear earl, I fear neither the judgement of men nor the accusation of myself, in the hope that from this the mercy of God will confer the gift of wisdom on you and me equally.

The more I see the headlong rush of the world to its ruin, the more my thoughts are directed to the fearful sentence of divine judgement falling without doubt upon all who have been driven mad by bestial insanity. What then? In this situation the chosen can only be counselled to heed the commands of their Saviour who, when He predicted the awful destruction of the world, added 'when these things begin to come to pass, look up and lift up your heads, because your redemption is at hand'.[2]

Shortage of time precludes a longer letter.

137   [1] Cf. John 6: 37.   [2] Luke 21: 28.

138

To Simon de Montfort, earl of Leicester

(1250 × 1251)

Illustri uiro, comiti Leycestriensi Frater Ada, salutem et post gratiosa certaminum merita gloriosa triumphorum premia.

Si rupti federis et affectionis ficte responsa recipiatis, quid aliud quam quod antea cogitastis postea toleratis? Nempe quod expectauit presentia hoc experientia representat. Meminit, ni fallor, prudentie uestre clara circumspectio quam frequenti sollicitorum examinum colloquio auribus nostris inuicem ingessimus, quam aspicimus oculis execrandam seductiue calliditatis impudentiam, licet ob imminentes falsitatis stupende suspiciones, considerata fidelitatis animose fiducia, ambiguum pregrandis negotii discrimen subire nequaquam formidauerit.

Sed quid? Certe mitigant afflictionum presentiam premeditationes periculorum, secundum amplexandam diuini Gregorii sententiam, qua dicitur, 'Minus feriunt iacula que preuidentur, et nos tolerabilius mundi mala suscipimus si contra hec per prouidentie clipeum munimur'.[1] Hec est etenim circa fidelem electorum militiam saluifica dispensatio, ut sublatis secularis confidentie subsidiis, totaliter se conferat triumphalis militantium fortitudo ad superne uirtutis insuperabile presidium, que de se seculis omnibus clamat, dicens (Prou. 8),[a] 'Meum est consilium et equitas, mea est prudentia, et mea est fortitudo. Per me reges regnant et legum conditores iusta decernunt; per me principes imperant et potentes decernunt iustitiam. Ego diligentes me diligo, et qui mane uigilant ad me inuenient me.'[2]

Qualiter, inquies, illam diligens ad illam uigilabo? Audiamus illum ad magistratus mundi directum precipue prophete sermonem (Mich. 6),[a] 'Indicabo tibi, O homo, quid sit bonum, et quid Dominus querat a te. Utique facere iudicium et diligere misericordiam et sollicitum ambulare cum Deo tuo.'[3] Ut, uidelicet, ab hiis qui presunt in iudicio per censuram districtionis plectantur discoli, in misericordia per affectum mansuetudinis subleuentur deuoti, in sollicita diuini comitatus ambulatione per cultum diuinitatis

---

138   *a   The copyist here reproduces Adam's arabic numerals.*

138

To Simon de Montfort, earl of Leicester

(1250 × 1251)

Brother Adam to the illustrious earl of Leicester, greetings, and the glorious reward of triumph after the grace and merit of the struggle.

If you are receiving the responses of a broken treaty and feigned affection, are you enduring anything other than what you had expected? Surely what you anticipated is fulfilled by your experience. Unless I am mistaken, with your clear-sighted wisdom you recall the frequent anxious conversations in which we afflicted each others' ears with tales of the detestable treachery and cunning which we now see with our eyes; yet with your lively trust in fealty, you have not in the least feared to incur the uncertain risk of a large-scale undertaking, despite your insistent suspicion of amazing bad faith.

What then? Afflictions are mitigated by anticipation of perils, according to the judgement of St Gregory, which we should adopt, where he says 'Darts that are foreseen are less wounding, and the evils of the world are more bearable if we are armed against them by the shield of foresight'.[1] For the warfare of the saints has this saving dispensation, that when confidence in worldly assistance is gone, the triumphant courage of the warriors becomes entirely dependent upon the invincible strength and protection of heaven, which in all ages cries aloud of itself with the words 'Counsel and equity is mine; prudence is mine; strength is mine. By me kings reign, and lawyers decree just things; by me princes rule, and the mighty decree justice. I love them that love me; and they that in the morning early watch for me shall find me.' Prov. 8.[2]

How, you will ask, shall I keep watch for that which I love? Let us listen to the speech of the prophet, especially addressed to the governors of the world: 'I will show thee, O man, what is good and what the Lord requireth of thee: verily, to do judgement and to love mercy, and to walk solicitous with thy God.' Mich. 6.[3] That is, the malicious are to be strictly admonished by those who preside in judgement; the loyal are to be supported by gentleness, and affection; all are to be ordered through divine worship to walk carefully in the

138 [1] Gregory the Great, *Homiliae in Evangelia* 35: *PL* lxxvi. 1259.
[2] Prov. 8: 14–17.   [3] Mic. 6: 8.

ordinentur uniuersi. Hec igitur solummodo sunt in quibus ad Christum, Dei uirtutem et Dei sapientiam, maxime uigilabitis, et Ipsius nichilominus comprobabitis dilectionem, per quem solum triumphaliter agitur in hostibus et ciues sapienter gubernantur.

Breuiaui epistolam, nolens inter tot perstrepentium curarum uarietates auribus tam multipliciter occupatis importunos sermones importare; sciens quoque quod studiosa uestre serenitatis industria ex paucis multa prudenter extrahet ad salutem. Hoc exopto, hoc obtestor, hoc rogo, ut salutarem diuinorum eloquiorum consolationem, ex frequenti sacrarum Scripturarum inspectione, ruptis, quoad fieri poterit, secundum rationis sustinentiam sepius intermissis perturbantium sollicitudinum uehementiis, uobis summopere comparare studeatis. Pernecessarium uestre discretioni fore puto, ut capitula .xxix., .xxx., .xxxi., libri Iob, et cetera statui uestro in eodem libro conuenientia, cum suauissimis expositionibus Sancti Gregorii, diligenti scrutinio, prout diuinitus dabitur, frequentetis.

Locutus est michi dominus rex de facto uestro, qui, ut credo, libenter consiliis uestris adquiesceret, plurimum de integritate fidei uestre confidens, si in hac parte ipsum fauorabiliter sua fulcirent latera.[4] Allocutus sum et ego dominam reginam diligenter super agendis uestris, que ad omnia rationabiliter et benigne respondit, de uobis etiam magnam habens spem subuentionis.

Benedictus Deus, ualet dominus Lyncolniensis et insignes liberi uestri indolis eximie et magne spei de die in diem in bono proficientes. Statum regni, cui Dominus subueniat, dominus Iohannes de la Haye[5] uobis melius poterit referre. Scripsistis michi nuper de uariis periculis mundo imminentibus. Audita autem sunt postmodum apud nos omnibus hominibus inexplicabiliter terrifica.

Valeat excellentie uestre desiderabilis incolumitas in Christo semper et beatissima Virgine.

---

[4] The word *latera* which Adam uses here is slightly ambiguous; it could also mean the king's intimate counsellors.

company of God. These alone are, therefore, the things in which you
shall be most watchful for Christ, the power of God, and the wisdom
of God, and you shall no less attest the love of Him, through whom
alone you may triumph over enemies and citizens may be governed
with wisdom.

I have shortened my letter, not wanting to bother your ears with
unseasonable words when you are preoccupied with the clamorous
demands of various matters. I know, too, that your serenity's zeal and
concentration will extract from a few words much that is relevant to
salvation. This I long for, this is my entreaty and request, that you are
careful to procure for yourself the consolation of the words of God by
frequently consulting the Holy Scriptures, taking a break, so far as is
reasonably possible, from the exigencies and worries of your duties. I
think it is most necessary for your discerning lordship, as the Lord
affords you opportunity, frequently and diligently to study chapters
29, 30, and 31 of the book of Job, and other passages in that book that
are relevant to your condition, together with the delightful commentaries of St Gregory.

The lord king has spoken to me about your matter. He would, I
believe, freely give his consent to what you advise, if his relatives[4]
gave their favour and support in this matter, as he has much
confidence in your complete loyalty. I have also spoken earnestly to
the lady queen about your proposals, and she replied reasonably and
kindly to everything, being very hopeful of your receiving a subvention.

The lord bishop of Lincoln is well, blessed be God, and your
distinguished children, whose outstanding talents give us great hopes
of them, daily progress in virtue. As to the state of the kingdom,
which may the Lord succour, Sir John de la Haye[5] will be better able
to give you a report. You recently wrote to me about various dangers
threatening in different parts of the world. Shortly afterwards we
came to hear of terrible things which no man can explain.

Farewell and safety to your dear excellency, ever in Christ and the
Blessed Virgin.

---

[5] John de la Haye was a knightly tenant of the honour of Leicester, and frequently a
member of Montfort's household, to whom he remained a loyal supporter in the 1260s:
Maddicott, *Simon de Montfort*, pp. 66–8.

139

To Simon de Montfort, earl of Leicester

f. 54 Comiti Leycestriensi Frater Ada.

Breuitas temporis et uarietas occupationum et cursoris uestri acceleratio non permiserunt, licet hoc plurimum optarem, hac uice prolixius scribere. Idcirco litteram pariter et incipio et finio, hoc monens, hoc obsecrans, hoc obtestans, ut quanto diuinitatis clementia nomini suo dans gloriam, et uestre deuotioni dans gratiam supra quam estimare poterit, magnifica sua uoluntatis negotia per laborosiam uestre sollicitudinis efficaciam prosperiori fauore dinoscitur, tanto misericordia indulgentiori et fideliori ueritate, directiori iustitia et tranquilliori pace, ex tota cordis affectione, ex tota anime districtione, ex tota uirtutis intentione amplius in auctorem salutis assurgat saluifica mentis generose dilectio.

Quid enim? Quanti sceleris fore putabitur, si inde contra diuinitatem insollescere contingat arrogantia? Unde secundum assertionem Scripture, 'peccatum maximum et negationem contra Deum altissimum'[1] admittere conuincitur, diuinam ordinationem dampnabiliter euacuans, qui ex Ipsius muneribus non proficit. In ipsum formidandum est iudicium ingratitudinis que legitimum exheredat filium.

Libuit littera, quod uoce non licuit, adire uidelicet desideratam uestre serenitatis presentiam. Quod utinam concedatur michi diuinitus cum opportunitate maturiori personaliter adimplere. Superuacuum putaui scribere uobis de hiis que plenius uobis scripsit uenerabilis dominus Lyncolniensis,[2] qui, benedictus Deus, corpore ualet et spiritu. Valent et amabiles liberi uestri, ut spero, proficientes etate pariter et gratia. Agendum est iugiter piis precaminum instantiis ut malignorum molimina reprimat omnipotentis sapientie pietas.

Locutus fui de negotio subuentionis uobis faciende per indulgentiam apostolicam, sicut expedire putaui. Concepi autem spem indubitatam in Domino quod illud bene prosperabitur per sollicitudinem domini Lyncolniensis et domini Wygorniensis,[3] uobis inter mortales omnes speciali amicitia fauorabiliores.

Conseruetur, oro, uestre serenitatis incolumitas in Christo semper, etc.

139 [1] Job 31: 28.   [2] Robert Grosseteste.
[3] Walter Cantilupe, bishop of Worcester 1236–66.

139

To Simon de Montfort, earl of Leicester

Brother Adam to the earl of Leicester.

Shortness of time, my various engagements, and the haste of your courier have not allowed me to write at greater length this time, much as I would have liked to. So I am beginning and ending my letter all at once. This I admonish, entreat and implore you, the more the mercy of God glorifies your name and gives grace beyond human telling to you in your devotion, and with his favour is seen to be performing the magnificent works of his will through the effective instruments of your toil and care, all the more the salvific love of your generous mind should be directed to the author of salvation, by exercising more forgiving mercy, by greater faithfulness to truth, by straighter justice, and by greater peace and tranquillity, stretching out to Him with all the love of your heart and all the strength of your soul.

Well then, what a sin we shall think it if on this account one should be puffed up with pride, thereby insulting the deity. According to Scripture, he who does not profit from His gifts, and to his damnation makes God's dispensation void, is guilty of the greatest sin and denial of the Most High.[1] It is to be feared that he incurs the charge of ingratitude, which disinherits the lawful son.

It has given me pleasure to address your dear lordship by letter, as it was not possible to do so by word of mouth. Would that God would grant me an earlier opportunity to see you in person. I thought it superfluous to write to you about matters which the venerable lord bishop of Lincoln has written to you about more fully.[2] He is well in body and spirit, blessed be God. Your dear children are also well and are, I hope, advancing in both age and grace. We must always persevere in our prayers that the goodness and wisdom of the Almighty may repress the endeavours of the wicked.

I have spoken about the business of providing you with a subvention by a papal grant, as I thought it expedient. I have in my mind an unwavering hope in the Lord, that it will succeed through the efforts of the lord bishop of Lincoln and the lord bishop of Worcester,[3] who favour you among all men with their special friendship.

I pray your serenity may be preserved ever in Christ, etc.

140

To Simon de Montfort, earl of Leicester

(1253–4)

Comiti Leycestriensi Frater Ada.

Si uirum honorabilem, dominum decanum Lyncolniensem,[1] nobilitati uestre beneuolentia spirituali fideliter obnoxium, cui iuxta morem ecclesie sue in solempni Beate Virginis natalitio,[2] utpote nuper in decanie dignitatem sublimato, solempne conuiuium instruere tam honoratioribus quam popularibus sollicite[a] incumbit, grato subuento ferine uenationis censueritis honorandum,[b] reor uobis erit honorificum et deuotis uestris acceptum. Quod et frater Gregorius[3] una mecum fieri precatur.

141

To Simon de Montfort, earl of Leicester

(1250)

Inclito domino Simoni comiti Leycestriensi Frater Ada salutem, et post discrimen certaminis triumphi felicitatem.

Ignoraui quid scriberem, pernesciens quid ageretur circa desiderabilem uestre nobilitatis excellentiam. Licet mentem suspensam uaria uarie referentium assertio, nunc secura nunc periculosa preferens, uacillare compellat inter sollicite formidinis angustias et latitudines expectationis letifice, intolerabilem quoque hesitationum molestiam ingereret, si non et metus diffidentiam adimeret, et exhiberet confidentie securitatem longanimis patientia et consolatio salutaris Scripturarum; in quarum loco quodam ait Dominus exercituum, dispensatoriam maiestatis sue clementiam etiam in uestre strenuitatis sudoribus bellicis depromens, 'Ecce ego mittam angelum—uidelicet Christum, Dei Filium, Dei uirtutem, Dei sapientiam—qui precedat te et custodiat in uia, et introducat ad locum quem paraui. Obserua eum et audi uocem eius, nec contempnendum putes, quia non dimittet cum peccaueris, et est nomen

---

140   [a] sollicius *MS.*   [b] honorendum *MS.*

140

To Simon de Montfort, earl of Leicester

(1253–4)

Brother Adam to the earl of Leicester.

It is a serious obligation of the honourable lord, the dean of Lincoln,[1] your lordship's faithful spiritual servant, as he was recently elevated to the decanal office, to provide a solemn feast for both the dignitaries and people on the solemnity of the Nativity of the Blessed Virgin,[2] in accordance with the custom of his church. If you considered he should be honoured with a gracious subvention of game, I think it would honour you and would please your devoted servants. I, and Brother Gregory[3] with me, beg it should be done.

141

To Simon de Montfort, earl of Leicester

(1250)

Brother Adam to the illustrious lord Simon, earl of Leicester, greetings and after the trial of conflict the happiness of triumph.

I have not known what to write, as I have no knowledge of what has been happening to your noble lordship. I have had varying reports, now with news of your safety, now of your being in danger, which cause me to vacillate between anxiety and fear for you and relief, hope, and joy. The uncertainty would be unbearable if I were not released from my fears and given faith and reassurance by my long-suffering patience and the consolation of the Scriptures. In one passage, the Lord of Hosts extends the merciful kindness of his majesty even to your labour and warfare, where He says 'Behold I will send my angel' (that is, Christ, the Son of God, the power and wisdom of God) 'who shall go before thee and keep thee in the way to bring thee to the place I have prepared. Look out of him and hear his voice, and do not think him one to be condemned, for he will not forgive when thou hast

---

140 [1] Richard Gravesend, who first appears as dean in a papal dispensation for plurality, 28 Aug. 1254: *CPL* i. 305; *Fasti* Lincoln, p. 10.
[2] 8 Sept. [3] Gregory de Bosellis; cf. Letters 1 n. 2, 142, 133, 155, 168.

meum in illo. Quod si audieris uocem eius, et feceris omnia que
loquor, inimicus ero inimicis tuis, et affligam affligentes te. Pre-
cedetque te angelus meus.'[1]
Et post pauca, 'Terrorem meum mittam in precursum tuum,
cunctorumque inimicorum tuorum coram te terga uertam. Non
eiiciam eos a facie tua anno uno, ne terra in solitudinem redigatur
et crescant contra te bestie. Paulatim expellam eos e conspectu tuo,
donec augearis et possideas terram.'[2]
Et alibi, 'Custodi ergo precepta et ceremonias atque iudicia'—
scilicet precepta in forma uiuendi, ceremonias in ritu colendi, iudicia
in censura iudicandi—'que ego mando tibi hodie ut facias. Si
postquam audieris hec et feceris, custodiet Dominus Deus tibi
pactum et misericordiam, quam iurauit patribus tuis, et diliget te et
multiplicabit, benedicetque fructui uentris tui. Benedictus eris inter
omnes populos. Quod si dixeris in corde tuo "Plures sunt iste gentes
quam ego. Quomodo potero delere eas?" Noli metuere. Non timebis
eos, quia Dominus tuus in medio tui est, Deus magnus et terribilis;
ipse consumet nationes in conspectu tuo paulatim atque per partes.
Non poteris eas delere pariter, ne forte multiplicentur contra te bestie
terre. Dabitque Dominus Deus tuus in conspectu tuo, et interficiet
illos donec penitus deleantur. Dabitque reges eorum in manus tuas, et
disperdes nomina eorum sub celo; nullus poterit resistere tibi donec
conteras eos.'[3]
Ex propositis diuinorum eloquiorum testimoniis profecto cernit
illustris uestre claritatis industria, quod non nisi diuine legis custodia
repugnantiam legis diuine poterit edomare. Quis enim ambigit,
preterquam is quem obtenebrauit perfidei caligo, quin rabiem
immanem crudelium misericordium benigna mansuetudo subigat;
quin fallacem calliditatem perditorum fidelium simplicitas ueridica
refellat; quin iniquam persuasionem diripentium distribuentium
largitio recta obtineat; quin inquietam perniciem discordium con-
cordantium pacifica sedulitas trihumphet? Hec est certe superni
regiminis prouida moderatio, per quam sudoris uestri uigor inuictus
in uirtutibus misericordie et ueritatis, iustitie et pacis, crudelitatum et
seductionum, rapacitatum et discidiorum[a] uitia superabit.

141 ᵃ discidionum MS.

141 ¹ Exod. 23: 20–3.   ² Ibid. 23: 27, 29–30.   ³ Cf. Deut. 7: 11–24.

sinned, and my name is in him. But if thou wilt hear his voice and do all that I speak, I will be an enemy to thy enemies, and afflict them that afflict thee. And my angel shall go before thee.'[1]

And a little further on: 'I will send my fear before thee, and I will make all thine enemies turn their backs unto thee. I will not drive them out from before thee in one year, lest the land become desolate and the beasts of the field multiply against thee. By little and little I will drive them out from before thee, until thou be increased and inherit the land.'[2]

And in another place: 'Keep therefore the precepts and ceremonies and judgements' (namely precepts for how we live, ceremonies in the service of divine worship, judgements in the office of a just judge) 'which I command thee this day to do. If after thou hast these judgements, thou keep and do them, the Lord thy God will keep his covenant to thee, and the mercy which he swore to thy fathers, and he will love thee and multiply thee, and will bless the fruit of thy womb. Blessed shalt thou be among all peoples. But if thou say in thy heart: these nations are more than I. How shall I be able to destroy them? Fear not. Thou shalt not fear them, because the Lord thy God is in the midst of thee, a God mighty and terrible. He will consume these nations in thy sight by little and little and by degrees. Thou wilt not be able to destroy them altogether, lest perhaps the beasts of the earth should increase upon thee. But the Lord thy God shall deliver them in thy sight, and shall slay them until they be utterly destroyed. And he shall deliver their kings into thy hands, and thou shalt destroy their names from under heaven. No man shall be able to resist thee, until thou destroy them.'[3]

From the foregoing testimony of the divine word your lordship's attentive mind readily perceives that only by adhering to the divine law can those who reject it be overcome. For only one whose mind is darkened by unbelief doubts that the kindness and gentleness of the merciful shall put down the great ferocity of the cruel; that the truthful simplicity of the faithful shall rebut the cunning and deceitfulness of the lost; that the upright generosity of those who give to others shall conquer the wicked persuasions of those who scatter and break asunder; that the pacific efforts of those who seek harmony shall prevail over the balefulness of those who sow discord. This is surely the provident governance of heaven, by which your indomitable energy and toil will, by virtue of mercy and truth, justice and peace, overcome the vices of cruelty and seduction, greed and discord.

Sed numquid impetu subitaneo et non dispensatiuo tractu? 'Non eiiciam eos a facie tua anno uno, ne terra in solitudinem redigatur, et crescant contra te bestie. Paulatim expello eos de conspectu tuo donec f. 54ᵛ augearis | et possideas terram.'⁴ Ait ergo, 'Non poteris eos delere pariter',⁵ ne cessante hostilitatum incursu uelut solitudo terra sileat, et tam facinorum quam flagitiorum demoniales bestie per otiosam lasciuientis ineptie uecordiam et crescant et multiplicentur contra te, animorum uim euacuentes et eneruantes robur corporum et, quod absit, parta laudabiliter, uituperabiliter collabantur. Quin potius militia triumphalis castigata pauore solicito et uigenti exercitio roborata, non tam in propria strenuitate gratiose consistat, quam proficiat gloriosius ex peruersitate aliena.

Huic accedit euidenter illud beati Augustini ⟨in⟩ libro De Ciuitate Dei quod prudentia Scipionis 'nolebat emulam olim imperii Romani armis subactam Cartaginem dirui, et decernenti ut dirueretur contradicebat Catonis astutie, timens infirmis animis hostem securitatem, et tanquam pupillis ciuibus idoneum tutorem necessarium uidens esse terrorem. Nec eum fefellit sententia reipsa quantum et quam uere diceret; deleta quippe Cartagine, magno scilicet terrore Romane reipublice depulso atque extincto, tanta de rebus prosperis orta mala continuo subsecuta sunt, ut corrupta disrupta est concordia, prius seuis cruentisque seditionibus, deinde mox malarum connexione causarum. Bellis etiam ciuilibus tante strages ederentur, tantus sanguis effunderetur, tanta cupiditate proscriptionum ac rapinarum ferueret immanitas, ut Romani illi qui uita integriore mala metuebant ab hostibus, perdita integritate uite, crudeliora paterentur a ciuibus.'⁶

Et quibusdam interpositis, 'Auarus uero luxuriosusque populus secundis rebus effectus est, quod Scipioᵇ Nasica ille prouidentissime cauendum esse censebat, quando ciuitatem hostium maximam, fortissimam, opulentissimam, nolebat auferri, ut timore libido premeretur, libido pressa non luxuriaretur, luxuriaque prohibita nec auaritia grassaretur; quibus uitiis obseratis ciuitati utilis uirtus floreret et cresceret, eique uirtuti libertas congrua permaneret.'⁷

ᵇ Scipio *inserted above the line.*

---

⁴ Exod. 23: 29–30.   ⁵ Deut. 7: 22.
⁶ *De civitate Dei,* i. 30: *CSEL* xxx (1898), pp. 53–4.   ⁷ Ibid. i. 31.

But will this really be accomplished by a sudden onslaught, and not rather by provident negotiation? 'I will cast them out from thy face in one year, lest the land be brought into a wilderness, and the beasts multiply against thee. By little and little I will drive them out from before thee, till thou be increased, and dost possess the land.'[4] He says therefore 'Thou wilt not be able to destroy them altogether'[5] lest when the assault of your enemies ceases and the earth is deserted and silent, the beastly demons of sin and shame should grow and multiply against you through sloth and folly, depriving men's spirits of their power, weakening the strength of their bodies, and, which God forbid, things praiseworthy at their origin should collapse in ruin and common censure. But rather let a triumphant soldiery, disciplined by fear and concern and strengthened by vigorous exercise, not so much stand thankfully in its own strength, but advance more gloriously through the failings of the enemy.

Clearly that text in the blessed Augustine's book *The City of God* is relevant to this, where the prudence of Scipio 'would not have Carthage, once the rival of the Roman Empire, to be utterly destroyed after it was defeated in arms, but contradicted Cato's cunning decree that it should be destroyed, because he feared that security would be harmful for weak spirits; he considered that fear was a necessary and suitable tutor for citizens under instruction. Nor was he mistaken in his judgement: the event itself afforded sufficient proof of how truly he had spoken. For afterwards, when Carthage had been razed and the great dread of the Roman state had been put down and extinguished, straightaway such great evils arose from prosperity that the bonds of concord were broken asunder, first through brutal and bloody seditions, then soon after through the alliance of evil factions. In fact, civil wars produced so much slaughter and bloodshed, so monstrous were the proscriptions and robberies produced by greed, that those Romans who lived in more honest times feared harm only from their enemies, but now having lost the honourable life, suffered far worse cruelty from their fellow citizens.'[6]

With some intervening words, he goes on: 'The people were made so avaricious and voluptuous by prosperity that that Scipio Nasica when he did not wish the greatest, strongest and richest enemy city destroyed, it was because he believed with the greatest foresight that they should have a care that lust should be repressed by fear, and being repressed, would not have free rein, voluptuousness would be restrained, nor would avarice run riot. Once these vices had been restrained, virtue beneficial to the city would flourish and grow, and liberty, fitting this virtue, would be lasting.'[7]

Igitur si auctoritatum sententiis, si rationum efficaciis, si sapientum exemplis adquiescimus, clementem diuini^c moderaminis ordinationem circa uestram uigilare presumimus discretionem, potissimum ex hoc quod hostes profani rupti federis maligna molimina tranquillitati perturbande conantur excitare. Proinde si ad Altissimum timoratam deuotionem, si ad ecclesiam piam emulationem, si ad proceres socialem honorationem, si ad tyrones munificam subuentionem, si ad plebes regituram defensionem, si ad calamitosos affluentem miserationem, si ad modestos fauorabilem beneuolentiam, si ad federatos inuiolatam pactionem, si ad discolos districtam cohertionem, si ad uniuersos ordinatam dilectionem, procurantes omnimodis et adiutoria ualida et consilia diserta et munda ministeria et iudicia examinata perseueranter seruaueritis, et inter terrificos tubarum clangores et inter horribiles conclamantium uociferationes et inter diros armorum stridores, inter stipatos castrorum congressus et inter precipites corruentium occasus et inter profluos sauciorum cruores et inter miserabiles morientium ululatus, de aduersariis profecto illud diuinitus implebitur, 'Fugit impius nemine persequente'; de uobis uero, 'Iustus ut leo confidens absque terrore erit'.[8] Quod si ducem magnanimum saluandis hominibus ⟨ex⟩ rebus humanis contingat excidere, quid unquam estimabitur aut gloriosius aut decentius aut salutaris, quam propter causam uiuendi, uiuendi finem facere?

Succingo sermonem, sciens quod in cartulis alias uestre discretioni destinatis, licet minus eleganter, non tamen inaniter, caracteres pinxerim. Nichil scribere non permisit amoris solliciti pauens affectio. Ceterum cum attonita mente consideramus fulgurantem hastam diuine districtionis seculis omnibus inauditas formidandarum ultionum immensitates hiis diebus exercentem et super prelatum et super cleros et super principes et super populum, que et summa rerum culmina et deiecit et dissipauit et attriuit, quid aliud quam desipientia humanitatis reuocatur ad Diuinitatis sapientiam, que 'attingit a fine usque ad finem fortiter et disponit omnia suauiter'?[9]

De tam necessario salutis negotio quod nostis in regno Anglie operando, cuius mora summum indubitanter trahit periculum, dolendum fore permaxime censeo, aspiciens illud nescio quo frustratum in Omnipotentis iudicio.

---

^{c} diuine *MS.*

[8] Prov. 28: 1.   [9] Wisd. 8: 1.

If, therefore, we assent to the considered judgements of our
authorities, to the effective arguments of reason, and to the examples
of the wise, our presumption is that the merciful governance of God
is keeping watch over your discreet lordship, especially considering
the fact that your enemies have profanely broken a sworn engagement
and are making malicious efforts to disturb the peace. Thus, if you
persevere in maintaining your pious devotion to the Most High and a
religious zeal for the Church, if you honour the nobles with your
society, if you offer generous help to young recruits, if you defend the
people, show abundant compassion for those who are ruined, favour
and kindness to the virtuous, if you offer your allies an unbroken
covenant, stern force to rebels, and order and love to all, providing in
all respects vigorous assistance, clearly expressed counsel, the service
of incorrupt agents and considered judgements, then even amidst the
dreadful clamour of trumpets, the fearful shouts and the grim
screeching of arms, the pressing concourse of combatants, the
sudden death of those who fall, even amidst the blood streaming
from the wounded and the piteous cries of the dying, that judgement
of God shall assuredly be fulfilled upon your adversaries: 'the wicked
man fleeth, when no man pursueth' and regarding you, 'the just, bold
as a lion, shall be without dread'.[8] But if the great-hearted captain
should happen to lose his life to save his men, what will ever be
judged more glorious or more seemly or salvific than to end one's life
for the sake of the living?

I am shortening what I say, in the knowledge that I have depicted
the signs of the times in letters sent to your lordship at another time,
albeit with small elegance but not to no purpose. My loving concern
and fear did not allow me to write nothing. But when we consider
with stupefaction the flashing spear of the divine judgement in these
days inflicting an immense, and for all ages unheard of and terrifying
vengeance upon prelates and clergy, princes and people, which has
cast down and scattered and worn down the supreme powers of the
world, what else is this but the recalling of human foolishness to the
wisdom of God, 'which reacheth from end to end mightily and
ordereth all things sweetly'?[9]

I consider the delay of the most necessary business, of which you
know, that has to be conducted in the English kingdom, is very much
to be regretted and will certainly be extremely dangerous. As I see it
the business has in some way been frustrated by the judgement of the
Almighty.

Occurrit quiddam artius eminentie uestre commendandum, licet
magnanimitatis sit conceptum corde sermonem, liberiori audentia non
habito personarum delectu, patenter proferre, tum omnimodis opportunum est magnanimo intra cordis domicilium lingue motus moderari,
ne dum immoderatius, ut libet laxata locutio, ad offensam prouocat,
magnifica magnanimarum uirtutum opera prepediantur; propter quod
ait Dei sapientia 'In ore fatuorum cor eorum, et in corde sapientum os
illorum'.[10] 'Totum spiritum suum profert stultus; sapiens differt et
reseruat in posterum':[11] 'Homo sapiens tacebit usque ad tempus;
lasciuus autem et imprudens non seruabunt tempus.'[12] Attendendum
quoque non segniter puto, quod tam in diuinis quam in humanis
litteris inter uirtutum excellentias, loquendi circumspectio uigilantiori
commendatione precipitur, cum inconsideratio sermocinandi secundum sapientie testimonia et religionem diuinam et humanam necessitudinem perniciosius euertere dinoscitur.

Circa festum Sancti Luce[13] indignationis regie motus incurri, ut
reor, propter uerba uite. Vnde nec ad presentiam domini regis aut
regine michi fas est accedere. Fiat uoluntas Domini. Mitto uobis
transcriptum litterarum papalium pro lamentabili depopulatione
partium Anthiocensium domino Cantuariensi directarum, si forte
tante hostilitatis uastitatem Terre Sancte tam periculose imminentem
aut fame relatio aut signatio littere nondum ad uos usque detulerit;
transcriptum etiam littere michi a domino Cantuariense pro memorato negotio transmisse, cui ego litteratorie cum quanta ualui instantia
supplicaui, ut me a memorata commissione exoneraret et illam in
aliquem prelatorum Anglie transferret.[14] Mitto, inquam, memoratam
litteram michi directam, ut si opus fuerit ope uestra, liberari
f. 55 insufficientia mea ualeat a tam molesto | grauamine. In confectione
autem presentium adhuc ipsius responsum super hoc expectaui.

Gauisus sum cum intellexi quod karissimus frater Gregorius de
Bosellis de Lugduno in Vasconiam ad uos profectus fuisset,[15] qui tam
uobis quam domine comitisse, quam et ceteris uos contingentibus,
prouidum sicut uobis in Christo deuotissimus poterit auxilium
exhibere. Et cum sit prudens eloquii mistici, minus curandum
putaui explanandis Scripture testimoniis superius positis insistere.

[10] Ecclus. 21: 29.
[11] Prov. 29: 11.
[12] Ecclus. 20: 7.
[13] 18 Oct.
[14] The commission Adam sought to escape was doubtless the papal commission to
preach the crusade.

Something occurs to me that I would pressingly recommend to your eminence. Although it belongs to your generous nature to speak openly, freely, and boldly the thoughts in the heart, without distinction of persons, yet it is always advantageous for a generous man to use his heart to govern the utterance of his tongue, lest, while it is pleasant to speak more freely, lack of restraint causes offence and may hinder fine works of generosity and virtue. On this account the wisdom of God says 'The heart of fools is in their mouth; and the mouth of wise men is in their heart'.[10] 'A fool uttereth all his mind; a wise man deferreth and keepeth it till afterwards.'[11] 'A wise man will hold his peace till he see opportunity: but a babbler, and a fool will regard no time.'[12] I think we should not be slow to notice that in both sacred and humane letters, among the excellent virtues circumspection in speech is a precept that is closely commended; for it is acknowledged from the evidence of wisdom that thoughtlessness in speaking is the downfall of both holy religion and human need.

About the feast of St Luke,[13] I incurred the king's displeasure, I think, on account of (preaching) the words of life. On account of this I am not permitted access to the lord king or the queen. The Lord's will be done. I am sending you a copy of papal letters, addressed to the lord Archbishop of Canterbury, regarding the lamentable depopulation of the region of Antioch, in case perhaps oral report or letters have not yet reached you about the threatening waste of the Holy Land by the enemy; also a copy of the letter sent me by the lord of Canterbury for the business I have mentioned; I have implored him, with all the force I could, to exonerate me from the said commission and to transfer it to some other English prelate.[14] I say I am sending you the letter that was sent me, so that if need be, my inadequate person may be freed from such a grievous burden by your intervention. While writing the present letter, I am still awaiting his reply to this.

I was delighted when I understood that our dearest brother Gregory de Bosellis had set off from Lyons to join you in Gascony.[15] He is most devoted to you in Christ, and he will be able to offer prudent assistance to both you and the lady countess and others connected with you. As he is well versed in mystical language, I thought I needed to take less pains to expound the texts of Scripture cited above.

---

[15] Gregory de Bosellis accompanied Archbishop Boniface to the papal Curia at Lyons; from there he was authorized by his Provincial to proceed to join the Montforts in Gascony: see Letters 155, 168.

Contristaret excessus pie recordationis magistri Radulfi de Cantuaria,[16] ni ad letificandum occurreret uidelicet presumptio quod in conspectu Domini pretiosa sit mors ipsius,[17] quam precessit usque ad exitum uita laudabilis. Poterit autem uestra discretio, si placet, cum domina comitissa et fratre Gregorio michi signare quod expedire uideatur de successore eidem substituendo, necnon de personis ad ministerium uestrum euocandis, ne in hac parte tedium inferat diuturnior expectatio certitudinis.

Non sine causa uestram exhortor in Christo pietatem, anxissime obsecrans quatinus scribere uelitis Ricardo de Aueriges,[18] ut non permittat ministeriales uestros in Anglia, quibus est rerum commissa custodia, animas pro quibus mortuus est auctor uite pernecabiliter trucidare.

Conseruet inter mundane uicissitudinis pericula serenam sublimitatem uestram ad gloriam sui nominis Altissimus in Christo Iesu semper et beatissima Virgine.

Valet dominus Lyncolniensis. Valent liberi uestri, sit Saluatori superexaltata benedictio.

142

To Simon de Montfort, earl of Leicester

Illustri domino Simoni comiti Leycestriensi Frater Ada.

Satis est michi molestum quod uobiscum et cum domina comitissa loqui non potui hactenus sicut optaui. Sed si dilationem presentem pia patientia perferamus, spero indubitanter quod expectatio cedet ad salutem et complacentiam, Saluatore melius disponente secundum occultum sui beneplaciti, quam secundum planum nostri desiderii.

Ceterum super negotio, quod nosti, uidetur michi nichil fore scribendum hac uice, presertim cum agatur de re maxima, et hinc speretur salus summa, illinc uero timeantur extrema pericula, et secundum sensum sapientis mortua littera unicum sensum preferat, uox autem uiua plures formas demonstrat, et nullatenus muta scriptura sic respondere ualet sollicitis interrogationibus sicut potest sermonis multiplicitas. Et scio certissime quod nullo modo innotescunt aut tam prudenter aut tam salubriter ea que sunt agenda,

---

[16] Cf. Letter 97.　　　　　　　　　　　　　　　　[17] Cf. Ps. 115: 15.
[18] Richard of Havering was Montfort's steward and general manager of the earl's estates: CPR 1233–37, 1145: Maddicott, *Simon de Montfort*, p. 67.

The death of Master Ralph of Canterbury[16] of pious memory would be saddening were it not for our joyful presumption that his death, preceded by a life that was praiseworthy to the end, is precious in the sight of the Lord.[17] Could your discreet lordship together with the lady countess, if you please, indicate to me what should be done to provide a substitute in his place, and also the persons to be summoned to your service, so that you may not be troubled by uncertainty or delay in the matter?

Not without cause I exhort your goodness in Christ, beseeching you most anxiously to be so good as to write to Richard of Havering,[18] instructing him not to allow his agents in England who are entrusted with guarding property, to slay souls for whom the Author of life died.

May the Most High preserve your highness amidst the dangers and changes of the world to the glory of his name, ever in Christ and the Blessed Virgin.

The lord bishop of Lincoln is well. Your illustrious children are well, blessed be our Saviour.

142

To Simon de Montfort, earl of Leicester

Brother Adam to the illustrious lord Simon, earl of Leicester.

It quite troubles me that I have not yet been able to talk with you and the lady countess, as I desired. But if we put up with the present delay with good patience, I have no doubt that the waiting will be turned to our salvation and mutual pleasure, and that our Saviour is ordering everything according to his hidden good pleasure better than by fulfilling all our desire.

But regarding the business, of which you know, it seems to me that nothing should be written this time, especially as we are dealing with a very great matter from which we may have on the one hand high hopes of safety, but on the other fear of great danger; and as according to the mind of the wise, a dead letter presents a single meaning, but the living voice communicates many figures, and mute writing cannot at all answer anxious questions in the way that can be done by the multiplicity of living speech. And I know very well that courses of action, above all those relating to great matters, are in no way so prudently or

maxime circa res grandes, per caracteres scripture, que copiose et utiliter per diligentiam tractatuum et multiformitatem discussionum ex illuminationibus patefiunt diuine clementie, cum honor Dei sincere queritur et propter uitam eternam laboratur.

Nonne propterea et beati apostoli, quorum unusquisque inestimabilem Spiritus Sancti affluentiam suscepit, et tota ecclesiasticarum personarum discretio et mundi principes, qui tanta splenduerunt sapientia, et populorum secularium contiones, a temporum exordiis per colloquiorum uiuaces disquisitiones ea que recta sunt inuestigare non desistunt et ea que exsequenda sunt disponunt? Proinde rogo uestre non displiceat serenitati si de illo facto tam ambigue formidinis, secundum quod uoluistis, non rescribo, quia nullo modo uideo expedire, ne forte per aliquam incuriam, quam nescio cauere, per scriptum causis salutaribus, quod absit, ingeratur irreparabilis detrimenti periculum.

Grates uobis refero quod michi communicare uoluistis rumores Terre Sancte, quamuis plurimum tristes et permaxime timendas.

Valete semper in Christo et beatissima Virgine.

Habetis presentiam dominorum Lyncolniensis, Wygorniensis, Fratris Gregorii, in quibus ut credo, est spiritus consilii, qui uobis diuinitate propitia satisfacere poterunt longe melius quam mea insufficientia super requisitis, presertim ⟨hiis⟩ que differri nequeunt.

Iterum ualeat, etc.

143

To Simon de Montfort, earl of Leicester

(May–June 1250)

Illustri uiro, domino Simoni comiti Leycestriensi Frater Ada, salutem in Domino.

Terrifica diri fulminis tonitrua nostris auribus passim ingesta, proth dolor, de sancto rege Francie, imo de negotio Domini seculorum, O gemitus! O suspiria! O singultus! O angustie! ob immanitatem horroris, et uoces lamento congruentes premunt et exprimunt insiccabiles lacrimarum inundationes.

Cuius enim uel execrabilem animam non consternat, adeo quod ultra non sit spiritus, cum considerat felicissimum catholicorum potentatuum regem, uictoriosos castrorum fidelium duces, bellicosos

so properly communicated through written words as are those that are openly transacted thanks to the illumination of the divine mercy through diligent negotiation and many-sided discussions, when men sincerely seek the honour of God and work for eternal life.

Is not this the reason why the blessed Apostles, each of whom received an immeasurable outpouring of the Holy Spirit, and the totality of ecclesiastical persons in their discretion, and the princes of the world with their shining wisdom, and the assemblies of lay people, have not ceased from the beginning of time to search for what is right and to decide on courses of action through lively discussion and inquiry? So I ask your serene lordship not to be displeased if I do not write back to you as you wish about that matter where there is such uncertainty and grounds for fear. I see it to be most inexpedient, in case through some carelessness, which I know not how to guard against, my writing might endanger or do irreparable harm to a good cause.

Thank you for being good enough to communicate to me the the current reports of the Holy Land, very sad and most dreadful though they are.

Farewell in Christ and the Blessed Virgin.

You have with you the lords of Lincoln and Worcester, and Brother Gregory, who have, as I believe, the spirit of counsel, and who can, with God's favour, satisfy your requirements far better than my inadequate self, especially those that cannot be postponed.

Again, farewell.

143

To Simon de Montfort, earl of Leicester

(May–June 1250)

Brother Adam to the illustrious lord Simon, earl of Leicester, greetings.

The news of the holy king of France, and indeed of the entire project of the Lord, strikes our ears like a frightful peal of thunder. O what groans, what sighs and sobs! O what distress, what immense dread, what a chorus of lamentation and floods of tears!

Whose spirit, even a profane one, would not be dismayed and drained of courage, when he contemplates the king, the most auspicious of Catholic potentates, the victorious leaders of the

Christiani certaminis proceres, preualidos deuote militie populos, qui
cum tanta fidei certitudine, cum tanta fortitudine fiducie, cum tanto
dilectionis feruore, cum tanto timore diuinitatis, cum tam potenti
uirtute, sollicitudine tam uigili, tam pia emulatione, constantia tam
longanimi, ad hoc se accingere meruerunt inspirati diuinitus ut, pulsis
hostibus regni Dei, ad diuinam formam uiuendi, ad diuinam censuram iudicandi, ad diuinum ritum colendi restituerent hereditatem
Dei, et profusas opum copias exponentes, et armantes robustos
bellatorum exercitus, et grauidas classium multitudines instruentes,
et iura celestis imperii latius distendentes? Quis, inquam, post tot
stupores miraculorum, post tot discriminum terrores, post tot sudores
preliorum, post tot gentium strages, ista uel cecutiens conspicatur et
non scissi pectoris corde saucio, pallidi uultus sanguine exinaniti, sub
ferali barbarice atrocitatis rabie et mundane uastitatis gloriam, et
letitiam orbis Christiani, et ecclesiastice salutis protectionem, et
defensionem sanctitatis celice, tam spectabilem regie celsitudinis
maiestatem tam ignominiose captiuari,[1] tam trihumphalem inclite
expeditionis multitudinem tam calamitose trucidari, et uniuersam
humani status excellentiam in tanti horroris subuersionem precipitari,
desolati meroris inconsolabili planctu non deplorat?

Quis hinc ferre ualebit et insultationes perfidorum et subsannantium irrisiones et scandala credentium et sanctorum blasphemias?
Non enim frustra iudicat Deus, nec Omnipotens subuertit quod
iustum est. Nonne cum flagello attriuisset et subleuasset in beneficium incorrigibilem[a] Pharaonis peruicaciam ⟨et⟩ ipsam nouissime
immutabili horrende mortis sententia dissipauit? Nonne Joram regem
Israel, postquam ipsius perfidiam seueritatis iuste uerberibus casti-
gauit et releuauit blandimentis pie consolationis, tamen cum interitus
atrocissimi supplicio ipsum et uniuersam cognationem per inaudite
stragis effrenationem a facie terre deleuit?[2] Numquid Is, 'apud quem
non est transmutatio nec uicissitudinis obumbratio'[3] antiquam consiliorum ordinationem poterit mutare? Absit.

Hec breuiter perstrinxerim, ut ea sollerti prudentie uestre con-
siderationi pertractanda fre [. . .][b] beneuolum [. . .] suauiter affectum
uellem in fide et lenitate.

143 [a] *The remainder of this letter was written by the copyist in a smaller script in the margin below the last line of fo. 55.*   [b] *The concluding words of the letter have been lost by the paring of the lower margin of the manuscript.*

143 [1] Outmanoeuvred in Egypt, Louis IX was taken prisoner and the crusading army was forced to capitulate on 6 Apr. 1250.

armies of the faithful, the noble warriors of the Christian battle, the valiant people devoted to the holy warfare; who, with such unshakeable faith, such trust and fortitude, such fervent love, so much fear of the Lord, so strong in virtue, with such caring and vigilance, such pious zeal, such patient perseverance, were worthy of the divine inspiration to arm themselves for this purpose: that, after expelling the enemies of the kingdom of God, they might restore God's inheritance to the form of life divinely ordained, to justice in accordance with divine law, and to the due celebration of divine service, providing abundant resources; equipping armies of vigorous warriors with arms; furnishing fleets of laden ships, and widely extending the boundaries of the holy empire; who, I say, after so many astonishing miracles, so many fearful crises, the sweat of so many battles and the slaughter of so many of the heathen, viewing these things even with blinded sight, does not lament inconsolably, with broken heart and paling countenance to see so admirable a royal majesty, the glory and joy of the Christian world, the protector of the Church and defender of heaven's holiness, made ignominiously captive[1] under the deadly fury of the barbarians, and the whole world laid waste, the calamitous slaughter of such a triumphant multitude of the noble expedition, and the whole excellence of the human condition so dreadfully cast down and ruined?

Who after this will be able to endure the insults of unbelievers, the derision, and the scandal to believers and the blasphemies against the saints? For the Lord does not pass judgement in vain, nor does the Almighty overthrow what is right. Had He not worn down the incorrigible stubbornness of Pharaoh by flagellation and raised him again for his good, and finally routed him with an unchangeable sentence of dreadful death? Did He not restore Joram king of Israel, with gentle words of consolation after castigating him for his perfidy with the lash of just severity, and yet punished him with a savage death, erasing him and all his kindred from the face of the earth by unheard of slaughter?[2] Can He, 'with whom there is no variation or shadow of change',[3] change the ancient ordinance of the councils? God forbid.

I have touched on these things briefly, so that the matters that are to be brought to your prudent consideration . . .

---

[2] See 4 Kgs. (2 Kgs.) 9: 16–26.
[3] James 1: 17.

144

To Simon de Montfort, earl of Leicester

(1250)

f. 55ᵛ Illustri uiro, domino Simoni comiti Leycestriensi, Frater Ada salutem in Domino.

Notum est uniuersis, quos rationis expertes non uexat insania, quia periculosa laboris bellici certamina et dignum initium et iustum processum et salutarem exitum sortiri diuinitus cognoscuntur, cum et uirtus impauida et sensus inerrans*a* uel disertus, et zelus deuotus, per omnia satagit ut, subactis pie pacis hostibus, ordinate, pacifice Dei populus quod 'prudenter discernit gerat*b* fortiter, temperanter cohibeat,*c* distribuat*d* innocenter'[1] ad cultum summe diuinitatis, ubi pax nichil aliud est quam ordinatissima et concordatissima iucunditas fruendi Deo et inuicem in Deo; 'illum uidelicet felicitatis finem indesinenter referat, ubi est Deus benedictus, Deus beatus saluator, rex pacificus, omnia in omnibus eternitate certa, pace perfecta',[2] secundum prelibationem in terris et secundum satietatem in excelsis.

Quid enim aliud docemur in illo monarchie mundialis principe,[3] qui ait, 'Cum pluribus gentibus imperarem et uniuersum mee ditioni subiugassem, uolui nequaquam potentie abuti magnitudine, sed clementia et lenitate gubernare subiectos, ut absque ullo terrore uitam silentio transigentes optata cunctis mortalibus pace fruerentur'.[4] Ad hoc sane secundum supernarum legum decreta desudant exercitia preliorum, ut regni Dei aduersarios ferrum edomet, quos uerbum non emendat, et ⟨ad⟩ instar uiuentium in polo disponantur degentes in solo.

Sed quid? Qualiter hoc fieri continget? Profecto non aliter nisi ut secundum exempla castrorum triumphalium, tam gloriam Dei et populi liberationem emulantium, in confessione propriarum iniquitatum et diuinarum bonitatum consideratione cum gratissimis lacrimarum profusionibus hominibus insufficientiam et omnipotentiam Creatori rependamus incessanter, cum illis de quibus canit tam solempniter ecclesia, 'In hympnis et confessionibus benedicebant Dominum, qui magna fecit in Israel, et uictoriam

144 *a* inerratus *MS.*   *b* gerit *MS.*   *c* cohibet *MS.*   *d* distribuit *MS.*

---

144 [1] Cf. Augustine, *De ciuitate Dei*, xix. 20; *CSEL* xl, ii. 407.
[2] Ibid.   [3] Artaxerxes, the king of Persia.
[4] Esther 13: 2.

144

To Simon de Montfort, earl of Leicester

(1250)

Brother Adam to the illustrious lord Simon, earl of Leicester, greetings in the Lord.

Every reasonable person, who is not distracted by madness, knows that heaven grants the people of God a worthy beginning, a just continuance, and a salutary outcome to the perils and toil of their warfare, when they act with fearless courage, unerring feeling, zeal, and devotion, and having defeated the enemies of a rightful peace, they endeavour in everything to carry out prudent decisions with resolution, moderation, and restraint, and with blameless distribution,[1] to the honour of the high Godhead, where peace is nothing but well regulated and joyful concord in the fruition of God, and of one another in God. That is, 'it should ceaselessly relate to that end of felicity where God is blessed, where God our blessed Saviour, the king of peace, is all in all, in sure eternity and perfect peace',[2] with a foretaste of it on earth and its fulfilment in heaven.

For what else are we taught by that prince of worldly monarchy[3] who says: 'Whereas I reigned over many nations and had brought all the world under my dominion, I was not willing to abuse the greatness of my power, but wanted to govern my subjects with clemency and gentleness, that they might live quietly without any terror, and might enjoy peace, which is desired by all men.'[4] Indeed, according to the decrees of divine law this is the object of the toil and sweat of battle: that those adversaries of the kingdom of God who are not amended by words may be tamed by the sword, and that those living on the ground may be reconstructed in the likeness of those living in heaven.

But what follows? How can this come about? Surely not otherwise than by following the examples of triumphal armies that are zealous for the glory of God and the freedom of the people, by confessing our own iniquities and being mindful of God's goodness to us, while with tears of gratitude we ceaselessly acknowledge the insufficiency of men and the omnipotence of the Creator, together with those of whom the Church so solemnly sings 'with hymns and thanksgiving they blessed the Lord, who had done great things in Israel and given

dedit illis'[5] Dominus Omnipotens. Nunquam, oro, clementissimi cordis catholica magnanimitas horum sustineat obliuisci.

Dominus rex, dominus archiepiscopus, domina regina, dominus Ricardus comes, dominus Petrus de Sabaudia, ceterique nonnulli prelatorum et procerum erga personam uestram in regno Anglie, sicut ex euidentibus sermonum indiciis coniici potest, longe sereniorem solito, sit benedictus Deus pacis et dilectionis, conceperunt beneuolentiam.

Cum liberaliter concessisset karissimus pater Fratrum Minorum Anglie minister,[6] ut Frater Gregorius de Bosellis, uobis et uestris in Christo fidelissimus, ad uos uenire acceleraret iuxta quod domina comitissa requisiuit, quoniam ego instanti anno lecturus Oxonie nullatenus euadere potui quin suspensa lectione domino archiepiscopo Cantuariensi assisterem, nisi per Fratrem Gregorium absentie mee defectus suppleretur,[7] cum magna de benignitatis uestre discretione fiducia ordinatum est ut me, secundum quod Dominus dederit, impendente eruditionem Oxonie, memoratus Frater Gregorius stet cum prefato domino Cantuariensi; unde dilata est ad presens eius ad uos profectio, impleturus per Dei gratiam beneplacitum uestri opportuniori tempore.

Ab aliquot diebus intimis uisceribus flagrans desiderium, ut speo celitus, concepi desiderabili serenitatis uestre frui colloquio, confidens de gratia clementissimi Saluatoris quod per inuiolabilem fidei uestre serenitatem, adiutorium pariter et consilium, peccatis meis non obsistentibus, diuinitus prestabitur, ut per uiam rectitudinis proficiam ad tam diu suspiratam pacis diuine felicitatem. Licet per ineffabilem Illius clementiam, cuius proprium est misereri semper et parcere, celestium illuminationum euentus miraculosi orbem Christianum hiis diebus letificauerint, tamen plurimum formidandum fore creditur quod, nisi uias suas catholica fidelium nationum cum dignis penitentie fructibus et nequaquam, ut est hodie, addens preuaricationem, correxerit ecclesia, implebit diuinorum iudiciorum dira districtio ⟨secundum⟩ quod scriptum est, 'ante ruinam exaltatur cor et extrema gaudii luctus occupat'.[8]

them the victory'.[5] Never, I beg you, allow your great and catholic heart to forget these things.

The lord king, the lord archbishop, the lady queen, the lord earl Richard, lord Peter of Savoy, and not a few of the other prelates and nobles are more kindly disposed towards your person than usual in the English kingdom, as can be gathered from clear indications of what is being said. Blessed be the God of peace and love for it.

Our dear father, the minister of the Friars Minor in England,[6] freely granted that Brother Gregory de Bosellis, who is most devoted to you and yours, should hasten to you, as the lady countess requested, but because I am about to lecture at Oxford this year, and could in no way avoid suspending my lectures and accompanying the lord archbishop unless the defect of my absence was made good by Brother Gregory, it has been decided, trusting in your great kindness and discretion, that while I dispense learning at Oxford, Brother Gregory should stay with the lord of Canterbury;[7] hence he has been delayed in setting off to you at present, but hopes by God's grace to fulfil your pleasure at a more opportune time.

For some days I have felt a burning desire within me—I hope of heavenly origin—to enjoy a conversation with your serene lordship. I trust in the grace of the most merciful Saviour that through the inviolable serenity of your faith, help, and counsel that, notwithstanding my sins, God will show me how to advance by a straight path to the happiness and holy peace I yearn for. Although through the ineffable mercy of Him, whose property is always to be merciful and to pardon, the Christian world has in these days been given joy by miraculous occurrences and heavenly illumination; nevertheless it is much to be feared that unless the Catholic Church of the faithful peoples corrects its ways by the fruits of worthy penance, without prevaricating, as is the case today, the fearful severity of divine judgement will be fulfilled, of which it is written 'Pride goeth before destruction, and mourning taketh hold of the end of joy'.[8]

---

[5] 2 Macc. 10: 38.

[6] William of Nottingham, English Provincial 1240–54.

[7] Gregory de Bosellis accompanied Archbishop Boniface to the papal Curia in June 1250 in place of Adam; cf. Letter 168.

[8] Prov. 16: 18 and 14: 13.

145

To Peter, count of Savoy

Illustri uiro et domino suo Petro de Sabaudia[1] Frater Ada, post
laboriosa certaminis discrimina triumphalia felicitatis premia.

Nequaquam mirandum est si anxiorem saucio cordi molestiam
littera uestre dominationis ingesserit, insinuans quod inclitus comes
Cornubiensis tantam maximi negotii cogentiam prorogandam censuit
per tam magnum periculosi temporis interuallum. Augmentauit
etenim quam plurimum angustiam quod ad memoratum negotium
salubriter expediendum summe necessariam nobilitatis uestre presentiam quantacumque rerum magnitudo subducit, sicut reor, cum
non mediocri salutis optate detrimento.

Sed quid? Contra formidabiles ambiguorum euentuum exitus hoc
infallibile semper recurrit remedium, quod secundum salutaria
exempla uirorum triumphalium Illi diligentia indefessa supplicetur
de quo scriptum est, 'Tu autem, Domine uirtutis, cum tranquillitate
iudicas, et cum magna reuerentia disponis que circa nos'.[2] Cum
etenim ignoramus quid agere debeamus, omnem sollicitudinem
nostram in Ipsum proiciamus qui amat animas. Hec est certe sapientie
celestis dispensatio, ut nonnunquam presidium auferat desperabili
causarum difficultati quibus magnifice disponit diuinum prestare
patrocinium, cunctis seculis perpetua clamante uigilantia: 'Cum
placuerint Domino uie hominis, inimicos quoque eius conuertet ad
pacem.'[3] Ceterum quales, obsecro, benignissime serenitati ⟨uestre⟩
gratiarum actiones modicitatis mee poterit referre deuotio, per quam
tam exilis meriti pauperculo[a] tante dignationis beneuolentiam tam
liberaliter scribere uoluistis?

De hiis hactenus. Ad hoc, O domine desideratissime, annon
nefarium iudicabitur, iuxta quod persuadent exempla nobilium,
conuincunt efficacie rationum, precipiunt auctoritates sapientum, si
quos et dignitas generis et[b] sanguinis, et claritas ingenii, et strenuitas
militie titulis illustrant clarioribus, nequaquam et irreprehensibilis
forma uiuendi et inflexibilis censura iudicandi et inuiolabilis ritus
colendi spectabilioribus insigniant uirtutibus? Quale namque fore
putabitur si, quod absit, quem nature gloria honorandum sublimauit,
f. 56 hunc deiiciat conculcandum | ignominia uitiorum?

145   [a] paupercule MS.   [b] et generis MS.

145

To Peter, count of Savoy

Brother Adam to the illustrious lord Peter of Savoy,[1] after the toil and strife, the triumphant reward of happiness.

Be not surprised if I am made anxious and troubled in my heart by your lordship's letter informing me that the noble earl of Cornwall has decided to postpone so great and urgent a business for such a long and dangerous time. Indeed, my distress has been greatly increased by the fact that affairs, however great, take your lordship from us, when your presence is supremely necessary for the successful expedition of the said business with, as I think, no little detriment to the safe outcome we desire.

But what is to be done? The infallible remedy for our fear of events that are uncertain is to follow the example of men who triumph and with untiring perseverance supplicate Him of whom it is written 'Thou, O Lord of power, judgest with tranquillity; and with great favour disposest of us'.[2] Indeed, when we do not know what we ought to do, let us cast all our care upon Him who loves souls. Surely it is a dispensation of heavenly wisdom that sometimes removes human aid from desperately difficult causes, for which in all ages He designs divine protection with that cry of eternal vigilance: 'When the ways of man shall please the Lord, he will convert even his enemies to peace.'[3] But what thanks, I ask, can my poor but devoted self offer your most kind serenity for being willing to write so freely to one undeserving of such condescension?

So much for this. To the point, my dear lord, will it not be judged disgraceful if those who are distinguished by high birth and blood, the brilliance of their talents and the greater brilliance of their martial valour, are not also distinguished by more admirable virtues thanks to their irreproachable way of life, the unbending justice of their judgements, and the purity of their divine worship, as we are persuaded by the example of noble souls, effectively convinced by reason, and commanded by the authority of the wise? For what shall we think of it if, which God forbid, one whose glorious nature has elevated him to a noble estate should be cast down and made contemptible by ignominious vices?

145 [1] See Letter 30 n. 4. [2] Wisd. 12: 18. [3] Prov. 16: 7.

Studeat ergo iugiter eximia uestre serenitatis industria, ut eidem sit facies hilaris, hoc ⟨est⟩ sint oculi pudici, sint aures disciplinate, sit lingua discreta, sint manus ualide, sint pedes honesti, sit pectus pium, sit cor latum, sit conscientia pura, sit gestus maturus, sit habitus moderatus, sit opinio integra, sint consiliarii fideles, sint ministri sinceri; apex quoque uester sit deuotus ad prelatos, sit fidus ad principes, sit consultus ad proceres, sit socialis ad milites, sit affabilis ad plebes, sit amabilis ad omnes, sit seuerus ad rebelles, sit suauis ad unanimos, et ut sit ad unum dicere, seruetur ad superiores obedientia et reuerentia, ad compares honor et amicitia, ad subditos miseratio et munificentia.

Hec idcirco sub modulo breuitatis perstrinxerim, ut qualitercunque commonefiat ingenue mentis eminentia ⟨inter⟩ tam grandium occupationum turbamina, sicut sapientis monet eloquium, qui ait, 'Da occasionem sapienti et sapientior erit'.[4] Propter quod oro pia suscipiat dignatio quod sollicita presumpsit affectio. Licet sermo conceptus in prolixum extendi conaretur, compescuit calamum ad succingendam epistolam temporis angustia.

Ad magnifice regine famulatum, quamuis non sufficiam, ut iussistis, quantum tamen ualuero, prout diuinitus dabitur, operam adhibebo sedule promptitudinis. Concedat, oro, uestre nobilitatis uigilantie Dei altissimus Filius, ut in omnibus que 'prudenter discernitis, agitis fortiter, cohibetis temperanter, iusteque distribuitis, ad illum finem referatis in quo est Deus omnia in omnibus, eternitate certa et pace perfecta'[5] in Christo semper et beatissima Virgine.

Propter formidandam examinis districti sententiam, cum accesserit opportunitas, sic prouideatis sanctuario Domini exclusa penitus mundane considerationis necessitudine, ne ad curam animarum, pro quibus benedictus Saluator pio cruore uiuifice crucis rubricauit patibulum, unquam^c presentare consentiatis nisi quos ad hoc superna dispensatio decernit euocandos, dicens, 'Date e uobis uiros sapientes et gnaros, quorum conuersatio sit probata in tribubus suis, et dabo uobis eos principes'.[6]

Iterum et in eternum ualeatis.

---

^c nunquam *MS*.

Therefore let your serene lordship take care constantly to have a cheerful countenance, that is, let your eyes be modest, your ears well instructed, your tongue discreet; let your hands be strong, your feet honourable, your breast pious, your heart big, your conscience pure, your bearing mature, your dress restrained, your judgement sound, your counsellors faithful, and your ministers true. May your highness also be devoted to prelates, faithful to princes, considerate to the nobles, sociable to the knights, affable to the people, amiable to all, stern to rebels, agreeable to those who seek concord, and to put it all in one: maintain obedience and reverence towards superiors, honour and friendship towards peers, and compassion and generosity towards subordinates.

I have touched briefly on these things so that your eminence may recall them to mind in whatever manner while you are in the whirl of great affairs, like the admonition of the wise man, who says, 'give an occasion to a wise man, and wisdom shall be added to him'.[4] On this account, I pray your good lordship will condescend to accept what I have presumed to say out of solicitude and affection. Although my thoughts tempted me to prolixity, lack of time compelled my pen to shorten the letter.

Inadequate though I am, I shall with God's help render the noble queen my prompt service, as you have commanded, so far as I am able. I pray that the high Son of God may grant your vigilant lordship that in all things which 'you discern with prudence, perform with resolution, constrain with moderation, and distribute with justice, you direct them to that end where God is all in all, eternity is sure and peace is perfect',[5] ever in Christ and the Blessed Virgin.

Having in mind the dread sentence of the judgement, when occasion arises, so provide for the sanctuary of the Lord that you wholly exclude consideration of worldly needs, and never agree to present to the cure of souls (for whom our Blessed Saviour reddened the living cross with his blood) any person except those whom heaven has called to this, saying 'Let me have from among you wise and understanding men, and such whose conversation is approved among your tribes, that I may appoint them your rulers'.[6]

Again and for ever farewell.

---

[4] Cf. ibid. 9: 9.
[5] Cf. Augustine, *De civitate Dei*, xix. 20. Cf. Letters 74, 76, 90.
[6] Deut. 1: 13.

146

To Sir Geoffrey Despencer

Nobili uiro, domino Galfrido Dispensatori[1] Frater Ada salutem, et post gratiam uite temporalis gloriam eterne felicitatis.

Benedicta sit Saluatoris clementia, que saluandis animabus inspirauit salutis consilium. Igitur serenitatis uestre litteram, tam honoris diuini deuotum amorem quam pium desiderium ecclesiastice promotionis proferentem, digno suscipiens[a] gaudio, post diutinam deliberationem, quam nimirum tante rei requirebat periculum, dominum Petrum presbiterum, custodem Hospitalis de Luterwrthe,[2] uirum honesta conuersatione laudabilem et in animarum regimine probatum, celesti scientia preditum, et in exteriorem pietate spectabilem, dominationis uestre discretioni, iuxta tenorem mandati uestre designare curaui presentandum, diuintate propitia, si uestre benignitatis sederit beneplacito, propter contemplationem diuini nominis ad ecclesiam illam[3] de qua modicitati mee tam pio concepto scribere uoluistis.

Valeat uestre nobilitatis incolumitas in Christo semper et Beatissima Virgine.

147

To lord John of Lexington

Nobili uiro, domino Iohanni de Lexinton,[1] domini regis iusticiario, Frater Ada salutem, et in ueritate iudicii misericordie mansuetudinem.

Licet modicitatem meam meritorum pauperies reuocauerit, tamen serenitatis uestre clementiam ob claram illustris anime pietatem quam erga me, sit uobis sempiterna retributio, perpendi fuisse serenam, fiducialiter interpellare[a] consensi. Proinde serenitatis uestre supplico beneuolentie, rogans obnixius quatinus Thome de Marisco, consanguineo meo,[2] uestre dominationi supplicius obnoxio, in negotio suo,

---

146   ^a suscipere *MS.*

147   ^a interpellari *MS.*

---

146   ¹ Cf. Letters 65 and n., 123.

146

To Sir Geoffrey Despenser

Brother Adam to the noble lord Geoffrey Despenser,[1] greetings, and after the grace of life in time the glorious happiness of eternity.

Blessed be the mercy of our Saviour, who for the saving of souls has inspired you with saving counsel. I have received with fitting joy your serenity's letter, showing both your devotion for the honour of God and a pious desire for the advancement of the Church. After the prolonged deliberation demanded by the peril of so great a business, I have taken care, in accordance with your instruction, to nominate to your lordship Sir Peter, priest and warden of Lutterworth Hospital,[2] for presentation, with God's favour and your lordship's good pleasure and out of regard for the divine name, to that church[3] about which you wrote to my humble self with such a pious idea. He is a man of upright life, tested in the direction of souls, equipped with heavenly doctrine, and of admirable piety in the conduct of external affairs.

Wishing your noble lordship health, ever in Christ and the Blessed Virgin.

147

To lord John of Lexington

Brother Adam to the noble lord John of Lexington, justice of the lord king,[1] greetings, gentle mercy in true judgement.

Although want of merit deterred my humble self from writing, on pondering your lordship's manifest kindness and goodness towards me—for which may you receive an eternal reward—I felt confidence in appealing to you and I agreed to write. I am therefore supplicating your kind serenity with a request that you would condescend to grant your gracious favour to Thomas Marsh,[2] a blood-relative of mine,

---

[2] Letter 65 n. 1.   [3] Sulby (Northamptonshire); ibid. n. 3.

147 [1] John of Lexington was steward of the king's household; he served as judge of Coram Rege in 1246; acted as unofficial keeper of the Great Seal 1249–50; he was appointed chief justice of the forests north of Trent in Nov. 1252: R. C. Stacey in *ODNB* xxxiii. 682–3.

[2] On Thomas Marsh see Introduction, p. xix.

quod ipse uestre discretioni, si placet, uiua uoce expositurus est, quatenus iustitie non obuenitur et inheretur miserationi, propensioris gratie fauorem beneuolum impertiri non ducatis indignum.

Valeat pietatis uestre incolumitas, etc.

148

To William of Beauchamp

Nobili uiro, domino Willelmo de Bello Campo[1] Frater Ada salutem, et sincerum in Domino debite dilectionis affectum.

Ad piam karissimorum fratrum instantiam pro dilecto michi in Christo S. Druel, milite uestro, serenitati uestre presentem consensi dirigere petitionem, rogans humiliter quatinus eundem in negotio suo, quod in curia uestra habet expedire, quatenus misericordia seruatur et iustitia non offenditur, benigni fauoris gratiam impertiri uelitis, nequaquam, si placet, presumptioni ascribentes quod pro uestro milite qualiscunque uester uestram interpellat nobilitatem.

Valeat serenitatis uestre incolumitas in Christo, etc.

149

To the prioress of Godstow

f. 57 Venerabili domine prioresse de Godestowe[1] Frater Ada salutem, et promptum sincere dilectionis affectum.

Ex illa quam de uestre religionis pietate, licet immeritus, in Christo concepi fiduciam, apud discretionis ⟨uestre⟩ beneuolentiam, presertim in hiis que et iustitia compellit et requirit honestas, precum rationabilium effectus impetrare non diffido. Proinde uestre circumspectionis industriam suppliciter rogo quatinus uiro commendabili, domino Willelmo de Cyrnecestria super debito quo eidem, ut dicitur, obligata tenemini sine more dispendio, si placet, satisfacere uelitis, ob quod a modicitate mea benignitati uestre memoratus dominus Willelmus destinandam hanc obtinuit petitionem. Propensius quippe Ipsius attendenda est reuerentia qui per apostolum suum cunctis clamat 'Nemini quippiam debeatis nisi ut inuicem diligatis'.[2]

---

148 [1] William de Beauchamp had been sheriff of Worcester since the death of his father, Walter, who had in practice made good his claim that the shrievalty was hereditary in his

your lordship's humble subject, in his business, which he will, if you please, explain to your lordship by word of mouth, so far as justice is not obstructed and compassion maintained.

Wishing your good lordship health, etc.

148

To William of Beauchamp

Brother Adam to the noble lord William Beauchamp,[1] greetings, and the true affection due in the Lord.

At the request of my dearest brethren I have agreed to send your serene lordship this petition on behalf of my beloved in Christ S. Druel, your knight, with a humble request that you would grant him your kind favour in his business that he has to conduct in your court, so far as mercy is preserved and justice is not obstructed. I trust you will not think it presumptious for a servant of yours of whatever kind to appeal to your lordship on behalf of your knight.

Farewell; your serenity, in Christ, etc.

149

To the prioress of Godstow

Brother Adam to the venerable lady, the prioress of Godstow,[1] greetings and affectionate service.

Unworthy though I am, I have in Christ gained a trust in your religious devotion that gives me confidence in appealing to your kind discretion with reasonable requests, especially in matters where justice compels us and honour makes the request. So I humbly beg your attention with a request to satisfy the commendable Sir William of Cirencester in respect of the debt in which you are, as is said, under obligation to him, without delay, if you please. On this account the said Sir William got my humble self to send you this petition. Surely we should more readily heed Him who cries to all of us through his apostle 'owe no man anything, but to love one another'.[2]

family: D. A. Carpenter, *The Minority of Henry III* (1990), p. 125. William accounted at the Exchequer for the farm on 24 June 1251: *Close Rolls 1247–51*, p. 464.

149 [1] Emma Bluet (Bloet), prioress of Godstow 1248–69: *Rotuli Grosseteste*, p. 49; Smith and London, *The Heads of Religious Houses*, p. 562.   [2] Rom. 13: 8.

De hiis hucusque. Ceterum cum ad regimen uirginum sub institutione regulari Deo famulantium uos electio diuina uocauerit, quid aliud uestre satagendum est sanctitati quam ut sit apud ipsas intrinsecus religio, non illecta lasciuiis, non decepta fallaciis, non peruersa nequitiis, non oppressa uiolentiis; sed sit sana per innocentiam, sed sit ualida per constantiam? Quod ni fiat per uos et tota affectione, et tota ratione, et tota uirtute, ecce coram formidando superni examinis iudicio nullatenus de suscepto ministerio in condempnationem capitis Domino seculorum ualebitis reddere rationem.

Si autem memoratum beatissime caritatis studium, iuxta quod nunc tactum est, implere satageritis, temporalia ad subsidium presentis miserie monasterio uestro exterius adiacentia et temperanter, et prudenter, et equaliter, et stabiliter administrari faciet clementie celestis benedicta dispensatio, perhibente*a* sermone paterno, qui ait 'Primum querite regnum Dei, et omnia hec adiicientur uobis'.[3]

Valeat professionis uestre sancta perfectio in Christo Iesu semper et beatissima Virgine.

150

To Queen Eleanor

f. 58 Illustrissime domine Alionore, Dei gratia regine Anglie, domine Hybernie, ducisse*a* Normannie, Aquitanie, comitisse Andegauensis, Frater Ada, pacem in terris et gloriam ⟨in excelsis⟩.

Quum paratis cordis deuoti desideriis inclite dominationis uestre cupiam in Domino non tam preces perficere quam parere preceptis, non aliter, reor, insinuari posset, nisi uotorum affectibus affectuum uices ex equo, quod fieri nequit, correspondere ualerent.

Proinde iuxta prouidam reginalis excellentie circumspectionem, si superiorum auctoritas hoc exegerit, ut Angliam exeant hii de quibus per amicissimum in Christo dominum Walterum de Bradele[1] signare uoluistis, quoad fieri poterit, inoffensa diuinitate, quantum sufficiet exilitatis mee possibilitas, ad mutandam ordinationis edite sententiam operam dare curabo, scientes quod iugiter illo tendit serenitatis uestre clementissima sollicitudo quo requisitio compellit iuste necessitatis aut utilitatis pie deducit intentio.

149 *a* presentis *MS.*
150 *a* duce *MS.*

---

[3] Matt. 6: 33.

So much for this. Since divine election called you to govern virgins serving God in a regular institute, what else should preoccupy your holiness except ensuring that they practice an interior religious life, not enticed by lewdness or deceived by delusions, not led astray by wickedness or oppressed by violence, but that their religion should be healthy and blameless, and strong through their perseverance? Unless this comes about through you, through the application of all your affection, all your mind, and all your strength, see, you will in no way be able to render account to the Lord of the ages for the ministry you have received at the dread judgement which will lead to your capital sentence.

But if you are active and zealous to perform this blessed task of charity in the way I have mentioned, heaven's blessed dispensation will ensure that the temporal possessions of your monastery will be administered with restraint, prudence, justice, and stability, for the relief of your present unhappy condition, in accordance with the Father's word, who says 'Seek ye first the kingdom of God, and all these things shall be added to you'.[3]

May your holy profession flourish and be perfect, ever in Jesus Christ and the Blessed Virgin.

150

To Queen Eleanor

Brother Adam to the most illustrious lady Eleanor, by the grace of God queen of England, lady of Ireland, duchess of Normandy and Aquitaine, countess of Anjou, peace on earth and glory in the highest.

Since with the readiness of my devoted heart I desire not so much to answer your noble ladyship's prayers as to obey your commands, I could not, I think, put it in any other way, unless my affections could requite your kind wishes in equal measure, which cannot be.

Accordingly if, as your far-sighted royal excellency intimates, those you indicated through my dear friend in Christ, Walter de Bradley,[1] have been required by higher authority to leave England, so far as can be done without offending divinity, I will exert my efforts to change the decision and orders that have been issued. I know that the very kind concern of your serene highness is always directed to what is demanded by a search for what is just and necessary or to what is good and useful.

150   [1] Walter de Bradley; see Letter 108 and n.

Concedat, oro, altissimi Dei benedicti predestinatio domino regi, uestre pietati, clarissimis liberis uestris, et sublimitatem potentie et profunditatem sapientie et latitudinem innocentie et longitudinem permanentie, ad gloriam sui nominis et regni uestri salutem, in Christo Iesu semper, etc.

151

To Queen Eleanor

Excellentissime domine Alionore, Dei gratia regine Anglie, domine Hybernie, ducisse*a* Normanie, Aquitanie et comitisse Andegauensis, Frater Ada, tranquillitatem in tempore gratiosam et gloriosam in eternitate felicitatem.

Cum apud liberalem cordis latissimi magnificentiam amplius pietatis inclinatio prouocet ad interpellandum, quam ab interpellando reuocet celsitudo maiestatis, in necessariis salutarium causarum articulis ad clementiam uestram confidenter recurrit deuotorum uestrorum qualiscunque modicitas. Proinde placitam sublimitatis*b* uestre serenitatem humiliter rogo, supplicans attentius quatinus pro domino Willelmo de Hamton, quem inspirationis diuine celeste desiderium flagrantius accendit, de consueta clarissime dignitatis beneuolentia apud honorabilem uirum, dominum Robertum de Manneby, magistrum fratrum Hospitalis Ierosolimitanis in Anglia, spirituali uel littere uel uocis interuentione dignum ducatis, ob Saluatoris contemplationem, satagere, ut memoratus dominus Willelmus in sacram prefatorum fratrum religionem, intemeratis per omnia tam euangelicis sanctionibus quam traditionibus canonicis, sine ulterioris more dispendio, sub salubri recipi ualeat obseruantia; tanto, si placet, presentem religiose petitionis deuotionem propensiori prosequentes gratia, quanto benignius alias—sit uestre dignationi sempiterna retributio—pro eodem Willelmo eidem domino Roberto super eodem negotio petitoriam dirigere consensistis.

Conseruet dominum regem, conseruet uestram sublimitatem, conseruet inclitos regni uestri heredes Omnipotens Rex celorum per interuentum Regine Angelorum. Amen.

Dame, si ws a la feste de ceste resurrectiun uoilez treiter oueke le contesse de Leycestr' ententiuement de la saluatium des almes as queles, tant cun en ws est, ws auez si benettement presente,[1] je espeir

I pray that the high providence of God may grant the lord king, your good person, and your children sublime power, profound wisdom, deep integrity, and long life, to the glory of his name and the salvation of your kingdom, ever in Christ, etc.

151

To Queen Eleanor

Brother Adam to the most excellent lady Eleanor, by the grace of God queen of England, lady of Ireland, duchess of Normandy and Aquitaine and countess of Anjou, grace and peace in time and glory and happiness in eternity.

Piety more inclines me to appeal to the generosity of your most generous heart than your majesty's highness deters me from doing so, for in particular cases relating to salvation any of your devoted subjects, however humble, has confidence in having recourse to your clemency. Thus I am humbly making a request to your gentle and serene highness on behalf of Sir William of Hampton, who has been inspired by divine inspiration with heavenly desires. I ask that with your customary kindness you would make a spiritual representation, either by letter or word of mouth, to the honourable Robert of Manneby, master of the brothers of the Hospital of Jerusalem in England, that the said Sir William may be received without delay into the holy religion and pious observance of the said brothers, provided that neither the sanctions of the Gospel nor canonical tradition are thereby violated. You will, if you please, the more readily forward this devout religious petition as you kindly agreed elsewhere to send a request on the same subject—may your ladyship receive an everlasting reward for it—to the same Sir Robert on behalf of the same Sir William.

May the Almighty King of Heaven preserve the lord king, your highness, and the noble heirs of the kingdom, through the intercession of the Queen of Angels. Amen.

Lady, if at this Easter you wish to have a serious discussion with the Countess of Leicester about the salvation of souls for whom, inasmuch as it is in your hands, you have so piously offered support,[1]

151 [1] The Anglo-Norman *presente* is ambiguous; it could equally mean 'requested'. The subject for discussion is evidently that of ecclesiastical patronage, in which the queen showed a keen interest.

en la grace le beneit Fiz Deu ke il, par la uertu de sa gloriuse resurrectiun, i mettra conseil a la glorie de sun num, ke mener ws pusse a la ueie de salu pardurable. Aman. Aman. Awekis.

152

To Queen Eleanor

Excellentissime domine Alionore, Dei gratia regine Anglie, domine Hybernie, ducisse*a* Normanie, Aquitanie, comitisse Andegauensis, Frater Ada, et in presenti prosperitatem gratie et glorie felicitatem in futuro.

Nouerit clarissima reginalis eminentie serenitas quod qualiscunque modicitatis mee humilitas non tam dignam quam debitam uoluntatis in Domino gerit promptitudinem ad obtemperandum celsitudinis uestre beneplacito, michi iam secundo per dignationis uestre litteram insinuato, iuxta quod hoc ipsum et benigna pietas compellit et desiderate salutis requirit ministerium. Proinde cum propitia diuinitas opportunitatem indulserit, non cunctabor, quantum in me est, uestre dominationis diligenter implere iussionem.

Conseruetur, oro, per Reginam Angelorum regine et sanctus amor et timor castus diuini nominis, ad ecclesie edificationem et gubernationem regni per tempora longissima.

153

To Queen Eleanor

Excellentissime domine Alionore, Dei gratia regine Anglie, domine Hibernie, ducisse*a* Normanie, Aquitanie et comitisse Andegauensis, Frater Ada, pacem in terris et gloriam in excelsis.

Ecce coram uenerandissima uestre serenitatis celsitudine et cor saucium dolor anxiat et obducit rubor confusam faciem, pro eo quod iuxta cogentem uestre iussionis efficaciam honorabilem magnifice sublimitatis presentiam, obsistentibus difficilium causarum detinentiis, hac uice personaliter adire non sufficio. Accedit tamen in hac parte ad meorum molestaminum qualecunque remedium, quod ad supplices modicitatis mee obsecrationes, quas per presentem litteram

152 *a* duce *MS.*
153 *a* duce *MS.*

I hope in the blessed Son of God that by the power of his glorious resurrection, he will give you counsel for the occasion to the glory of his name, that may lead you into the way of eternal salvation. Amen.

152

To Queen Eleanor

Brother Adam to the most excellent lady Eleanor, by the grace of God queen of England, lady of Ireland, duchess of Normandy and Aquitaine and countess of Anjou, grace and prosperity in the present and glory and happiness in the world to come.

Your royal and serene highness will know that my humble person is willing in the Lord and ready, as is seemly and fitting, to comply with your highness's good pleasure, which you have indicated to me a second time by your letter. In this I am compelled by your piety and kindness and by your desire for my ministry of salvation. Therefore, when God's favour affords an opportunity, I shall not be slow to carry out your ladyship's command as far as lies in my power.

I pray that through the Queen of Angels the queen may be preserved in holy love and chaste fear of the divine name, for the building-up of the Church and the governance of the realm for a very long time.

153

To Queen Eleanor

Brother Adam to the most excellent lady Eleanor, by the grace of God queen of England, lady of Ireland, duchess of Normandy, Aquitaine, and countess of Anjou, peace on earth and glory in the highest.

Before your serene highness I confess that it pains my heart and makes me blush for shame because I am detained by difficult matters so that I am unable on this occasion to comply with your urgent command and come to your highness in person. My vexation gains some relief from the reflection that in response to my humble entreaties conveyed by this letter, your kind ladyship will be willing

153   [1] 29 Nov.
      [2] Richard, earl of Cornwall, 1225–72; cf. Letters 21, 30, 48, 145.

humiliter represento, quod implere non ualet tristis deuotio clemens uolet ignoscere. In uigilia beati Andree[1] dominationis uestre litteram cum ea que decuit reuerentia suscepi. Quo die uix raptim propter uarias interruptiones potui conficere presentia.

Cum domino comite Cornubie[2] fui dominica prima aduentus, cuius motus, ut uideo, quos ipse in audientia uestra seuerius expressit, suauior mitigauit consideratio. Astruit autem protestatione firmiori suam beneuolentiam circa omnia que contingunt salutem pariter et honorem, sicut dignissimum est, tam domini regis quam heredum suorum.

Conseruetur, oro, optabilis generositatis uestre prosperitas in Christo semper et beatissima Virgine.[b]

154

To Sanchia, countess of Cornwall

f. 59 Illustri domine Sanchie, comitisse Cornubiensi,[1] Frater Ada, pacem et salutem in terris et in celis gloriam et honorem.

Pro eo quod exilitatis mee statum et uoluntatem sibi precepit insinuari serenissima uestre dominationis eminentia, licet non ad quantas uolo, ad quantas tamen ualeo, assurgo gratiarum actiones, obsecrans ut quod mea nequit insufficientia superna uobis satisfaciat summe maiestatis affluentia pro multiplici beneficiorum pariter et honorum largitione michi per innatam beneuolentie uestre liberalitatem frequentius exhibita. Igitur sit benedictio diuino nomini.

Oxonie cum fratribus ibidem degentibus dies ago in presentiarum, corporali sospite subnixus, ad honorabile serenitatis uestre beneplacitum deuotam in Domino gerens promptitudinem. Ceterum uestra nouit excellentia karissimum fratrem Willelmum Batale[2] in conuentu Fratrum Minorum Norhamtone de ordinatione superiorum nostrorum, quousque ipsi aliud de ipso statuendum censuerint, secundum religionis nostre obseruantias consistere.

Valeat inclitus comes, dominus uester. Valeat et nobilitatis uestre prosperitas. Valeant et insignes liberi uestri. Valeat et uniuersa domus uestra. Valeant et cuncti profectus uestros fideli desiderio prosequentes in Christo Iesu semper et beatissima Virgine.

---

[b] Following this letter the last eight lines of fo. 58 and the reverse of the folio are blank.

to pardon me for what my sad devotion could not accomplish. I received your ladyship's letter on the vigil of St Andrew[1] with the reverence that was fitting. This was the day on which I was scarcely able to compose this letter hurriedly on account of various interruptions.

I was with the lord earl of Cornwall[2] on the first Sunday of Advent. His anger, which he expressed rather sternly in your hearing, has, it seems to me, been softened by gentler thoughts. As is most fitting, he strongly protests his good wishes for everything touching the welfare and honour of both the lord king and his heirs.

I pray that your excellency may be preserved and may prosper ever in Christ and the Blessed Virgin.

154

To Sanchia, countess of Cornwall

Brother Adam to the illustrious lady Sanchia, countess of Cornwall,[1] peace and greetings on earth and glory and honour in heaven.

I rise to expressions of thanks to your serene ladyship which are not as great as I would wish, but such as I am capable of, for having given instructions to be informed about the condition and wishes of my miserable self. I pray that the supreme Majesty may requite you from his riches, as I cannot, for the manifold benefits and honours frequently conferred on me by your kindness and generosity. For this blessed be the name of God.

I am at present spending my days at Oxford, enjoying bodily health, together with the brethren residing there, ready to render honourable and devoted service to your serenity in the Lord. But be it known to your excellency that Brother William Batale[2] is staying in the convent of the Friars Minor at Northampton following the observances of our religious life by order of our superiors, until they decide otherwise concerning him.

Wishing health to your lord, the earl; wishing prosperity to your noble self, and health to your noble children and to your whole house, and to all who faithfully serve your progress, ever in Christ and the Blessed Virgin.

154 [1] Sanchia, daughter of Raymond Berengar V of Provence, wife of Richard of Cornwall, 1242–61.
[2] Cf. Letter 183 *infra*.

155

To Eleanor de Montfort, countess of Leicester

(May/June 1250)

Inclite comitisse domine Alionore, comitisse Leycestriensi,[1] Frater Ada salutem.

Benignissimam uestre serenitatis industriam rogo suppliciter, ut acceptare uelitis dilationem aduentus fratris Gregorii de Bosellis ad honorabilem excellentie uestre presentiam, quem pater uenerabilis minister Fratrum Minorum Anglie licentiauit sui gratia, ut sine more dispendio ad uos in Vasconiam proficisceretur. Ordinatum est enim per deuotos uestros in Domino ut memoratus frater moretur ad tempus cum domino Cantuariensi propter maxima salutarium causarum negotia.[2]

Ad hec, quoniam cum presentia conficerentur, michi non uacauit in prolixum epistolam protrahere, hoc exoro, hoc moneo, hoc adopto, ut ea que modicitatis mee insufficientia uobis, quantum sufficit in Christo, beneuolentissime[a] et uoce et littera piissime serenitatis uestre recordationi curauit frequenter imprimere, salutari benigni conatus effectu satagitis secundum Deum adimplere. Desiderabile michi foret per omnia, si uestro sederet beneplacito, per proximum nuntium a uobis mittendum in Angliam super optabili status uestri et domini comitis et domus uestre et aliorum uestram dominationem contingentium litteratorie certificari.

Valeat eximia sublimitatis uestre generositas in Christo, et.

156

To Eleanor de Montfort, countess of Leicester

(1251–1252)

Illustri domine Alionore, comitisse Leycestriensi, Frater Ada, salutem in Domino.

Benedicta gloria Domini de loco suo que et uestram non spernit deuotionem et orationem respexit, concedens uobis et a periculis

---

155   [a] beneuolentissima *MS*.

155

To Eleanor de Montfort, countess of Leicester

(May/June 1250)

Brother Adam to the noble lady Eleanor, countess of Leicester,[1] greetings.

Our brother Gregory de Bosellis was licensed by our venerable father, the minister of the Friars Minor in England, as a favour to proceed to join you in Gascony without delay. I humbly beg your most kind serenity to accept that his arrival will be delayed, for it has been decreed by your devoted servants in the Lord that the said brother should stay for a time with the lord archbishop of Canterbury on account of business of major concern to the work of salvation.[2]

In addition, because when I was composing this letter I lacked the leisure to write at length, I beg this, this is my admonition and my desire: that you would, according to the will of God, make every effort of good will to fulfil for your salvation those things that my humble and inadequate self has often striven to impress upon your ladyship's most kind and pious memory both orally and by letter, so far as is possible in Christ. I would desire above everything to be informed by letter, if you please, when you next send a courier to England, about everything desirable concerning your state and that of the lord earl and your house, and that of others of your ladyship's following.

Farewell your gentle serenity in Christ, etc.

156

To Eleanor de Montfort, countess of Leicester

(1252)

Brother Adam to the illustrious lady Eleanor, countess of Leicester, greetings in the Lord.

Blessing and glory to the Lord, who has not despised your devotion and has heard your prayer, and granted you delivery from anxiety and

---

155   [1] Cf. Letter 25 n. 3.

   [2] Gregory de Bosellis accompanied Archbishop Boniface to the papal Curia at Lyons in June 1250 to assist the archbishop in pursuing his case against the bishop of London, who had resisted his visitation: cf. Letters 144, 168.

anxioribus liberationem et exultationem de prole gratiori.[1] Quid ergo? Hoc super omnia dumtaxat consultum fore dinoscitur, ut et iuge diuini nominis preconium et laudabilem emendatioris uite consortium profectum intentissimo corde de die in diem celesti clementie rependamus. Valeat uestra serenitas. Valeant et liberi. Valeant et amici. Valeant et ministri uestri in Christo semper et beatissima Virgine.

157
To Eleanor de Montfort, countess of Leicester

Inclyte domine Alionore, comitisse Leycestriensi, Frater Ada. Breuiter scripsi, quia prolixius scribere non uacauit. Ex illa Dei sententia qua dicitur 'Faciamus ei adiutorium simile sibi'[1] euidenter instruimur, quia uxor uiro districtissime tenetur et per uigoris constantiam, et per discretionis prudentiam, et per benignitatis clementiam, iugem iuuaminis impendere sedulitatem ad omnia in quibus aut Deus colitur, aut iuste uiuitur, aut recte iudicatur; propter quod omnis anima coniugalis, que modis omnibus hoc implere non satagit indiuiduum uite consortium, in quod secundum legem matrimonii intemerate seruandum coniurauit, dampnabiliter uiolare conuincitur.

Cuius preuaricationis reatum pre cunctis mentes incurrere comprobantur, que per demoniales irarum furores amantissimam coniugii pacem perturbare non formidant. Proinde contra tales formidabiliter illud occurrit, 'Virum stultum (id est animum) interficit iracundia et paruulum occidit inuidia'.[2] Nempe dum per iram mansuetudo amittitur, diuine ymaginis similitudo uitiatur, sapientia perditur, uita amittitur, iustitia relinquitur, socialitas destruitur, concordia rumpitur, ueritas obumbratur.

De ira rixe, tumor mentis, contumelie, clamor, indignatio, pusillanimitas, blasphemie proferuntur. Quam necessario sequitur tristitia, de qua malitia, rancor, pusillanimitas, desperatio, torpor circa precepta, uagatio mentis erga illicita nascitur. In ira cor palpitat, in concussionem proximi propellit, in maledictionem linguam impingit, mentem intus deuastat, odium karissimorum generat et fedus amicitie dissoluit. Absit ut tam execranda pestis animum, tam multiplici

156   [1] This probably refers to the birth of Eleanor's fifth son, Richard, who was born at Kenilworth in the autumn of 1251; but the chronology of the Montforts' later children is uncertain. Among them was a daughter born to them in Gascony, who died soon after her birth, between 1248 and 1251: see discussion by Maddicott, *Simon de Montfort*, pp. 43–4.

danger and joyfulness for a beloved offspring.[1] What shall we say then? This advice will at any rate be in place: that we should repay the divine mercy day by day with constant praise of the divine name, accompanied by a laudable and heartfelt amendment of life.

Farewell your serenity. Farewell also your children. And farewell your friends and your servants, ever in Christ and the Blessed Virgin.

157

To Eleanor de Montfort, countess of Leicester

Brother Adam to the noble lady Eleanor, countess of Leicester.

I have written briefly as I had no leisure to write at greater length. That judgement in which God says 'Let us make him a help like unto himself'[1] clearly teaches us that a wife is most strictly bound to her husband by her strength and constancy, her prudence and her meekness and kindness, to give him constant help and care for everything relating to the worship of God, righteous living, and right judgement. For this reason the soul of any spouse who does not make the effort to perform this in every way is guilty of damnably breaking the bond of their lifelong association, which she swore to keep inviolate according to the law of matrimony.

Those whose minds do not fear to disturb the love and peace of their married life by demonic fits of anger are proved to be guilty of a violation of this duty. Therefore to such people is applicable that fearsome text: 'Anger killeth the foolish, and envy slayeth the little one.'[2] For indeed by anger gentleness is lost, and our likeness to the divine image is spoiled, wisdom is dissipated, life is lost, justice is abandoned, companionship is destroyed, concord broken, and truth obscured.

Anger is the source of quarrels, mental disturbance, insults, shouting, indignation, faint-heartedness and blasphemy. Necessarily these are followed by sadness leading to malice, rancour, pusillanimity, despair, sloth in regard to the commandments, and a mind straying into things that are illicit. Anger makes the heart palpitate, drives one to batter one's neighbour, drives the tongue to cursing, inwardly devastates the mind, generates hatred of those dearest to us, and dissolves the ties of friendship. Heaven forbid that such a

157 [1] Gen. 2: 18.   [2] Job 5: 2.

illustrium titulorum gloria sublimatum, in ignominiam exitialis
baratri detestabilem detrudat. Subueniat, oro, placidissima piissime
Virginis gratia apud benedictum auctorem pacifice dilectionis, ut 'pax
Dei, que exsuperat omnem sensum custodiat cor uestrum et intelligentiam uestram'.[3]

Nec miretur, obsecro, perspicue considerationis subtilitas quod
rem acerrimam ex sanctorum eloquiis acrius sum insecutus; ceterum
quid cultus lasciuior matronalem pudicitiam in sinistram ducit
suspicionem? Numquid non discrepabunt meretricii uultus et facies
castitatis? Quis est qui hanc insaniam non execratur, que cum tantis
sumptuum impensis, cum tot ministrantium occupationibus, indies
continuatur, uesanum studium ornatus superflui, per quem et diuina
Majestas prouocatur et offenduntur aspectus honesti nec nisi leno-
num placet petulantiis? An non est diuinitatis iniuria speciem, quam
uenustatis[a] decorauit priuilegio, nescio quibus ineptiis peregrine
superinductionis fucare?

Audiamus diuinos apostolos, quorum princeps sic ait: 'Mulieres
subdite sint uiris suis, ut et si qui non credunt uerbo, per mulierum
conuersationem lucrifiant, considerantes in timore sanctam conuersationem. Quarum sit non extrinsecus capillatura aut circumdatio
auri aut indumenti uestimentorum cultus; sed qui absconditus est
cordis homo in incorruptibilitate quieti et modesti spiritus, qui est
in conspectu Dei locuples.'[4] Doctor etenim gentium, qui omnia
omnibus factus est, ut omnes lucrifaceret, cunctis clamat mortalibus
'mulieres in habitu ornato, cum uerecundia et sobrietate ornantes
se, non in tortis crinibus, aut auro, aut margaritis, uel ueste
pretiosa; sed quod decet mulieres, promittentes pietatem per
opera bona'.[5]

f. 59ᵛ   Vtinam perspicuum pectus panderet quanta sit | anxietas cordi
pauido, pro eo quod oportet dissuadendis tante perniciei nugacitati-
bus insistere inter tot salutis negotia, de quibus, nisi per huiuscemodi
fatuitates excluderentur, sermo tam necessarius foret habendus ad
splendidissimam uestre pietatis industriam. Non incassum, obsecro,
propter Dei uulnera tela celestis emulationis in sancta uibrauerim
precordia. Confido quod, diuinitate propitia, de cetero penitus in
neglectum deuenient ob studium honeste maturitatis luxus profusior
ornatus perituri tam diutius protractus imperitia. Ignoscatur michi,
obsecro, quia anxia sollicitudo calamum obiurgationis aspere, immo

detestable disease should affect a mind so elevated by glorious titles and thrust it into an execrable pit of dishonour. I pray that the grace of the most holy Virgin may plead with the blessed author of peace and love to secure that 'the peace of God, which surpasseth all understanding, may keep your heart and mind'.[3]

I beg you, with your fine perspicacity, not to be surprised at my having pursued a very hard subject rather harshly with words quoted from the saints. Further, why does a wanton style cause matronly modesty to be suspected of impropriety? Is there no difference between the face of a whore and the face of chastity? Is there anyone who does not detest this madness, the demented zeal for superfluous adornment, which goes on daily with such expense and occupies so many servants, which both provokes the divine Majesty and offends decent eyes, and pleases no one except shameless pimps? Is it not an insult to God to paint your face, which He has privileged with beauty, plastering it with some foreign absurdities?

Let us hear the holy apostles, the prince of whom says, 'let wives be subject to their husbands, that if any believe not the word, they may be won without the word by the behaviour of their wives, considering your behaviour with fear; whose adorning let it not be the outward plaiting of the hair, or the wearing of gold, or the putting on of apparel, but the hidden man of the heart, in the incorruptibility of a quiet and a meek spirit, which is rich in the sight of God'.[4] Indeed the doctor of the gentiles, who became all things to all men for the profit of all, cries aloud to all mortals, 'women also (should be) in decent apparel, adorning themselves with modesty and sobriety, not with plaited hair, or gold, or pearls, or costly attire; but as it becometh women, professing godliness with good works'.[5]

How I wish you would open your discerning heart to embrace the heartfelt anxiety I have, because I must needs press to dissuade you from such ruinous follies, in the midst of so many matters relating to your salvation. About these matters, if they were not excluded from the subject by silliness of this kind, I should address a necessary word to your shining piety. I beg you, for the wounds of God, let me not have brandished the weapon of heavenly zeal at your holy heart in vain. I trust that henceforth with divine help, out of zeal for true perfection, your extravagance in perishable adornment, so long continued thoughtlessly, will be altogether abandoned. Forgive me, I beg you, for not having restrained my pen from harsh reproof or

³ Phil. 4: 7.   ⁴ 1 Pet. 3: 1–4.   ⁵ 1 Tim. 2: 9–10.

salutifere suasionis, non compescui, cum ignorem utrum in carne
morari diunitus concedatur quousque desiderabili sublimitatis uestre
fruar colloquio. Succingo epistolam uel inuitus. Esset enim, si daretur
opportunitas, super quam plurimis tractu prolixiori sermo proten-
dendus. Valeat karissima nobilitas uestra. Valeatque comes illustris. Valeat
et uestri proles eximia. Valeat quoque digna domus uestra in Christo
semper et beatissima Virgine.

<h1 style="text-align:center">158</h1>

To Eleanor de Montfort, countess of Leicester

(1249–50)

Illustri domine Alianore, comitisse Leycestriensi, Frater Ada salutem
in Domino.

Melius nouit uestre serenitatis industria, quam sit difficile uel
unicum inuenire sacerdotem, qualis domino comiti uobisque et
familie uestre foret necessarius. Tantum enim talis requirendus esse
cognoscitur, qui sit in sacramentis diuinis deuotus, et strenuus in
officiis ecclesiasticis, in moribus honestus et circumspectus in
agendis. Plus autem omnino carendum fore non dubito penitus
ecclesias talium hominum ministerio, quam huiusmodi pestes
quales, proth dolor, communiter aspicitis, in domesticum suscipere
contubernium, per quos et Dei maiestas prouocatur et uiolatur
societas hominum. Nempe tunc in immensum fatuitas peruagatur
cum propter reuerentiam ordinis stultus ordinatur.

Propter hoc non nisi unum in hac parte consilium ualere poterit;
uidelicet ut Is suppliciter interpelletur, qui non iudicat secundum
faciem sed intuetur cor, 'potens de lapidibus suscitare filios Abra-
hame'.[1] In hoc autem et in aliis statum uestrum contingentibus, si
quid apud modicitatem meam esse poterit, adiutorii, prout Dominus
dederit, libenter laborabo. Parcite michi, rogo, quoniam ignoro si non
quantum res expostulauit et litteris et mandatis uestris responderim,
etsi non ut uolui, tamen ut ualui.

Valete in Christo.

rather from salutary advice, out of my anxiety and solicitude; for I did not know whether God may let me remain in the flesh long enough to enjoy the conversation with your highness that I long for. I am cutting my letter short, yet unwillingly; for, if opportunity permitted, our discussion should be extended over a great many things.

Wishing health to your most dear ladyship, to the illustrious earl, to your distinguished offspring, and also to your worthy house, ever in Christ and the Blessed Virgin.

158

To Eleanor de Montfort, countess of Leicester

(1249–50)

Brother Adam to the illustrious lady Eleanor, countess of Leicester, greetings in the Lord.

Your serene ladyship well knows how difficult it is to find even a single priest of the sort needed by the lord earl and yourself and your household. For one knows that what is sought is simply a man devoted to God in the sacraments, energetic in performing his ecclesiastical duties, upright in his conduct, and circumspect in action. But more than anything, I have no doubt that it would be better for churches to do without altogether the ministry of such men, than that pests of a kind one so commonly sees, alas, should be received into a family household—persons who provoke the majesty of God and soil the society of men. Indeed the folly is widespread when fools are ordained out of reverence for their social class.

For this reason, there can be only one piece of advice to offer in this matter, and that is to appeal humbly to Him who judges not according to appearances, but sees into the heart, He who had 'the power to raise sons for Abraham out of stones'.[1] But in this and other matters touching your situation I shall be glad to work for you if, as the Lord provides, I can be of any help. Forgive me, I beg you, if I do not know whether I have answered both your letter and your instructions to the extent that the case demanded. I have done as much as I was able, not as much as I desired.

Farewell in Christ.

---

[2] Ralph of Canterbury served in the Montforts' household in Gascony, where he died in 1250; see Letters 97, 141.

Tedium ingerit de facto fratris Iohannis tam longa uocum uanitas. Salutare erit, puto, si de cetero quantum ad illum pertinet, totiens prelocute rei non differatur effectus. Iterum in eternum ualete. Consultum erit in Domino ut diligenter conferatis cum magistro Radulfo[2] et magistro Wydone, aliisque uiris prudentibus et timoratis de sacerdote ydoneo in domum uestram assumendo, cum, sicut pretactum est, res sit periculosa et difficilis. De profectione uestra erga Regnum Anglie, cauendum est omnino ne fiat sine magna deliberatione et prouisione discreta, et non debet esse molesta in hoc negotio circumspecta dilatio.

159

To Eleanor de Montfort, countess of Leicester

(1249 × 1250)

Excellenti domine Alionore, comitisse Leycestriensi, Frater Ada salutem et post meritorum gratiam gloriam premiorum.

Si inclitus comes, uir uester, propter Dei honorem et ecclesie salutem, propter fidem domini regis et populorum utilitatem uirtute magnifica, de Saluatore confisus, quasi desperatum pregrandis periculi negotium ad saluandam memorato domino regi, fratri uestro, et heredibus suis terram Vasconie ex deliberato discretorum tractatuum consilio, per diuinum adiutorium, de quo spero indubitanter quod ad laudabilem perducetur consummationem, assumpsit magnifice, uestra serenitas[a] necnon et uniuersi[b] memorato comiti fideli dilectione copulati[c] in letam diuinitatis laudem glorifice debent assurgere.

Quod si per inconsiderationem humanam, tamen ex intentione laudabili, aut pactiones aut federa aut contractus minus ⟨caute⟩ quam oporteret assecutus, cum immoderatiori pecuniarum effusione, tamen, ut uidetur, rerum necessitate coactus inierit, uestrum erit per piissimam benigne circumspectionis industriam, penitus semotis irritantium rixarum contentionibus, in spiritu lenitatis ipsum ad cautius negotiandum de cetero per tranquillitatem consiliorum dirigere.

Super eo quod mandastis de Fratre Gregorio, loquar, Domino propitio,[d] ⟨ministro⟩ in breui cum michi concedetur opportunitas. Benedictus Dei Filius, ualet dominus Lyncolniensis. Valent et incliti

---

159 [a] serenitati *MS.*   [b] uniuersis *MS.*   [c] copulatis *MS.*   [d] *The copyist has clearly omitted something after* propitio.

Such prolonged empty talk about the matter of Brother John is tedious. For the future it will, I think, be for the best if what has been said so many times before should, so far as it concerns him, be put into effect without postponement. Again, for ever farewell. You would be well advised in the Lord to confer carefully with Master Ralph[2] and Master Wido, and other God-fearing men, about a suitable priest to be taken into your house since, as I have already said, it is a dangerous and difficult business. As regards your setting off for the realm of England, you must take care not to do it without much consultation and discreet precaution; in this business a prudent delay ought not to be harmful.

159

To Eleanor de Montfort, countess of Leicester

(1249 × 1250)

Brother Adam to the excellent lady Eleanor, countess of Leicester, greetings, and after the grace that accrues from merit, the reward of glory.

If, for the honour of God, the safety of the Church, acting out of fealty to the lord king and for the service of the people, the noble earl, your husband, with his magnificent strength and trust in the Saviour, has after considered advice and wise deliberation taken on the land of Gascony, to save it for the lord king, your brother, and his heirs, an almost hopeless and very dangerous task, which will, as I confidently hope, be brought to a praiseworthy conclusion, your serene highness and all who are bound to the earl by fealty and love ought to render joyful praise to the glory of God.

If, on the other hand, through human frailty, though acting with laudable intentions, he has entered into pacts or treaties or contracts with less caution than was necessary, making extravagant payments of money, seemingly forced by the demands of the situation, it will be your part, through your very good efforts and benign prudence, avoiding any provocation or contention by the gentleness of your spirit, to direct him with quiet advice to negotiate with more care in future.

As regards your commands about Brother Gregory, I shall, with the Lord's favour, speak shortly to the minister, when I have an opportunity. The lord bishop of Lincoln is well, blessed be the Son of

liberi uestri, iugiter de bono in melius proficientes.[1] Concessit michi domina regina quod ageret apud magistrum Hugonem de Mortuo Mari,[2] ut ad tempus in pace dimittat magistrum Radulfum de Cantuar'[3] et dominum Willelmum de la Hose. Quid inde fiet nescio. Valeat nobilitatis uestre dignissima sinceritas in Christo semper et beatissima Virgine.

Statum domini regis, domine regine, prelatorum et procerum, cleri et populi in regno Anglie, dominus Iohannes de la Haye[4] dominationi uestre melius insinuare ualebit. Iterum in eternum ualeatis.

160

To Eleanor de Montfort, countess of Leicester

Excellenti domine Alionore, comitisse Leycestriensi, Frater Ada salutem et laudabiles consiliorum salubrium effectus.

Tactus dolore cordis intrinsecus et foris faciei rubore suffusus, iam a diebus pluribus inhonestioribus fame crebrescentibus molestiis, super dedecentiis statum uestrum maculantibus non mediocriter audiui, que mens amaricata nec immerito plangere non cessat. Quamobrem ob contemplationem Saluatoris qui, cum sit 'pater misericordiarum et Deus totius consolationis',[1] uenientem ad se non eiicit foras,[2] cui dictum est 'Misereris omnium, quia omnia potes, et dissimulas peccata hominum propter penitentiam; parcis autem omnibus que tua sunt, Domine, qui amas animas'[3], rogo, moneo, et adiuro, ut de cetero benefacientes multiplicibus honestatum incrementis, et conscientiam serenare coram Altissimo, et ad homines opinionem reformare studeatis, modis omnibus in hiis que uirum uestrum et liberos uestros, familiam uestram, et communiter proximos uestros contingunt, uigilanter, rationabiliter et pacifice, secundum exempla matronarum laudabilium uosmetipsas iugiter exhibentes; sciture quod ego cum ceteris amicis uestris, secundum quod diuinitati placuerit et expedire uidebitur, indefesse laborabo ad salutem uestram pariter et honorem, dum tamen huic suasioni, immo preceptioni diuine, consentire uestra benignitas uoluerit cum effectu. Valete.

159 [1] Montfort's first and third sons, Henry and Amaury, were placed in Grosseteste's household for their education; cf. Letters 25, 52.
[2] Hugh de Mortimer was Official to Archbishop Boniface until c.1250; cf. Letter 131 n. 1.
[3] Master Ralph served Montfort in Gascony, but died in 1250; cf. Letters 97, 141, 158.
[4] John de la Haye; cf. Letter 138.

God, and your noble children are also well and continue to make good progress.[1] The lady queen has granted me that she would put it to Master Hugh de Mortimer[2] to dispatch Master Ralph of Canterbury[3] and Sir William de la Hose in peace for a time. What will happen over that I do not know.

Farewell your noble ladyship ever in Christ and the Blessed Virgin.

Sir John de la Haye[4] will be better able to inform your ladyship about the condition of the lord king, the lady queen, and that of the prelates and nobles, clergy and people in the English kingdon. Again, may you for ever farewell.

160

To Eleanor de Montfort, countess of Leicester

Brother Adam to the excellent lady Eleanor, countess of Leicester, greetings, and a laudable outcome to salutary counsel.

For several days now it has pained my heart and made me blush to have heard an increasing number of unpleasant and vexatious reports of improprieties that are soiling your reputation not a little, something that I continually lament with bitterness of spirit. Therefore I ask you, out of regard for our Saviour who, since He is 'the Father of mercies and the God of all comfort',[1] does not cast out one who comes to Him,[2] to whom it is said, 'thou hast mercy upon all, because thou canst do all things, and overlookest the sins of men for the sake of repentance. Thou sparest all because they are thine, O Lord, who lovest souls',[3] I admonish you, I adjure you to multiply your good deeds for the future and both to make a zealous effort to make your conscience clear before the Most High, and to repair your reputation with men, showing yourself in every way, in matters that affect your husband and children, your household and in general those closest to you, ever watchful, reasonable, and peaceable, following the example of praiseworthy matrons. You will know that I, with the rest of your friends, will, according as it pleases God and seems expedient, work tirelessly for your salvation and likewise for your honour, so long however that you will give your kind and effective consent to this counsel or rather this divine precept.

Farewell.

---

160 [1] 2 Cor. 1: 3.   [2] Cf. John 6: 37.   [3] Wisd. 11: 24, 27.

161

To Eleanor de Montfort, countess of Leicester

Illustri comitisse Leycestriensi Frater Ada salutem, et post securam pacem temporis gloriam eternitatis.

Grates refero dominationi uestre quantum ualeo, pro eo quod meam modicitatem super magnificis euentibus domino comiti et uobis per Dei clementiam concessis, in litteris tam diligenter conscriptis, statum quoque memorati comitis et uestri, liberorumque uestrorum, desideranti animo innotescere non omisistis. Sit benedictio superne dispensationi per omnia, que si obstiterit diffidentie

f. 60 pusillanimitas, indubitanter | nouit quod sub diuino patrocinio, in angelorum presidio, cum sanctorum adiutorio, cunctas salutarium difficultates in manibus memorati comitis, siue seuiant hostes, siue proditores moliantur, siue obloquantur detractores, siue peruersores insaniant, trihumphali celebritate consummabit.

Absit a serena regii cordis excellentia uana ficti timoris ignauia. Numquid hesitare poterit humana suspicio ubi dignatio diuina ex preteritorum exhibitione expectationem futurorum consummare curauit? Sit ergo uobis in auctore salutis certitudo infallibilis, quod ea que ratione salutari sunt inchoata salubriter adimplebit, propter nominis sui gloriam et de se fideliter sperantium consolationem.

162

To Eleanor de Montfort, countess of Leicester

(1249 × 1251)

Excellentissime domine Alionore, comitisse Leycestriensi, Frater Ada salutem in Domino.

Etsi non quantis uolo, cum quantis tamen ualeo gratiarum actionibus benigne serenitatis uestre dominationi assurgit mee deuotionis exilitas, pro eo quod, sicut per benignam dignitatis uestre litteram michi nuper innotuit, inter tanta uariarum occupationum molestamina status mei sedulam geritis sollicitudinem. Ceterum nichil nobilitatis uestre pio pectori consultius fore comprobatur quam ut, quanto clemens diuinitas gratia propensiori uotis aspirare

161

To Eleanor de Montfort, countess of Leicester

Brother Adam to the illustrious Countess of Leicester greetings, and after a trouble-free peace in time the glory of eternity.

I thank your ladyship with all my might for remembering to tell me in your letter to my poor self, so carefully written, about the splendid outcome granted to the lord earl and yourself by the clemency of God, and also of how things are with the aforesaid earl and with yourself and your children, of which I much desired to hear the news. Blessed be divine providence through everything, which despite the hindrance of fear and mistrust knew with certainty that by the hands of the earl, acting under the divine patronage, the protection of the angels and with the help of the saints, it would accomplish its ends in glorious triumph over all the obstacles to salvation, whatever the fury of enemies, the efforts of traitors, the abuse of detractors or the madness of subversion.

Do not let your excellency's royal heart be touched by a baseless pusillanimity and false fear. Can there be a place for human mistrust where the divine condescension has worked to perfect our hopes of what is to come by the manifestation of things in the past? Have infallible certainty in the Author of salvation, that He will safely fulfil what has been begun with sound reason, to the glory of His name and to the comfort of those who faithfully hope in Him.

162

To Eleanor de Montfort, countess of Leicester

(1249 × 1251)

Brother Adam to the most excellent lady Eleanor, countess of Leicester, greetings in the Lord.

My poor devoted self cannot thank your kind ladyship enough for being, as you recently indicated to me in your kind letter, sedulously concerned about my condition, while you are in the midst of such great, varied, and troublesome preoccupations. Otherwise, I can offer your ladyship's devout heart no more prudent advice than to say that the more the merciful God condescends to inspire our prayers with increasing grace, the stronger should grow our humility and fear of

dignatur, tanto diuini nominis et timor humilius uigeat, et uiuat sublimius amor in deuotione cordium, que dignam celicis illuminationibus gratitudinem rependere non postponunt.

Contra malignantium insidias summopere curetis, obsecro, Dei patrocinio, angelorum presidio, sanctorum adiutorio, placidis pie conuersationis precibus cum iugitate saluifica commendare que domini uestri et uestri ipsius in tantarum necessitatum articulis contingunt. Cum presentia conficerentur, prolixius scribere non uacauit.

Valeat uestre serenitatis incolumitas in Christo. Valet dominus Lyncolniensis. Valent et insignes liberi uestri. Valeo et ego qualiscunque uester, benedictus Deus per omnia.

163

To Ida Beauchamp

Nobili domine Yde[1] de Bello Campo Frater Ada salutem et quod potest oratio pauperis et deuotio peccatoris.

Pro dilecto michi in Christo domino S. Druer uestro deuoto milite, fratrum meorum caritate compulsus, serenitati uestre presentem direxi petitionem, rogans attentius quatinus eundem in negotio suo, quod in curia domini Willelmi de Bello Campo,[2] excellentis uiri uestri, quatenus pietati seruitur et nequaquam obuenitur, per benigni fauoris gratiam iuuare dignemini, nequaquam, si placet, indigne ferentes quod pro uestro milite qualiscunque uester uestram rogat eminentiam.

Valeat dominationis uestre benignitas in Christo semper et beatissima Virgine.

164

To John of Parma, Minister General of the Friars Minor

(1254)

Clementissimo in Christo patri, Fratri Iohanni, Ordinis Fratrum Minorum generali ministro,[1] Frater Ada humilem obedientialis reuerentie famulatum cum gloria honoris et opere fortitudinis.

---

163 [1] *Sic* in MS; but possibly for Isabelle (Mauduit), wife of William III Beauchamp, c.1235–68: vid. E. Mason, *The Beauchamp Charters*, PRS, NS xliii (1980), pp. xxiii–xxxi.
   [2] i.e. the Beauchamp honorial court.

the divine name, and the more sublimely should love dwell in the devotion of our hearts, which do not delay repaying heavenly illuminations with worthy gratitude.

Against the designs of malicious people take care, I beg you, to commend to the patronage of God, the protection of the angels, and the assistance of the saints, with saving constancy in quiet prayers and goodness of life, all the things involving your lord and yourself where the need is so great. When composing this letter, I had no leisure to write at greater length.

Farewell. I wish your serenity good health in Christ. The lord of Lincoln is well; and your noble children are well. I too am well, yours in what way so ever; blessed by God in all things.

163

To Ida Beauchamp

Brother Adam to the noble lady Ida[1] de Beauchamp, greetings and what can be offered by the prayers of a poor man and the devotion of a sinner.

Urged by the charity of my brethren, I have addressed this petition to your serene ladyship on behalf of my beloved in Christ Sir S. Druer, your devoted knight, with the earnest request that you should condescend to help him with your gracious and kind favour in his case in the court of the lord William de Beauchamp,[2] your excellent husband, so far as piety is served and by no means obstructed, trusting that you will in no way think it improper for anyone of yours to petition your eminence on behalf of your knight.

Farewell, your kind ladyship, ever in Christ and the Blessed Virgin.

164

To John of Parma, Minister General of the Friars Minor

(1254)

Brother Adam to the most kind father in Christ, Brother John, Minister General of the Friars Minor,[1] humble and obedient service, with honour and glory and fortitude in your work.

---

164   [1] John of Parma, Minister General July 1247–February 1257.

Utinam, sicut semper liberet, liceret sepe uestre sanctitatis anime
deiformi pectoris aneli spiritum auidum presentare per littere
colloquium, quod per officium lingue non ualeo. Obsistit hic
nempe absentia corporalis amicitialibus animis, iuxta sapientum
sententiam, licet non sine planctuum anxiamine ferenda, tamen
quam dispensatio legitima salubriri necessitate mortalibus defectibus
adesse compellit.

Numquid non Ille inuiolabilis amicitie superamabilis*ᵃ* federator eis,
quos sui ipsius supercelesti dignificauit amicitia, 'Vos', inquiens, 'dixi
amicos, quia quecunque audiui a Patre meo nota feci uobis';² iam
iamque corporali uiduaturus presentia premittere curauit: 'Ego ueritatem dico uobis, expedit uobis ut ego uadam';³ uidelicet ne quantumcunque delectabili gratie tamen carnali hereatis infirmitati, sed ex
ea, per eam, super eam insuper desiderabilem gloriam certe spiritualem
conscendatis alacriter. Huic consentit illud apostoli, 'Etsi cognouimus
secundum carnem Christum, sed nunc iam non nouimus'.⁴

Porro hic occurrit admodum mirandus Perypatetici principatus
preceptor primus, qui corporalem absentiam inter maxima ueracis
amicitie dampna deputari contendit.⁵ Quomodo namque ueri amici,
quorum amicam necessitudinem solummodo conciliat uerus amor
bonitatis, iuxta quod probat memoratus sapientum primicerius,
arbitrari poterunt ⟨quibus⟩ amicitie felici quod quicquam detrahat
corporalis disiunctio? Immo potius illam et equanimiter sustinent et
exoptant longanimiter, cum eam aut compellit humanitatis impendende necessitas aut suauitas diunitatis inspiciende requirit. Et eo
amplius diuinitus conceditur singulis et omnibus ueri nominis amicis
in supersimplicem originem fontalis amicitie superseculariter pergere,
ubi propter simplicem summe bonitatis essentiam ueraces amici
eidem coherendo unus*ᵇ* spiritus effecti, presentialius inuicem adu-
nantur in indiuiduum beate uite consortium, quam quiuis eorum
possit quantumcunque secum sit presens esse sibi.

Delectabat licet sermonis inculti ieiuna macie, tamen affectu
feruido desiderantis animi adminiculo litterali ad piam paternitatis
uestre disertitudinem proponere istud tantillum de re tanta, ueritus
ulterius uestre sinceritatis auribus seriem prolixiorem ingerere. Sed
pigebat nacta opportunitate optabili serenitati (uestre) nichil omnino

164 *ᵃ* superamabilis *written above the line.*   *ᵇ* unus: uno *MS.*

² John 15: 15.   ³ Ibid. 16: 7.
⁴ 2 Cor. 5: 16.   ⁵ Aristotle, *Nicomachean Ethics*, viii. 5.

How I wish it were often granted, as it was always my delight, to convey to the godly soul of your holiness the longing spirit panting in my breast through a conversation by letter, which I cannot do by word of mouth. Here physical absence is indeed, as wise men have said, an obstacle to souls linked by friendship, yet what a rightful dispensation has made one of the inescapable human limitations out of the need for salvation, is still not to be borne without anxiety and lamentation.

Did not that most lovable maker of inviolable friendships say to those whom he dignified with his own superheavenly friendship 'I have called you friends, because all things whatsoever I have heard of my Father, I have made known to you?'[2] Again and again, when He was about to deprive them of his bodily presence, He took care to tell them in advance 'I tell you the truth: it is expedient to you that I go';[3] that is, lest you should cling to the weakness of the flesh, how great soever the delight of its grace, but that you should swiftly rise from it, through it, and above it, to the glory of your desire, which is truly a spiritual one. The apostle accords with this in saying 'We have known Christ according to the flesh, but now we know Him no longer'.[4]

On the other hand, we are met here by the first teacher of the Peripatetics, whose pre-eminence is wonderful, who argues that bodily absence is to be counted among the things most harmful to true friendship.[5] For how can they be thought real friends who are united in a necessary bond solely by a real love of the good, according to the aforesaid leader of the wise, when bodily separation deprives them of something of the happiness of friendship? Indeed do they not rather endure separation with equanimity, and patiently wish for it when it is forced upon them by human necessity or imposed by the sweetness of divine contemplation? All the more is it granted by God to each and every one of the friends of the True Name to proceed beyond the world to the transcendent source and origin of friendship, where true friends, cleaving to the simple essence of the supreme good, are made one in spirit and are united to one another in their undivided share of the blessed life, by which each of them can be more intensely present to the other.

It was a pleasure to offer you, my eloquent father, these scrappy thoughts on such a great matter by means of a letter, albeit in meagre and untutored language, but with the fervent affection of my spirit; I feared to inflict a more prolix piece on your generous ears. But I was reluctant, given the opportunity, to write and seal nothing at all to

sigillatim scribere. Ceterum in benedicto Dei Filio exorabiles pietatis uestre pedes complexus, effuso uisceralium affectionum profluuio, propter pium glorifici Redemptoris cruorem, propter districtum terrifici iudicis examen, propter honorem Dei, propter profectum hominum, una cum ceteris Anglicane prouincie fratribus sicut petitione communi, sic speciali supplicatu humillime rogo, attentissime deprecor, quatinus uirum honorabilem apud considerationem uestram excellenter estimatum, Fratrem Willelmum de Notingham, in ministrum administrationis ⟨prouincie⟩ Anglicane pie consensionis unanimi concordia solempniter electum[6] et per uestre prelationis auctoritatem uestri gratia canonice confirmatum, ad salutem celicam et perenne solatium filiis uestris, inter mortales uobis deuotissimis filiis, fratribus memorate ministrationis, per prouisiuam paternitatis uestre dispensationem remittere uelitis in patrem et pastorem, id agentes, diuinate propitia, ut tante multitudinis diuina desideria in Deo compleantur.

Valeat beatitudinis uestre prospera sospitas in Christo Iesu semper et beatissima Virgine.

165

To John of Parma, Minister General of the Friars Minor

(1250)

Reuerendissimo ac desideratissimo patri, Fratri Iohanni, ministro generali, Frater Ada.

Benedicta sit superni Saluatoris dispensatio, per quam ad eximiam multimode salutis operationem desiderabilem persone uestre presentiam, amotis innumerabilium occasionum impedimentis, prouincie remotiores suscipere meruerunt.[1] Succingo scripturam, confidens quod per linguam fieri poterit tempore opportuno quod in presenti nequit expediri per calamum. Ceterum pro karissimo fratre W.,[a] quem plurime meritorum laudabilium commendant eminentie, languoris diuturni molestia pregrauato, humiliter supplico, quatinus ob Christi contemplationem uelitis mittere N., ut diuinitate propitia dicto W. consilium mitigande ualetudinis impendere ualeat.

165   [a] N in MS; the copyist's mistake is apparent from the last sentence of the letter.

---

[6] William of Nottingham left England in 1254 to attend the general chapter of the Order at Metz. In his absence the English provincial chapter unanimously re-elected him, unaware

your serenity. But in the blessed Son of God embracing your compassionate feet with an outpouring of my heart's affection, by the holy blood of our glorified Redeemer, by the severe examination of the dread Judge, for the honour of God and the progress of men I, together with the rest of the brethren of the English Province, thus joined in a common petition, most humbly ask and urgently implore you by a wise dispensation of yout fatherly care to send back to us as our father and shepherd our honoured brother William of Nottingham, greatly esteemed in your eyes, who has been solemnly and by common agreement unanimously elected minister to govern the English Province[6] and canonically confirmed by the grace of your prelatical authority, for the heavenly salvation and perpetual consolation of your sons, who are of all mortals those most devoted to you; doing this in order that by divine favour the holy desires of such a great multitude may in God be fulfilled.

Farewell, your beatitude, wishing you good health ever in Christ Jesus and the blessed Virgin.

165

To John of Parma, Minister General of the Friars Minor

(1250)

Brother Adam to the most revered and beloved father, Brother John, Minister General.

Blessed be the dispensation of our heavenly Saviour, by which for their excelling and manifold works of salvation the more distant provinces have, after the removal of innumerable obstacles, deserved to receive your personal presence as they desired.[1] I am writing briefly in the belief that at an opportune time it will be possible to do with my tongue what cannot be accomplished by pen. But I make a humble request on behalf of our dearest brother W., commended by the prominence of his merits and much praise, who is burdened by a troublesome daily sickness, that out of regard for Christ you would send him brother N., so that with God's favour he may be able to counsel the said W. to alleviate his illness.

that the general chapter of Metz had discharged him from the office of provincial which he had held for fourteen years; Eccleston, p. 100 and n. 3a; cf. Letter 208 below.

165 [1] John of Parma visited Greece in 1249 on a papal mission, returning to Italy in autumn 1250; cf. Letter 48 n. 15.

166

To Bonaventure, Minister General of the Friars Minor

(1259)

f. 61ᵛ Reuerendissimo in Christo patri et uotis intimis semper exoptando, Fratri Bonauenture,[1] Fratrum Minorum ministro generali, Frater Ada dictus de Marisco, 'omne datum optimum et omne donum perfectum desursum descendens a patre luminum',[2] cum supplici humillime deuotionis obedientia.

Pro pia disertitudinis uestre littera, quam michi nuper rescribere curauit benigna paternitatis uestre consideratio, sanctitati uestre ad plures quam ualeam assurgo gratiarum actiones in gratia Saluatoris. Verum non merui ut super quibusdam articulis requisitionum mearum expressum per litteram responsum habuerim. Satisfacit tamen, sicut dignum est, plenius in hoc et in aliis modicitati mee sinceritatis uestre beneplacitum. Aggrauata sunt super me uehementer usque ad confectionem presentium multiformia ualetudinum discrimina; propter quod affectu uiscerali deprecor humilius ut, si quomodo libet hoc saluifica ratio sustineat, mittere dignemini ad me personaliter uenerabilem patrem Fratrem Iohannem, ministrum prouincialem,[3] sine cuiuslibet more dispendio, per quem diuinate propitia in euentum omnem et inter transeuntia dirigar, et erigar in permanentia.

Super mora uestra in prouincia Anglie, quam dispensationis diuine prouisiua bonitas ac gloriam nominis sui et sui regni profectum opportuno tractu protelare condescendat, si commode fieri posset, plurimum optarem certificari, quo si, Domino largiente, uita comes fuerit, ualeam etiam inestimabilia necessitatum pregrandium desideria per uiue uocis colloquium, ex Altissimi patrocinio, propensius explicare optato cum effectu.

Valeat preoptabilis sanitatis uestre sospitas in Christo Iesu semper et beatissima Virgine. Amabilem comitiuam uestram, cui me in Christo recommendo, saluet semper Auctor salutis.

166

To Bonaventure, Minister General of the Friars Minor

(1259)

Brother Adam, called Marsh, to the most reverend father in Christ, greatly sought for in our prayers, Brother Bonaventure,[1] wishing him 'every best gift and every perfect gift from above coming down from the Father of lights',[2] with humble obedience and devotion.

I cannot thank your holiness enough in the grace of our Saviour for the eloquent letter that your fatherly kindness recently wrote to me. Really I did not deserve a reply to all the details of my requests set out by letter; yet your sincere goodwill renders my poor self full satisfaction, as it should, in this and in other things. Up to the time of composing this letter I have had worsening crises of health, on account of which I humbly beg you with heartfelt affection to send me in person our venerable Brother John,[3] our provincial minister, without delay, if in any way this may be acceptable in the cause of salvation. Through him, God willing, I shall be set to rights in transitory matters and raised up for things everlasting.

I should very much like to be informed about your stay in the English Province, if it could be conveniently done, which may the goodness of divine providence opportunely condescend to prolong for the glory of His name and the advancement of His kingdom. By this, if the Lord grants that I am still alive, I should be able, with the aid of the Most High, to set out to you more readily in conversation by word of mouth our very great needs and our boundless desires with desired effect.

Wishing you most desired health and safety ever in Christ Jesus and the Blessed Virgin. May the Author of salvation ever preserve your beloved headship, to which I commend myself in Christ.

---

166 [1] St Bonaventure was Minister General 1257–74.

[2] James 1: 17.

[3] John of Stamford, English Provincial Minister 1258/9–?64. This letter, which must be dated summer 1259, is the earliest reference to his being in office.

167

To Bonaventure, Minister General of the Friars Minor

(1259)

Reuerendissimo in Christo patri et domino, Fratri Bonauenture, Fratrum Minorum generali ministro, Frater Ada dictus de Marisco supplicissimos iugis obedientie famulatus cum salutari gloria et honore perhenni.

Mesti cordis meror anxius animam meam uehementius affligit, de eo quod in presentiarum desiderabilem presentie uestre iocunditatem, presertim in tantis pregrandium necessitatum exigentiis, sicut uereor admodum obsistentibus infelicitatis mee peccatis, personaliter adire non sufficio. Sed benedicta dispensationis superne clementia adhibet in hac parte remedium pacis longanimis per quam, Deo melius aliquid prouidente, qui cum magna reuerentia disponit que circa nos, secus ordinatur mortalium processus ad exitus optabiles quam eorum uota requirant aut inquirant consilia, pariter prouidens tam ipsorum desiderio quam solamini.

Quod igitur personaliter nequeo, hoc ut queo, ago litteraliter, scilicet latissime paternitatis uestre pietati qualiscunque filiationis spiritum contribulatum humillime represento, per prouisiuam sedulitatis uestre sanctimoniam manu ducendum*ᵃ* ad Eum qui dedit illum. Subministrat benedicti Saluatoris benigna miseratio michi adhuc cor habens fiduciam in Domino uidendi faciem uestram amabilem, et uobis fruendi in Domino ad beatum profectum ampliande caritatis et ueritatis contemplande. Sicut fuerit uoluntas in celo, sic fiat.

Satisfaciat uobis sempiterna retributio pro eo quod inter tot rationabilium detinentiarum uariamina uenerabilem patrem, ministrum Anglie,[1] ad meam paruitatem tanta sedulitate mittere uoluistis. Vtinam litteram qualem,*ᵇ* quam me memini uestre prelationi ⟨destinasse⟩ in partes ultramontanas maturius post susceptum a uobis ministerium, plenius fuisset lecta et intellecta, per quam conatus sum nonnulla, succincte licet, aperire continua uotorum meorum meditamina. Sed forsitan hoc exclusit assidua ingentium causarum urgentia hominis utriusque multimodas indigentias quibus premor indies. Perdilectis patribus Fratri I. et Fratri M., sociis uestris, ceterisque uobis spirituali necessitate coniunctis, si placet, uicibus

167 *ᵃ* manuducendum *MS.*   *ᵇ* qualem *repeated in MS.*

167

To Bonaventure, Minister General of the Friars Minor

(1259)

Brother Adam, called Marsh, to the most reverend father in Christ and lord, Brother Bonaventure, general minister of the Friars Minor, most humble and obedient service, with saving glory and eternal honour.

My heart is immensely afflicted with sadness because at present I cannot manage to come in person to enjoy the pleasure of your presence, being much hindered, I fear, by my unhappy sins, especially in my great and demanding needs. But the blessed and merciful dispensation of heaven provides in this case a remedy of patience and peace, for through it by the providence of God, who disposes all to do with us most awesomely, providing something still better, the doings of humans are directed to desirable outcomes other than those that our prayers look for or our counsels seek, providing the fulfilment of our desire and our consolation equally.

What therefore I cannot do in person, I perform by letter, that is to say, I most humbly present to your fatherly goodness and generosity my troubled and in every way filial spirit, to be led by your sacred and perspicacious hand to Him who gave it. The merciful kindness of our blessed Saviour aids me with a heart still confident in the Lord of seeing your beloved face and enjoying you in the Lord, to the blessed gain of enlarging charity and contemplating truth. Let it be as heaven wills.

May you receive an eternal reward for having been willing with so much concern, in the midst of so many and various preoccupations, to send our venerable father, the minister of England,[1] to my poor self. I could wish that the letter which I remember having dispatched to your headship overseas soon after you had received the office of minister, had been fully read and understood. By it I endeavoured to disclose, though briefly, some of my constant reflections and prayers. But perhaps the relentless pressure of great matters excluded attention to the manifold needs of the inner and outer man by which I am oppressed daily.

I beg to be frequently commended, if you please, to our dear Father J. and Brother M., your associates, and the others attached to

---

167 [1] John of Stamford; cf. Letter 166 and n. 3.

frequentatis obsecro recommendari. Sapientiam cordis et fortitudinem roboris continuet uobis Sapiens corde et Fortis robore per iugem
interuentum sue genetricis gloriosissime. Amen. Datum Lincoln'.
Hec est ultima littera quam dictauit pie recordationis Frater Ada de
Marisco.ᶜ

168

To William of Nottingham, provincial minister

(June 1250)

f. 62 Reuerendissimo in Christo patri, Fratri Willelmo, ministro Fratrum
Minorum in Anglia, Frater Ada salutem in Domino.

Inspecta littera pietatis uestre, cuius uel ferreum pectus frequentatis uicibus non transfigerent, dum per eam imprimerent uulnera
uulneribus limpidissime compassionis, iaculis iacula succedentia. Sed
quid? Certe mellifluum inflicti doloris solatium habundantius attulit,
cum nectarea suauissime dilectionis affluentia patulas plagarum
scissuras salubrius infunderet. Proinde ad rependendas condignas
gratiarum actiones amabili uestre sanctitatis liberalitati, quoniam
uocis succumbit eloquium, utinam prout celitus subministrabitur,
animi gestiat desiderium.

Ceterum postquam diutinis uehementium conaminum instantiis
per dominum Cantuariensem actum est iugitate inflexibili ut cum eo
ad Sedem Apostolicam tam ego quam Frater Gregorius[1] proficisce-
remur, hoc ipsum omnimodis domino rege et domina regina primo
quidem uolentibus, sed deinde ut moraremur in Anglia memorata
regina prout ualuit satagente, tandem obsistentibus michi mandatis
apostolicis et auctoritate deficiente per quam dictum iter arripere-
mus,ᵃ [2] in hoc resedit perpensis sollicite rerum circumstantiis exitus
deliberationis, ut prefatum dominum, me remanente, karissimi
Fratres Gregorius de Bosell' et socius eius Frater W. de Wygorn'
per obedientiam eisdem ut in Vasconiam pergerent dudum a uobis
iniunctam, comitarentur, quousque ob iter eis occurreret auctoritas
apostolica, per quam ad Curiam accedere ualerent; quam si

ᶜ *The copyist added these words in red below Letter 167. The rest of fo. 61ᵛ was left blank.*
168 ᵃ arripemur *MS.*

---

168 [1] Gregory de Bosellis; cf. Letter 1 n. 2.
[2] The obstacle to which Adam refers is a privilege of Innocent IV dated 24 Sept. 1245

LETTER 167

you by spiritual necessity. May He who is wisdom and strength
continue to confer wisdom on your heart and fortitude, through the
constant intercession of His most glorious mother. Amen. Given at
Lincoln.
This is the last letter composed by Brother Adam Marsh of holy
memory.

168

To William of Nottingham, provincial minister

(June 1250)

Brother Adam to Brother William, minister of the Friars Minor in
England, greetings in the Lord.

I have perused your letters, the successive darts of which would not
pierce even a breast of iron, as through it the wounds they implant are
those of purest compassion. But how? Surely it brings honeyed solace
more abundantly for the pain inflicted, since an affluent nectar of
sweetest love is poured soothingly into the open wounds inflicted by
the blows. O that the desire of my spirit might render fitting thanks to
your holiness for your amiable generosity in the way that heaven will
provide, for speech fails me.

Well, after insistent attempts the lord of Canterbury ordained with
an immovable determination that both I and Brother Gregory[1] should
set off for the Apostolic See with him, the lord king and the lady
queen being at first entirely in favour of this very thing. It was then
decided that we should stay in England, as the aforesaid queen
entreated as much as she could. At length, as papal mandates were
an obstacle for me and we lacked the authority to undertake the
journey,[2] when the circumstances of the case had been anxiously
considered, the discussion settled on this: that I should remain behind
and that our dearest Brother Gregory de Bosellis and his companion
Brother William of Worcester would accompany his said lordship,
acting under the obedience by which you had a short time ago
instructed them to proceed to Gascony, until papal authority reached
them authorizing their journey to the Curia. Should it happen that

forbidding bishops to include friars in their households for the purpose of conducting
business without special licence of the Apostolic See. The prohibition was repeated in the
privilege *Petitionibus vestris* of 13 Aug. 1247: Sbaralea, i, Inn. IV, no. 100, p. 383.

contingeret non obtinere, uersus Vasconiam tenderent. Igitur, ipsis proficiscentibus, a mari regressus sum die beati Antonii[3] mandatum apostolicum apud dominum regem, prout Saluator dederit, expleturus.

Una cum honorabili uiro Fratre Petro,[4] ministro Colonie, omni precum piarum instantia supplico rogans obnixius quatinus dilectum Fratrem Paulinum, qui cum Fratre Waltero de Maddeley ante aliquot dies per obedientiam memorati ministri in Angliam rediit, de consueta latissimi sinus clementia obuia sedulitate suscipere et confouere pia paternitate dignemini, meliorandi moris gratia eundem sancto fratrum prouincie uestre collegio aggregantes. Hoc idem nequaquam per dictum ministrum interpellatus uestram rogo beneuolentiam modis quibus ualeo de prefato Fratre Willelmo de Maddele.

Mitto uobis litteras michi a uenerabili patre domino Lyncolniensi a Curia destinatas, sciens quam sit benigne sanctitati uestre de profectu causarum salutarium leta consideratio. Audiui etiam quod prosperatis negotiis dictus dominus a Curia cum salute reuertitur. Que presenti cartule desunt dilectissimus Frater Iohannes de Stanford[5] uestre discretionis insinuabit arbitrio.

Valeat desiderabilis uestre paternitatis incolumitas, et.

169

To Brother William of Nottingham, provincial minister

(1250–1)

Fratri Willelmo, ministro Anglie, Frater Ada salutem in Domino.

Inspectis diligentius et plenius intellectis paternitatis uestre litteris, non obstantibus causis quas et efficaciter et prudenter et salubriter tam ex attributis negotio quam personis, quam et necessitatibus obtendistis, si quo modo fieri posset quominus Wyntoniam ad instantem Natiuitatem Domini accederetis,[1] uisum est Fratri Willelmo Batale et michi, quod ruptis omnibus modi quibuscunque importunitatum detinentiis, in hac parte regiis uos oportet obtemporare mandatis.

169   *a* diligenter *added in margin of MS.*

---

[3] St Antony of Padua, 13 June.
[4] Peter of Tewkesbury: Eccleston, p. 91 and n. He was subsequently head of the Oxford custody, 1236–*c*.1248, and English provincial 1254–8. Little, *Greyfriars in Oxford*, p. 127.
[5] John of Stamford; cf. Letter 34 n. 13.

this authority was not obtained, they would proceed on their way to Gascony. So as they set off, I returned from the sea on St Antony's day,[3] to discharge the papal mandate with the lord king, as the Saviour shall help me.

Together with the honourable Brother Peter,[4] minister of Cologne, I beg you with the urgency of our pious prayers that you would with your customary kindness deign to receive, and like a good father to cherish our dear Brother Paulinus, who out of obedience to the said minister returned to England some days ago with Brother Walter de Maddely, aggregating him, for the sake of improving his behaviour, to the holy association of the brethren of your province. I ask you, not at all by request of the said minister, but in such a way as I can, if you would be so kind as to do the same in regard to the said Brother Walter de Maddely.

I am sending you the letter sent me from the Curia by our venerable father the lord bishop of Lincoln, knowing how gladly your kind holiness contemplates the progress of salutary causes. I have in fact heard that his lordship is safely returning from the Curia with his business having prospered. Our beloved Brother John of Stamford[5] will present to your prudent judgement the things that are missing from the present letter.

Fare you well, dear father.

169

To Brother William of Nottingham, provincial minister

(1250–1)

Brother Adam to Brother William, minister of England, greetings in the Lord.

Your letter, father, has been carefully read and fully understood. Notwithstanding the causes which you effectively and prudently plead arising from both business and personal commitments and from unavoidable circumstances to prevent you, if it were in some way possible, from going to Winchester for the Nativity of the Lord,[1] it seems to Brother William Batale and me that you should put aside everything whatsoever that detains you, and in this matter bow to the

---

169 [1] The palace of Winchester, to which Brother William was invited, was King Henry's favourite venue for celebrating Christmas.

Nempe hoc exigere uidetur crucis predicatio et tam solempniter impetrata et tam diligenter*a* commissa, tantam preferens salutem, tantis agenda periculis, ut priusquam de regno exeatis,[2] prouide circumspectionis sollicitudo uigilantior, quantum fieri potest, Domino concedente, ad humanam salutem et diuinum honorem memorate predicationis executionem dirigat, iuxta quod ex hiis que audituri estis doceri poteritis.

Ad rem etiam pertinere cognoscitur ut priusquam ab Anglia recedatis domino regi et domine regine ualefacientes, eorundem patrocinio religionis nostre deuotionem in Christo recommendetis. Quod si regie maiestatis mandata suscepistis, ⟨et⟩ contingeret uos tam prope positos regalem declinare presentiam, maxime cum uigeat causa, quam dominus rex non irrationabiliter tanti estimat,[3] nec insolentioris supercilii notam, nec odibilioris ingratitudinis oblocutionem, nec uehementioris indignationis motus aliquatenus sicut creditur, effugeretis. Denique illustres animi sapientum ex consideratione secularium fantasmatum in pomposis solempnitatum celebritatibus nitorem lanuginis preferentium, sublimiter proficiunt ad insignem mendacis mundi contemptum. Super omnia uerba uite contra tanta celice saltis pericula impauide sanctitatis sapientia non tacebit, si hoc inspirauit Is qui omnium est artifex, omnem habens uirtutem, quique ante reges et presides incogitatos sermones subminstrat ad salutem.

Valeat uobis inuicte uirtutis salutaris industria in Christo, etc.

170

To Brother William of Nottingham, provincial minister

(1251)

Fratri Willelmo, ministro Anglie, Frater Ada salutem et subiectam debite deuotionis obedientiam.

Hoc ago littera quod lingua nequeo; uidelicet alloquor desiderabilem mansuetudinis uestre paternitatem. Iuuat enim quos salutaris nectit necessitudo per scripturam spirituum exhibere presentiam, cum personalem excludit necessaria dispensatio.

[2] Presumably William's expected departure was to attend the general chapter of the Order in 1251. The triennial chapter that should have met in 1250 was postponed owing to the absence of the Minister General, John of Parma, in the East; cf. Letter 8 n. 13.
[3] Henry III took the cross on 6 Mar. 1250.

royal commands. For indeed the preaching of the cross seems to demand this; for it was so solemnly petitioned for and so earnestly committed to us; it offers such great promise of salvation and is to be executed in so much danger, that before you leave the kingdom[2] the execution of this preaching should be guided by your provident circumspection and care as much as possible, the Lord granting it, for the salvation of men and the honour of God, according to what you learn from the things you are going to hear.

It is recognizably to the point that before you leave England you should bid farewell to the lord king and the lady queen, and commend our devoted religious order to their patronage. But, if you have received the commands of his royal majesty, and it were to happen, nevertheless, that you declined the royal presence when you were in the vicinity, especially when there is a vital cause which the lord king not unreasonably values so highly,[3] you would not, we believe, escape being branded with arrogance or insolence or odious ingratitude, or the strength of his displeasure. In the end, the noble spirits of the wise, contemplating the images of the worldly in the solemnity of their pompous celebrations and the brittle splendour they prefer, are transported to a noble contempt for the mendacious world. The fearless wisdom of holiness will not withhold the words of life preached against such great dangers to our heavenly salvation, if thus inspired by Him, the author of all, who having all power, supplies spontaneous words to speak before kings and unconsidered rulers for their salvation.

May your saving efforts and unconquered strength prevail in Christ, etc.

170

To Brother William of Nottingham, provincial minister

(1251)

Brother Adam to Brother William, minister of England, greetings and humble and devoted obedience.

I am doing by letter what I cannot do by word of mouth, that is addressing your dear fatherly kindness. For it is pleasant for those bound together by the needs of salvation to convey their spiritual presence by writing when the necessity of their situation prevents

Verum intolerabilibus uestrarum occupationum iugitatibus impor-
tunitatem prolixi sermonis ingerere non tam improbum quam
noxium fore putaui. Quid ergo? Ut quid multa? 'Porro unum est necessarium.'[1] Et quid
hoc? Nonne hoc quod diuinum Moysen docuit Is qui ait 'Sine me
nichil potestis facere',[2] et alibi 'In mundo pressuram, in me autem
pacem habebitis'?[3] Et adhuc inquiens 'Quid hoc est?' Hoc est profecto
sine quo superior locus ecclesiastici regiminis nisi prouocande
diuinitati et perdendis animabus non tenetur.

Nostis autem, et quis melius? hoc esse illud, quod cum seuirent
rebellantium uiolentie, cum insanirent insultantium conuicia, cum
urgerent malignantium molimina, pro quibus ait, 'Aut dimitte eis
hanc noxam, aut dele me de libro quem scripsisti',[4] ipsi legislatori tam
salutaris iussionis uigilantia precepit Deus: nunc montis ascensum,
nunc introitum tabernaculi. Et quid per ascensionem montis nisi
limpida superne ueritatis contemplatio? Quid per introitum tabernaculi nisi ignitum orationis sacrificium? Quorum illud sine tranquillitate uacationis, suspensis quantumcunque salutaribus exercitiis, non
attingitur. Istud uero sine mortificatione passionum, repressis motibus quantecunque sedulititatis nequaquam celebratur. Propterea
ignorare nequit, nisi quem aut excecauerit astutia seculi aut carnis
illecebra captiuauit, quam sit execrandus qui celice pastionis ministerium profitetur et tamen in hiis que dicta sunt, secundum summam
intentionis estimationem iugiter pergens in Deum, cui est cura de
omnibus, non immoratur.

Hec igitur scripserim non ut indefessam uestre sanctitatis sollici-
tudinem aut doceam aut reprehendam, sed ut secundum | sententiam
Salomonis deuota filiatio pie paternitati prestet occasionem. De hiis
usque sufficiat. Noui namque quam efficaciter in hac parte et in
similibus sibi persuaserit desuper uobis data sapientia. Scripsit michi
domina regina litteram affectuosam et efficacem ut, cum opportunitas
se offerret, presentiam ipsius non omitterem; quod michi non
mediocriter foret graue et molestum. Instat etiam domina comitissa
Leycestriensis quod ad eam ueniam circa instans festum Sancti
Michaelis,[5] et etiam per aliquem magnum super similibus sum
sollicitatus. Vestrum erit super hoc quod uobis sederit michi, si
placet, signare. Quid me uelit uestra paternitas facere post presentem
autumpnum precor expresse signare.

f. 62ᵛ

170 [1] Luke 10: 42.   [2] John 15: 5.   [3] Ibid. 16: 33.
     [4] Exod. 32: 32.   [5] 29 September.

bodily presence. Truly I thought it would be as wicked as it would be tiresome to impose the nuisance of a prolix speech upon the constant and intolerable burden of the business matters that occupy you.

So what am I to say? and why so much? 'But one thing is necessary.'[1] And what is this? Is this not what the divine Moses was taught by Him, who says 'without me you can do nothing',[2] and in another place, 'In the world you shall have distress, but in me you may have peace'.[3] And still He cries 'what is this?' Truly this is that without which one cannot hold a senior position of ecclesiastical governance except by provoking God and destroying souls.

But you know, and who better? This is what God with such saving care commanded the legislator: now the ascent of the mountain, and now the entry into the tabernacle, when we are reviled by those shouting abuse and are oppressed by the contrivances of the wicked, on whose behalf He says, 'either forgive them this trespass or strike me out of the book of life that thou hast written'.[4] And what is signified by the ascent of the mountain except the clear contemplation of heavenly truth? what by the entry into the tabernacle except the burnt offering of prayer? Of these the former is not achieved without tranquillity and leisure and for a time suspending salutary activity; the latter is not celebrated without mortifying the passions and sedulously repressing the obtrusiveness of sensual motions. Therefore it cannot be ignored, except by someone blinded by worldly cleverness or enslaved to the enticements of the flesh; how accursed is one who professes the heavenly ministry of a pastor, yet in these things I have said does not continue with his utmost intent to seek God, who cares for all.

I have written this not in order to instruct or reprehend the untiring solicitude of your holiness, but that, in accordance with the judgement of Solomon, a devoted son may offer an opportunity to a kindly father. Enough of this, for I know how efficaciously in this respect and in others like it you are guided by the wisdom given you from above. The lady queen has written to me an affectionate and forceful letter requesting that I should not neglect to visit her when I have an opportunity. This would be no small burden and irksome for me. The countess of Leicester is also pressing me to come to her around the feast of St Michael,[5] and I have even been solicited with similar requests from a magnate. It is for you to signify to me, if you would, what you decide about this. I beg you, father, to indicate clearly what you wish me to do after the present autumn.

Valeat uobis, oro, et uirtus inuicta, et sensus indeceptus, et zelus irremissus ad illius operis consummationem, quod propitia diuinitas uobis et quibusdam filiorum uestrorum ad ueram ordinis reformationem nuper inspirauit.[6] Genua pietis uestre complexus deprecor humiliter, supplicius obsecrans ut mee paruitatis insufficientiam diuine uelitis miserationi per saluifica uestri et filiorum uestrorum, fratrum minorum, suffragia, eosque qui mecum per uestram laborant ordinationem. Salutari peto obsequio mei karissimos patres et fratres, fratrem R., fratrem W., ceterosque fratres filios uestros in Auctore salutis.

Valeat uestra paternitatis incolumitas, etc.

171

To Brother William of Nottingham, provincial minister

(January–March 1250)

Fratri Willelmo, ministro Anglie, Frater Ada.

Postquam, proficiscente domino Lyncolniense ad Curiam Romanam, per inexorabilem, licet multiformiter attemptatam, domini regis, domine regine, domini Cantuariensis detinentiam moratus sum in Anglia, uel inuitus, cum intolerabili laborum, sollicitudinum, ⟨et⟩ anxietatum molestia domini Cantuariensis contubernio aggregatus,[1] inestimabilia celestium illuminationum detrimenta, uidelicet eternitatis in mente, ueritatis in ratione, tranquillitatis in uoluntate, propter immensas terrenarum caliginum uoragines, me miserum in dies perferre sub luctuosis continui planctus gemitibus non desisto. Hec idcirco dixerim, quia licet uideri posset legibus amicitie derogari, cum desperabiles cause discriminosi doloris, quod sine cruciatu diro fidelis amici fieri nequit, patefiant euidenter, tamen fiduciam suscitat remedii pectori transfixo cum letale telum uigenti, clementi educendum pie panditur paternitati.

Proinde cum non appareat qualiter iter aperiatur euasioni, nisi per benignam fauoris apostolici gratiam, obtestor, obsecro, deprecor, omni precum genere congesto, quatinus animam, pro qua apud formidande maiestatis examen sub tante districtionis inexcusabili

---

[6] The reform of the Order to which Adam refers is most probably the restoration of a stricter rule of poverty, which had been relaxed by Innocent IV's bull *Ordinem Vestrum*. William of Nottingham, assisted by Brother Gregory de Bosellis, succeeded in persuading the general chapter of Genoa (1251) to suspend the concessions made by the bull: Eccleston,

Wishing you, I pray, unvanquished strength, undeceived understanding, and inexorable zeal to complete that work which a merciful God has recently inspired you and some of your sons to undertake for the true reform of the Order.[6] Embracing your knees, I humbly beg with a request that you would commend my little and inadequate self, and those who by your ordinance work with me, to the divine mercy through the saving prayers of yourself and of the Friars Minor, your sons. I ask, as a favour, greetings to my dearest fathers and brothers, Brother R., Brother W., and the rest of the brethren, your sons, in the Author of salvation.

Wishing you, father, good health, etc.

171

To Brother William of Nottingham, provincial minister

(January–March 1250)

Brother Adam to Brother William, minister of England.

After the lord of Lincoln set off for the Roman Curia, I stayed in England, being detained by the irresistible, albeit variously formulated, demands of the lord king and the lady queen, and my lord of Canterbury, and against my will was added to the company of the lord of Canterbury's associates,[1] causing me intolerable trouble, work, and anxiety. Wretched me, every day, without ceasing I suffer with groaning and lamentation the incalculable harm to heavenly illumination, that is to thoughts of eternity, truthful reasoning, or a tranquil will, on account of [being sucked into] the darkness of a vast abyss of worldly concerns. I say this because, although it may seem contrary to the rules of friendship to disclose desperately painful and dangerous subjects, which are bound to torment a loyal friend, yet a pierced heart trusts to find a remedy when the deadly shaft is shown to a strong and kind father to have it mercifully plucked out.

Therefore, since there appears to be no way of escape except through the kindly grace of the Apostolic favour, I beg you, I implore you, with every kind prayer heaped upon prayer, by ways that seem

p. 42 and n. The terms of Adam's letter suggest that William had already left England to attend the chapter.

171 [1] Adam was pressed into accompanying Archbishop Boniface on a visitation of the dioceses of Canterbury, Rochester, and London in Apr. and May 1250; cf. Letters 32, 52.

410   LETTERS OF ADAM MARSH

sponsione sanctitatem uestram defixistis, cui dictum est, 'Virum hunc custodi, qui si lapsus fuerit, erit anima tua pro anima illius',[2] modis quibus congruere censuerit suauissima sedule paternitatis circumspectio, absque amaricantis more odibili dispendio, per amantissimi patris, Fratris Iohannis, domini pape nuntii,[3] adiutorium, a tanto precipitiorum imminentium horrore studeatis eripere, restituendo tam desiderabilem stabilium profectuum ordinem.

Ceterum aptissimum fratrem filium uestrum, Robertum de Thornham,[4] diuino desiderio flagrantem et humane salutis auidum, cum expeditione castrorum[5] pro celici cultus sublimatione, non sine feruore triumphalis martirii se fiducialiter accingentium ad passagium instans diuinitate propitia profecturum, noui indubitanter quoniam uestre strenuitatis pia sedulitas tanto propensiore fauore prosequetur, quanto dilectione[a] feruentiori Redemptori rependere satagit quod redemptus accepit.

Ad hec, cum honorabili patre, Fratre Petro, ministro Colonie,[6] quam necessaria, quam rationabili, quam affectuosa ualeo, humillime supplico deprecatione, quatinus propter Dei gloriam, propter ecclesie salutem, propter fratrum caritatem, beneuoli fauoris auditum leto cum affectu eidem, manifeste pietatis causam agenti, inclinare non ducatis indignum. Longe fiat a pia latissimi cordis[b] magnificentia detestabile diffidentie uitium quo mens blasphema desperat Dei uirtutem, Dei sapientiam, Dei sanctificationem, aut posse aut nosse aut uelle cum multiplici superne largitionis feruore sibi impensa refundere. Denique de mandato ministri generalis de prouincia superioris Alemannie, duos fratres, Hugonem et Iordanum, iuuenes, benignos, idoneos et bone spei, ad uos ut in diuinis proficiant eloquiis destinatos, attentius rogo prouisiua benignitate suscipere, dirigere, promouere uelitis in Domino.

Valeat desideratissima uestre sanctitatis incolumitas, etc. Gemens sub aquis uix ista rauci gutturis susurrio carptim submurmuraui, quem abissalis horror opprimentium occupationum profundat immensium.

171   [a] dilectioni MS.   [b] MS adds vigil, expuncted.

[2] 3 Kgs. (1 Kgs.) 20: 39.
[3] The Franciscan Brother John was papal nuncio in England 1247–51; cf. Letter 94 and n.
[4] Robert of Thornham (Norfolk) was formerly warden of Lynn and was custodian of Cambridge in 1250, when he resolved to go crusading in the Holy Land: Eccleston, p. 89.
[5] Adam frequently uses the word castra to mean armies.
[6] Peter of Tewkesbury was head of the Oxford custody 1236–c.1248: Little, The

fit to you, most gentle father, to whom it is said 'Keep this man: and if he shall slip away, thy life shall be for his life',[2] to act without delay and use the help of our dear Brother John, the nuncio of the lord pope,[3] to deliver my soul from the fear of imminent catastrophe and restore to me the stability and ordered progress I so desire; inasmuch as your holiness has pledged to answer for my soul with an inescapable engagement at the dread judgement of the divine Majesty.

I know without doubt that you, with your kindly and assiduous energy, will favour our well-equipped brother, your son Robert of Thornham,[4] who is burning with desire for God and hungry for the salvation of men, and is about to set off, with God's favour, on the coming crossing overseas with the armed expedition[5] to exalt divine worship, faithfully girding itself, not without a fervent desire for triumphant martyrdom. I know that you favour him all the more readily as he is eager to repay our Redeemer with the fervent love he received when he was redeemed.

Together with the honourable father, Brother Peter, the minister of Cologne,[6] I most humbly beg you with all the reasonable and affectionate insistence that I can, that for the glory of God, the safety of the Church, and the love of the brethren, you would be so good as to grant him a favourable hearing with joyful affection, as he is pursuing a manifestly holy cause. May the vice of distrust be far removed from your magnificent and most generous heart, a vice by which a blasphemous mind despairs of the strength of God, the wisdom of God, the sanctifying power of God, or of the ability or the knowledge or a willingness to repay what has been bestowed on him with fervent generosity. Lastly, I urgently request you to receive with kindness and care the two brothers, Hugh and Jordan, from the province of Upper Germany, young, pleasant, and suitable youths of good promise, sent to you by the command of the Minister General, to advance their study of Sacred Scripture, and that you would direct them and help them on.

Farewell, your most dear holiness, etc. I am groaning under the waters. I have barely muttered this bit by bit, with a hoarse throat, my voice deepened by the utter dread and pressure of endless business.

Greyfriars in Oxford, p. 127; Eccleston, p. 34; he was provincial minister of England 1254–58; Eccleston refers to him as minister of Germany, ibid. p. 91 and n.

172

To William of Nottingham, provincial minister

Fratri Willelmo, ministro Anglie, Frater Ada salutem et reuerentialem in omnibus obedientiam. Karissimum fratrem A. de Hereford, quem michi pia uestre circumspectionis sedulitas assignauit pro socio, inueni benignum affectibus et moribus honestum, docilem ingenio et litteratura prouectum, efficacem adiutoriis et officiis operosum, suauem socialitate et conuictu gratiosum. Quamobrem indubitanter credi debet quod, diuinitate propitia, ante prolixa temporum curricula, ad honorem Domini et cleri doctrinam et populi salutem, si eidem de continuitate studii prouideatur, laudabiliter proficiet ad predicationem uerbi Dei in eloquii promptitudine, qua preditus esse cognoscitur; quo etiam nonnulli longe inferiores ad officium eruditionis impendende, ut opinor, in Scriptura Sacra sunt designati de discretorum consilio.

Verum oculata fide conspicio, secundum quod cogit mea necessitas et utilitas mea requirit, quia quicunque fratrum michi in adiutorium tam uarii et tam continui laboris fuerit associatus, postposito ecclesiastici sudoris exercitio, illum iugiter oportebit defectibus meis supplendis, et uiis meis dirigendis et oneribus meis supportandis insistere, et nonnunquam sibi^a ipsi geminaretur et uirtus et industria et longanimitas. Absit igitur a me ista tyrannidis impietas ut uellim in prefato fratre tantos diuine dispensationis profectus aut attenuari aut retardari aut impediri ob priuate commoditatis considerationem, presertim cum michi sine communi dispendio in competenti consortio, sicut hactenus uestri gratia factum est, ualeat per Saluatoris misericordiam prouideri. Per experientiam quoque coniicio quod nequit, quantecunque sit mansuetudinis seu quanticunque uigoris, prefatus Frater A. sine corporis grauamine et mentis inquietudine nisi quatenus urgentia mitigat obedientie salutaris diurnos estus et uigilias nocturnas mecum indeficienter sufferre.

Cum igitur per certissima compererim argumenta, quod ad subueniendum meis insufficientiis, quantum secundum Dominum fieri
f. 63 ualebit, perfectam in Christo | gerat uoluntatem, uestre discretionis inolita benignitas fiducialiter rogo quatinus, si uestre non displicet

172   ^a sibi: si *MS*.

I72

To William of Nottingham, provincial minister

Brother Adam to Brother William, minister of England, greetings, reverence and obedience in all things. With your prudent and holy solicitude you assigned Brother A. of Hereford to me as my companion. I have found him to be kind and sympathetic in his disposition, upright in his conduct, talented and teachable and accomplished in letters, an effective helper, industrious in performing his duties, and a gracious and charming companion. It must therefore be unquestionably thought that, with God's favour, if it is arranged for him to continue with his studies, before long he will go on to preach the Word of God with the ready eloquence with which we know he is endowed, to the honour of the Lord, the instruction of the clergy, and the salvation of the people. In my opinion, some persons far inferior to him have been appointed to the office of teaching Sacred Scripture by the advice of wise men.

Truly, I see with my own eyes, as my need compels me and my usefulness demands, that whoever of the brethren is associated with me to help with such varied and continuous work, putting aside his ecclesiastical tasks, will continually be obliged to apply himself to making up for my failings, giving me guidance, and supporting my burdens, and sometimes it would mean combining his own strength with industry and patience. So let me not be guilty of the impious tyranny of wishing, out of consideration for my personal convenience, to diminish, delay, or hinder the said brother's great progress through divine dispensation; especially since it is possible through the mercy of the Saviour to provide me with an adequate associate without expense to the community, as has been done hitherto thanks to you. Also I conclude from my experience that, however great his gentle compliance and however great his energy, the said brother cannot unfailingly endure with me the heat of the day and the watches of the night without physical harm and mental disturbance, except insofar as they be mitigated by the pressing dictates of saving obedience.

From most certain proofs I have concluded that in your kindness and prudence you are perfectly willing in Christ to come to my assistance in my inadequacy, as far as it can be done according to the will of the Lord. I therefore trustfully ask, if you please, father, that

sancte paternitati, desideratum in Christo Fratrem Laurentium de
Sutthon ad me sine more dispendio in subsidium societatis, si tamen
in hoc ipsum ipse consentiat, remittere dignemini; prefatum fratrem
A. Londinum ad studendum, intuitu Christi, quod et ipse, si uestro
sederit beneplacito, plurimum desiderat, nichilominus maturius
mittere consentientes.

Si autem dictus frater Laurentius aliquem satis tolerabilem patiatur
defectum, insignitus tamen est quam plurimis ad assistendum mee
paruitatis idoneitatibus, quamuis uulgaris pertinacia non sic sentiat.
Nunquam tamen formidat sapiens odibilem inconstantie notam, ubi
superne ueritati constanter inheretur, que secundum rerum trans-
mutabilium uarietates diuersas, tamen eadem manens, precipit
uicissitudines consiliorum. Quod quia stultorum superba iactantia
peruicaciter exhorrescit, ipsi recedentes ab incommutabili ueritate et
mutabilium euentibus innitentes, illud incurrunt cum despicabili
ignominia quod ex inani gloria fugiunt, adeo quod contra ipsos
loquitur sapientia, dicens 'Stultus ut luna mutatur, cum sapiens
sicut sol perseueret'.[1]

Valeat paternitatis uestre sanctitas, etc. Tanto propensiori diligentia prescripte petitionis effectum precor maturare uelitis, quanto dum
pendet anceps exitus arbitrii uestri in hac parte series tranquillitatis
non mediocriter emulanda desiderandi moderaminis patietur detrimentum. In eternum ualete. Si petita superius concesseritis, bene
quidem. Sin autem, quod bonum est in oculis uestris fiat per
Dominum. Expediui secundum quod michi desuper dictum est
apud dominum Lyncolniensem que mandastis.

173

To Brother William of Nottingham, provincial minister

Fratri Willelmo, ministro Anglie, Frater Ada salutem et tam debitam
quam deuotam in auctore salutis obedientiam.

Cum intellexissem per karissimum fratrem N. de Amlyeres
causam satis rationabilem profectionis sue in ministrationem Francie, discussis rei circumstantiis cum eodem fratre, fratris Petro de
Theokesbyr'[1] et mee paruitatis consiliis adquiescentibus,[a] presentem
petitionem paternitati uestre censui dirigendam, suppliciter rogans

173 [a] adquiescente *MS*.

you would be good enough to send me the desired Brother in Christ Laurence of Sutton without delay to assist me, provided, however, that he agrees to this; also that you would consent to send the said Brother A. to London to study earlier, out of regard for Christ, which he too, if you please, very much desires.

If the said Brother Laurence suffers from some failings that are quite tolerable, he is nevertheless distinguished by a great many qualities that fit him to assist my puny self, though this is not the general opinion. But the wise man never fears the odious label of inconstancy where he clings with constancy to heavenly truth, which, according to the changing conditions of transitory things, though it remains constant, demands changes of counsel. But as the pride and boastfulness of fools are frightened by this, relying on the accidents of mutable things, they themselves abandon changeless truth, and out of vainglory incur that judgement from which they flee with contemptible disgrace, so much so that Wisdom says against them, 'The fool changes like the moon, but the wise man is as constant as the sun'.[1]

Farewell, holy father, etc. I pray you to make haste to deal with the above request the more carefully and readily, for as long as your decision remains in doubt, it will be detrimental to continued peace, which is much to be desired in this matter, and harmful to your desirable authority. For ever, farewell. If you grant the above request, well and good. But if not, let that be done through the Lord which is good in your eyes. I have dispatched with my lord of Lincoln what you commanded, in accordance with what was told me from above.

173

To Brother William of Nottingham, provincial minister

Brother Adam to the minister of England, greetings with due and devoted obedience in the author of salvation.

When I understood from my dearest Brother N. de Amilyeres the quite reasonable cause why he was setting off for the province of France, after examining the circumstances of the case with him, and with the agreement of Brother Peter of Tewkesbury[1] and my little self, I decided to send you, father, this humble request that, saving

172 [1] Cf. Ecclus. 27: 12.

173 [1] Peter of Tewkesbury; see Letter 171 n. 6.

quatinus, salua dispositione ministri generalis circa ipsum eidem fratri concessa, si ministri Francie consensus accesserit, clementi pietate prouidere uelitis locum certum, ubi dictus frater per uestre discretionis ordinationem moram facere ualeat in deuotionis tranquillitate et fretus honestatis exemplo ad eruditionem Sacre Scripture proficiat; tanto propensiori gratia hanc, si placet, prosequentes supplicationem quanto desiderabilius fore censetur, ut iuuenis docilis ingenii, boni moris et spei laudabilis, per uestre benignitatis diligentiam ad Dei honorem et salutem multorum, diuinitate propitia, promoueatur. Accedit autem ad impetrandam fauoris beneuolentiam fratri Petri sedula deuotio.

Videtur denique, si uestro sederit beneplacito, opportunum fore aut ut Oxonie, aut Cantebrugie, aut Londini dictus frater studendi gratia collocetur usque ad tempus unius aut duorum annorum, secundum quod minister suus uiderit ordinandum. Voluntatem uestram placeat, oro, per latorem presentium michi signare.

Valeat sanctitas uestra in Christo, etc.

174

To William of Nottingham, provincial minister

Fratri Willelmo, ministro Anglie, Frater Ada salutem et deuotam subiecti famulatus obedientiam.

Ob contemplationem specialissime caritatis qua non immerito circa karissimum filium uestrum I. de Beuerlaco affici compellor, presentem sanctitati uestre direxi petitionem, rogans attentius quatinus iuxta paternam prouide discretionis emulationem, perpensis cause sue circumstantiis, uobis, si placet, per dilectum patrem fratrem Martinum, gardianum Oxonie,[1] uiua uoce exponendis, clementie uestre beneplacitum[a] sine more dispendio secundum deliberatam rationis exigentiam insinuare non ducatis indignum.

Valeat, etc.

---

174   [a] Beneplacito *MS.*

the arrangements of the Minister General accorded to this brother, and if the consent of the minister of France be given, you would be so good as to provide a fixed place where the said brother could stay by your ordinance in peace and devotion, relying upon an honourable example, to advance his learning in Holy Scripture. We ask that you favour this request the more readily, please, as it is considered to be very desirable that a youngster of teachable talent, good conduct, and praiseworthy expectation should, with divine favour, be advanced by your care and kindness for the honour of God and the salvation of many.

Finally, it seems appropriate, if it pleases you, for the said brother to be placed to study at Oxford, or Cambridge, or at London, for up to one or two years, according to what his minister ordains. May it please you, I pray, to signify your will to me by the carrier of this letter.

Farewell, your holiness, in Christ, etc.

174

To William of Nottingham, provincial minister

Brother Adam to the minister of England, greetings with humble service and devoted obedience.

I have directed this petition to your holiness out of regard for the very special charity that deservedly moves me towards your dearest son, brother J[ohn] of Beverley, with a pressing request that you would deign to indicate your good pleasure without delay, according to your fatherly wisdom, having regard to the circumstances of his case that are to be explained to you, if you please, by word of mouth by the dear father Brother Martin, the warden of Oxford.[1]

Farewell, etc.

---

174 [1] To be distinguished from the Brother Martin of Alnwick listed in Eccleston as 32nd lector of the friars at Oxford, p. 54, who was at Oxford c.1300: A. G. Little and F. Pelster, *Oxford Theology and Theologians, c.* AD 1282–1302 (Oxford, 1934), p.275.

175

To William of Nottingham, provincial minister

Fratri Willelmo, ministro Anglie, Frater Ada (salutem) et tam debitam quam deuotam subiecti famulatus obedientiam.

Non putaui ad prouide circumspectionis uestre discretionem utendum fore rationibus persuasoriis, sed solummodo ad paternam benignitatis uestre pietatem summendas esse humiles deuotarum precum instantias. Proinde suauitatis uestre supplico clementie, cum quanta ualeo rogans intentione quatinus, perpensis studii urgentia cum angustia temporis, corporis ualetudine cum animi molestia, parcat michi uestre sanctitatis pietas intuitu sancti Saluatoris et piissime Virginis, ne cogar cum multiplici mentis et corporis discrimine, sicut nuper michi scripsistis, apud Bedeford uobis occurrere, beneplacitum honorabilis reuerentie uestre per latorem presentium mee paruitatis humilitati signantes, Domino propitio, per omnia sicut dignum est, iussionibus uestris super id modicum quod potest obtemperare.

Prefata que tetigi discrimina tam menti quam corpori, si laborem aggrediar quem michi precepistis, magis eligo sub silentio preterire quam uestre pietatis auribus tot interpellantium uocibus incessanter occupatis cum prolixitate sermonis ingerere. Habetis karissimum patrem Petrum de Theokesbyr',[1] qui qualecunque sensum meum in hiis de quibus tracturi estis, ut reor, non ignorat. Habetis etiam prouidum amplexandum societatis uestre consilium. Habetis quoque, ut credo, maturioris industrie uiros, quos ut uobis occurrant euocastis, quibus adhuc alios aggregare uideri poterit superuacuum, quantumcunque magna fuerint negotia, de quibus per diuinitatis gratiam estis tracturi. Quod si quid consilii a me paternitas uestra iudicat fore requirendum, poterit illud, prout preceperitis, uobis per litteram insinuari.

Valeat, etc.

175

To William of Nottingham, provincial minister

Brother Adam to Brother William, minister of England, greetings with humble service and due and devoted obedience.

I have not thought it proper to use persuasive arguments in addressing you in your far-sighted prudence, but only to press your fatherly kindness with my insistent and devoted prayers. Thus I beg your gentle indulgence with all my strength that, in view of the pressing needs of the studium, the short time available, my bodily health, and my troubled spirit, your holiness would, out of regard for our holy Saviour and the most blessed Virgin, spare me from the obligation of meeting you at Bedford, as you recently wrote to me, with the manifold hazards to my mind and body; and that you would signify to my humble self, by the favour of the Lord, through the bearer of these letters your reverence's good pleasure how to comply with your commands to the limited extent within my power.

I prefer to keep silent about the risks to both mind and body that I have mentioned, rather than to burden your devout ears with excessive verbosity when they are ceaselessly occupied by so many importunate voices, if I should undertake the labour that you have bidden me. You have our dearest father Peter of Tewkesbury,[1] who is not unaware of any opinion of mine regarding the matters that you are, I think, going to discuss. You have indeed the prudent advice of your order to embrace. You also have, I think, men of more mature experience, whom you have summoned to meet you. To add still more to their number may appear pointless, however great the business with which, by God's grace, you are going to deal. But if, father, you judge any advice is required from me, it can, as you command, be conveyed to you by letter.

Farewell, etc.

---

175   [1] Peter of Tewkesbury; see Letter 171 n. 6; cf. Letters 173, 175.

176

To William of Nottingham, provincial minister

Fratri Willelmo, ministro Anglie, Frater Ada salutem et deuotam humilis obedientie reuerentiam.

Cum secundum tenorem mandati uestri karissimum Fratrem Eustachium de Normanuill'[1] secundum formam quam competere putaui allocutus fuissem, et digestus considerate deliberationis tractatus per dies aliquot tenderetur, tandem perpensis rei difficilis circumstantiis pretendens diutinam corporis ualetudinem et aptitudinem mentis imparatam, asseruit se in officio lectionis exhibende nullatenus posse desiderio fratrum Northwyci prout ratio requireret satisfacere. Proinde uestre paternitatis prouide circumspectioni supplicat obnixius, obsecrans quatinus sibi clementer in hac parte parcat sancte pietatis consideratio, parato, sicut dignum est et salutis sue requirit exigentia, uestris iussionibus cum promptitudine deuotionis obtemperare. Non igitur uideo quid fiat in hac parte consultius quam ut fraterno solamini sedula condescensione prouideatur.

f. 63ᵛ Frater Walterus de Euesham, missus nuper in Angliam pro statu | fratrum Hybernie meliorando, fratrem Iohannem de Stanford[2] et me super quibusdam articulis officium Fratris Andree de Lexinton[3] in memorata prouincia contingentibus, diligenter consuluit; quibus ego respondere distuli usque super eisdem discretionis uestre diffinitio michi patefieret; propter quod transcriptum littere obedientalis, si forte eam non uideritis, per quam minister generalis prefato fratri Andree suam commisit auctoritatem, simul cum littera predicti Fratris Walteri dictam consultationem continente, uobis presentibus inclusam transmitto, rogans ut in causa tante salutis quid facto opus sit michi rescribere uelit benignitatis uestre sollers industria.

Pro Fratre Ada de Bechesoueres et Fratre R. de Waltham, sicut alias feci, non piget iterum interpellare paternitatis uestre sollicitudinem, ut eosdem in pacifica consolatione, sicut noueritis et uolueritis, propter intuitum Saluatoris salubriter lucrifacere studeatis, quod

176 [1] Eustace of Normanville, canonist and chancellor of Oxford, entered the OFM by 1251; incepted as lector to the friars at Oxford c.1253; then resumed as lector at Cambridge: Eccleston, pp. 51, 58; Little, *Franciscan Papers, Lists and Documents*, pp. 133–4; *BRUO* ii. 1364. Cf. Letter 177.

176

To William of Nottingham, provincial minister

Brother Adam to Brother William, minister of England, greetings with humble obedience, reverence, and devotion.

When, in accordance with the sense of your mandate, I had spoken to our dear Brother Eustace of Normanville,[1] following a form of words which I thought appropriate, various points were considered and mooted for some days. At length, after the difficult circumstances of the question had been pondered, he raised the long-standing question of his health and his mental unpreparedness for the task, and declared that he could in no way satisfy the desire of the brethren of Norwich in the capacity of their lecturer as reason would require. Therefore he vehemently begs you, father, of your provident prudence and consideration mercifully to spare him in this matter. He is ready to obey your orders with promptitude and devotion, as is fitting and his own salvation demands. I do not see, therefore, what is advisedly to be done in the matter, except to provide him with brotherly comfort and reassurance.

Brother Walter of Evesham, who was recently sent to England to improve the condition of the brethren in Ireland, has earnestly consulted Brother John of Stamford[2] and me about certain points concerning the office of Brother Andrew of Lexington[3] in that province. I have postponed answering his inquiries until your discreet decision on these points is clear to me. For this reason I am enclosing a copy of the letter of obedience by which the minister general committed his authority to the said Brother Andrew, in case you have not seen it, enclosed together with Brother Walter's letter in which he consults us; this with a request that with your usual care you would kindly write back to me to say what needs to be done in a case of such moment for salvation.

May it not displease you if I appeal to your fatherly solicitude again for Brother Adam of Bechesoveres and Brother Richard of Waltham, as I have done before, to make a salutary effort to win them over by offering them peaceful consolation, out of regard for our Saviour, as

---

[2] John of Stamford; cf. Letter 123.
[3] Andrew of Lexington; cf. Letters 206, 211, 225, 240.

et Domino propitio sine difficultate ualebitis. Forsan*a* expediret ut, ubi ego moror, maneret etiam supradictus Frater A.

Petitionibus meis, quas apud suauitatem uestram semper uestra*b* gratia ⟨numquam inhibet⟩*c* desperatio displicendi, specialiter inserere curaui subiectam humilitatis obsecrationem, uidelicet ut sine more dispendio ad reformandam plenius uenerabilis patris Fratris Iohannis de Rading[4] sanitatem, que per diuinitatis gratiam in proximo prouentura speratur, sepe dictum Fratrem Adam de Bechesoueres Oxoniam iuxta fratrum desiderium remittere non ducatis indignum.

Ad supplicem fraterne compassionis instantiam apud pium paterni pectoris arbitrium noui non mediocriter fauorabilem, cum quanto possum affectu deprecatoriam adiungo petitionem, ut Fratrem Philippum de Londino,[5] quem, ut spero, ad cumulum meritorum manus Domini misericorditer tetigerit, cui sicut audio citra requisitionem impendende caritatis ad fratris tam afflicti solatium in subsidiis prouidetur uictitandi, maxime quantum ad loci et societatis competentiam ita recommendare curetis, dilectissimis patribus et fratribus uestris curam fratrum Londini agentibus, prout et diuine uoluntati seruiatur, et infirmitatis necessitatibus subueniatur, et salutaribus fratrum exemplis consulatur in Domino.

Valeat, etc.

177

To Brother Robert of Thornham

Amantissimo sibi in Christo patri, Fratri Roberto de Thornham,[1] Frater Ada pacem in terris et gloriam in excelsis.

Ad inolitam benigni moris suauitatem, pro eo quod non condignus occurrit effectus, affectus assurgit supplex gratissimis benedictionibus studiose uarietatis, multiplicem suauis anime dulcedinem rediuiua frequentatione patenter insinuantibus, licet non ut uellet, tamen ut ualet, prosequens obnixius amabilem uestre liberalitatis amicitiam.

176 *a After* Forsan *MS has* desperatio displiciendi *expuncted.*   *b* uestri *MS.*
c nunquam inhibet *MS has* n repellit, *inserted over a deletion in another hand. The editor's suggestion is only tentative.*

---

[4] John of Reading was abbot of Oseney when he joined the Franciscans in 1235: *Ann. Mon.* iv. 82; Eccleston, p. 18.
[5] Philip of London was listed by Eccleston (p. 27) as one of the first friars to be appointed to the office of preacher general.

you know how and desire. With the Lord's favour, you will be able to accomplish this without difficulty. Perhaps it would be expedient for the said Brother Adam even to stay where I am residing.

I have taken care to graft on to my requests to your kind self, whereby I am not discouraged by a fear of ever displeasing you, a humble entreaty from your subject that you would not consider it unsuitable to send the aforesaid Brother Adam of Bechesoveres back to Oxford without delay in accordance with the brothers' desire, to restore the health of the venerable father, Brother John of Reading,[4] more fully, of which by the grace of God there is hope in the near future.

Moved by brotherly compassion, I add with the greatest possible affection a supplicatory prayer—one that I know without doubt finds favour in your fatherly breast—that you would earnestly commend Brother Philip of London[5] to your beloved fathers and brothers caring for the brethren at London. He has, as I hope, been mercifully touched by the hand of the Lord to the full measure of his merits. In accordance with a request to bestow charity, I hear that provision will be made for the consolation of the so-much afflicted brother by additional food on the greatest scale within the means of the place and the community, so that God's will may be observed and the needs of the sick man met, and that consideration may be given in the Lord to salutary examples for the brethren.

Farewell, etc.

177

To Brother Robert of Thornham

Brother Adam to the most beloved father in Christ, Robert of Thornham,[1] peace on earth and glory in the highest.

Because the outcome you desired is not forthcoming, my humble affection rises to embrace your natural sweetness and the kindness of your conduct with most grateful and various blessings, that manifold sweetness of the spirit reflecting our renewed association, as I strive, not as I would wish, but as I am able, to oblige the delightful friendship of your liberal mind.

---

177   [1] Robert of Thornham was warden of the friars at Lynn, then custodian of Cambridge, before setting out on crusade to the Holy Land: Eccleston p. 89 and n. e.

Ceterum karissimi fratris Eustachii de Normanuil',[2] quas habet multimodas presentium importunitatum obsistentias, quominus in presentiarum impleri queat quod uestri et filiorum uestrorum optauit pia consideratio,[3] puto penitus excusatas habebit, cum uobis innotuerint, fraterna circumspectio. In hac parte, sicut arbitror, sufficientem dedit operam rationis iusta requisitio, quamuis non prouenerit expetitus intentionis exitus, Deo melius aliquid disponente,[a] propter quod constat fore consultum ipsi committere quod concupiuimus. Quoniam reuerendi patris ministri nostri ad instans festum Natalitium presentiam adire disposuistis, per quem plenius de singulis innotescere poterit causis exprimendis, supersedendum esse censui. Precipiat michi, qualicunque uestro uestra digna dilectio. Valeat uobis status integri sancta sinceritas in Christo, etc.

178

To William of Nottingham, provincial minister

(1253–4)

Fratri Willelmo, ministro Anglie, Frater Ada deuotum supplicis obedientie famulatum.

Distantia mille passuum inter Montem Oliueti et ciuitatem Ierusalem obtineat michi et ceteris filiis uestris cursu ueloci breuiter explicare orationis uestre longanimitas indeficiens peruenturis ad sabbatum in utroque homine delicatum, certe placidam tranquillitatis perfecte requiem in affluentissimis dulcedinem absconditarum deliciis, cuius in littere uestre primordio sub affectuoso meministis desiderio. Sic scilicet ut dextris sequacium diuinitus apprehensis in diuine Maiestatis manductione perpeti pariter pertingamus ex Monte Oliueti per iter sabbati in ciuitatem Ierusalem, uidelicet ex sabbato gratie per uiam uite in sabbatum glorie; uiam, aio, uite excellentiorem, uiuifice caritatis directionem, quam inestimabiliter extollens apostolus, 'Adhuc,' inquit, 'excellentiorem uiam uobis demonstro. Si linguis loquor hominum et angelorum, caritatem autem non habeam, factus sum uelud es sonans aut cymbalum tinniens.'[1]

177   [a] disponente *written above the line, over* exponente *expuncted.*

[2] Eustace de Normanville had incepted at Oxford in canon law and served as chancellor of Oxford before entering the Franciscan Order; *BRUO* ii. 1364; cf. Letter 176.
[3] The duties for which the brethren of Lynn had chosen him was that of their lector. As

But I think our dear Brother Eustace of Normanville[2] will be wholly excused from the office for which you and your sons have thought fit to choose him, when you know the many and various importunities and hindrances that at present prevent him from fulfilling your request.[3] In this matter, I think, your rightful request was perfectly justified, although the desired outcome was not attained, as God disposed better otherwise, on account of which it will certainly be advisable to commit your wishes to Him. As you have decided to go to our reverend father, our minister, at the coming feast of the Nativity, through whom it will be possible for clearer explanations to be given regarding reasons that have to be made plain, I have decided I should refrain from doing so. I am at the command of whatever your love commands.

May your holy integrity flourish undiminished in Christ, etc.

178

To William of Nottingham, provincial minister

(1253-4)

Brother Adam to Brother William, minister of England, devoted and obedient service.

By the distance of a thousand paces between the Mount of Olives and Jerusalem, may your patient and unfailing prayer swiftly gain for me and the rest of your sons on their way to the sabbath that assured rest of perfect peace, overflowing with hidden sweetness, delightful to both the inner and outer man, to which you refer with longing desire in the beginning of your letter: that thus, our right hands divinely clasped, led for ever by the divine Majesty, we may together reach the city of Jerusalem after a sabbath's journey from the Mount of Olives; that is by the sabbath of grace, through life's journey to the sabbath of glory. The route, I say, is the straight and more excellent way of life-giving charity, which is boundlessly extolled by the apostle, saying 'I show you a more excellent way. Though I speak with the tongues of men and of angels, but have not charity, I am become as sounding brass or a tinkling cymbal.'[1]

Adam continues below, he had better things in mind for Eustace, and in fact he was appointed lector and regent in theology first at Oxford, then at Cambridge.

178   [1] 1 Cor. 12:31–13: 1.

Iter reuera sabbati, quo speciosis bone uoluntatis plebibus tam pie quam feliciter ambulatur, a monte gratiose pietatis ad ciuitatem felicitatis, mille misticarum dimensionum passibus, hoc est mille uiuificarum*a* uirtutum profectibus spiritualiter integrato productis ex uitalis decalogi denario, secundum quod est apud denariam effectuum sanctitatem, secundo proficiat millenarium mille uiuificarum uirtutum passibus quod nunc dictum est iter sabbati 'uiam uite' uiuifice distinguentem, in uno sui terminorum habentem montem letifice miserationis, in alio ciuitatem pacifice uisionis, in utroque sabbatum delicatum hominis utriusque; porro secundum gratiosam pregustationem in tempore, sed gloriosam satietatem in eternitate.

Forsitan exiet nescio quis nemo, omnis ueritatis omnino nescius, qui ex uesaniori demonialis arrogantie cecitate altissima celestium eloquiorum misteria blasphemare non formidans, deridendus deridere presumens, quippe ridere potes de ridiculoso, illud quod ingenii tardioris angusta tenuitas hunc nunc exprimere conata est. Vtinam affectu simplici, quo de Domino sentitur, in bonitate et in simplicitate cordis queritur de ratione denarii bis ducti ad productionem millenarii, conficientis integraliter iter sabbati, quem ex derisione terribilem obiurgans auctor eloquii mistici, ait 'Qui erudit derisorem, ipse sibi iniuriam facit';[2] et iterum, 'Eice derisorem et exibit cum eo iurgium'.[3] Numquid que in utroque Testamento tam subtili commendantur exquisitione numerorum rationes uacare putabimus a misteriis? Legamus, si libet, doctorum ecclesie Gregorii, Augustini, Bede, et ceterorum commentarios, si doceri dignemur quam sint inuestigande rationum numeralium archane potestates, pre ceteris uniuersitatis perfecte speciebus, ad patefacienda saluifica misticorum eloquiorum latibula. Si tamen, ut fieri fere semper assolet, tam ignauie quam insolentie in cunctis non queramus solatia, miseri et miserabiles, curarum spiritualium et carnalium concupiscentiarum abyssali uoragine captiuati, misericors Miserator miseris miserere, Amen.

f. 64　Opus esset hic | sermo longus et interpretabilis, si non rectius eligeret inspientis affectio animo sapientis Scripturarum studioso, ut sit sapientior occasionem prestitisse. Ceterum respiciant superclementes summe celsitudinis oculi humilem sanctitatis uestre condescensum, quem non pigebit per accuratum subtilioris epistole tenorem

178　*a* uiuifice *MS.*

[2] Prov. 9: 7.　　　　　　　　　　　　　[3] Ibid. 22: 10.

Truly the sabbath journey on which the beautiful people of goodwill walk in piety and happiness, from the mount of grace and piety to the city of felicity, measuring a thousand mystical paces, is spiritually accomplished by advancing in a thousand life-giving virtues, drawn from the coinage of the vital Decalogue, inasmuch as it relates to a tenfold holiness in action. Secondly, let the millennium be forwarded by a thousand paces of life-giving virtues, which is now called the sabbath journey, designating the vital way of life, having as one of its ends the mountain of joyous compassion; and as the other the city of peaceful vision, each of them delightful to either man, in turn through a gracious foretaste in time, and a glorious satiety in eternity.

Perhaps some nobody—I know not who—will set out wholly ignorant of all truth, who out of blindness and mad with diabolical arrogance will be unafraid to blaspheme the high mysteries of heavenly speech and presume to mock them as worthy of derision; to be sure one can ridicule what the narrowness of my slow mind has here tried to express. Would that the computation of the coinage twice brought forth to prolong the millennium, which constitutes the entire sabbath journey, be sought in goodness and simplicity of heart, with that simple love one feels for the Lord. He who is dreadful in his derision is rebuked by the author of mystical speech, saying 'He who teaches one to mock does an injury to himself';[2] and again, 'Cast out the mocker, and the reproach will go with him'.[3] Shall we think the computation of numbers which is commended in each Testament with such refined research is devoid of mystery? Let us read, if you like, the commentaries of the doctors of the Church, Gregory, Augustine, Bede, and the rest, if we are fit to be taught the importance of investigating the secret powers of the computation of numbers, above other forms of the perfect universe, to make evident the hidden and saving meanings of mystical speech. But if, as nearly always happens, we do not seek consolation out of both cowardice and lack of habit, in all things wretchedly and pitiably imprisoned in an abyss of spiritual anxieties and carnal concupiscence, have mercy upon us wretches, O Merciful One. Amen.

There would be need of a long and interpretative discourse, if the affection of a foolish man did not more rightly choose to offer the mind of a scholar wise in the Scriptures an opportunity to be wiser still. But may the supremely merciful eyes of the Most High look upon the humble condescension of your holiness, whom it has not

consternatam lacrimose mentis mestitiam et animare uigentius et consultius edocere, et letificare iocundius et stabilius confirmare ex necessariis causarum multiformium considerationibus.

Ad hoc, consummato uisitationis officio in Londinensi, Helyensi, Norwycensi, Lyncolniensi episcopatibus, cum omnium et singulorum placida consolatione, sit exaltata superne dispensationis*b* benedictio, dominus Cantuariensis in die beati Martini[4] regressus est Londinum; in cuius comitiua per plures dies postea moram traxi, quousque inter memoratum dominum et capitulum Lyncolniense occasione diocesane iurisdictionis exercende in episcopatu Lyncolniensi sede uacante, quam utraque pars sibi uindicauit utrimque allegando pro se et ius commune et quasi possessionem acrius concitate litium compugnantie, in ecclesie dicte, sicut apparuit, ruinam irreparabilem, per auctorem pacis pacifica repressit ordinatio; uidelicet ut dominus archidiaconus Cantuariensis[5] (et) Magister Robertus de Marisco,[6] super iure et proprietate prefate iurisdictionis sine strepitu iudiciali, secundum formam iurium inter partes fixam proferant diffinitionem inuiolabiliter, si fieri potest, citra Natiuitatem beati Iohannis Baptiste[7] proximo uenturam; supradicto domino archiepiscopo interim prenominatam auctoritatis diocesane iurisdictionem plenius in cunctis exercendo penitus absque preiudicio partis aduerse.

Quibus celitus expletis, adhuc cum prescripto domino Cantuariensi michi morandum fore putaui usque ad festum beati Barnabe,[8] suspensam ducens expectationem tempore medio, iuxta mee modicitatis modulum anxioribus contristati spiritus instantiis, tam littera quam lingua, et ex eloquiorum testimoniis et ex rationum argumentis, et ex sanctorum exemplis, prout diuinitas annuit, sibi subinde succedentibus opportune importunitatis uicibus, secundum cogentissimam dignitatis sue requisitionem intimo eiusdem archipresulis affectui,*c* et arguendo et increpando et obsecrando et exhortando et promittendo et comminando et blandiendo et perterrendo, nunc nocte nunc die satagens ingerere uerba salutaria, utinam cum effectu salutari non obsistentibus indigni presumptoris excessibus, cogito autem sepe nominati domini et suorum superatus obsecratione, instans festum Natalis Domini cum ipso in partibus Cantie, si

---

b dispensationi *MS.*   *c* affectu *MS.*

[4] Translation of St Martin, 4 July.
[5] Master Stephen of Vienne, archdeacon 1249–69.
[6] Robert, Adam's brother or cousin, had been a canon of Lincoln since 1244; cf. Letters 33, 51.

displeased to revive my perplexed and tearful mind in its sadness through the caring tenor of your fine letter, to instruct it with good advice, to give it joy, stability, and strength with regard to the many and various matters that have to be considered.

As to this, my lord of Canterbury returned to London on St Martin's day,[4] having completed the task of visiting the bishoprics of London, Ely, Norwich, and Lincoln, to the consolation and peace of each and all, blessed be the dispensation of heaven. I stayed on in his company many days afterwards until, through the Author of peace, a peace-making ordinance put an end to the fiercely fought litigation between the said archbishop and the chapter of Lincoln over the exercise of *sede vacante* jurisdiction in the Lincoln diocese, which each side claimed for itself, both parties claiming for themselves both common right and as it were possession, to the seemingly irreparable ruin of the said church. The ordinance decreed that the lord archdeacon of Canterbury[5] and Master Robert Marsh[6] would produce, by the next feast of the Nativity of St John the Baptist,[7] a determination without litigious conflict in a legal form established between the parties, of the legal entitlement to the said jurisdiction; this to be inviolably observed by each party for every occasion; the said archbishop in the meantime fully exercising the aforesaid diocesan jurisdiction in other respects, entirely without prejudice to the opposing party.

When with heaven's help this was completed, I thought I should stay on with the said lord of Canterbury until the feast of St Barnabas,[8] my hopes being suspended in the meantime; according to the measure of my limited capacity, urged on by the anxiety of my troubled mind, arguing both by letter and speech, from written testimony and proofs of reason and from the examples of the saints, as God allowed, and as one opportunity for nagging followed another, in keeping with the compelling demands of the archbishop's dignity and his affectionate intimacy, chiding, pleading, exhorting, promising, threatening, flattering, and frightening, striving, night and day, to interpose salutary words of peace; would that they were effective, despite the transgressions of my unworthy presumption. Overcome, however, by the pleading of the said lord and his officers, I am considering spending the coming festival of the Lord's Nativity with him in the region of Kent for the purpose of achieving

[7] 24 June.   [8] 11 June.

Deus uoluerit, alicuius utilitatis causa transigere, dum tamen prouidentie uestre non interueniat prohibitio.

Meminerit Sanctus sanctorum uestre sanctitatis in bonum, qui tam sancta sollicitudine, tam sanctis suffragiis, sanctam memoriam sancti presulis,[9] sicut sancti confidunt, in ardentissimis flagrantium sanctitatum luculentiis, secundum latissimam diffuse caritatis amplitudinem, indefessa iugitate commendare curatis ad Ipsius, qui solus bonus est, benedictam gloriam, per quam idem sancte recordationis antistes apud felicem inuicti cursus consummationem spiritu et uirtute Helye efficacissime animatus 'exultauit audacter pergens in occursum armatis, contempsit pauorem, nec cesset gladio'[10] contra scelesterrimam immanitatem triumphalem animum patenter accingere non formidans, imperterritam illam responsionem, de qua scripsistis tam prudenter quam eloquenter, quam uehementer conscriptam, seculis uere omnibus Altissimo presidente profuturam, ad formidandam quam nostis maiestatem destinando.[11]

Rogo per presentis carte portitorem, si placet, michi uoluntatem uestram euidentius insinuari.

Valete.

179

To William of Nottingham, provincial minister

(1251)

Fratri Willelmo, ministro Anglie, Frater Ada.

Scripsit michi reuerentie uestre diligentia suauior litteram quaterna petitione comprehensam; quarum prima continebat quod nec ad precatum pontificis,[1] nec ad fratrum desiderium, nec ad hortatum beneuolorum, nec ad necessitatum requisitum, consensistis pernoctare Bugeden,[2] sed per horrendam rigorum hyemalium iniuriam processu precipiti, sabbato uiolato, Cantebrugiam properastis. Causa leuis, grauis instantia, admirari cogunt recusationem inexorabilem. Si mansuetudo, si consideratio, si sanctitas, si longanimitas exhibende caritati et ueritati conspiciende, presertim in diuinissimarum solempnitatum tantis concurrentiis, solicius accomodande

---

[9] Robert Grosseteste died 9 Oct. 1253. Archbishop Boniface attended his funeral at Lincoln: *Chron. Maj.* v. 412.   [10] Job 39: 21–2.
[11] The reference is to Pope Innocent IV, to whom Grosseteste addressed his famous remonstrance in 1250.

something of use, provided, however, that your providence does not
interpose a prohibition.

The Holy One of the saints will remember to reward your holiness,
who are taking pains with such pious solicitude and such holy prayers
to commend the sacred memory of the holy bishop,[9] as the saints
trust in the shining light of his sanctity displayed by his vast and
widely diffused charity, commending him with untiring constancy to
the blessed glory of Him who alone is good, by which that same
bishop of holy memory, unvanquished at the happy finish of his race,
most effectually inspired by the spirit and strength of Elias rejoiced
boldly, 'going forth to meet armed men, he mocketh at fear, neither
turneth he back from the sword',[10] and feared not to arm his
triumphant spirit against the monstrosity of wickedness, directing
to the dread majesty whom you know,[11] that fearless reply of which
you wrote, written with such wisdom and eloquence, truly for the
advantage of all under the headship of the Most High.

I ask you, please, to indicate to me your wishes more clearly
through the bearer of the present letter.

Farewell.

179

To William of Nottingham, provincial minister

(1251)

Brother Adam to Brother William, minister of England.

Your reverence has been kind enough to write me a letter containing
a twofold request, the first of which contained a statement that you
would not consent to spend the night at Buckden,[2] whether at the
request of the bishop[1] or at the desire of the friars or at the exhortation
of people of good will, or in response to their needs, but that you had
rushed off in haste to Cambridge, through the frightful rigours of
winter, and in violation of the sabbath. The trivial reasons you give and
the serious urgency of your invitation make one wonder at the
inflexibility of your refusal. If you truly recognize the gentleness, the
regard, the holiness, the patience that should be accorded to the
exercise of charity and the perception of truth, the more carefully to

---

179   [1] Robert Grosseteste.
       [2] Manor and palace of the bishops of Lincoln; cf. Letters 34, 50, 120, 121.

ueracius cognoscantur, numquid non secus faciendum fuisse iudicabitur?

Dum insuper et celsitudinem pontificalem et filialem devotionem et emulationem et rationabilem persuasionem, rupta cuiuscunque necessitudinis obsistentia, conculcare non pigeat, hic certe reor formidandam exercende potestatis ambitionem. Videamus an exemplum a documento dissideat. Sed esto, dum punitur hostis, ciuem trucidare delectet, annon ueraciter atrocitatis piaculum committitur dum innocens comitiua piorum filiorum tanta uexatione personarum periculis exponitur?[3] Reuera tam uobis quam illis illud conuenire perhibetur: 'Nec fortitudo lapidis fortitudo mea, nec caro mea enea.'[4] Si audentia presumptionis repellitur, rogo susicipiatur sedulitatis inuigilantia. Nequiui conceptum tenere spiritum quominus in hac parte saltem occasionem prestiturus sapienti, licet non uolui, tamen ut ualui, hoc tantillum urgentius exprimerem.

Super eo quod uenerabilem matronam dominam de Tholeslund[5] contingit, prout uobis placere insinuastis, operam dare propono apud dominum Lyncolniensem. Consuete pietatis uestre, quam erga me, sit uobis sempiterna retributio, iugiter experior flagare fulgentius, pro eo etiam quod non interpellanti uoluistis apud predilectum patrem custodem Cantebrugiensem,[6] quoad fieri potuit, expedire negotium nostrum. Pro eo utinam condignas refero gratiarum actiones.

Remitto uobis transcripta litterarum domini regis Francie et domini Thuscaloniensis de excidio exercitus Christiani in Egypt et statu Terre Sancte.[7] Sobrietatem, prudentiam, iustitiam, uirtutem, quibus nichil est utilius hominibus in uita saluandis animabus, per sanctitatis uestre ministerium doceat Dei sapientia in Christo Iesu semper, etc.

be observed in such a great concourse of solemn religious celebrations, will you not consider that you should have done differently?

Furthermore, if it does not trouble you to trample upon the bishop's eminence, filial devotion, friendly zeal, and reasonable persuasion, having broken through any necessary impediment, then surely you must, I think, be fearful of having an excessive desire to exercise power. Let us see whether the example is at variance with the evidence. But be it so: while punishing the enemy, one may take pleasure in slaying an innocent citizen. Is not a misdeed really committed when your pious sons in their innocence, who accompany you, are exposed to danger with so much distress to them?[3] Truly that saying is applicable to both you and them: 'Neither is my strength that of stone, nor my flesh that of brass.'[4] If you reject my daring presumption, acknowledge, I ask, your failure to attend to serious obligations. I was unable to contain what was in my mind, in this case at least to offer an occasion to a wise man, but I was unable to stop myself from inflicting this little reproach upon you.

As regards the matter touching the matron, the lady of Toseland,[5] I propose to work on it with the lord bishop of Lincoln, as you indicated it was your pleasure. I constantly experience your customary goodness towards me ever more intensely. May you receive an everlasting reward for being willing to expedite our business, as far as was possible, with our dear father, the custodian of Cambridge,[6] even though I did not appeal for your help. For this I offer my thanks—would they were adequate.

I am returning to you the transcripts of the letters of the lord king of France and the lord of Tusculum concerning the disaster of the Christian army in Egypt and the condition of the Holy Land.[7] May the wisdom of God teach us sobriety, prudence, justice, and strength, than which nothing is more useful to men for the salvation of their souls, through the ministry of your holiness; ever in Christ Jesus.

---

[3] i.e. the friars attendant on the Provincial Minister as his council, who were in this case exposed to the rigours of a winter journey.

[4] Job 6: 12.

[5] ? Toseland (Huntingdon).

[6] Robert of Thornham was custodian of Cambridge in 1250: Eccleston, p. 89 and n. Cf. Letter 177.

[7] Cf. Letter 23 and n.

180

To William of Nottingham, provincial minister

(August 1253)

Fratri Willelmo, ministro Anglie, Frater Ada humilem deuoti famulatus obedientiam.

Quoniam karissimus Frater Ioannes, custos Oxonie,[1] sicut intellexi ad auctoritatis uestre iussionem, super omnibus progressum nostrum in partes ultramarinas et ab eisdem regressum contingentibus,[2] cum f. 64ᵛ ceteris que insinuanda putauit | pietati uestre, litteratoriam fecit certitudinem, superuacuum censui illorum sollicitudinis importune narrationibus iterare, succinctiori compendio, que in presentiarum uidebantur intimanda nequaquam preteriens sub silentio.

Siquidem postquam de presumpto uestre sanctitatis assensu, et de consensu mei custodis expresso, domino Cantuariensi tam Londini quam alias in episcopatu Londiniensi urgentioribus uictus instantiis, locis pluribus in exercitio uisitationis, quam—sit benedictio diuino nomini—et iugiter et prudenter et clementer et constanter, cum concordi cunctorum expediuit tranquillitate,[3] personaliter astiteram de memorati domini sustinentia, dimissis cum eodem dilectis fratribus Roberto de Rostun et G. de Ver, ex consulta gardiani Londiniensis prouisione, residuo uisitationis in dicto episcopatu perficiendo, reuersus Londinum ob uaria grandium causarum negotia in crastino beati Iacob,[4] indeque profectus, ueni Bugeden' in festo Sancti Petri ad Vincula,[5] ad dominum Lyncolniensem, de corporali ualetudine Dei misericordia melioratum tam secundum consistentiam carnis quam secundum spiritus sanctimoniam super humanam estimationem, propitiatione diuina melius aliquid prouidente.[6]

Vbi memorati patris domini Cantuariensis per cursorem, portitorem presentium, litteram recepi in crastino beati Syxti[7] preferentem magnum dignitatis sue desiderium ut per prouisiuam considerationis uestre beneuolentiam eidem concedatur prefatus Frater Robertus de Rostun saltem usque ad festum Sancti Michaelis[8] ⟨ad⟩ optatum sue

180   [1] John of Stamford was custodian of Oxford in 1253: Eccleston, p. 64 and n.

[2] Adam had made a frustrated effort to accompany Archbishop Boniface to the papal Curia in 1250 (Letters 52, 168). Here he refers to an otherwise unrecorded visit to the Continent, which must have occurred in 1253.

[3] Matthew Paris, reporting this second visitation of St Paul's and elsewhere in the London diocese in the summer of 1253, commented that the archbishop proceeded

180

To William of Nottingham, provincial minister

(August 1253)

Brother Adam to Brother William, minister of England, devoted service and humble obedience.

Since our most dear Brother John, the custodian of Oxford,[1] has, acting on your command as I understand, informed you by letter about everything concerning our progress overseas and our return,[2] with the rest of the things he thought you should be told, I regarded it as superfluous and unsuitably bothersome to repeat the story, by no means passing over in silence what it seemed necessary at present to intimate to you in a shorter form.

After I had been overcome by strong pressure to accompany the lord of Canterbury personally both at London and elsewhere in the diocese of London, presuming on the agreement of your holiness and with the express consent of my custodian, I was personally present to support his lordship in many places in the task of visitation, which, blessed be the divine name, he carried out always prudently and kindly and unflaggingly to everyone's peace and concord.[3] Brothers Robert de Rostun and G. de Ver, who were with him, having been discharged with the foresight and counsel of the guardian of London, with the rest of the visitation in the diocese to be completed, I returned to London on the morrow of St James[4] for the purpose of various business of great moment, and proceeding thence I reached my lord of Lincoln at Buckden on the feast of St Peter-in-chains.[5] His physical health is improved by the mercy of God, both in the soundness of his flesh and his mental health, by a dispensation of divine mercy beyond human expectation.[6]

While there I received on the morrow of St Sixtus[7] a letter from the said father, the lord of Canterbury, by the courier carrying these letters, expressing his lordship's great desire that you would be so considerate and kind as to grant him the said Brother Robert de Rostun as a desired helper with his visitation at least until the feast of St Michael.[8] Also that with your kind advice he should not be denied

cautiously and was received more kindly than he had been on the previous visitation: *Chron. Maj.* v. 382.   [4] 26 July.

[5] 1 Aug.   [6] Grosseteste died at Buckden on 9 Oct. 1253.

[7] 7 Aug.   [8] 29 Sept.

uisitationis adiutorium; mei quoque qualiscunque non negetur assis-
tentia personalis ad id ipsum, de benigno discretionis uestre consilio;
a cuius domini metropolitani primatu cum presertim hiis diebus
pessimis tanta pendeat in regno Dei, sicut ecclesiis omnibus notum
est, salutis celice reformatio, euidentem mee modicitatis insufficientiam maiestatis ipsius indeficiens obsecratio, quid e duobus malim
compellit ambigere: uidelicet aut ipsius actuoso copulari contubernio,
aut mei otioso iocundari silentio. Nempe nescio. Deus scit quid sibi
uelit, quod longe amplius retro temporibus humilitatem meam sua
sublimitas, ut uideo, et obtemperanter audit, et attendit intelligenter
et diligenter excipit, et sustinet perseueranter in sanctitatis amplec-
tande utcunque monitis insistentem.

Proinde si secundum considerata congruentium temporum inter-
ualla prouisiua dispensationis uestre disertitudo, quantum ad meam
attinet aut alterius cuiuscunque fratrum personam, sepe dicti domini
Cantuariensis obsecrationibus, tam sancta saluifice pietatis contemplatione subnixis, condescendum*a* salutari sedulitate censuerit ob
saluatoris intuitum, fateri compellor, ipso prestante uie gratiam et
gloriam patrie, tam in clero quam in populo cumulatius ampliabitis,
ut reor indubitanter, maxime quousque fratre Gregorio de Bosellis
reuerso, per Altissimi dispositionem de uestra circumspectione super
hiis et aliis salubriter ordinetur, et michi, si Deus uoluerit, parcatur ab
occupationum uarietatibus ad illas in ueritate minime reputabiles.*b*
Vtinam michi celitus donetur uiuo paternitatis uestre in Domino
maturius frui colloquio.

Conseruetur pietati uestre sincera sospitas in Christo, etc.

181

To William of Nottingham, provincial minister

Fratri Willelmo, ministro Anglie, Frater Ada supplicem deuoti
famulatus obedientiam.

Si non cause salutaris exigentia, quam instantia fraterne pietatis
hoc apud meam obtinuisset exilitatem, ad persuasam spiramine
diuino clementiam cunctarer admodum destinare petitoriam, ut
adolescens Willelmus, portitor presentium, quem et indoles probatior
et litteratura competentior et uenustas etatis et claritas sanguinis, ex

---

180   *a* condescentium *MS.*   *b* reputabili *MS.*

my personal presence in whatever way for the same purpose. When a heaven-sent reform of the pastoral care in the kingdom of God, especially in these very evil days, depends so much upon this primacy of the lord archbishop, as is known to all the churches, his majesty's ceaseless entreaty makes my humble and obviously inadequate self doubtful which of the two I prefer: that is to be joined to his very active company, or to enjoy the pleasure of leisure and silence. I really do not know. God knows what is his will. His lordship listens to my humble self much more readily than in times past, it seems to me, heeds and understands me, diligently takes up my advice, and perseveringly puts up with me when I press upon him my admonitions to embrace holiness.

Hence, so far as your wise dispensation concerns my person or any other of the brethren, if, after an interval you consider appropriate, you decide out of regard for Our Saviour to give way to the entreaties of the said lord of Canterbury, based, as they are, upon such a holy regard for saving piety, I am bound to acknowledge that you will, as the event will show, hugely increase the way of grace and glory of their homeland for both clergy and people. This I think without doubt, especially until after the return of Gregory de Bosellis, when sound arrangements will be made by your prudence for these and other matters, through the disposition of the Most High; and, if God wills, I shall be spared a variety of occupations which are really of very little relevance. How I wish heaven would grant me sooner a live conversation with you in the Lord, father.

May your good person keep well in Christ, etc.

181

To William of Nottingham, provincial minister

Brother Adam to Brother William, minister of England, humble obedience and devoted service.

If it had not been won from my poor self by the pressure of fraternal charity as much as by the demands of someone's salvation, I would be very hesitant to send you, whose kindness has ever been swayed by divine inspiration, a petition that William, a youth who is the bearer of this letter, may in accordance with the heavenly desire with which he is aflame, be admitted happily by a command of your

gratia superni muneris insigniunt, iuxta conceptam celestis desiderii
flagrantiam ad beatam religionis nostre militiam, per prouisiuum
magistratus uestri presidium felicius applicetur.

Verumptamen ut
ualuerit, uiderit, uoluerit circumspecta patris benigni sinceritas,
utinam ob benedicti Saluatoris intuitum sanctos salutis affectus
expedire curet ad gloriam Altissimi et electorum letitiam.

Conseruetur consueta sanctitatis uestre benignitas in Christo etc.

Placeat, opto, ut si diuinitate propitia interuentum presentem
admiseritis, is pro quo interuenitur extra nostri uiciniam nequaquam
mittatur instituendus, si sic uestro sederit beneplacito.

182

To Brother William of Nottingham, provincial minister

Fratri Willelmo, ministro Anglie, Frater Ada non tam debitam quam
deuotam subiecti famulatus obedientiam.

Cordis saucii mestam animam refocillauit nimirum paternitatis
uestre littera. Siquidem preferebat uisceralem affectus benigni compassionem cum prouisiua sensus diserti directione. Sit summe
sollicitudinis uestre suauitati cum illuminatione celica salus sempiterna. Habito consulte deliberationis tractatu, prout diuinitus datum[a]
est, iuxta iussionis uestre tenorem cum predilectis patribus Iohanne,
domini papa nuntio,[1] Thoma de Eboraco, et Ricardo Cornubiensi,[2]
accito ad ipsum uiro prouido gardiano Oxfordie,[3] super mandato
ministri generalis dicto fratri Cornubiensi directo, licet concorditer
uisum fuerit quod idem Frater Ricardus propter multimoda ualetudinum suarum discrimina missis excusatoriis ad ministrum generalem, non tam secura conscientia quam obedientia intemerata
remanere ualeret in consuetis studiorum exercitiis Oxonie, tamen
prouisum est per memoratos fratres quod idem Frater Ricardus
propter temporis angustiam maturitate celeri[b] uestram Londini
adeat presentiam, ut per uestre circumspectionis industriam quid
facto opus sit conuenientius innotescat.

182   [a] datum *written above the line.*   [b] sceleri *MS.*

---

182   [1] Cf. Letters 94 n. 3 and 171.
   [2] Richard (Rufus) of Cornwall succeeded Thomas of York as fifth lector to the Oxford
school of the Franciscans in 1256. For his career and commentary on the *Sentences* see P.
Raedts, *Richard Rufus of Cornwall and the Tradition of Oxford Theology* (Oxford, 1987). Cf.
Letters 190, 197, 198, 203.

watchful magistracy to the blessed militia of our religion. He is well fitted for it by his nature, his competence in letters, and the grace of his age and the nobility of his blood by the gift of divine grace. Nevertheless, as your prudent and kind fatherhood considers best, sees, and wishes, I pray that you may, out of regard for our blessed Saviour, be minded to further his holy desires for salvation to the glory of the Most High and the joy of the elect.

May your holiness's customary goodness be preserved in Christ, etc. May it please you, I wish that if by God's favour you allow this intervention, he for whom the intervention is made, be by no means sent outside our neighbourhood for his induction, if this is your pleasure.

182

To Brother William of Nottingham, provincial minister

Brother Adam to Brother William, minister of England, with due and devoted obedience and humble service.

Your fatherly letter greatly revived my sad spirit and my wounded heart. Indeed it displayed your heartfelt compassion, your affection and kindness, the foresight of your guidance, and the clarity of your understanding. May your gentleness and supreme solicitude be rewarded in eternity by the light of heaven. In accordance with the tenor of your command, we have had a long and careful discussion, as heaven allowed us, with the beloved fathers John, the nuncio of the lord pope,[1] Thomas of York, and Richard of Cornwall,[2] calling in the prudent guardian of Oxford,[3] concerning the mandate of the Minister General addressed to the said brother of Cornwall. Although it seemed agreed by all that Brother Richard could remain with a clear conscience and inviolate obedience participating in the customary academic exercises at Oxford, having sent letters of excuse to the Minister General on the grounds of various crises of health, it was, however, proposed by the brothers named that because time was short the said Brother Richard should present himself quickly and at an early date to you at London, to be informed by your prudent wisdom what needs to be most appropriately done.

[3] John of Stamford, subsequently minister provincial c.1258–64: Little, *Franciscan Papers, Lists and Documents*, p. 191. Cf. Letters 123, 196, 168, 211, 218.

Faciat omnimodis, obsecro, benigna uestre sanctitatis indulgentia
karissimum Fratrem * * *⁴ personaliter adesse, Deo dante, cum
Londinum uenerit,ᶜ de quo propter Dei Filium et Dei regnum
suadelas supprimo; exprimo supplicatus ⟨ut⟩ ordinare uelitis, ut
postquam uobis locutus fuerit,ᵈ propere proficiscatur ad dominum
Cantuariensem, adiutorium sue assistentie, quo non mediocriter
indiget supradictus dominus, ut asserit, in presentibus causarum
salutarium urgentiis eidem domino exhibiturus. Non est estimanda,
ut reor, si a pietatis uestre non dissideat beneplacito, in tante salutis
necessitatibus mora modici temporis, que cum tantis domini requir-
itur instantiis.

Quum recessi a Rading', et fuerat ibi Comitissa Arundel,⁵ sicut credo
uobis signatum est et facta et dicta per ipsam ibidem innotuerunt. Dixit
dilectus * * *⁶ quod super omnibus de quibus actum est coram uobis
humiliter ueritatem confitebitur et regulari discipline se subiciet per
f. 65 omnia, insinuans quasi per dictam comitissam etsi non locutus fuerit, |
quodᵉ rememoratio ueritatis supra qua prius certus non fuerat, tam
dictorum, quam factorum, quam etiam scriptorum, quam inficiatus
fuit coram uobis, ei est innouata. Dixi eidem Fratri * * *⁶ quod a
Rading' tenderet Oxoniam iturus Leycestr' sicut precepistis, nisi per
uestrum mandatum reuocaretur antequam illuc ueniret; ut reformatio
status sui fieret super omnibus de quibus actum est hactenus, quantum
ad factum obligationum dicte comitisse in manibus ipsius factarum.
Cum presentia conficerentur, nondum uenit Oxoniam.

183

To William of Nottingham, provincial minister

Fratri Willelmo, ministro Anglie, Frater Ada deuotissimum obedientie debite famulatum.

Tam instantia reginalis excellentie, quam pietas cause salutaris,
exilitatem meam ad interpellandam paternitatis uestre clementiam
per presentis petitionis humillimam affectionem compulit diligentiori
uigilantia, ut predilecti in Christo fratris Willelmi Batale¹ optabilis

---

ᶜ uenero *MS.*   ᵈ fuero *MS.*   ᵉ quod *added in another hand.*

---

⁴ Name omitted in MS.
⁵ Isabella d'Albini, foundress of Marham abbey for nuns.
⁶ Name omitted in MS.

By all means, by your holiness's kind indulgence have Brother
* * *[4] come in person when, God grant, he gets to London. I refrain
from attempting persuasion on his account, for the Son of God and
the kingdom of God. I humbly express a petition that, after he has
spoken to you, you would make arrangements for him to proceed to
the lord archbishop of Canterbury to act as his help, of which the said
lord has no small need, as he says, to provide him with assistance in
meeting the pressing demands of cases important for the work of
salvation. If it is not contrary to your good pleasure, I think a short
delay is invaluable where there is so great a need of salvation and the
pressure of his lordship's request is so great.

When I left Reading, the Countess of Arundel[5] was also there, as I
believe you were informed, and what she said and did there has been
made known to you. Our beloved * * *[6] will humbly confess to you
the truth of everything that was done, and will submit himself to
regular discipline in all things, making known as it were through the
said countess, even though he has not actually said it, his recollection
of the words and acts and of even what was written, about which he
was previously uncertain and which he withdrew in your presence,
has been refreshed. I said to the same brother that he should proceed
from Reading to Oxford on the way to Leicester, as you bade him,
unless he was summoned back by your command before he got there;
in order that his position should be restored relating to everything
that has been done hitherto as regards the deed of the countess's
obligations executed in his hands. When this letter was composed, he
had not yet got to Oxford.

183

To William of Nottingham, provincial minister

Brother Adam to Brother William, minister of England, due obedience and devoted service.

Both a pressing request of the queen's excellence and piety in the
cause of salvation have impelled my poor self, out of loving
watchfulness, to appeal to your fatherly kindness with this most
humble and affectionate petition that our beloved in Christ Brother
William Batale[1] may without difficulty or trouble be presented to the

---

183   [1] William Batale resided at the friary of Northampton; his services had also been
sought by the Countess of Cornwall: cf. Letter 154.

copia secundum presentiam personalem ob singularem anime medelam temporibus et locis, que per prouide circumspectionis industriam
competere dinoscuntur, sine difficultatis grauamine exhibeatur piissime domine regine.

Prestat autem pleniorem fiducie certitudinem quod persone quibus
in hac parte summa discriminis posset imminere formido, quibus et
sollertia est sollic⟨it⟩ior de prospicienda securitate secundum rerum
requirendas circumstantias, omnimodis contra quecunque pericula
urgentius cauere incumbit. Quocirca uenerabili sanctitatis uestre
sedulitati omni qua possum intentione supplico, rogans quatinus per
inolite benignitatis uestre mandatum, quam in salutis eterne negotiis
noui, karissime, flagrantiori feruere beneuolentia, rescribere uelitis
amicissimo nostro memorato fratri Willelmo, ut secundum discretionem sibi diuinitus inspiratam ualeat inoffense de uestre paternitatis
obedientia salutari tam salutaribus uotis tante maiestatis, propitia
Saluatoris miseratione, satisfacere salutarius, tanto propensiori fauoris
gratuiti dulcedine qualiscunque seruli uestri rogatum prosequentes,
quanto quod petitur emulationem sinceriorem respicere presumitur, et
pro qua petitur propter huiusmodi spiritualis gratie celeste desiderium
ampliorem rectissime promeretur in Domino consensum.

Valeat sanctum sinceritatis uestre patrocinium in Christo, etc.

184
To Brother William of Nottingham, provincial minister

Fratri Willelmo, ministro Anglie, Frater Ada humilem obedientie
deuotionem pariter et honorem.

Pater benigne, suppliciter obsecro quatinus amicissimum michi
nimirum in Domino Fratrem R. dictum monachum, cum fiducia
supplici reuertentem humillime ad uos· tanquam ad pastorem et
episcopum animarum nostrarum,[1] una mecum, sub consueto suauis
clementie patrocinio, ob pium Ipsius intuitum qui ait, 'Eum qui uenit
ad me non eiciam foras',[2] in benignam lati cordis gratiam misericorditer admittentes, eidem ut ualueritis, uideritis, uolueritis, prospicere uelitis ad pacem simul et salutem.

Valeat gratiosa uestre sanctitatis incolumitas in Christo Iesu
semper et beatissima Virgine.

184 [1] Cf. 1 Pet. 2: 25.   [2] John 6: 37.

most pious lady queen. His desirable capability as regards his personal presence and the uniquely healing quality of his spirit, demonstrated in times and at places through his foresight and prudence, are known to meet the case.

It shows the fullest assurance of our trust, that persons who can in this role be subject to fear of their perilous position, who have to be more careful and adroit over their preservation by foresight as circumstances demand, are under a pressing need to be on their guard against all kinds of dangers. For this reason, I beg your venerable holiness with all the earnestness in my power to use your customary goodness, which I know, dearest father, burns more fervently in questions of salvation, and to write to our very dear brother William to say that he can safely satisfy the salutary wishes of her great majesty, according to the judgement afforded him by divine inspiration by the merciful favour of the Saviour, without prejudicing his holy obedience to your fatherly person. In so doing you will be pursuing the request of your little servant, whatever his kind, all the more readily with the sweetness of a freely bestowed favour as what is sought is presumed to have a regard for most genuine zeal, and the lady on whose behalf this request is made most justly deserves, because of her heavenly desire for spiritual grace of this kind, the fullest consent in the Lord.

May your true holy fatherly protection flourish in Christ, etc.

184

To Brother William of Nottingham, provincial minister

Brother Adam to Brother William, minister of England, humble obedience and devoted service.

Kind father, I humbly implore you mercifully to admit to the kindness and grace of your generous heart my dearest brother in the Lord, Brother R. called Monk, who is humbly returning to you as to the shepherd and bishop of our souls,[1] with trusting supplication, together with me, subject to your usual fatherly kindness, out of regard for Him who says, 'He who comes to me I will not cast out',[2] and that as you can, as you see fit, as you will, you would provide at the same time for his peace and salvation.

Farewell, your holiness, ever in Christ and the Blessed Virgin.

Hoc rogaui, pater benigne, fraterna uictus instantia, quod scio faceretis omnimodis et in contrarium adiurati per quemcunque ne fieret. In eternum ualete.

De karissimis fratribus R. dicto monacho, Fratre A. de Bechesoueres, R. de Sancta Cruce, in receptione littere uestre ubi inueniri possent penitus ignoraui, duorum ipsorum, scilicet Fratre A. et Fratre Roberto iam profectis in Franciam ad ministrum generalem, cum litteris modicitatis mee supplicatoriis sigillatim pro ipsorum singulis memorato patri destinatis. Promisit dictus Frater A., quod et credo, Deo dante, promptius adimplebit, se maturius rediturum in Angliam, et regulari discipline per omnia sub obedientie uestre patrocinio humiliter obtemperaturum. Circa Fratrem R. dictum monachum quid actum sit nondum intellexi. Predilectus Frater G. de Londinio quartam decimam quatarne perpessus accessionem, super uexamine ualetudinis post alleuiationem qualemcunque Londini expectat a clementia Saluatoris salutare remedium; uice cuius michi solitario subuenit de uoluntate gardiani sui karissimus Frater Iohannes de Kemesing'.

185

To Brother William of Nottingham, provincial minister

Fratri Willelmo, ministro Anglie, Frater Ada deuotam humilis obedientie reuerentiam.

Karissimum Fratrem Iohannem de Dingtone, sanctitati uestre supplicantem pro diutine ualetudinis optabili remedio, humiliter obsecro, ad sollicitam eiusdem fratris instantiam, benigne paternitatis prouisiua circumspectio, ut ualuerit, uiderit, uoluerit, suscipiat in Omnipotentis sermone qui sanat omnia.

Valeat uestre pietatis sospes incolumitas, etc.

186

To Brother William of Nottingham, provincial minister

(February 1253)

Fratri Willelmo, ministro Anglie, Frater Ada obedientialem debite deuotionis famulatum cum reuerentia pariter et honore.

I have made this request, kind father, vanquished by fraternal pressure, which I know you would do, even in opposition to anyone who had sworn it should not be done. For ever farewell. On receiving your letter, I had no knowledge where our dearest Brothers R. called Monk, Brother A. de Bechesoueres, and Brother R. of Holy Cross could be found. Two of them, namely Brothers A. and Robert, had already set out to France to the Minister General, with sealed letters from my humble self pleading for each one of them, directed to the said father general. The said Brother A. has promised— and I believe that by God's help he will fulfil the promise—to return to England earlier and in all things humbly to comply with the discipline of the Rule in obedience to your fatherly person. As regards Brother R. called Monk, I do not yet understand what has been done. Our beloved Brother G. of London, who has suffered a fourteenth attack of fever, after some relief from his troubled health, is at London awaiting a genuine remedy from the mercy of Our Saviour. In his place my very dear Brother John of Kemesing has come to assist me in my solitude with the goodwill of his guardian.

185

To Brother William of Nottingham, provincial minister

Brother Adam to Brother William, minister of England, reverence and humble obedience.

I humbly implore you, at the earnest instance of our dearest Brother John of Dington, who is supplicating for a desired remedy for his long-term infirmity, that with the foreseeing prudence of your fatherly kindness you would, as you can, as you see fit, as you will, support him with the word of the Almighty, which heals all things. Wishing your goodness health and safety.

186

To Brother William of Nottingham, provincial minister

(February 1253) ·

Brother Adam to Brother William, minister of England, obedience and devoted service and likewise reverence and honour.

Cum iam iamque recessurus esset dominus Cantuariensis a Londino pridie kal. Februarii dedi operam ut cum eo colloquium haberem, presentibus domino Herfordensi[1] et domino archidiacono Cantuariensi[2] et magistro Hugone de Mortuo Mari,[3] precipuis consiliariis prefati domini, cui secundum quod tunc concessum fuit celitus causas prout uideri potuit perefficaces proposui quibus obsistentibus fieri nequit aliquatenus ut ad ipsius familiarem assistentium accedam. Quarum obsistentiarum tunc et alias propositarum quasi primaria fuit quod uos, qui michi uice Dei presidetis, de fratrum nostrorum consensu, michi officium eruditionis impendende in sacris eloquiis imposueratis, cuius iussionibus non obtemperare animo uolenti et deuota promptitudine michi fore cognoscitur nepharium scelus preuaricate professionis.

Alia autem fuit insufficientie mee multomodi defectus, quos coram throno maiestatis protestatus sum, licet huius rei ambiguitas non cogeret longissime subsistere citra sufficientiam et ualidissime uirtutis et clarissimi sensus et emulationis sanctissime et constantissime stabilitatis et preter hec amplius ⟨apud⟩ uniuersos opinionis integerrime, que quidem omnia ineuitabili necessitate requiruntur in uiris qui tanto archipresuli ex decreto celesti debent assistere in potentibus adiutoriis, in consiliis timoratis, in ministeriis mundis.

Tertia quoque fuit iam fatiscentis etatis annosa prolixitas, propter quam potissime michi summopere consultum erit, ut satagam deinceps omnimodis et frequentias curiales et aulica exercitia penitus declinando, sub regularibus professe religionis obseruantiis actuosam f. 65ᵛ sollicitudinem diminuere et augmentare uacationem otiosam, | si quo modo concederetur rebus humanis post dies paucos excessuro pregustare diuinas iocunditates in tempore, quibus satiandi sumus in eternitate, ut illuc inoffense feratur inter turbamina temporalium discriminum liberum absolute mentis desiderium 'ubi est Deus omnia in omnibus, eternitate certa et pace perfecta'.[4]

Quarta etiam fuit priuilegium apostolicum[5] pro me a fratribus impetratum, cui obuenire non debeo, ne cogar in alicuius prelati aut principis domestico laborare contubernio. Quintum insuper fuit districtum domini regis mandatum quo interdictum fuit domino archiepiscopo ne me, uelut proditorium inimicum ad comitiuam

186 [1] Peter d'Aigueblanche, bishop of Hereford 1240–68.
 [2] Master Stephen of Vienne, archdeacon of Canterbury 1248–69.
 [3] Hugh Mortimer was Official of Archbishop Boniface until 1251; cf. Letters 131, 159.
 [4] Augustine, *De civitate Dei*, xix. 20, a favourite valediction of Adam's; cf. Letters 8 n. 14 and 124 n. 3.

On the 31st January, just as the lord of Canterbury was about to leave London, I managed to have a conversation with him, there being present the lord of Hereford,[1] the lord archdeacon of Canterbury,[2] and Master Hugh Mortimer,[3] his lordship's foremost counsellors; and to the extent that heaven helped me, I placed before him very cogent grounds of objection on account of which it was impossible for me to join him as a member of his familia. The first of these objections, and the principal one then and at other times, was that you, who are my superior representing God, had with the agreement of the brethren imposed on me the duty of teaching Sacred Scripture It is recognized that failure on my part to comply with this command with a willing spirit and ready devotion would be a heinous sin of violating my religious profession.

Another objection that I protested before the throne of his majesty was my failings and inadequacy, though any doubt on this score would make it unnecessary to tarry at length on the sufficiency of energy, clear-headed good sense, most holy zeal, and unshakable loyalty required, and besides these qualities a reputation with all people for the utmost integrity, all of which are inescapably demanded of men who are by heaven's decree obliged to support such a great archprelate with powerful assistance, God-fearing counsel, and impeccable service.

The third objection was the weary prolixity of my feeble age, on account of which it will be highly advisable for me to be careful and henceforth in every way to avoid frequenting courts and the business of palaces, and reduce my active concerns, while keeping the observances of the Rule professed by our religion, and increase my time of freedom and leisure; if it may be allowed to one who has few days left before he will take his leave of human affairs, to taste in time the divine pleasures with which we are to be sated in eternity. So amidst the disturbance of worldly troubles the longing mind, set absolutely free, may be borne without hindrance to that place where 'God is all in all, in sure eternity and perfect peace'.[4]

The fourth objection was the apostolic privilege obtained for me by the brethren,[5] which I ought not to contravene, to the effect that I should not be obliged to work in a household association of any prelate or priest. Moreover, fifthly there was the strict command of the lord king that the lord archbishop should not call on me to join his

[5] The reference is apparently to the mandate of Innocent IV, dated 24 Sept. 1245. Cf. Letter 168 n. 2.

suam euocaret. Sexta nichilominus fuit commissiones causarum inter dominum regem et dominum Meneuensem,[6] et inter eundem dominum et dominum abbatem Glouerniensem,[7] propter quas, licet michi alias concederetur agere de iudicio, nequaquam personali presentia dominum archiepiscopum comitari.

Septima denique fuit, que super omnia in hac parte cogitabilia me maxime faciunt exhorrescere ipsius domini archiepiscopi personalem assistentiam, seculis omnibus atrocitas superstupenda de strage animarum, que, proh nefas, iugiter hactenus fieri assueuit, pro eo quod nunc auctoritate prouisionum,[8] nunc iurisdictione metropolitana, nunc ratione patronali, si personaliter adessem, indesinenter aspicerem ecclesiam Dei dissipari, sanctuarium Dei prophanari, Filium Dei conculcari, sanguinem testamenti pollui, curis gregum dominicorum traditis nunquam curaturis, ignauis, impiis et peruicacibus, sed eosdem uastaturis, direpturis, demoniali rabie superatrocissimi furoris concitatis. Quibus tam superhorrendis spectaculis si assistens reclamerem, nichilominus exercebuntur facinora tam nepharie crudelitatis. Sin autem conniuendo sileo, quod absit, mors michi erit.

Cum igitur nunc septem proposuissem causarum obsistentias quominus fieret de me quod fieri uoluit sepe dictus archiepiscopus, ad omnia rationabili respondit prosecutione secundum estimationem astantium, promittens se secundum mee modicitatis insinuationem erroribus correctionem adhibiturum. A domina regina quoque, ut ipse michi postea dixit, obtinuit litteras cum propriis petitoriis ad uos, pro beneplaciti sui complemento[a] destinatas, qui postquam ueni Oxoniam misit michi litteram, quam presentibus inclusam uobis transmitto.

Dominus autem comes Leycestriensis per litteras suas, quarum nouissimam[b] nichilominus presentibus inclusi uobis, si placet, legendam, et etiam domina comitissa Leycestriensis ad me personaliter accedens, me summa sollicitarunt instantia, ut sine more dispendio Boloniam me transferam, cum eodem comite super arctioribus negotiorum articulis collocuturum in Domino. Hec modo scripsi licet ipsa dicta uel facta scriptura non equiparet, ut si dignum duxeritis, que et qualiter uolueritis rescribatis.

---

186 *a Here* ad uos *is repeated by the copyist in error.*   *b* nouissime *MS.*

[6] Thomas Waleys, bishop of St David's 1248–55.
[7] John de Felda, abbot 1243–63.

company, as I was a traitor and enemy. There was also a sixth, namely the commissions dealing with the cases between the lord king and the lord bishop of St David's[6] and that between the lord king and the lord abbot of Gloucester,[7] on account of which, although elsewhere I would be allowed to act as judge, I was in no way to accompany the lord archbishop or to be personally present.

Finally there was the seventh, more objectionable than anything conceivable, an outrage amazing for all time, that makes me most dread being a personal assistant of the lord archbishop: I refer to the slaughter of souls, which, for shame, customarily and hitherto constantly occurs, now by the authority of provisions,[8] now by the exercise of metropolitan jurisdiction, or again by reason of patronage. If I were personally present, I would ceaselessly see the Church of God destroyed, the sanctuary of God profaned, the Son of God trampled underfoot, the blood of the testament polluted, the pastoral care of the Lord's flocks handed over to the idle, the irreligious, and unrepentant, who will never care for them but will be moved by demonic madness to plunder them and tear them asunder. If I were personally present to see such frightful things and cried out against them, these cruel crimes will be committed just the same. But if I connive at them by remaining silent, which God forbid, it will be the death of me.

When therefore I had set out seven grounds of objection to the archbishop doing with me what he wished, he answered all of them with a response that all those present judged to be reasonable, and promised that he would see that all the errors indicated by my miserable self would be corrected. Also he has obtained letters from the lady queen, as he himself afterwards told me, addressed to you with their own request to fulfil his good pleasure. After I had come to Oxford he sent me the letter, which I am sending to you enclosed with this one.

Nevertheless, the lord earl of Leicester has asked me by his letters (the last of which I enclose for you to read, if you please), as has also the countess of Leicester, who approached me personally, with the utmost urgency to cross to Boulogne without delay, to have a discussion in the Lord with the earl about the more difficult articles of their negotiations. I have written this now, although the actual words and facts will not correspond to what will be written, so that if you consider it proper, you may write back what and how you wish.

[8] i.e. papal provisions to parish livings, a favoured instrument by which the king obtained benefices for his clerks.

450 LETTERS OF ADAM MARSH

Ceterum uestre innotescat paternitati, inter dominum Cantuariensem et dominum Wyntoniensem[9] discordiarum discrimina nuper exorta, post plurimos diutinorum tractatuum labores in hac forma conquieuisse: uidelicet quod dominus electus iuramento solempni coram domino archiepiscopo, in presentia suffraganeorum, comitum et baronum, et complurium aliorum clericorum et laicorum, suam purgauit innocentiam super iniuriis contra dictum dominum Cantuariensem in manerio de Lamee et alibi presumptis.[10] De offensis autem et excessibus ex utraque illatis compromissum est in duos episcopos ad hoc datos a domino Cantuariensi, uidelicet dominum Wygorniensem[11] et dominum Norwycensem.[12] Secundum quod ipsi decreuerint emende fiant hinc inde, ad honorem Dei et ecclesie. De controuersia autem hospitalis in Suwerk, que fuit occasio omnium dissensionum in hac parte, compromissum est in dominum comitem Cornubiensem, qui per se uel coassumptis sibi ad hoc duobus episcopis uel pluribus neutri parti suspectis super omnibus hanc controuersiam contingentibus immutabilem proferat diffinitionem.

Videtur, benedictus Deus, quod unanimitas firma, contra spem mortalium, erit inter dominum archiepiscopum et suffraganeos suos, et eorum omnium ad inuicem, in prosecutione omnium causarum ecclesie apud summum pontificem et dominum regem, ut sanctis omnibus optata qui in terra sunt, ecclesie et regni reformatio proueniat, prout fuerit propitia diuinitas; sicut fuerit uoluntas in celo, sic fiat. Verenda est in hac parte peccaminum obsistentia. Maior tamen est Altissimi misericordia quam nostra miseria.

Actum est uicissim per septem dies ante confectionem presentium apud cancellarium et magistros uniuersitatis Oxoniensis, ut de benedicto eorum assensu karissimus Frater Thomas de Eboraco, sit benedictio diuino nomini, propter eminentiam moris, ingenii, litterature et experientie, apud magnos et multos commendabilis, cathedram ordinarie regendi in Sacris Scripturis ascenderet.[13] Extitit autem obtinendi difficultas, obicientibus eidem aliquibus quod nequaquam in litteralibus rexerat cathedraliter.[14] Anceps expectabatur euentus

[9] Aymer de Valence, elected bishop of Winchester in 1250, consecrated 16 May 1260, after his expulsion from England at the request of the baronage.

[10] On the attack on the manor of Lambeth sponsored by Aymer de Valence see Letter 56 n. 1.

[11] Walter Cantilupe, bishop of Worcester 1236–66.

[12] Walter Suffield, bishop of Norwich 1245–57.

[13] On the inception of Thomas of York, see Little, *The Greyfriars in Oxford*, p. 236 and cf. Letter 196. He was regent in theology 1253–6.

For the rest, let me inform you, father, that the dangerous dispute that arose recently between the lord of Canterbury and the lord of Winchester[9] has, after very many long and laborious negotiations, been laid to rest in this manner: namely that the lord bishop-elect has by solemn oath before the lord of Canterbury in the presence of his suffragans, earls, and barons and many others both clerks and laymen, purged his innocence regarding the alleged injuries to the lord of Canterbury on the manor of Lambeth and elsewhere.[10] But for the offences and transgressions emanating from either side, it was agreed to arbitration by two bishops appointed for the purpose by the lord of Canterbury, namely the lord of Worcester[11] and the lord of Norwich.[12] Amends are to be made on either side according to what they decide, for the honour of God and the Church. As regards the dispute over the hospital of Southwark, which was the occasion of all the disputes in this case, the lord earl of Cornwall was to arbitrate, who either by himself or with two bishops associated with him for the purpose or with more persons suspect to neither party, is to produce an unchangeable judgement on all things touching this controversy.

It seems, blessed be God, that, contrary to human hopes, there will be firm unanimity between the lord archbishop and his suffragans, and between each and all of them, and the lord king, in prosecuting all ecclesiastical cases at the court of the Supreme Pontiff, so the reform of church and kingdom desired by all the saints in the land may come about. As it is His will in heaven, so let it be done; it is to be feared that sins will be an obstacle to this, but the mercy of the Most High is greater than our misery.

Seven days before the composition of this letter, it was enacted by the chancellor and masters of the University of Oxford, with the blessed assent of all—blessed be the divine name—that our very dear Brother Thomas of York should be raised to a chair of a regent master to give the main lectures on Holy Scripture,[13] on account of his distinguished conduct, his intellectual gifts, and his proven learning, which commend him to many and great persons. But there was difficulty in securing this, as some objected to him on the grounds that he had never held a chair as regent in Arts.[14] The outcome of this

[14] The Franciscans, like the Dominicans, did not permit their members to attend the university schools in Arts, but provided the necessary instruction in their own houses. At Oxford the congregation waived the requirement in the case of Thomas of York by a special grace; but following this, enacted a statute disbarring anyone from incepting to teach theology who had not been regent in Arts: *SAUO*, p. 49.

super hoc in profectione portitoris presentium. Benedicta sit gloria Domini de loco sancto suo quicquid unquam nobis accidat.

De facto illo pro quo presentiam uestram uice mei amicissimus pater, Frater Iohannes, custos Oxoniensis, suppliciter adire consensit, doleo admodum quod nequaquam placuit prouisiue paternitatis discretioni, secundum formam que petita fuerit, litteras concedere super recessu meo a regno Anglie, cum hoc nulla conditione nisi preurgenti necessitate compulsus eligerem. Credo namque quod si obtente fuissent a clementi sanctitatis uestre circumspectione, saltem ad tempus ualeture, plurimum per omnem modum prodessent, non sine desiderato affectu ad pacem pectoris et salutis profectum in Christo Iesu Domino nostro. Propter Dei Filium si aliud uobis Spiritus Dei non suggesserit adhuc, oro studiosius nunc tacte petitioni ad uotum attendite, considerantes inter tantas succrescentium oppressionum uoragines affectu paterno filialem animam anxie deprecantem. Rescribet uobis in breui, Domino propitio, dilectissimus pater, Frater Iohannes, custos Oxoniensis, super hiis que occurrent uobis innotescenda.

Rescripsi domino archiepiscopo ad singulos articulos littere sue, secundum quod michi competere uidebatur in Domino, adiciens quasi necessitate compulsus quod laborabo, quatenus licito modo fieri potuit, personaliter adire presentiam eius circa instantem mediam quadragesimam,[15] ut habeatur secundum Deum fixa deuotio super eo quod ipse tam uigili petit instantia. Scripsi etiam domine comitisse Leycestriensi per cursorem suum a uobis redeuntem, quod si fieri poterit opportune accelerabo Boloniam accedere secundum comitis Leycestriensis et eiusdem comitisse petitiones, non uidens f. 66 quid aliud ei signare conueniret de hoc | in presentiarum.

Finiat, oro, supernus Saluator in salutem sempiternam ista tam intransmutabilia uicissitudinum uolumina. Quocunque me uertam? Vbi et semper tolero—utinam longanimiter—intolerabilia uariarum inquietationum examina? Precipiat super ipsis quod beneplacitum est in oculis suis et profuturum electis suis, omnia subiciens sub pedibus eorum uelociter, Verbum Domini quod in eternum permanet,[16] quod est, quia 'uelociter currit sermo eius',[17] fidelis minister. Ipso preduce uos proficitis in domo eius. Amen.

Abscidi tria uocabula de litteris domini archiepiscopi, manente sensuum integritate, quia insinuabant sine fraude, ut reor, aliquid

---

[15] Sunday, 30 Mar. 1253.   [16] Cf. 1 Pet. 1: 25.   [17] Ps. 147: 15.

was uncertain when the carrier of this letter set out. Blessed be the glory of the Lord from His holy place, whatever happens to us.

Regarding the matter for which my dear friend Brother John, the custodian of Oxford, consented to approach you acting in my place with a petition, I am very sorry that your fatherly discretion was in no way disposed to grant letters authorizing my departure from the English kingdom according to the form that had been requested; for I would not have chosen this for anything, unless I had been driven by the most urgent necessity. For I believe that if I had obtained them from your kind and discreet holiness, valid for a time at least, they would have been greatly advantageous in every way, and not without your affectionate desire for my peace of mind and the advancement of my salvation in Christ Jesus Our Lord. For the sake of the Son of God, if the Holy Spirit has not yet suggested to you another course, I beg you most anxiously heed now the longing expressed in the petition in your hand, and consider with fatherly affection the soul of a son pleading with anxiety amidst such turbulence and violent oppression. With the Lord's favour, Brother John, the custodian of Oxford, will shortly write back to you, dearest father, to inform you what will happen.

I have written to the lord archbishop replying to each point in his letter as it seemed to me appropriate in the Lord, adding as it were compelled by necessity that I shall work, so far as can be done in a lawful way, to be personally with him about the coming mid-Lent,[15] so that, God permitting, he may have a firm assurance of my devoted service regarding what he himself sought with such vigilant insistence. I have also written to the countess of Leicester through her courier on his return from you, to say that, if I have the opportunity, I shall hasten to Boulogne, in accordance with the request of the earl and countess of Leicester, as I do not see what else it would be proper to say to her about the matter at present.

I pray Our heavenly Saviour may for my eternal salvation make an end to these unchanging eddies of change. Where am I to turn? where I always suffer—hopefully with patience—insufferable trials and various disturbances? May the word of the Lord which endureth for ever,[16] which is, 'for his word runneth swiftly',[17] his faithful minister, prescribe in these matters what is pleasing in His eyes and will be of advantage to His saints, swiftly subjecting all things beneath their feet. With Him as leader, you go forward in his house. Amen.

I have cut off three words from the lord archbishop's letter while keeping the entirety of the sense, lest they should perhaps cause

quod non uidi utrum sic se haberet rei ueritas, ne forte sine causa preferrent displicentiam. De omnibus hiis, si placet, quid facto opus est signate, precor, in Christo Domino; quia sicut uideo hoc precari debeo ut, sicut scripsi domino archiepiscopo, ⟨et⟩ domine comitisse Leycestriensi; fiat sub uestre sanctitatis obedientia. Spero siquidem quod tempestiue postmodum dabitur diuinitus desideriis preconceptis directio salutaris. Amen.

187

To Brother William of Nottingham, provincial minister

Fratri Willelmo, ministro Anglie, Fratres Iohannes, custos Oxoniensis, Thomas de Eboraco, Ada de Marisco, deuotissimam humilis obedientie promptitudinem.

Apud gratiosam lati cordis suauitatem quis metuere poterit repulse seueritatem, cum petitio filialis pro filio reconciliando patri paternam mansuetudinem interpellat? potissime ubi ad impetrandi gratiam efficacius accedit per superbenigni Spiritus saluificam dulcedinem, preter spem humanam prestitum angelis in celo gaudium super uno quocunque sed insigni peccatore penitentiam agente.[1] Hugonem Cote loquimur, quondam obedientie uestre subiectum, in tantam barathralis abyssi uoraginem precipitatum, per inexcogitabilem prouisiue dispensationis clementiam Ipsius, de quo sapientale diuinitatis eloquium, 'Misereris', inquit, 'omnium, quia omnia potes, et dissimulas peccata hominum propter penitentiam; diligis enim que sunt et nichil odisti eorum que fecisti. Parcis autem omnibus quoniam tua sunt, Domine, qui amas animas. O quam bonus et suauis est, Domine, spiritus tuus in nobis. Ideoque hos qui exerrant corripis, et de quibus peccant admones[a] et alloqueris, ut relicta malitia credant in te, Domine',[2] a sceleratioris apostasie piaculis perditissimis non sine iusto stupore reuocatum, ad piam obsecrationis fraterne suadelam in sacro die pii pontificis Nicholai.[3]

Igitur austro spirante et secedente aquilone, fluxerunt aromata iustitie. Nempe memoratus Hugo singulis sua restituendi concepto

---

187   [a] admonent *MS*.

---

187   [1] Cf. Luke 15: 10.
   [2] Wisd. 11: 24–5, 27–12: 1–2.
   [3] The reference is unclear. Adam is evidently not referring to St Nicholas. Possibly the

displeasure, for they implied, without I think intended deception, something which I did not see to be true. If you please, signify, I beg you, in Christ the Lord, what needs to be done in all these matters; for, as I see it, I ought to make this entreatty, as I have written to the lord archbishop and the lady countess of Leicester; let it be done under obedience to your holiness. I hope indeed that shortly at the right time we shall be given from God saving direction to our preconceived desires. Amen.

187

To Brother William of Nottingham, provincial minister

Brothers John, custodian of Oxford, Thomas of York, and Adam Marsh, to Brother William, minister of England, most devoted, humble and ready obedience.

Who can fear the severity of a rejection from the graciousness of your generous heart when your sons are petitioning your fatherly clemency for the reconciliation of one of your sons? especially when their intercession is efficaciously assisted by the surpassing kindness and saving sweetness of the Spirit, showing that beyond human hope there is rejoicing among the angels in heaven over one sinner, whoever and however conspicuous, doing penance.[1] We are speaking of Hugh Cote, a former obedient subject of yours, fallen into such an abyss, but now recalled through the mercy and inconceivably wise providence of Him of whom the wise word of the godhead says 'Thou hast mercy upon all, because thou canst do all things, and overlookest the sins of men for the sake of repentance. For thou lovest all things that are and hatest none of the things which thou hast made. But thou sparest all because they are thine, O Lord, who lovest souls. O how good and how sweet is thy spirit, O Lord, in all things! Therefore thou chastisest them that err little by little: and admonishest them, and speakest to them, concerning the things wherein they offend: that leaving their wickedness, they may believe in thee, O Lord.'[2] He has been recalled, not without justified wonder, from the most abandoned sin of apostasy on the sacred day of the most holy pontiff Nicholas.[3]

Thus have the perfumes of righteousness flowed at the breath of the south wind, following after the wind of the north. For indeed the

words refer to Nicholas of Farnham, bishop of Durham 1241-9, who resigned the see on 2 Feb. 1249.

celitus spiritu, equos tres pretii grandioris, minus recte adquisitos et quedam alia uetitis usibus congruentia, singulos et singula iustis eorum dominis, prout placuit fratribus, destinauit assignanda, et percepto confessionis beneficio, pollicitus est coram tribunali formidandi examinis se de cetero apud piam paternitatis uestre sanctitatem, amplexata cuiuscunque rigoris animaduersione, salutis sue negotia indefessa prosecuturum perseuerantia. Quid ergo? Prouisiuum cure pastoralis officium, presertim in precipua tante sublimitatis professione, contra terrificam eterne districtionis sententiam, Deo reducente, repellet quod perierat seducente diabolo.?

Quid multis morer? Beneuolam auctoritatis uestre prouidentiam pedibus uestris prouoluti, effusa totius conaminis affectione rogamus, deuotissime supplicantes, quatinus ob Ipsius contemplationem qui obstinate prodigalitatis filium post deuoratam substantiam cum dissolutiori luxuria, de regione dissimilitudinis ad paternam reuersum miserationem, non tam in pristini gradus gratiam restituendum censuit, sed honore cumulatiori liberalius ampliauit,[4] intra consuetum misericordioris clementie sinum memoratum Hugonem una nobiscum admittere non ducatis indignum. Vbi necesse est ad exemplum summi iudicis, sic censura seuiat ut non excludat clementiam; sic clementia leniat ut non emolliat censuram. Credimus indubitanter quod, prout expedire censueritis, quousque peccator penitens pulsando perseuerat, ipsum periclitari non permittetis pre penuria uictualis subsidii secundum reficiende necessitatis exigentiam.

Conseruet, oramus, sospitem paternitatis uestre, salus omnium, in Christo Iesu semper et beatissima Virgine.

188

To William of Nottingham, provincial minister

(November 1253)

Fratri Willelmo, ministro Anglie, Frater Ada subiectum supplicis obedientie famulatum.

Sincerissimam pietatis uestre litteram, que non tam suauem emulationem quam sollicitudinem officiosam placide religionis erga

[4] Cf. Luke 15: 13–24.

said Hugh, with a heaven-sent idea of restoring to each individual his property, has determined that three horses of greater value, which had been improperly acquired, and certain other things suited to forbidden use, should each and all be assigned to their rightful owners, as it pleased the brethren; and after receiving the benefit from confession, he has promised before the dread tribunal of judgement that, having accepted from your paternal holiness a punishment of whatever severity, he will pursue the business of his salvation with tireless perseverance. What therefore? Shall the prudent duty of pastoral care, especially in such a sublime profession as ours, act against the frighteningly strict judgement of the eternal, and repel that which God has recovered, which else had perished through the seduction of the Devil?

Why delay further? Casting ourselves at the feet of your kind and providential authority, we entreat you with all the affection we can and most devotedly request you to be pleased to admit the said Hugh with us to the bosom of your mercy and customary kindness, out of regard for him who, after his obstinately prodigal son had wasted his substance with dissolute and riotous living in a far country and returned for his father's pity, decided not simply to restore him to his grace and original status, but generously enlarged him and heaped honours upon him.[4] Where there is need, after the example of the Supreme Judge, let the sentence not be so harsh as to exclude mercy; let mercy not be so gentle as to make the sentence soft. We believe without a doubt that as far as you consider it expedient, so long as the repentant sinner perseveres in his penance, you will not allow him to be endangered for shortage of food according to the demands of necessary sustenance.

We pray that the Saviour of all may keep you safely, good father, in Christ Jesus and the Blessed Virgin.

188

To William of Nottingham, provincial minister

(November 1253)

Brother Adam to Brother William, minister of England, an entreaty with obedience and humble service.

I received your very candid letter on Monday after the feast of

modicitatem meam—sit, oro, sanctitati uestre sempiterna retributio—se tota preferebat, in partibus Londonii constitutus, suscepi feria secunda proxima post festum Sancti Luce.[1] Veni quoque in crastino Sancti Leonardi[2] Oxoniam, ibidem secundum quod propitia fuerit superna dispensatio quoad fieri ualebit, iuxta benignum sententie[a] uestre beneplacitum moraturus.

Nempe licet domino Londinensi[3] et Fratri Iohanni de Sancto Egidio, necnon et michi, per litteram apostolicam delegata sit cognitio iudicialis in causa[b] que uertitur inter dominum regem ex una parte et dominum Meneuensem[4] ex altera parte, et nichilominus exilitati mee incumbat ad mandatum papale cognoscere iudicialiter in causa que uertitur inter Meneuensem ex parte una et dominum abbatem Glouerniensem ex parte altera, cum quibus collegis nescio; et insuper dominus Cantuariensis et domina regina cum beneuolis eorum uehementibus egerint instantiis, ut ipsius domini domestico iungerer contubernio; prouisiua dispensationis diuine clementia michi, spero, prospexit misericordius ab hiis et huiusmodi molestissimis intolerabilium angustiarum occupationibus, per imperiosam regie maiestatis obsistentiam,[5] eximi pro tempore, sit diuino nomini gratiosa benedictio, Deo melius aliquid prouidente. Oxoniam regressus, uix respiro inter sibi succedentia turbaminum horrendorum cruciamina. Imperet Dei Filius, excitantibus ipsum uiris apostolicis, uentis et mari ut fiat tranquillitas magna.[6]

Acceptissimo patri nostro, Fratri Roberto de Thornham,[7] paternitatis uestre filio probatissimo, quem multiplicius, ut uos potissime nostis, duplici honore conuersationis et regiminis dignificant eminentie clariores, iuxta presentem sue ualetudinis exigentiam, quanta possum affectionis diligentia rogo consolatiua lati cordis industria subuenire curetis, propter diuini honorem nominis et considerationem fraterni profectus. Scio ad celitus persuasum importunum erit insistere supplicatoriis. Credo fore consultum, ut dum medele corporali datur opera, memorato fratri | uicarius[c] prouideatur cure spiritualis. Spero quod in hiis et in aliis docebit uos unctio que docet de omnibus.

De officio resumendo eruditionis impendende nescio si ante instans

f. 66ᵛ

188 [a] *Sic in MS, but possibly the copyist's misreading of* serenitatis.   [b] causa: eam *MS.*
[c] uicario *MS.*

188 [1] In 1253 Monday, 20 Oct.   [2] 7 Nov.
[3] Fulk Basset, bishop of London 1241–59.
[4] Thomas Waleys. See Letter 186 n. 6.

St Luke[1] while I was in the London area, displaying in its entirety your delightful zeal and your official solicitude, a product of peacefulness and religion, towards my humble self; I pray your holiness may receive an eternal recompense for it. Also I reached Oxford on the morrow of St Leonard,[2] to stay there according to your judgement and good pleasure, according to what is favoured by heavenly dispensation within the bounds of possibility.

For indeed, although the lord bishop of London[3] and Brother John of St Giles and also myself, have been appointed judges-delegate by apostolic letters in the case arising between the lord king on one side and the lord bishop of St David's[4] on the other; nevertheless my wretched self is required by papal mandate to take cognizance as a judge, with which colleagues I know not, of the case arising between the lord bishop of St David's on one side and the lord abbot of Gloucester on the other. Moreover, the lord of Canterbury and the lady queen have strongly urged me with kind insistence to join the household of the lord archbishop. The foreseeing kindness of divine providence has, I hope, mercifully procured me exemption for the time being from these and other most tiresome and intolerably exacting commitments of this kind, by means of the imperious opposition of the king's majesty[5]—grateful blessings on the divine name—God providing something better. Having returned to Oxford, I can scarcely draw breath amidst a succession of frightful trials and torments. May the Son of God, aroused by the apostles, command the winds and sea, that a great calm may descend.[6]

With all possible concern, I ask you to be solicitous and with your generous heart to console our most esteemed father, Brother Robert of Thornham,[7] as his condition of health demands for the honour of God's name and out of concern for brotherly well-being; he is, as you above all know, distinguished in manifold ways by both the nobility of his life and of his regime. I know that it will be unsuitable to add pressing entreaties to persuasion from heaven. I think that while effort is made to provide bodily healing, it will be advisable to provide the said brother with a vicar to exercise his spiritual care. I hope that in these matters and others you will be instructed by the unction which teaches us in everything.

As regards resuming my teaching position, I do not know whether

[5] Cf. Letter 186, pp. 447–9.
[6] Cf. Mark 4: 38–9; Matt. 8: 24–6.
[7] Robert of Thornham. Cf. Letters 171, 177.

Natalitium Domini fieri poterit quod opto, uobis hoc uolentibus. Memini me Hereford' iuxta coniecturam meam insinuasse discretioni uestre quod ante memoratum tempus hoc aggredi non ualerem. Cogito tamen hoc maturare prout Dominus donauerit. Sicut fuerit uoluntas in celo, sic fiat. Concedat, oro, Altissimus studiorum salutaribus exercitiis spiritum infallibilis consilii et fortitudinis insuperabilis, per Iesum Christum semper ad interuentum beatissime Virginis. Pro uestibus sacris uestiat uos sacrum lumen quo amiciamini sicut uestimento.

In eternum ualete. Amen.

189

To a spiritual director (John of Stamford)

(1253)

Iohanni, patri et preceptori discreto,[1] Frater Ada filialis obedientie famulatum supplicem.

Cum inter corporis uexamina et molestamina mentis etiam optatam studii litteralis uacationem penitus excludentia, per dominum Cantuariensem et comitem Cornubiensem hiis diebus non mediocrem hominis utriusque inquietationem sustinuissem, idem dominus archiepiscopus, afflictionibus addens afflictiones, miserum pregrauauit miserabilem. Nempe satagebat omnimodis personalem exilitatis mee presentiam exhiberi ad instans festum Sancti Hylarii[2] Londini in congregatione pontificum ⟨me⟩ ante memoratam solempnitatem undecim diebus ad ipsum nichilominus personaliter accessurum, ut quatenus superclemens diuinitas aspirauerit, sedandis formidabilis diffidentie seditionibus tam dudum excitatis quam nuper obortis in prelatis et proceribus, in clero et populo ecclesie et regni Anglie, detur opera salutaris diligentioris uigilantie.

O Domine Deus exercituum, quid exiguis et tantis negotiis! Quid infime abiectioni et altitudini horribili! Quid extremo peccatori et supreme saluti! Nempe longe a peccatoribus salus. Adiecit quoque prefatus archipontifex, importuniori urgentia curans omnimodis renitentem inducere, ut in uisitationibus faciendis per ipsum in

189   [1] The address is defective: a space after the word *discreto* is blank. Adam's reference to obedience due to the recipient and to his precept to resume teaching at Oxford indicate the recipient was John of Stamford, custodian of Oxford; cf. Letter 180.
   [2] 14 Jan.

what I desire will be possible before the coming Nativity of the Lord. I remember that I suggested to your prudent person at Hereford that, as I conjecture, I would not be in a position to undertake this before the time I have mentioned. However, I have it in mind to make it earlier, so far as the Lord grants it. As it is His will in heaven, so let it be. I pray the Most High may grant the salutary exercises of our studia the Spirit of infallible counsel and unconquerable resolution, ever through Jesus Christ and the intercession of the Blessed Virgin. For sacred vestments may you be clothed by sacred light like a garment.

Farewell for ever, Amen.

189

To a spiritual director (John of Stamford)

(1253)

Brother Adam to John, his father and prudent director,[1] filial obedience and humble service.

Among the physical vexations and mental trials that utterly exclude the leisure I desire for study of letters, and the by no means slight disturbance of body and spirit that I have suffered these days through the lord of Canterbury and the earl of Cornwall, I have been greatly burdened in my misery by further torments, one after another, added by the lord archbishop. In fact, he badgered my wretched person by every means to be present at the congregation of bishops at the coming feast of St Hilary[2] in London, my coming to him in person nevertheless eleven days before the said solemn assembly, so that, as far as the surpassing mercy of God provides inspiration, saving labour and diligent care may be given to calming the fearsome disloyalty and sedition that was stirred up some time ago and has recently arisen among prelates and nobles and among clergy and people of the English church and kingdom.

O Lord God of hosts, what great business for such little men! What a fearful elevation for the lowliest and most abject! What has an extremely sinful man to do with the salvation of the highest? Surely salvation and sinners are far apart. To all this, the said archbishop has also added, taking pains by every means and importunate pressure in the face of my resistance, to persuade me that I should by no means

prouincia sua post dies paucos, sicut proponit, eidem sicut olim assiduitate iugi nullatenus cuncter asssisterem; quod cum quantis terribilium discriminum inundantiis utique fieret, uos nostis melius quam ullus nouerit. Ad que cuncta cum optenderem euidentiores defectuum meorum insufficientias, et cogentiorem paternitatis uestre preceptionem, non sine fratrum instantia concordi super officio resumendo eruditionis impendende diuinorum eloquiorum, quod hactenus, ut reor, occasione ipsius domini diutius est intermissum, et insuper in hac parte seuientem regis maiestatis indignationem cum minationibus prohibitionis districte uehementiis; cum, inquam, horum et similium uectes et ostia ponerentur ubi certe uorago abyssalis confringeret tumentes fluctus[3] perstitit dominus sepe dictus auctoritate iussionum, ratione persuasionum, supplicatione petitionum, coactione priuilegiorum, agens improbitate grandiori ne in tanta negotiorum quam asserit necessitate, sue intentionis sustineat quantalibet conditione repulsam.

Igitur ecce coram clementi auctoritatis uestre patrocinio si pateret scisso pectore cor saucium nequaquam panderet merentis anime superanxias acrimonias, rediuiua redundantia uite domicilium non sine luctu letum minitante concutientes atrocius. Quid enim? Si hoc quod uereor inexplicabilius euenerit, non uideo nisi ut in omne tempus, si tamen modicum restet, quoad uixero suspendatur, quod absit, et studium uiuifice ueritatis agnoscende et otium saluifice sanctitatis assequende. Quorum detrimenta, ne dicam dampna, presertim exitu propinquante, quis nisi perditissime uesanie uecordes excecati non uidet insiccabilis lacrime lamento prolixiori assequanda? Hic est enim planctus Vnigeniti, quem ut ualuit sermo prophetalis aperuit: 'Quis' inquiens, 'dabit capiti meo aquam et oculis meis fontem lacrimarum, et plorabo die ac nocte interfectos filie populi mei?'[4] In tetra spiritus mesti caligine atro liquore,[a] cordis lingue calamus intinctus presentes pinxit caracteres nocturnus, diurno quippe non uacauit. Denique quid dicam? Sileo quia nescio.

Sit uobis, oro, Christus Dei uirtus, Dei sapientia, Dei sanctificatio, et uigor inuictus et sensus indeceptus et zelus irremissus in hiis et in omnibus, per interuentum superbenedictum beatissime Virginis. Non tam temporis quam mentis angustia angustauit epistolam. Rescribite

189 *a* liquoris *MS.*

---

[3] uectes . . . fluctus: cf. Job 38: 10–11. [4] Jer. 9: 1.

hesitate to assist him, as once before, with continuing assiduity on the visitations he is to make in his province, as he proposes to do a few days later. You know better than anyone what a frightful deluge of difficult matters would be involved. To all this, when I objected my defects and obvious inadequacy and, more compelling, your fatherly precept, issued not without the pressing agreement of the brethren, about my resumption of teaching the word of God, which has hitherto been too long posponed on account, as I think, of the said archbishop, and also in this case by the raging indignation of the king's majesty and his strict and vehement prohibition. When, I say, bars and doors like these have been interposed, where the swelling waves would be broken by a profound chasm,[3] the said lord archbishop persisted with authoritative commands, with rational persuasion, with humble entreaties and the compulsion of privileges, urging me greatly and beyond measure that in business of such great necessity, as he asserts, he would not in any circumstances suffer a refusal.

Therefore see, before the patronage of your kind authority if it were available, the wounded heart within my torn breast would by no means expose to you the anxiety and bitterness of my grieving spirit, now that the overwhelming pressures are renewed, darkly threatening and striking at the happy abode of my life. What then? If what I fear inexplicably comes about, it seems to me that for all time—if, however, a little time remains—both the study to acquire life-giving truth and, which heaven forbid, the leisure to pursue saving holiness will be suspended as long as I live. Who except those blinded by irrecoverable madness fail to see the damage, not to say loss, of these things and the ensuing extended lamentation and unquenchable tears, especially when my end is near? For here is the lament of the Only-Begotten, which, as it was valid, the word of the prophet revealed: 'Who will give water to my head and a fountain of tears to my eyes, and I will weep day and night for the slain of the daughter of my people?'[4] My pen, the tongue of my heart, has traced these letters dipped in black liquid, in the darkness of my sorrowful spirit, by night, for there was no time during the day. In the end, what am I to say? I am silent because I know not what.

I pray that Christ, the strength of God, may be with you, and the wisdom of God, the holiness of God, invincible energy, and undeceived understanding and an unrelaxed zeal in these and in all matters, through the most blessed intercession of the Blessed Virgin. Stress of both time and mind have shortened my letter. I pray you,

maturius, precor, quod inspirauerit spiraculum Omnipotentis. Talibus litteris scripsi qualibet quod uolui, quamuis ut uolui non ualui; amplius tamen expressi. Sit, opto, pietati uestre recommendatioris[b] Hugonis Cote,[5] per angelorum presidium et uestrum ministerium, diuinitus edomanda indomabilis peruicacia. Amen

190

To Brother William of Nottingham, provincial minister

(March 1253)

Fratri Willelmo, ministro Anglie, Frater Ada obedientie reuerentialis famulatum.

Vt sancte paternitatis uestre discretioni processus hiis diebus super facto Fratris Thome de Eboraco promouendi ad officium eruditionis impendende diuinorum eloquiorum,[1] iuxta quod in presentiarum et utilitas pia requirit et compellit iusta necessitas, plenius innotescat, presentem cartam seriem rerum continentem, deliberatione preuia sinceritati uestre destinare consensi.

Igitur cum supplicationum diligentia per quindenam integram a festo Cathedre Beati Petri[2] sub aliquo interuallo usque ad sabbatum uigilie xl Martyrum[3] pro negotio memorato sollicius apud uniuersitatem protensa[a] fuisset, secundum quod uobis plenius, ut reor, retulit karissimus pater Iohannes, custos Oxoniensis, memorato sabbato conuenerunt cancellarius et magistri et bachelarii quidam, qui prius elegerant de se septem commissarios ut ordinarent super eo quod petitum est de prefato Thoma, et formam statuti conciperent super incepturis in theologia deinceps. Qui septem commissarii ordinauerunt quod, sicut petitum est, hac uice Frater Thomas inciperet, non obstante impedimento obiecto eidem, scilicet quod in artibus non rexerit; insuper statuentes uice cancellarii et uniuersitatis quod in posterum nullus incipiat in theologia nisi prius inceperit in liberalibus et unum librum canonis aut Sententias legerit, et publice in uniuersitate predicauerit.[4]

---

[b] recommendatior *MS.*

190   [a] protenso *MS.*

---

[5] Hugh Cote: cf. Letters 187, 192.

190   [1] Cf. Letter 186.   [2] 22 Feb.   [3] 8 Mar.

write back to me soon with what inspiration the Spirit of the Almighty offers. In this letter I have written what I wished, but as I wished, not as I could have done; but I have expressed more than enough. I wish the indomitable obstinacy of Hugh Cote,[5] who is highly commended to your goodness, may be tamed by divine intervention through the help of the angels and your ministry. Amen.

190

To Brother William of Nottingham, provincial minister

(March 1253)

Brother Adam to Brother William, minister of England, obedience, reverence, and service.

In order to inform your fatherly discretion more fully of the process followed these past days in promoting Brother Thomas of York to the office of teaching the word of God[1]—according to the demands of piety and service and the obligation of justice and necessity—I have after previous discussion agreed to dispatch to you this letter containing the succession of events.

When, therefore, diligent supplication to the university for the said case had been drawn out for a whole fortnight, from the feast of the Chair of St Peter,[2] with an interval until Saturday, the vigil of the Forty Martyrs,[3] as I think has been fully reported to you by our very dear Father John, the custodian of Oxford, the chancellor, masters, and certain bachelors met on the Saturday I have mentioned, having first chosen from their number seven commissioners to make an ordinance regarding the supplication for the said Thomas and to think out a form of statute concerning those who will incept in theology for the future. These seven commissioners ordained that this time Brother Thomas should incept as had been supplicated, not withstanding the alleged impediment that he had not been regent in arts; in addition, they decreed on behalf of the chancellor and the university that in future no one might incept in theology unless he had previously incepted in the liberal arts, and had lectured on one book of the Bible or the Sentences, and had publicly preached in the university.[4]

---

[4] This is the earliest account of legislative procedure at Oxford. See the text of this statute in *SAUO*, p. 49. On the objection of the university see Letter 186 n. 14.

Et si quis pro[b] aliquo qui hunc defectum patitur, preces magnatum
f. 67 auctoritate armatas impetrauerit, penitus uniuersitatis | priuetur
priuilegio, et quod huic statuto subscriberent et cancellarius et
omnes magistri regentes in Sacra Scriptura, et Frater Hugo de
Mistretune,[5] et ceteri magistri regentes in decretis et legibus, et
duo[c] rectores pro artistis, et Frater Ada de Marisco. Que cum recitata
fuissent coram omnibus et quia non consensi ut scriberem propter
causas quas obtendebam, dilatum fuit colloquium usque in crastinum,
scilicet dominicam Quadragesime. Quo die, cum ob plures causas,
quas prius obtenderam, et assererem me nullatenus subscripturum,
post uarias altercationes ab hucusque in feriam secundam continuo
secuturam, prorogatum est negotium.

Quum presentibus cancellario et magistris et scolaribus iteraui
adhuc rationes, aliquibus additis, propter quas non adquieui in hac
parte eorum uoluntati, ut sint[d] omnes quasi aggregate, quia quando
alias actum est multum instanter, ut tale statutum roboretur auctoritate uniuersitatis, ego ipse quantum ualui egi omnimodis ne hoc
fieret, contradicens, sicut uisum fuit, non sine assignatione causarum
maiorum exceptione qualicumque. Semper etiam et continue post hoc
hucusque dissentiens, reatum leuitatis incurrerem si subscriberem,
cum causis sentiendi similiter se habentibus super eodem dissimiliter
sentirem. Adhuc etiam quod uitium falsi euidentius admitterem si
quasi uictus cupiditate optinendi quod petebam, statuto subscriberem, quod michi non placuit, corde a digitis dissidente. Et
nichilominus cum uideatur infallibiliter, quod in frequentes euentus,
licet cancellarius et uniuersitas sibi retinuerint potestatem dispen-
sandi ex causis opportunis contra statutum huiuscemodi, tamen sicut
fieri assolet presertim in huiuscemodi uniuersitatibus sicut frequens
docet experientia, per contradictionem uniuscuiuspiam posset talis
gratia aut perperam retardari aut impediri penitus. Vnde etiam ille
repelleretur in quem clarior gloria concurreret meritorum, et quem
diuinitas approbaret reprobaret inhumanitas.

Insuper quod non expediret nec deceret ut mei assensus uel
subscriptio requireretur ad sua statuta roboranda, qui iam per
triennium quasi foras factus cessauerim a docendi officio in eorum
uniuersitate. Demum quod ipsorum gratia tam humili totiens

---

[b] pro: *inserted above the line by another hand.*   [c] duobus *MS.*   [d] sicut *MS.*

[5] Hugh de Misterton was a Dominican friar, regent in theology *c.*1250–2: W. A.
Hinnebusch, *The Early English Friars Preachers* (1951), p. 369; *BRUO* ii. 1285.

Also [they decreed that] if anyone shall procure supplications, armed by the authority of great persons, on behalf of anyone who suffers from this disqualification, he shall be utterly deprived of the university's privileges; and that this statute should be subscribed to by the chancellor and all the masters regent in Sacred Scripture, and by Brother Hugh de Misterton[5] and the rest of the masters regent in decretals and law, and by two rectors for the Arts faculty, and by Brother Adam Marsh. When these proposals had been read out before everyone, because I had not agreed to subscribe for reasons that I put forward, the discussion was postponed until the next day, that is the Sunday of Lent. On this day, since for numerous reasons that I had previously advanced, I stated that I would in no way subscribe, after various altercations the business was prorogued until the following Monday.

When in the presence of the chancellor, masters, and scholars, I repeated the reasons advanced hitherto, plus some additional ones so that all reasons might be grouped together; since when on another occasion urgent action was taken to get a similar statute confirmed by the authority of the university, I acted as far as I could by all means to prevent this being done, contradicting the motion, as it appeared, not without pleading an exception of some sort on major grounds. As I have always continued to dissent from then until now, I should incur a charge of frivolity if I were to subscribe, since I would judge the same thing differently while the reasons for my opinion were unchanged. Moreover, I would be admitting an obvious offence of deceit if, overcome by a desire to get what I was seeking, I were to subscribe to a statute which I did not approve, with my heart opposed to what my fingers were doing. Notwithstanding, since it seems infallibly certain that on frequent occasions, although the chancellor and university retain the power to dispense from a statute of this kind for appropriate reasons, yet as customarily happens, especially in universities of this kind, as frequent experience teaches us, such a grace [of dispensation] could be either wrongfully delayed or totally obstructed by the contradiction of any one person whatsoever. Consequently one whose merits were clearly agreed to be more splendid would be repelled, and one approved by God would be rejected by inhumanity.

Moreover, that it would be neither expedient nor fitting that my consent or subscription should be required to confirm their statutes, as I had for three years now been like an outsider, having retired from a teaching post in their university. Finally, their grace, so many times

postulata supplicatione, inhonestius uiolata degeneraret in seuitiam, quam michi nisi sub extorta consensione non concederent. Subfuit pre omnibus hiis ratio potior, quam suppressi de iudicio, que uehementius obstitit quominus in hac parte requisitis cancellarii et uniuersitatis preberem assensum. Preter que omnia, sicut prefatis sabbato et die dominica, feria secunda precise asserui coram omnibus in hec uerba: 'Ego isti statuto uestro nec subscribo nec illud statuo, nec consentio nec etiam contradico, cum licet sit periculosum admodum et michi non complacitum, non uidetur secundum planum ⟨sensus⟩ sui preferre iniquitatem', rogans ut precibus supplicum suorum tam frequenter interpositis beneuolum adhiberent assensum. Quibus sic excursis factum est, ut de uoluntate cancellarii et uniuersitatis memorati commissarii seorsum fierent omnibus presentium negotiorum articulis sine more dispendio finem imposituri. Ego autem cunctis corde ualefaciens, de concione recessi, expectans super uniuersis responsum cancellarii, qui michi per cartulam presentibus inclusam manu propria statim conscriptam respondere sui gratia curauit.

Post hec autem omnia feria quarta sequente, scilicet die Beati Gregorii,[6] profectus sum Tyngehyrst ad dominum Lyncolniensem, multis ex causis ualetudinem satis molestam sustinens oculorum. Sit benedictio diuino nomini, relicto honore, quem michi ademptum non doleo, dilectissimo patri Fratri Petro de Manners[7] presidendi in inceptione Fratris Thome de Eboraco, ad gloriam diuini nominis, preconsulto super eodem omni gratia dignissimo patre honorabili, Fratre Matteo, priore Fratrum Predicatorum in Anglia; cuius inceptionis uespere in crastino Beati Gregorii, feria quinta, et ipsa inceptio dispensatione feria sexta proxima sequente expedite sunt in Domino.

Cogitaui in confectione presentium transferre me maturius Radinges, ualetudinis leuigande causa per Saluatoris medelam qui sanat omnia. Succinxi scripturam, sperans per amicissimum patrem, Fratrem Iohannem de Stanford apud clementiam uestram satacturum et modicitati mee satisfacturum super urgentibus necessitatum mearum articulis, de benigna circumspectionis uestre uigilantia, per strenuam interuentus sui sedulitatem. Concedat, oro, Dominus Deus uirtutum pietati uestre, ut in omnibus quod prudenter discernit, agit

---

[6] 12 Mar.
[7] Peter de Manners was a Dominican regent in theology: *BRUO*, ii. 1215–16. This

humbly supplicated, was dishonourably violated and degenerated into cruelty when they would not grant it to me unless their consent was obtained by force. Before all these there was a stronger reason, which I judiciously held back, which was strongly opposed to my giving my assent to the requests of the chancellor and the university: besides everything which, as on the said Saturday and Sunday, I briefly stated before them all on Monday in these words: 'I neither subscribe to this statute of yours, nor enact it, nor do I consent to it nor even speak against it, since, although it is somewhat dangerous and I do not like it, it does not, taken in its obvious sense, show its iniquity', while I asked that they would give their kind assent to the entreaties of those supplicating, which had been so frequently placed before them. When these matters had been dealt with, it was enacted by the will of the chancellor and university on their own that the aforesaid commissioners should without delay impose a conclusion to all the items of the present transactions. I, however, with a heartfelt farewell to all the rest, left the meeting, awaiting the chancellor's response to everything. He was gracious enough to reply to me immediately in his own hand, by a letter which I include with this one.

After all this, on the following Wednesday, that is St Gregory's day,[6] I set off for Tilehurst to see the lord of Lincoln. I am suffering from a rather tiresome eye complaint, from many causes. Blessed be the divine name, I having abandoned the honour of presiding over the inception of Brother Thomas of York—the loss of which does not grieve me—to the beloved Father Peter Manners,[7] to the glory of the divine name, having first consulted the honourable and most worthy and gracious father, Father Matthew, prior of the Friars Preachers in England, the vesperies of his inception were held on Thursday, the morrow of St Gregory, and the inception itself by dispensation in the Lord on the next Friday.

I thought while composing this letter that I would transfer myself to Reading earlier, for the purpose of relieving my complaint through the remedy of the Saviour, who heals all things. I have cut short what I have written, hoping that our dear father Brother John of Stamford will be actively and busily interceding with your kind person to satisfy my humble self in respect of the items I urgently need, thanks to your vigilant and kind prudence and his vigorous intervention. May the Lord God of power grant you, I pray, in all matters to refer that

passage is the earliest evidence of the practice of holding the vesperies and inception on separate successive days: Little and Pelster, *Oxford Theology and Theologians*, p. 45.

fortiter, temperanter cohibet, distribuit equaliter, ad illum finem iugiter referat ubi est Deus omnia in omnibus, eternitate certa et pace perfecta, in Christo Iesu semper et beatissima Virgine.

Obsecro, pater, consueta prouisionis uestre suauitas propter Dominum et in Deo karissimo Fratri Ricardo Cornubiensi,[8] uiro cui opus non est apud sollertem uestre paternitatis experientiam interpellatio commendaticia, prospicere uelit in adiutorio competenti secrete societatis in officio subueniendi et scribendi subsidio. Frater Thomas Bachun de conuentu Notingham putatur ad hoc fore non tam ydoneus quam uoluntarius. Plures, ut audio, reperientur opportuni ad nunc dictum fratris obsequium, si scripture quas ex studiosa prefati Fratris Ricardi uigilantia manibus suis conscripserint singuli sue concedantur in usus utilitatis priuate, tamen ad communitatis profectum ampliorem.

191

To William of Nottingham, provincial minister

Fratri Willelmo, ministro Anglie, Frater Ada.

Vna cum domino Thoma de Wyke, latore presentium, paternitati uestre humiliter supplico, rogans obnixius quatinus eidem, licet longe sit excellentior in ecclesiastice ierarchie dispositis diuinitus ordinibus presbiteratus monachatu, tamen impar humeris ecclesiastici regiminis onus declinanti et institutionis religiose securiorem uacationem studiis leuigandis[a] affectanti, cuius desiderii feruores Deus, ignis consumens, in ipsius corde, ut uideo, succendit ardentius, ianuam clementie salutaris ob Saluatoris contemplationem aperire uelitis; prouiso per omnia ut propter pia Filii Dei uulnera detur opera, quoad fieri poterit, fidelis, ne per ipsius cessionem faucibus Satane grex dominicus exponatur deuorandus.

Sed antequam sacrum induat habitum, apud sacrilegos, ut uereor, patronos, sicut immensa res expostulat, satagatur per ducatum f. 67ᵛ Omnipotentis salutare negotium agi | ad salutem animarum.

Sit uobis, oro, perenniter benedictionis celice illuminatio salutiua in Christo Iesu semper et beatissima Virgine. Qui solus bonus est

191   ᵃ leuigatis MS.

---

[8] Richard (Rufus) of Cornwall; cf. Letter 182 n. 2 and Letters 197, 198, 203.

which you discern with prudence, perform with resolution, constrain with moderation and distribute with justice, to that end where God is all in all, in assured eternity and perfect peace, ever in Christ Jesus and the Blessed Virgin.

I beg you, father, for the sake of the Lord, that you would with your customary goodness and foresight provide for our dear Brother Richard of Cornwall[8]—a man needing no advocacy or commendation to your fatherly sagacity and knowledge of him—the competent help of a secretary associate with the task of supporting him and assisting him with writing. Brother Thomas Bacun of the Nottingham convent is thought to be not so much suitable as willing for this. Many, I hear, will be found ready to serve the said brother, if they write up with their own hands the writings which are from the zealous care of the said Brother Richard and are given them for their private use, yet also for the greater advantage of the community.

191

To William of Nottingham, provincial minister

Brother Adam to Brother William, minister of England.

Together with Sir Thomas de Wicke, the bearer of this letter, I humbly beseech you, father, with an earnest request to open for him the gates of saving mercy out of regard for our Saviour. Although in the divinely disposed orders of ecclesiastical hierarchy the priesthood is far superior to the monastic profession, nevertheless, declining the burden of ecclesiastical governance, to which his shoulders are unequal, Thomas desires the surer freedom of the religious life to facilitate study, and his fervent desires are, as I see it, kindled in his heart more ardently by the consuming fire of God. This is provided that in everything, for the holy wounds of the Son of God, faithful care should be taken, as far as possible, that through his retirement the Lord's flock be not exposed to being devoured by the jaws of Satan.

But before he dons the sacred habit, as the greatness of the matter demands, let there be under the lead of the Almighty active representations to the patrons (profane ones, I fear) to provide for the salvation of souls.

May you receive, I pray, the perpetual blessing of heaven with a saving light in Christ Jesus and the Blessed Virgin. May He who is

uestri meminerit in bonum pro eo quod, ut iugiter experior, mei licet indigni apud piam recordationem uestram iugiter uiuit memoria.

Commendet, obsecro, uestre sanctitatis fidelissime caritas Symonem comitem Leycestriensem innouatione rediuiua sanctissimis filiorum uestrorum, fratrum nostrorum, suffragiis in Domino. Amen.

192
To William of Nottingham, provincial minister

Fratri Willelmo, ministro Anglie, Frater Ada deuotum humilis obedientie famulatum.

Hugonem Cote,[1] latorem presentium ad uos reuertentem, ad imitatum eius qui ait, 'Si occiderit me, sperabo in eum',[2] suadelis sermonum ad suasum diuinitus supersedens supplico, una cum eodem pietatis uestre pedibus prouolutus, ut propter sacrosanctum sanguinem testamenti, quem pro salute ipsius expresserunt pia uulnera Filii Dei, in fidei lenitate suscipiatis, ianuas miserationis eterne clementius aperientes, probitate[a] salutari perseuerantie[b] in salutis Auctore pulsati. Vtinam sapientia que desursum est, humane peritie radios igneos exsufflans excecet oculos, et non tantum 'attingat a fine usque ad finem fortiter, quam disponat omnia suauiter'.[3] Prestet Dei Verbum, oro, ut quod nequit necessarium eloquium obtineat silentium opportunum.

Valeat, etc.

193
To Brother W., vicar of the Friars Minor in England

Desideratissimo patri in Christo, Fratri W., uicario Fratrum Minorum Anglie,[1] Frater Ada salutem in Domino.

Ut quid uigenti uirtuti, circumspecte prudentie, pie affectioni pretenderem prophete Dauid confessionem, filii prodigi penitentiam, Petri Apostoli lacrimam,[2] et Fratris Robert de Konole, dilecti filii

---

192   *a* probitate *is preceded by* in *MS, apparently erroneously.*   *b* perseuerantius *MS.*

192   [1] Cf. Letter 187.   [2] Job 13: 15.   [3] Cf. Wisd. 8: 1.

193   [1] It has not been possible to identify the recipient. William of Nottingham served as vicar to Haymo of Faversham, 1239–40, before succeeding him as provincial: Eccleston,

only good remember to reward you for the fact that, as I always feel, you constantly remember me in your prayers, unworthy though I am.

May the faithful charity of your holiness commend Simon, earl of Leicester, with renewed earnestness to the most holy prayers of your sons, our brethren, in the Lord. Amen.

192

To William of Nottingham, provincial minister

Brother Adam to Brother William, minister of England, humble obedience and devoted service.

Together with Hugh Cote,[1] bearer of this letter, who is returning to you, imitating him who says, 'Although he should kill me, I will trust in him',[2] casting myself at the feet of your goodness, the persuasion of my speech surpassed by a persuasion divinely inspired, I beg you, for the sake of the most sacred blood of the covenant shed from the wounds of the Son of God for his salvation, to receive him gently in faith, kindly opening to him the gates of eternal mercy, impelled by saving proof of his perseverance in the Author of salvation. Would that the wisdom that is from above, breathing upon us its rays of fire, may blind the eyes of human knowledge and not only 'reach from end to end mightily, but order all things sweetly'.[3] I pray the Word of God that what necessary speech cannot achieve may be gained by opportune silence.

Farewell, etc.

193

To Brother W., vicar of the Friars Minor in England

Brother Adam to the most beloved father in Christ, Brother W., vicar of the Friars Minor in England,[1] greetings in the Lord.

The reason why I would draw the attention of your lively virtue, your prudent circumspection and pious affection, to the confession of the prophet David, the repentance of the prodigal son, and the tears of Peter[2] and those of Robert de Konole, your beloved son and our

---

p. 86; but during William's regime as provincial, his vicar was Gregory de Bosellis: ibid. pp. 42, 101.

[2] i.e. cf. Matt. 26: 75; Luke 22: 62. The three instances of remorse leading to repentance are intended to validate the repentance of Brother Robert de Konole, who had gone astray.

uestri et karissimi fratris nostri, causam agerem apud clementiam uestram, quam indubitanter dudum noui Christum egisse apud suauem caritatis uestre compassionem; uerum cum prefato fratre ad horulam nuper per iuuenilem inspectionem modicum digresso, et per compunctionem, quasi auersus non fuerit, reuerso, uestram pronus rogo beneuolentiam, supplicans anxius quatinus eundem ad ianuas misericordie uestre, cum uestri reuerentia et sui confusione pulsantem, intuitu Ipsius qui pulsanti aperit et petenti largitur,[3] ad reconciliationis gratiam admittere non ducatis indignum.

Valeat desideratissimus michi pater in Christo semper et beatissima Virgine.

Videte qualibus litteris scripsi uobis mea manu misera. Quicunque autem uolunt ⟨Deo⟩ placere in carne,[4] hii cogunt uos in hoc fratris casu et similibus indurari ad filios quasi non sint uestri, ut tamen crucis Christi cui se, ne dicam mentientes Spiritui Sancto, deuouerant, tribulationem non patiantur.

Iterum in eternum ualete.

194

To Brother J(ohn), custodian of Worcester

Dilectissimo patri in Christo, Fratri I⟨oanni⟩[1] custodi Wygorniensi, sui in omnibus deuoti Fratres Ioannes de Stanford, Ada de Marisco, Thomas de Eboraco, salutem in Domino.

Meritum circa animarum adquisitionem melius conicitur ex diuinissimo amore Saluatoris, qui pro earumdem reparatione unicam illam pretiosissimam ipsius animam exposuit, secundum quod Ipse dicit in Ieremia, 'Dedi dilectam animam meam in manu inimicorum eius'.[2] Propter quod circa animam Hugonis Cote,[3] latoris presentium, de faucibus infernalibus reuocandam sollicius insistentes, decreuimus caritati uestre labores uestros derelinquere, siquidem cum impetu ruine preceps gradiebatur, nostris monitis impetum suum dereliquit et ordinationi ministri omnino se supposuit. Vnde promptus existens ad suam salutem querendam accedit nunc ad ministrum, ut sequatur eum quocunque ierit,[4] donec uisitauerit

[3] Cf. Matt. 7: 8.　　　　　　　　　　　　　　　　[4] Rom. 8: 8.

194 [1] The identity of the custodian is uncertain; the editor's extension of the initial is hypothetical.
[2] Jer. 12: 7.　　　　　　　　　　　[3] Cf. Letters 187, 189, 192.

very dear brother, is in order to move his cause with your kind person, which I have long since known without doubt that Christ has moved through your sweet charity and compassion. Together with the said brother, who recently went somewhat astray for a time through his youthful indiscretion and has returned with compunction as if he had not fallen away, prostrate with him, I ask you earnestly, having regard to Him who opens to those who knock and gives to those who ask,[3] to be so kind as to admit him to the grace of reconciliation, as he knocks at the gates of your mercy with reverence for you and confusion in himself.

Farewell, my most dear father, ever in Christ and the Blessed Virgin.

You see what kind of letter I have written you with my wretched hand. But those who wish to please God in the flesh,[4] compel you in this case of our brother and in similar cases to be hard on your sons, as though they are not yours, yet so that they do not suffer the tribulation of the cross of Christ, to which—if I am not to say they lied to the Holy Spirit—they had vowed themselves.

Again, for ever farewell.

194

To Brother J[ohn], custodian of Worcester

To our dear father in Christ, Brother John,[1] custodian of Worcester, his devoted brothers in all things, John of Stamford, Adam Marsh, Thomas of York, send greetings in the Lord.

The cost of winning souls can be inferred from the divine love of our Saviour, who for their recovery offered that most precious soul of his, as He himself says in Jeremiah: 'I have given my dear soul into the hand of her enemies.'[2] On this account, regarding the soul of Hugh Cote,[3] the bearer of this letter, we who are anxiously pursuing his recall from the jaws of hell, have decided to leave to your charity the form your labours should take, since when he was moving to ruin, he checked his course in response to our admonitions, and has wholly submitted himself to the judgement of the minister; and thus being ready to seek his salvation, he is approaching the minister, to 'follow him whithersoever he goeth,'[4] until the dayspring from on high hath

---

[4] Rev. 14: 4.

eum oriens ex alto,[5] illuminetque abscondita tenebrarum,[6] et reuelet scientiam salutis in remissionem peccatorum[7] eius. Scimus enim eum multum offendisse et ob hoc offensam fratrum incurrisse. Propter hoc sollicita erit uestra pietas et fratrum commotiones, prout possibile est, sedare, et eiusdem infirma supportare, et etiam per suaues collationes, si que in eo incepte[a] sunt, confirmare, et eundem ad meliorem spem prouocare.

Ceterum cum et illa temporalia que habuit, per consilium uestrum dereliquit, uestram rogamus clementiam quatinus, quamdiu infra terminos uestros sit, eidem per prouidentiam uestram in uictualibus prouideatur; ei quidem sicut alii pauperi subueniri potest, et eo misericordius quo in seculo stetit periculosius. Rogamus insuper quatinus apud ministrum negotium eiusdem promouere uelitis.

195
To William of Nottingham, provincial minister

Fratri Willelmo, ministro Anglie, Frater Ada salutem et tam debitam quam deuotam per omnia subiectionis obedientiam.

Notum sit honorabili paternitatis uestre pietati quod, cum dilectus Frater de Maddele[1] ad me Oxonie accessisset et ego eundem, iuxta quod michi uisum fuit, secundum tenorem mandati uestri fuissem allocutus, ipse michi respondit se nequaquam procurasse apud ministrum generalem[2] ut per eius auctoritatem ab Anglia uocaretur in alia prouincia collocandus, asserens quod nec etiam adhuc huius rei gerit desiderium, cum certa pro incertis, sicut circumspecte protestatur, nullatenus sint deserenda. Ceterum tenorem mandati quod minister generalis ad uos destinauit pro fratribus mittendis Parisius, prius[a] ipse michi retulit quam eidem super hoc aliquid expressius insinuassem. Ad hec, de inuestigandis expositionibus Sacre Scripture in libris originalibus sanctorum cum eodem contuli, sicut mandastis, qui prompta deuotione paratum se optulit, ut dignum est, omnino non tam ad hoc quam ad omnia quecunque ei salutariter duxeritis iniungenda.

194　[a] incepta *MS.*
195　[a] prior *MS.*

---

[5] Luke 1: 78.　　　　[6] Cf. 1 Cor. 4: 5.　　　　[7] Luke 1: 77.

visited him',[5] and 'will bring to light the hidden things of darkness',[6] and 'give knowledge of salvation unto the remission of sins'.[7] For we know that he has greatly offended and has on this account incurred the anger of his brethren. For this reason you will be solicitous in your goodness both to quieten the agitation of the brothers, so far as is possible, and to support his weakness, and even to strengthen him with gentle conferences, if such have already begun with him, and to arouse better hopes in him.

For the rest, since he has through your advice abandoned the temporal goods he had, we ask you, so long as he is within your boundaries, to be kind enough to have him provided with victuals, just as another pauper can be supported, but the more mercifully as he stood in more danger in the world. We also ask you to assist his case with the minister.

195

To William of Nottingham, provincial minister

Brother Adam to Brother William, minister of England, greetings with due and devoted obedience in all things.

This is to inform you, good father, that when our dear Brother Madeley[1] came to me at Oxford and I had spoken to him, as it seemed best to me in accordance with the gist of your mandate, he replied that he had never procured it with the Minister General[2] that he should be called from England on the latter's authority to be placed in another province, asserting that he has hitherto had no desire for this since, as he prudently protested, one should by no means abandon a certain situation for one that is uncertain. Actually, he first related to me the gist of the mandate that the Minister General sent you for sending brothers to Paris, before I had suggested to him anything on this subject. I would add, I conferred with him about investigating the commentaries on Holy Scripture in the early books of the saints, as you commanded, and he offered himself as being wholly ready with prompt devotion, as is fitting, not only for this task but also for anything whatever that you consider should be profitably enjoined on him.

195   [1] Walter de Maddeley was socius to Agnellus of Pisa in 1235, when the latter died: Eccleston, p.77; he was then at Oxford: Little, *The Greyfriars in Oxford*, pp. 188–9; *BRUO* ii. 1202. It is not clear from the letter where he was serving as lector.
   [2] John of Parma, 1247–57.

Quoniam igitur modicitatis mee consilium super instanti articulo emittendorum fratrum de prouincia uestra requirere uoluit uestra circumspecta discretio, perpensis ut ualeo rerum circumstantiis, uobis innotesco quod, ut uideo, satius est, tam Fratre Iohanne de Westun[3] quam Fratre Waltero de Maddele in presentiarum apud uos retentis, per reliquos mandatum generalis impleatis, studio Parisiensi in presenti necessitatis urgentia prouidentes. Sic enim, ut puto, et opportunius diuino seruietur honori et fratrum utilitati cumulatius prospicietur, et commodius cari nostri, de quibus sollicita est uestra paternitas, ad ecclesiasticam utilitatem per eosdem in futuris temporibus efficiendam, propitia Diuinitate proficiant.

Adhuc in calce littere non exiliter mirandum censeo, quod f. 68 karissimo Fratri Waltero de | Maddele, qui onus diuine eruditionis impendende sibi iamdudum impositum diligenter hactenus continuauit, in obsequiali adiutorio, nescio per quam circumspectionis seueritatem, nondum fuit prouisum. Vnde cogitur nimirum non solum spiritum uitalem per studiorum uehementiam exhaurire, uerum etiam manu propria scriptitando in dies corporale robur atterere, cum non sit fortitudo lapidis fortitudo sua, nec caro eius caro enea est.[4] Et quid est quod ceteris fratribus officio legendi deputatis, presertim quibus successit, in magnis prouisum est uoluminibus et in sociorum subuenientium[b] adiutoriis, iste solus uidetur non curari; qui tamen, ut audio, hanc diuinitus est assecutus gratiam ut sit in legendo suauis, acutus in disserendo, in scriptis et eloquiis tam fratribus quam secularibus utilis et acceptus. Erit igitur uestrum, si placet, per sedulam pie paternitatis sollicitudinem in hac parte, sicut expedire noueritis, absque more dispendio et paci mentis[c] consulere et studentium prouidere prouectui.

Rogauit me dilectissimus michi in Christo Frater R. de Frille, gardianus Stanfordie, quod et quantum ualeo, ⟨et⟩ scio, uestram interpellare pietatem, ut ei in pacifica consolatione per paternam clementiam prospiciatis. Rogo, pater mi karissime, salutari obsequio meo,[d] si placet, sanctam et amabilem societatem uestram sigillatim[e] in Christo.

Since in your prudent discernment you express a wish for the advice of my poor self about the pressing matter of sending brothers out of your province, I have weighed the circumstances as far as I am able, and I would have you know that, as I see it, it is more than enough if at present you keep Brothers John de Weston[3] and Walter Madeley with you, and fulfil the general's mandate, providing for the urgent needs of the Paris studium through the rest. I think in this way the divine honour will be more conveniently served, and our dear ones, who are the subject of your fatherly concern, may with God's favour make progress for the advantage of the Church in times to come.

Hereto, at the foot of my letter, I regard it as no small wonder that my dear Brother Walter Madeley, who has continued until now to carry the burden of teaching divinity imposed upon him long since, has not yet been provided with the service of an assistant, through what strict parsimony I know not. As a result he is is forced excessively to exhaust his vital spirit by the fervour of his studies, and even to wear out his bodily strength by writing day by day with his own hand, though his strength is not the strength of stone, nor his flesh of brass.[4] Why is it that the rest of the brothers assigned to the duty of lecturing, especially those whom he is succeeding, have been provided with great volumes and the help of supportive associates, while he alone seems uncared for? Yet he, as I hear, has gained this grace from heaven that he lectures beautifully, is acute in debate, and in his writings and his words is valuable and accepted by both the brethren and seculars. You will therefore, if you please, apply your sedulous fatherly concern in this matter, as you know is expedient, without delay to look to his peace of mind and to provide for the progress of his students.

My very dear brother in Christ, R. de Frille, the warden of Stamford, has asked me, as far as I can and know, to appeal to your goodness, to help him by your fatherly kindness with gentle consolation. I ask you, my dearest father, to convey to your holy and lovable congregation individually my greetings and service.

[3] John of Weston served as fourth in succession of lectors at Cambridge: Eccleston, pp. 49, 58. Here as elsewhere Adam showed anxiety that the general's requests to send recruits to Paris should not denude the English province of its best academic talents.
[4] Cf. Job 6: 12.

196

To William of Nottingham, provincial minister

(1250 × 1251)

Fratri Willelmo, ministro Anglie, Frater Ada salutem, cum spiritu consilii salutaris et impauide fortitudinis.

Ascripsit michi nuper uestra pia paternitas, ut insinuarem uobis si in ea perseuerarem adhuc sententia de electione ministrorum quam aliquando uisus fui approbare. Ad quod non bene liquet quid respondeam, cum utrinque immineant, ut uideo, multiplicia dampnorum discrimina. Verumptamen secundum quod modicitatis mee tarditas in re tam magna ualet conicere, satis erit in hac parte sanctorum exemplis et traditionibus patrum, accedente eisdem rationum efficacia, adherere, quam coactis casse uociferationis persuasionibus acquiescere, secundum quod nonnunquam de hoc articulo meos qualescunque conceptus uestre aperui uiua uoce discretioni.

Mandastis etiam de tribus fratribus uobis per litteram exprimendis, quos ad ministerium uicarie in absentia uestra iam instante[1] exilitas mea censeret fore nominandos. Quamobrem perpensis personarum et negotii, prout potui, circumstantiis, primo quidem Fratrem * * *,[a] secundo uero Fratrem * * *,[a] tertio uero Fratrem * * *,[a] secundum preceptionis uestre tenorem designandos putaui ex ordine. Quorum primus propter auctoritatem uirtutis, secundus propter circumspectionis experientiam, tertius propter emulationem pietatis, omnes nichilominus propter note probitatis conuersationem, secundum nunc positam seriem occurrunt exprimendi.

De desideratissimis patribus Fratre * * *[a] et * * *,[a] ceterisque inter fratres uiris prouidis et discretis ad officium huiuscemodi ydoneis, hoc omnimodis affecto, in quo eisdem, ni fallor, consultius credo prouidendum ad Dei honorem, ad sui salutem, ad multorum edificationem, uidelicet ut post tam uaria et tanta occupationum pondera, post tot et tam distrahentes sollicitudinum lacerationes, post tot inestimabiles sancte uacationis perturbationes, ita consulatur

196   *a* *Name omitted in MS.*

196   [1] The minister's impending absence, which required the appointment of a vicar, was caused by his attendance at the general chapter, presumably the chapter of Genoa in 1251; see Letter 8 n. 13.

196

To William of Nottingham, provincial minister

(1250 × 1251)

Brother Adam to Brother William, minister of England, greetings with a spirit of saving counsel and fearless strength.

You recently wrote to me, good father, to indicate to you whether I still continued to hold that opinion concerning the election of ministers that I once seemed to approve. I am not very clear how I should reply to this since, as I see it, either way involves numerous risks of harm. Truly, as far as the slow wits of my humble self are able to form a conclusion in so great a question, it will be enough to abide by the examples of the saints and the traditions of the fathers in this matter, effectively applying to them the judgement of reason, rather than to yield to the persuasion of vain and vociferous arguments; as regards which, I have sometimes disclosed to your discreet self some ideas of mine on this subject by word of mouth.

You have also commanded me to state to you by letter my opinion of three brothers whom my wretched self might deem fit to be nominated to the office of vicar in your absence, which is now imminent.[1] Therefore, having pondered the circumstances of the persons and the business, as far as I could, in accordance with the sense of your command, I think that Brother * * * should be designated first, Brother * * * second, and Brother * * * third in order of choice; of these, the first on account of the strength of his authority, the second on account of his tried prudence, the third on account of the zeal of his piety. All of them, in the order stated, are none the less named on account of the known integrity of their lives.

As regards the dear fathers, Brother * * * and Brother * * * and the rest of the caring and discreet men among the brethren who are suitable for an office of this kind, what I desire for them in every way is this, by which I believe, if I am not mistaken, the honour of God will be more advisably assured, as will the salvation of each of them and the edification of many, that is that, after the burden of such various and great matters, after the laceration of so many and such distracting anxieties, after so much disturbance of their holy retreat, they may be given such consideration that, by strength of mind,

ut et per mentis uigorem, et rationis industriam, et affectionis diligentiam, imperfectum suum discutere et ad perfectiones diuinas karismata celestia affluentibus percepturi, ualeant conscendere, perceptaque cumulatius postmodum ad profectum aliorum dispensare. Numquid non angeli Dei sunt ascendentes et descendentes in scala, cui innixum Dominum uidit ille patriarcha?[2] Succingo sermonem, sciens cui loquor. Sufficit enim occasionem prestare sapienti.

Ad hoc signastis, ut de facto Fratris Thome de Eboraco, non immerito fratribus in Christo karissimo, uobis insufficientie mee consilium intimarem; propter quod discretionis uestre paternitati, quatenus michi ueritatis contuitus non obducitur, suadeo quatinus dictum Fratrem Thomam ob claritatem ingenii et litterature peritiam et moderamen honestatis, quibus diuinitus est insignitus, precipiatis studio diuinorum eloquiorum applicare, lectiones doctorum audiendo et inuestigando scripta dictorum, dum adhuc iuuenilis etas maturiora tardat experimenta, nequaquam eidem hac uice onus impendende eruditionis imponentes. Secundum coniecturam meam, si Frater Thomas de Eboraco in officio legendi fuerit occupatus, citius forte eueniet quod de ipso timetur. De quo michi bonum uidetur quod assignetur fratribus Oxonie pro lectore,[3] ipsum retinendi gratia ad multimodas, diuinitate propitia, utilitates. Alias, si sic Dominus de ipso ordinauerit, ut alibi quam in regno Anglie propter electorum utilitatem occupetur, non est securum per cautelas humanas superne dispensationi contrauenire.

Rogauit me Frater Hugo de Leukenor', frater boni moris et spei laudabilis, uestram interpellare pietatem, ut non displiceat sanctitati uestre iniungere, quibus est assignatus pro lectore, ut eidem prouidere, secundum quod competit, satagant, aut ipsum ab obligatione dicte assignationis, si sic uestro sederit beneplacito, absoluta non querantur.

Insinuarunt michi fratres quidam quod Fratris Thome de Maydenstan, nouitii, qui diutine ualetudinis dudum laborauit molestia, amotio de conuentu Oxoniensi plurium, de quorum conuersione concepta est spes non modica per Dei mediationem diuinitus operanda, dampnum animabus fore creditur illatura. Propterea cum memoratis fratribus, accedentibus ad hoc ceterorum fratrum

---

[2] See Gen. 28: 12.
[3] Meaning that Thomas should succeed to the lectureship of Oxford when the existing incumbent vacated it. The aim was that every house should have a lector and also a designated student friar who was preparing to succeed him. On the system of assignation

ordered focus, and and loving desire, they may shake off their imperfections and be able to ascend to divine perfection and the heavenly charismata that flow from it, and after a period of time to dispense what they have received for the profit of others. Was it not the angels of God ascending and descending on a ladder terminating in the Lord that the patriarch saw?[2] I am cutting short my remarks, knowing to whom I am speaking; for it is enough to offer a wise man an opportunity.

Added to this, you have signified that my inadequate self should intimate to you my advice about Brother Thomas of York, who is deservedly very dear to our brethren in Christ. On this account, in view of the bright genius, accomplished learning, and well-governed integrity with which Brother Thomas has been divinely endowed, I urge your fatherly discretion, so far as my perception of the truth is not overstretched, to command him to apply himself to the study of the word of God, to hear the lectures of the doctors, and examine their writings, and while his youth is yet untried by experience, by no means to impose the burden of teaching upon him at this time. My guess is that if Brother Thomas of York is occupied as a lecturer, what we fear in his case will probably quickly happen. It seems good to me that he should be assigned as future lector to the brethren at Oxford,[3] so as to retain him, with God's favour, for many kinds of service. Otherwise, if the Lord ordains for him to be occupied elsewhere than in the English kingdom for the benefit of those who choose him, it is not safe to adopt human precautions to oppose the dispensation of heaven.

Brother Hugh of Lewknor, a brother of good conduct and praiseworthy hopes, has asked me to appeal to your holiness to be so good as to instruct those to whom he has been assigned as lector to try to make suitable provision for his needs or, if such is your decision, not to complain at his release from the obligation of the said assignation.

Certain brothers have suggested to me that the removal from the Oxford community of Brother Thomas of Maidstone, a novice suffering from a long-lasting health problem, is thought to be damaging to many souls, whose conversion is much hoped for through the intervention of God. On this account I join with the brothers I have mentioned, added to the desires of the rest of the

see next para. and Little, *Franciscan Papers, Lists and Documents*, pp. 62–3. Each house was required to support its *lector assignatus* at his studies.

desideriis, rogo humiliter quatinus dictum Fratrem Thomam in collegio nostro ad presens morari concedatis.

Cum Fratre Iohanne de Stanford clementie uestre obnixius pulso pietatem, supplicans deuote quatinus dicto Fratri Iohanni concedere uelitis, ut secundum quod ordinatum est pro negotiis apostolicis ad partes accesserit aquilonares. Fratri Iohanni de Warewyk de sibi iniuncte penitentie grauaminibus aliquid consolatorie relaxationis temperamentum ualeat uice uestra, secundum quod Dominus inspirauerit, si tamen hoc merita penitentis requisierint, misericorditer impendere.

Valeat pie paternitatis uestre incolumitas in Christo, etc. Insufficientiam meam et Fratris Iohannis karissimam animam apud fratrum pias memorias, si placet, innouetis. Valeant, oro, karissimi fratres, socii uestri, et ceteri uestre sanctitatis filii, in benedicto Saluatore et ipsius piissima Matre.

197

To William of Nottingham, provincial minister

(1251)

Fratri Willelmo, ministro Anglie, Frater Ada salutem et deuotissimam subiecti famulatus obedientiam.

Quod facere in persona non ualeo, ut ualeo, facio per litteram, uidelicet paternitatis uestre piam profectionem[1] obsequali prosequor affectione, quam ad interuentum Regine celorum et Dei patrocinium protegat et muniat presidium angelorum et sanctorum contubernium adiuuet, et fulciat suffragium sacramentorum, ad gloriam nominis Altissimi et ecclesie sue salutem.

In facto Fratris Ricardi Cornubiensis[2] obnixius supplico iuxta consuetam benigne circumspectionis clementiam, habito cum eodem super statu suo tractatu familiarioris diligentie, optabilem fauorabilis opere gratiam propter Dominum exhibere non ducatis indignum. Mitto uobis per presentium portitorem tractatum Ricardi de Sancto Victore de Trinitate[3] corrigendum Parisius, secundum quod michi uestri gratia uiua uoce dixistis.

Valeat, etc.

---

197 [1] William was setting out to attend the general chapter of 1251 held at Genoa; cf. Letter 8 n. 13.

community, in humbly asking you to grant that the said Brother Thomas may remain for the present in our community.

With Brother John of Stamford I earnestly and devotedly beg you to permit the said Brother John to proceed to the northern parts for papal business, following what has been ordained; acting in your place, he could, as the Lord inspires him, mercifully console Brother John of Warwick with a measure of relaxation from the troubles of the penance enjoined on him, provided, however, that the merits of the penitent call for it.

Farewell, good father, in Christ, etc. Please remember my inadequate self and the dear soul of Brother John to our good brethren. My farewells to the dear brothers, your companions, and the rest of the sons of your holiness, in our blessed Saviour and his most holy Mother.

197

To William of Nottingham, provincial minister

(1251)

Brother Adam to Brother William, minister of England, greetings with devoted service and humble obedience.

What I am unable to do in person, I do, as I can, by letter, that is pursue your pious departure,[1] father, with my humble affection. May the guardian angels protect and fortify you, by the intercession of the Queen of Heaven and the protection of God, the company of the saints help you, and the sacraments give you support, to the glory of the name of the Most High and for the safety of his Church.

Regarding the matter of Brother Richard of Cornwall,[2] having had a full and intimate discussion with him about his situation, I earnestly request you, following your usual kindness and prudence, to be so good as to grant him, for the Lord's sake, the wished-for grace for his promising work. I am sending you by the hand of the carrier of this letter the treatise of Richard of St Victor *De Trinitate*[3] to be corrected at Paris, as you were kind enough to tell me by word of mouth.

Farewell, etc.

---

[2] Richard of Cornwall; see Letters 182 n. 2, 190, and 203.
[3] *De Trinitate libri sex*: *PL* cxcvi, 887–994; modern edn. by J. Ribaillier (Bruges, 1958).

Insufficientiam meam reuerendissimo patri, ministro generali;[4] ⟨et⟩ ceteris patribus et fratribus ordinis nostri, prout noueritis et uolueritis, rogo, si placet, recommendetis. Opto supradictum librum correctum ad me quantocius[a] remitti, si tamen uobiscum eum non contingat deferri.

Iterum ualete. Inexhaustam liberalitatis uestre munificentiam arbitror plus honorandam silentio quam eloquio prosequendam.

198

To William of Nottingham, provincial minister

(1251)

Fratri Willelmo, ministro Anglie, Frater Ada salutem et deuotissimum perhennis obedientie famulatum.

Non tam fraterne cause pietas quam benignitas clementie paterne fiduciam prestat interpellandi, ubi et saluti consulitur et inseruitur ueritati. Proinde acceptissimum Fratrem Thomam de Dokkyng,[1] quem et suauissime conuersationis honestas, et claritas ingenii perspicacis, et litterature prouectioris eminentia, et facundia prompti sermonis illustrant insignius, humiliter obsecro, rogans obnixius quatinus circumspecte discretionis liberalitate consueta benignius respicientes, Bibliam karissimi P. de Wygorn' pie recordationis eidem ad usum salutarem assignare uelitis; tanto propensiori fauoris seduli gratia presentem petitionem, si placet, suscipientes, quanto is pro quo petitur meritis clarescit insignibus, et id quod petitur iudicio maiorum censetur benignius exaudiendum. Insuper non desunt qui de pretio libri memorati cumulatius, ut audio, satisfaciant.

Valeat, etc.

Titulum[a] exclusit occupationum cogentia,[2] angustauitque litteram temporis angustia. Quasi simul recepi uestram et rescripsi meam. Paternitatis solamina filialem deuotionem magnifice letificarunt. Sed conceptum sermonem non cohibere[b] ualui de desiderabili filio uestro fratre Willelmo de Hedele. Si cedat hominis ratio prouidentie

---

197 [a] quantociens *MS.*

198 [a] Itulum *MS.*   [b] *After* cohibere *MS repeats* non.

---

[4] John of Parma.

198 [1] Thomas Docking was listed by Eccleston as the seventh lector to the Oxford

I ask you, if you please, to commend my inadequate self to our reverend father, the Minister General,[4] and to the rest of the fathers and brothers of our order, as you wish and know how. I wish the book mentioned above, when it has been corrected, to be returned to me as quickly as possible, if perchance you do not bring it with you.

Again farewell. I think your unexhausted generosity should be more honoured by silence than proclaimed by words.

198

To William of Nottingham, provincial minister

(1251)

Brother Adam to Brother William, minister of England, greetings and perpetual obedience with devoted service.

Both concern for a brother's case and your fatherly kindness give me confidence to appeal to you, when it is in the interest of both salvation and truth. So I humbly beg you to consider with your usual generosity, discretion, and discernment our most esteemed Brother Thomas Docking,[1] who is conspicuously distinguished by his upright and most gracious life, the clarity and perspicacity of his intellect, his outstanding progress in learning, and his ready and eloquent speech, and I earnestly request that you would assign to him for his religious use the Bible of our very dear P. of Worcester of pious memory; and that you would receive this request and, if you please, favour it, all the more readily as he for whom it is requested is distinguished by his shining merits, and the request is considered acceptable by the judgement of his superiors. Moreover, there is no lack of those who would, I hear, meet the price of the said book.

Farewell, etc.

Urgency of business has made me omit the address,[2] and shortage of time has shortened my letter. I have received your letter and written my reply as if simultaneously. Your fatherly consolation has given your devoted son much joy; but I could not hold back what I had in mind to say about your dear son Brother William of Hadley. If

school; on his career and commentaries see Little, *Franciscan Papers, Lists and Documents*, pp. 98-121, and *BRUO* i. 580, and J. I. Catto in *HUO* i. 493-4.

[2] Despite the absence of the addressee's title, the copyist set this out as a separate letter. I have followed Brewer in treating it as a postscript to Adam's previous letter to William of Nottingham.

diuinitatis, gaudendum fore putaui et longanimiter ferendum de irreuocabili Fratris Ricardi de Cornubia intentione.[3] Indignam mee modicitatis insufficientiam filiorum et nostrorum fratrum orationibus suppliciter rogo per uestre paternitatis sedulam in Domino recommendari beneuolentiam.

Valeat honoranda sanctitatis uestre suauitas in Christo, etc.

Molestum est, puto, sine causa quod tantum prorogatur uestre circumspectionis alloquium. De Fratre Eustachio de Normanuill',[4] cuius laudanda conuersatio fratribus ingerit dignam exultationem, sit per omnia diuino nomini superexaltata benedictio. Quod uobis supplicabitur exaudiri desidero dumtaxat hac uice per uenerabilem patrem gardianum Oxon'; necnon et de dilecto Fratre Hugone de Lyndun',[5] erga quem et mentis angustia et ualetudo corporis benigniorem inuitat clementiam.

199

To William of Nottingham, provincial minister

Fratri Willelmo, ministro Anglie, Frater Ada salutem et deuotum supplicis obedientie famulatum.

Cum secundum diuine districtionis sententiam inflexibilem superni examinis terrificam interminationem pastores animarum incurrant, non tam qui quod forte est custodire negligunt quam qui quod abiectum est reducere contempnunt, noui quod indefessa sancte sollicitudinis uigilantia, per quam cunctis ad pietatis uestre curam pertinentibus iugiter prouidere curatis, petitiones salutares ad fraternam reformationem suspirantes in sedule miserationis uiscerali suauitate nescit non admittere.

Quocirca paternitatis uestre per presentem litteram consuetam pulso benignitatem, supplicans humiliter et obnixe rogans, quatinus ob contemplationem Ipsius, qui uel qualicunque uiolatus iniuria uel scelere quantocunque offensus, saluificis adquiescentem consiliis ab immensa non repellit clementia, quondam filium uestrum et fratrem nostrum A. de Brangford', licet reum apostatice preuaricationis, tamen auidum salutifere restitutionis, misericorditer recipere et salubriter expedire non ducatis indignum, aut in pristinum ordinis deserti gradum ipsum admittendo, aut secundum formam sue impetrationis eidem viam saluationis aperiendo.

Valeat paternitatis uestre sincera sanctitas in Christo Iesu, et.

---

[3] Richard's intention was to transfer himself from Oxford to Paris to teach theology; see

human reason is to yield to divine providence, I think we should rejoice over the irrevocable intention of Brother Richard of Cornwall and bear it with patience.[3] I humbly ask that my unworthy and inadequate self may through your fatherly and persistent kindness be commended in the Lord to the prayers of your sons and our brethren.

Farewell, your honoured and gracious holiness in Christ, etc.

It is vexatious, I think, for me to be prolonging my address to your prudent person without a cause. Blessed and exalted be the divine name for Brother Eustace of Normanville,[4] whose praiseworthy life has made the brethren suitably joyful. I desire that the request that will be made to you, at least this time through our venerable father, the guardian of Oxford, be accepted; also that in regard to our dear Brother Hugh of Lyndun,[5] whose mental trouble and bodily health call for greater kindness and forebearance.

199

To William of Nottingham, provincial minister

Brother Adam to Brother William, minister of England, greetings amd humble obedience with devoted service.

Since not only the pastors of souls who neglect to watch over what is strong, but those who scorn to bring back what is cast away, incur the fearful, unbending, and endless sentence of divine judgement, I know with what tireless vigilance and solicitude you constantly provide for those committed to your care, and that your goodness never fails to admit with heartfelt mercy and sweetness petitions that sigh for the reformation of a brother.

Therefore, contemplating the immense clemency of Him who, whether profaned by any wrongdoing or however much offended by a sin, does not reject one who assents to saving counsels, with this letter I am beating upon the door of your habitual kindness with a humble request to be so good as to receive your former son and our brother, A. of Brangford, mercifully and take care of him, although he is guilty of apostasy, yet eager for saving restitution, either admitting him to his early rank in the order he has deserted, or opening for him a path of salvation according to the form of his application.

Farewell, your fatherly holiness in Christ, etc.

Letter 203; see comment by Peter Raedts, *Richard Rufus of Cornwall and the Tradition of Oxford Theology* (Oxford, 1987) pp. 5–8.

[4] Eustace of Normanville; see Letter 176 n. 1.   [5] Cf. Letter 202.

200

To William of Nottingham, provincial minister

(1250–1)

Fratri Willelmo, ministro Anglie, Frater Ada (salutem).

Quid dicam ignoro de facto ordinis nostri. Video enim quasi subuersum iri uniuersam*ᵃ* edificii sublimis in illo structuram, tam stupenda omnibus seculis dispensatione diuinitus erectam, presertim cum a fundamentis non tam negligatur per ignauiam, quam ex arbitrio dissipetur; nouicios quoque, quorum uigor ualidus et preclara ingenia et feruens deuotio curari nullatenus uidetur; sed non obstantibus etatis infirmitate, caloris flagrantia et inexperientia moris, postquam tamen in tanta multitudine tam electe persone celitus a seculo euocate collegiis aggregantur, quando (ut uos melius nostis, et quis uobis consideratius?) eis opus esset et doctrina celestis et salutis exemplum, et ante omnia deuotum sancte Dei uacationis otium, quasi carni et sanguini, quasi luto et lateribus, quasi lignis et lapidibus, quasi quibuscunque qualicunque compendiolo, mundanis questibus totum dandum esset, et perficiende sanctissime professionis beatitudini nichil omnino debeatur, non tam crudeliter quam insipienter quam et pernecabiliter. Iterum, passim et indifferenter postposita cura salutari circa illos adhibenda, occurrente quantulacunque occasiuncula in secularium pernicierum discrimina, a quibus sunt euecti per promissas celice religionis obseruantias usque ad angelorum contubernia, absque cuiuscunque districtionis delectu incessanter detruduntur. O horrendum facinus! O detestandam incuriam! O execrandam impietatem!

Quod diuina clementia, per tam pie prouisionis consilium ruenti regno Dei hiis nouissimorum dierum temporibus periculosis in tanta celebritate tam efficax prouidit subsidium,[1] dissipatur tam conculcabiliter in terra prophanatum, ut timeri possit quod uadant et ueniant super illud horribiles, quod tamen in fundamentali frequentia nouellarum animarum subinde—sit diuino nomini benedictio—ad |

---

200   ᵃ uniuersum *MS.*

200   [1] Here Adam echoes the opinion of many Franciscans who identified the friars with the 'spiritual people' prophesied by Joachim of Fiore to be provided by God to succour the faithful in the tempestuous last days of the world.

200

To William of Nottingham, provincial minister

(1250–1)

Brother Adam to Brother William, minister of England, (greetings).

I do not know what to say about the state of our order. For I see the entire structure of the sublime edifice, raised up by a divine dispensation such as should be the marvel of all ages, in danger of being destroyed, particularly since it is not so much being neglected in its foundations by sloth as willfully demolished by policy; the same goes for the novices, whose active strength, outstanding intelligence, and fervent devotion seem to be cherished not at all; but notwithstanding the weakness of their age, the heat of their passions and untried character, when such a multitude of characters chosen from the world by heaven are brought together in communities, when (as you know better than I, and who can judge better than you?) it was supremely necessary for them to have religious instruction and a salutary example, and above all, the devout leisure for holy time dedicated to God, all attention was given over, as it were, to flesh and blood, mortar and buildings, wood and stones, and to worldly alms-begging, and nothing at all is regarded as owing to the cultivation of the blessed perfection of our most holy profession; this is done not so much out of cruelty as foolishly, but with deadly effect. Again, everywhere and without discrimination the care that should be shown for their salvation is being disregarded, and at even the slightest little opportunity that occurs, without alternative choice they are thrust back into the wickedness and dangers of the world, from which they were extricated and raised to the company of the angels by the observances of heavenly religion. Oh what a dreadful sin! What a detestable failure of care! What an execrable lack of piety!

Effectual help of such a great throng, which the divine clemency has provided by His wise counsel to aid the collapsing kingdom of God in this dangerous time of the last days,[1] is scattered and profanely trodden underfoot, leading one to fear that it may be subject to the fluctuation of dreadful events; yet He has established it—blessed be the name of God—in its base with a continuous supply of new souls coming to us to complete it to perfection. He

f. 69 nos uenientium, ut perficiat ad perfectum, Ille constituit, cuius 'opera sunt perfecta, et omnes uie eius iudicia'.[2]

Cohibeo calamum, sciens quam efficaciter huius tante rei anime uestre caracteres impresserit beatus Dei digitus. Ut quid ergo anime presenti ulterius laborarem scripture prolixioris atramentum protrahere et imponere? Nullatenus credo quod securum sit labores profectionis uestre, quam Saluator protegat, assumere,[3] priusquam illam salutari sacrificio huius ruine reformande diuinitate placata cum omnimoda circumspectione muniueritis.

Conseruet animam uestram Saluator animarum.

201

To William of Nottingham, provincial minister

Pio patri, Fratri Willelmo, ministro Anglie, Frater Ada salutem et supplicem prompte deuotionis obedientiam.

Ad clementem piorum uiscerum affluentiam tanto fiducialius in pietatis acceditur negotiis, quanto et displicendi desperatio et spes impetrandi humilem ad interpellandum animant presumptionem. Quocirca pro karissimo michi in Christo Fratre Hugone de Lyndun'[1] familiaris amicitie mee modicitati dudum deuincto spirituali necessitate, paternitatis uestre supplico pietati, cum eodem humiliter obsecrans ut, perpensis suarum necessitatum articulis uobis per ipsius litteram exponendis, quatenus et cordis consolatio et remedium ualetudinis requirere cognoscitur, secundum quod beneplacitum uestre circumspectionis censuerit et sue saluti in Domino fuerit consultum, eidem fratri propensiorem pii fauoris gratiam prouidere non ducatis indignum; nequaquam putantes ad excessum quod aliquamdiu sub uestri patrocinii fiducia Oxonie moram traxerit, loci custodem expectans.

Valeat pia uestre sanctitatis incolumitas in Christo, etc.

Cum dilecto patre, Fratre Martino, gardiano Oxoniensi, ceterisque fratribus ibidem commorantibus, ego qualiscunque uestram per Christum rogo prouidentiam, quatinus fratrum, cleri et populi, ob diuinum honorem et ministerium salutare suscipientes desiderium,

---

[2] Deut. 32: 4.

[3] Referring to William's preparations to set out for the general chapter of the order to be held at Genoa in 1251, cf. Letter 8 n. 13.

201 [1] Cf. Letters 189, 202.

has constructed it, whose 'works are perfect and all His ways are judgement'.[2]

I restrain my pen, knowing how efficaciously the blessed finger of God will imprint upon your soul the particulars of this so important matter. Why, therefore, should I labour to expend more ink and impose more prolix writing on your receptive soul? I believe it by no means safe for you to undertake the labour involved in your setting off[3]—which our Saviour protect—before you have secured it by the salutary sacrifice of reforming this ruinous situation, appeasing God in every way with your prudent judgement.

May the Saviour of souls keep your soul.

201

To William of Nottingham, provincial minister

Brother Adam to his good father Brother William, minister of England, greetings and a supplication with prompt and devoted obedience.

In religious matters we approach the overflowing kindness of your heart all the more confidently because our hopelessness of displeasing you and our hope of gaining a request encourage our presumption to make an appeal. Therefore I am making a request on behalf of our dear brother in Christ Hugh of Lyndon,[1] a household friend long bound to my poor self by the bonds of spiritual necessity; together with him I humbly beseech you, after you have considered the details of his needs that are to be explained to you in his own letter, you would be so good as to grant him the more ready favour and grace, insofar as he is known to be in need of consolation and a remedy for his ill health, according to your good pleasure and prudent judgement and what is advisable for his salvation in the Lord. You may think it by no means out of the question that he should extend his stay at Oxford for some time in the confidence of your fatherly favour, awaiting the custodian of the place.

Farewell, your holiness, in Christ, etc.

Together with our dear father, Brother Martin, the guardian of Oxford, and the rest of the brothers residing there, I, such as I am, ask you of your providence in Christ to support the desire of the brothers, clergy, and people, and for the honour of God and the ministry of

ordinare uelitis, ut Frater G. de Sancto Eadmundo conuentui fratrum
Oxonie restituatur, litteram super hoc, si placet, scribentes sine more
dispendio.

Iterum et in eternum ualeat desiderabilis uestre benignitatis
clementia.

202

To William of Nottingham, provincial minister

Fratri Willelmo, ministro Anglie, Frater Ada salutem et tam debitam
quam deuotam humilitatis obedientiam.

Doleo, mi pater clementissime, quod paruitatis (mee) petitio
effectum non est assecuta, si ratio non obsistit quominus fieret de
karissimo Hugone de Lyndun'[1] ad incolumitatem corporis et spiritus
consolationem. Verumptamen licet faciem obducat improbitatis
repulse nutans uerecundia, mens auida fraterne pacis, sicut reor,
non cunctatur super eisdem cartas implere caracteribus, sciens quod
prestabit paterna benignitas que non meruit filialis deuotio. Hic est
ergo obsecrationis mee calculus, ut ad suauem uestre pietatis
sanctitatem cum accesserit memoratus Frater Hugo, cui me spiritualiter inter mortales teneri fateor, exposito[a] uobis uiua uoce sue
consolationis articulo, secundum quod requirit et corporis ualetudo
et quietatio spiritus eidem consuete miserationis gratia prouidere non
ducatis indignum.

Valeat suauis paternitatis benignitas in Christo Iesu semper et
beatissima Virgine.

203

To William of Nottingham, provincial minister

(1253)

Fratri Willelmo, ministro Anglie, Frater Ada supplicem deuote
promptitudinis obedientiam.

Quum quod omnimodo nolo, scribo, quid scribam uix inuenio.
Calamum tamen, quem recondit amor, timor exserit. Nostis, mi

202   [a] exposita MS.

salvation, to arrange for Brother G. of St Edmund to be restored to the convent of the friars at Oxford, and that you would, if you please, write a letter about this without delay.

Again and for ever farewell to your kind and gracious person.

202

To William of Nottingham, provincial minister

Brother Adam to Brother William, minister of England, greetings with due, devoted, and humble obedience.

I am sorry, kind father, that the request by my little self has had no result, unless there is a reason against my request regarding the bodily health and spiritual consolation of our very dear Hugh of Lyndon.[1] Nevertheless, though shame might hesitate, like one who has gone too far and been repulsed, my mind, eager for a brother's peace, as I see it, has no hesitation in filling parchment with letters on the subject, in the knowledge that your fatherly kindness will grant what my filial devotion has not merited. Therefore the sum of my entreaty is this: that when Brother Hugh, who is I confess among all mortals spiritually bound to me, comes to your gracious holiness and explains by word of mouth the particulars calling for his consolation, with your usual compassion and grace you will be good enough to provide him with what his bodily health and spiritual peace require.

Farewell, kind and gracious father, in Christ Jesus and the Blessed Virgin.

203

To William of Nottingham, provincial minister

(1253)

Brother Adam to Brother William, minister of England, devoted and prompt obedience and a humble request.

Since I write most unwillingly, I can hardly find what to say; but fear drives my pen to write what love would withold. You know, dearest father, how very dear the presence of Brother Richard of

---

202   [1] Cf. Letters 198, 201.

amantissime, quam sit karissima Fratris Ricardi Cornubie[1] filiis
uestris opportuna presentia, quam titulorum laudabilium eminens
euidentia fratribus uniuersis reddit desiderabilem, cui conuersationis
honestas et claritas scientie, pietas affectionis et opinionis integritas,
facultas erudiendi et disserendi subtilitas, sic ad notiora meritorum
suffraguntur argumenta, quod et ipsorum manifesta consideratio
nostre professioni magnorum, mediocrium et minorum, tam in
clero quam in populo, salutare contubernium pariter et fidelem
amicitiam conciliare cognoscuntur.

Proinde, cum ante dies aliquot ob uehementiores perturbationum
occasiones dictus Frater Ricardus inexorabile concepit propositum
transferendi se, secundum concessionem ministri generalis olim
indultam, in prouinciam Francie, secundum quod fuerit propitia
diuinitas Parisius aliquamdiu moraturum,[2] et sic eidem ulterius
angustie desolatio, cum ad manendum nobiscum ipsum cogat deti-
nentia prorogatior, non tam amantissimo fratri uoluntarie compatiens, quam inuite consentiens anxioribus eius instantiis, pro sepe
memorato Fratre Ricardo et cum illo, cum quantis possum affectuum
diligentiis et uice ceterorum fratrum eum ad eternam salutem
emulantium, obsecro suppliciter exorans obnixius ut, si preexhibitis
circumspectionis paterne remediis ad remanendum apud nos nullatenus induci ualeat, ex inolita benigne sedulitatis clementia, propter
superbenigni Saluatoris contemplationem, suspensum desiderii filialis
exitum, cum ydoneo societatis solatio et necessario codicum adiutorio, secundum celitus datam uobis industriam, pia prosecutione
maturare curetis. Insipiens factus sum. Postulantis urgentia me
coegit.

Valeat paternitatis uestre pietas.

Ne forte memorie uestre ⟨exciderit⟩ propter occupationum uar-
ietatem tenor indulgentialis littere, quam piissimus pater minister
generalis Fratri Ricardo in suo recessu reliquit,[3] dicte littere tenorem
signo memorati generalis signato, quem nuper aspexi adhuc penes
prefatum Fratrem Ricardum remanentem, sanctitatis uestre discretioni sub sigillo nostro mitto transcriptum.

Cornwall[1] is to your sons. His praiseworthy qualities, of which there is eminent evidence, win him the affection of all the brethren. The integrity of his life, his brilliant learning, his pious disposition and the soundness of his opinions, the abundance of his erudition and his subtlety in debate, are proofs of his merits that are well known. We know that regard for these qualities of his brings together people great, small, and of middle rank, both clergy and people, in a saving association with, and loyal friendship to our religious profession.

Well then, a few days ago the said Brother Richard has, on account of powerful forces destructive of tranquillity, made a decision to transfer himself to the French province to stay, if with God's favour, some time at Paris,[2] in accordance with a permit granted him by the Minister General; and he suffers further anguish because he is forced to prolong his stay with us. While not so much willing to sympathize with a well-loved brother, as unwillingly yielding to his anxious perseverance, I humbly implore, for and with the aforesaid Richard, with all the feeling I can and on behalf of the rest of the brothers, who are anxious for his salvation, with an earnest request that, if he can by no means be induced to stay with us when your fatherly prudence has offered him a remedy, then that you would with your native compassion and kind solicitude and out of regard for our supremely benevolent Saviour be kind enough to piously further and hasten the delayed departure your son desires, with the comfort of a suitable companion and the assistance of the books he needs. I have been made foolish. I have been forced by the pressure of his request.

Farewell, good father.

In case the contents of the letter of indulgence, which was left for Brother Richard by our good father, the Minister General on his departure,[3] should have escaped your memory on account of your various preoccupations, I am sending your prudent holiness a transcript of the contents of the said letter sealed with the seal of the Minister General, which I recently inspected when it was still in the possession of the said Brother Richard.

---

203 [1] Cf. Letter 182 n. 2; also Letters 190, 197.

[2] Raedts suggests that Richard was disturbed and sought a transfer to Paris because Thomas of York, a younger man, had been preferred before him as lector at Oxford: *Richard Rufus of Cornwall*, pp. 5–9.

[3] The reference is to the visit to England by John of Parma, Minister General, in 1248, when he presided over a provincial chapter at Oxford: Eccleston, p. 73; Little, *Franciscan Papers, Lists and Documents*, p. 210.

204

To William of Nottingham, provincial minister

Fratri Willelmo, ministro Anglie, Frater Ada.

Mitto uobis litteram michi a ministro generali destinatam, si placet, inspiciendam, ut, si fieri potest a uestre paternitatis circumspecta discretione, declinem tam dispendiosam animo corporique tam importunam in presentiarum uexationem. Nempe nostis apud me et uirtutis defectionem et tenuitatem habilitatis*a* et luminum teneritudinem et etatis prouectionem, et ualetudinum discrimina faciliter imminentia. Vnde studium quod indies, licet lento conatu, ut ualeo tamen nuper inchoatum actito, non mediocri dampno dissipationis subiacebit, cum euidenti persone dispendio, non sine anxiis noctis molestiis, si contra instantes inquietudines michi remedium non prouideatur.[1] Quale erit si me miserum cogat per dies amaros, per f. 69^v tempus infructuosum ad | festinum exitum paterne prouidentie dispensatio? Fateor quia, ni fallor, satis michi tolerabilius esset exilium, quantumcunque foret diuturnum.

Quomodo ad infelicitatis cumulum non accedat, si pro solamine, si pro clementi consilio, non sine derisionibus recipiam conuicia, recipiam uituperia, recipiam diras obiurgationes? Longe sint a patrum inolita benignitate et torui uultus et oculi terribiles, maxime contra subiectam deuotionem et famulatum obtemperantem.

Videtur michi quod si cursor occurrerit Bedeford die Beati Alexandri[2] ministro adhuc, ut signauit, tunc uenturo, cum litteris uestris et meis petituris pro mea quiete posset idem cursor feria quarta uel quinta proxima sequente ad me redire Rading'. Ego quoque feria sexto uel sabbato in equo ⟨possem⟩ uenire Bedeford, si nullatenus minister uelit assentire nostris petitionibus; si aliquid consilii poterit in me inueniri, super articulis qui modo instare cognoscuntur, nonne sine exhibitione corporalis presentie cum tanto mentis et corporis grauamine, possem illud litteratorie, si tamen opus esset, quod nullo modo credo, presertim ubi uos eritis, requisitus respondere?

Valeat, etc.

---

204   *a* ebetudinis *MS*.

204

To William of Nottingham, provincial minister

Brother Adam to Brother William, minister of England.

I am sending you a letter sent to me by the Minister General for your inspection, if you please, so that if it can be done through your fatherly prudence, I may avoid at present a vexation so costly to my spirit and so inopportune for my body. To be sure, you know my failing strength, the paucity of my skill, the feebleness of my sight, my advanced age, and the easily brought on crises of my health. From this[1] the studies recently begun, in which, though the effort is slow, I am engaged from day to day, will suffer greatly from harmful distraction, with obvious personal loss, not without anxiety and trouble at night, if I am not provided with a remedy for my constant disturbance. How will it be if the father's provident dispensation forces my wretched self into an early end through days of bitterness and fruitlessly spent time? I confess that, unless I am mistaken, exile would be more bearable, however prolonged.

How would it fail to add to my accumulated unhappiness if, in return for my consolation and kindly counsel I should receive altercation, not to say scorn, censure, and fierce reproof? Far be fierce faces and dreadful expressions from the natural kindness of the fathers, especially directed against humble devotion and obedient service.

It seems to me that if the carrier comes to Bedford on St Alexander's day,[2] when the minister will be coming there, as he indicated, with your letter and my petition, the carrier could for my peace of mind return to me at Reading on the following Wednesday or Thursday. I also could come to Bedford by horse on the Saturday, if the minister is not at all willing to accede to our petitions. If any counsel can be found in me regarding the articles which we now know to be pressing, could I not reply to questions by letter without showing my physical presence at so much trouble of mind and body, if however it was needed, which I do not believe at all, especially where you will be present?

Farewell, etc.

---

204 [1] i.e. from the task that the Minister General wishes him to undertake.

[2] 3 May: Alexander, pope and Martyr: *BHL* i. 44–5.

Nunquam credatis quod mandatis superiorum uelim aut repugnare aut non acquiescere, sit michi propitia diuinitas; sed contrarietatem iussionibus inherentem, ultra quam credi potest, admirari compellor. Si sic uobis uidetur, mittite presentem cartam uelociter patri ministro inspiciendam.

205

To William of Nottingham, provincial minister

(1252–3)

Fratri Willelmo, ministro Anglie, Frater Ada salutem et quam debitam tam deuotam in omnibus obedientiam.

Inter pregrauantes occupationum angustias fere intercepto uite spiraculo, uix aneli spiritus anxietas, rupto soporis silentio, noctem agens insompnem ut assolet, presentes uoces raptim emittere potuit. Vtinam scisso pectore transfixi cordis angores filiales pater pius aspiceret! Hec idcirco dixerim quoniam dolores remittit miseri ipsos insinuasse clementi. Stilum tremulum meror desolatus prolixius euagari necessitate confusa prohibuit, ut feruor animi uiolenter repressus uehementius inardescat. Sed de hiis hucusque.

Cum de benigna uestre paternitatis concessione, propter pia salutis dirigende negotia, karissimus Frater Gregorius de Bosellis ad inclitos comitem Leycestriensem et comitissam Leycestriensem in Vasconiam proficiscendi,[1] plurimis licet molestatis, licentiam*a* iam tamen obtinuisset; accedentibus rerum cogentiis, propter inestimabiles maiorum causarum considerationes, de mee modicitatis consilio pariter et desiderio plurium magnatorum, presertim ut ego redeundi ad onus eruditionis impendende, non sine pregrandi difficultate tandem eluctatam, inuenirem opportunitatem, quousque de uestre pietatis constaret beneplacito, in contubernio familiari domini Cantuariensis, precum mearum deuictus instantiis morari consensit, diuinitate propitia, ecclesiastice necessitati temporibus periculosissimis non mediocriter profuturus.*b*

Proinde beneuolentie humiliter supplico sedule sanctitati ut de stando et de standi forma cum domino memorato dictum fratrem nostrum et uestrum deuotissimum filium, in desiderio salutari satis

---

205 *a* licenter *MS.*   *b* profuturis *MS.*

Never believe that I wish to oppose or not accept the commands of my superiors, may God be merciful to me; but I am bound to marvel at a paradox inherent in the orders beyond belief. If it seems so to you, send the present letter swiftly to our father the minister for his inspection.

205

To William of Nottingham, provincial minister

(1252-3)

Brother Adam to Brother William, minister of England, greetings and due and devoted obedience in all things.

In the midst of most severe constraints imposed by business, with barely time to gasp and draw breath, interrupting quiet sleep and as usual with sleepless nights, in my anxiety I managed to produce this hasty communication. How I wish my good father could behold the anguish of his broken-hearted son. I say this because it relieves a wretched man's sorrow to have expressed it to a kind person. My grief and desolation have stayed my trembling pen from wandering on at greater length in compulsive confusion, so that from being violently repressed, my spirit burns more fiercely. But enough of this.

Since by your kind concession, father, our dearest brother Gregory de Bosellis obtained your permission to set off, though with much trouble, to join the noble earl and countess of Leicester in Gascony,[1] for the good purpose of giving guidance in a matter of salvation; through the compulsion of events, out of overriding considerations for greater issues, by the counsel of my humble self and at the desire of many magnates, especially so that I might find the opportunity, finally obtained not without a struggle and much trouble, to resume the burden of teaching. So far as it is at your good pleasure, overcome by my pressing requests, he has consented to stay in the household company of my lord of Canterbury, by God's favour to be of no small help to the needs of the Church in very dangerous times.

Therefore I humbly beg your kind and caring holiness, with your customary pity to comfort our said brother and your most devoted son, troubled as he is by a desire for salutary advice, with express

---

205   [1] Cf. Letters 141, 142, 168. Gregory accompanied the archbishop to the Curia at Lyons in 1250, and thence proceeded to join the Montforts in Gascony.

afflictum, cum expressis celestis obedientie mandatis de consueta miseratione uelitis consolari. Vt autem consultiori deliberatione rescribere ualeat, prout oportet uestre circumspectionis industria, reuerentie uestre transmitto per presentium portitorem litteras domini Cantuariensis, domine regine, et Fratris Gregorii, michi super premissis destinatas. Ceterum cui uidebitur quin sit equitandum memorato fratri, cum aut exigit hoc persone periculum aut pietas causarum hoc compellit?[2] Si non obsisteret uirosa oblatrantium calumnia, iugiter reor expediret quod uehiculorum uteretur subsidio. Quoniam maxime in huiusmodi rebus letalis erit uiuendi tractus si non fulciatur uita grauis iucundo socii fidelis adminiculo, propter auctorem concordie socialis in hac parte consolatorie prouideatis, oro, cum effectu.

Valeat uestre paternitatis incolumitas, etc.

206

To William of Nottingham, provincial minister

Fratri Willelmo, ministro Anglie, Frater Ada salutem et deuotam subiecte deuotionis obedientiam.

Letifice paternitatis uestre letus litteras suscepi, per quas exilitatis mee requisitionibus tam efficaciter tam rationabiliter tam diligenter, etiam inter tot negotiorum uexuras, satisfacere uoluit consueta benignitas. Ceterum de mora karissimi Fratris Andree de Lexinton' in prouincia Hybernie[1] quid aliud sentiam non uideo quam quod, prudenter perpensis rerum circumstantiis, cum consilii deliberatioris examine, uestra michi rescripsit sollers industria; uidelicet ut in memorata moretur prouincia prouinciale capitulum proximo futurum celebraturus, ne casso tantarum prouisionum conamine, tam salutarium causarum exitus desiderati, quod absit, frustrari contingant;[a] sed potius que per strenuam prefati fratris sedulitatem, propitia diuinitas, salubriter inchoauit ad gloriam diuini nominis et religionis humane

---

206   [a] contingat *MS.*

[2] The constitutions of Narbonne required friars at all times to go unshod, and they were forbidden to ride except in cases of *manifesta necessitas* approved by superiors: 'Die ältesten Redactionen der Generalconstitutionen des Franz-Ordens' in *ALKG* vi. 91. 104.

206   [1] Andrew of Lexington had received a commission from the Minister General to

orders under heavenly obedience relating to his standing and conditions of residence with the said lord [of Canterbury]. So that with your prudent care you can write back with more informed judgement, I am sending on to your reverence, through the carrier of this, letters of the lord of Canterbury, the lady Queen, and Brother Gregory, sent me about the aforesaid matters. But to whom will it seem that the said brother should not ride by horse when personal danger demands this or in cases where he is obliged to do so by pious duty?[2] If it were not for the virulent yapping of calumniators, I think it would always be expedient to use the help of transport. Because in things of this kind above all, the course of our life would be deadly, if life's burden were not supported by the cheerful help of a faithful companion, I beg you, for the sake of the Author of social concord, to provide us with effectual comfort in this case.

Farewell, father.

206

To William of Nottingham, provincial minister

Brother Adam to Brother William, minister of England, greetings with humble and devoted obedience.

I rejoiced at receiving your letter, father, by which you have with your customary kindness been so good as to satisfy the requests of my poor self so effectively, so reasonably, and so carefully, even when you were in the midst of so much tiresome business. For the rest, as regards the stay of our dearest Brother Andrew of Lexington in the Irish province,[1] I do not see what else to think other than what you have, after considering the circumstances and the deliberation and advice of your council, wisely written in your reply to me: namely that he should stay in the said province to celebrate the next provincial chapter, lest so much effort that went into making provisions should be in vain and—which heaven forbid—the desired outcome of such wholesome causes should be frustrated; but rather that we may rejoice that what God's favour began, acting through the energy and application of our said brother, has been happily accomplished, to the glory of the divine name and the advancement

visit and reform the friars of the Irish province: Letter 176 and E. B. Fitzmaurice and A. G. Little, *Materials for the History of the Franciscan Province of Ireland* (Manchester, 1920) and J. A. Watt, *The Church and the Two Nations in Medieval Ireland* (Cambridge, 1970).

profectum felici fine consummata gaudeamus, presertim cum com-
missio ministri generalis fideliter considerata, plane sic agi deposcat;
ministri quoque Hybernie, ut audio, cum nonnullis fratribus que Dei
sunt pia longanimitate querentibus, hoc feruens flagitet desiderium.
Quod etiam distinguentium articulorum acceptabilis urgentia circumspecte uirtutis emulatione non tam acceptari quam adimpleri, si
diuinitus detur, compellit modis omnibus.

Modicum erit formidanda, licet malignius inseuiat, seuitiosa rabies,
immo per ipsum qui dat 'equo fortitudinem, et circumdat collo eius
hynnitum, suscitans eum sicut locustas, exultandum est, pergendum
in occursum armatis, contempnendus est pauor, nec cedendum
gladio'.[2] Quid enim? Audiamus triumphalem castrorum celestium
propugnatorem: 'Si consistant', inquit, 'aduersum me castra, non
timebit cor meum. Si exsurgat aduersum me prelium in hoc ego
sperabo.'[3] Et alibi: 'Non timebo millia populi circumdantis me.
Exsurge, Domine, saluum me fac, Deus meus.'[4] Respondi que
docuistis. Epistolam abbreuiauit importunitatum prolixitas. Non
quia diu nolui scribere, tardaui; rogaui tamen donari michi hanc
iniuriam.

Valeat uestre paternitais incolumitas in Christo semper et beatissima Virgine.

207

To William of Nottingham, provincial minister

Fratri Willelmo, ministro Anglie, Frater Ada salutem et deuotum
supplicis obedientie famulatum.

Cum humilem nostre professionis assistentiam pia pontificalis
excellentie dignatio uigilantiori requirit sollicitudine, indubitanter
assensu occurrit promptiori, nisi qui uel dilectionem prosequitur
euidenti perfidia uel ficta fide mentitur emulationem. Numquid | non
Christus,[a] Dei uirtus, Dei sapientia, summos sacerdotes tam stabili
quam salutari decreto constituit, ut sint et sal terre, lux mundi,
portantes orbem, dispensatores salutis,[b] preparatores regni, consum-
matores[c] celi?

Quis ergo tam sancta culminis apostolici moderamina, nisi quem

f. 70

207   [a] Christi MS.   [b] salutem MS.   [c] Sic in MS, but perhaps predicatores better.

[2] Job 39: 19–22.   [3] Ps. 26: 3.   [4] Ps. 3: 7.

of man's religion, especially since the commission of the minister general, when faithfully considered, plainly demands that we should so act. All this is the fervent desire of the minister of Ireland, as I hear, together with that of some of the brothers, who seek the things of God with patient piety. This too the timely urgency of the various ordinances in all respects compels not so much their acceptance as their implementation with the zeal of well-judged virtue, if God grants it.

There will not be much to fear from rage and madness, malevolent though they are, truly supported by Him who 'gives strength to the horse and clothes his neck with neighing, lofting him up like the locusts, one must go forth to meet armed men; he despises fear; he turneth not his back to the sword'.[2] For why? Let us hear the triumphant warrior of heaven's armies: 'If armies in camp should stand together against me,' he says, 'my heart shall not fear. If a battle should rise against me, in this I will be confident.'[3] And elsewhere: 'I will not fear thousands of the people surrounding me; arise, O Lord; save me, O my God.'[4] I have answered in accordance with your teaching. The inconvenience of prolixity has shortened my letter. It was not because of unwillingness to write that I have delayed so long; but I ask you to allocate the blame for it to me.

Farewell, father, ever in Christ and the Blessed Virgin.

207

To William of Nottingham, provincial minister

Brother Adam to Brother William, minister of England, greetings with humble and devoted service.

When out of caring solicitude his excellency, a good bishop, asks for the humble assistance of our profession, it is undoubtedly at hand with a ready assent, unless it is someone who is presenting love with evident dishonesty or who lies about his zeal with a pretence of trust. Did not Christ, the power of God, the wisdom of God, establish high priests by a lasting and saving ordinance to be the salt of the earth, the light of the world, the supporters of the globe, the dispensers of salvation, the heralds of the kingdom, the agents of heavenly perfection?

Who then does not support such holy apostolic governance with all

profana demonialis peruicacie deliramenta captiuant, totius potentie, totius prudentie, totius clementie, totius perseuerantie sacris subsidiis non prosequitur? Maxime quum cuncti cernimus—proh nefas—hiis diebus dampnatissimis familiarium inimicitias, uersutias fallacium, lasciuorum petulantias, malitias pertinacium intus illis obsistere, et opprimere illa foris atrocium uiolentias, peruasiones rapacium, assentantium blanditias, afflictiones perurgentium, et non tam intus quam foris conglobatos grassatores, et occidendis animabus innocentium, et pauperum uictualibus diripiendis, canine uoracitatis impudentiam inexplebili rabie perurgere. Igitur quantum rationis cogat necessitas, quantumque pie intentionis requirat utilitas, etiam ex seculari calliditate cecutientibus, dummodo prorsus ipsos deus huius seculi non excecauerit, evidenter non innotescit inter tam formidanda perdite condempnationis discrimina, illis qui uice Saluatoris saluandis omnibus episcopalis apicis ministerium salutare diuinitus suscipere, funditus postpositis simulate religionis ineptiis, irreuocabili benigne sedulitatis diligentia aptas adhibere personas ut^d iusta iudicia iugitate procurent indefessa?

Coarctandis caracteribus presenti cartule manus anxia cordis amaritudine intinxit. Ecce coram paternitate uestra^e non mentior. Sane quum uenerabilis pater dominus Sarisberiensis[1] dilectum Fratrem H. de Syreford in auxilium pontificalis officii, sicut audio, sibi non mediocriter necessarium, fratrem, sicut uos melius nostis, ardentem^f animo, acrem ingenio, promptum eloquio, ydoneum officio ⟨quem⟩, reor, super cuiuscunque sceleris admissi transgressione, nec euidentia conuincit nec accusat existimatio, licet ut libet lingue loquantur, tanta petit instantia; quid erit si prouisiua uestre sanctitatis circumspectio memorato domino dictum fratrem concedendum censuerit, aut cum eodem iuxta formam sue petitionis moraturum, aut ad ipsum de loco competenti a uobis assignando uicissim, secundum rerum exigentias, accessurum, cum dictum fratrem a dicto domino contigerit euocari?[2] Vt uideo, in presentiarum istud est in hac parte cui secundum modulum meum non dissentio, commonito fratre ⟨per⟩ discretam paternitatis uestre persuasionem super conuersationis maturitate et moderamine sermonis.

Conseruet Dominus uestre pietatis incolumitatem, etc.

---

^{d} et *MS.* ^{e} *MS adds* quum. ^{f} audentem *MS.*

207 [1] William of York, bishop of Salisbury 1247–56.
  [2] This elaborate arrangement was suggested by Adam as a way of adhering to the papal

his strength, his prudence, his clemency and perseverance, unless he is captive to profane and demonic madness? Especially when we all see, alas, in these most abandoned days that it is opposed within by the hostility of its household members, by the cunning of deceivers, by the wantonness of the lascivious, and is oppressed from without by the violence of scoundrels, the plundering of the rapacious, the blandishments of flatterers, the blows of its oppressors, and not only from within but from without by myriads of idle wretches who press with inexhaustible fury and canine greed to slay the souls of the innocent and to carry off the food of the poor. Therefore, is it not obvious even to those whose vision is not obscured by worldly wisdom, so long as the god of this world has not blinded them, how compellingly reason requires it as necessary and how pious intention demands it as useful, that those who have by divine will received the ministry of episcopal headship in place of the Saviour to save all from condemnation and loss, having put behind them the follies of religious pretence, are supplied by our diligence and unshakable concern with suitable persons as helpers untiringly to procure just judgements for all time?

To restrict the verbiage of this letter in my anxiety I have dipped my pen in the bitter gall of my heart. You see, father, before you I do not lie. To be sure, as our venerable father the lord bishop of Salisbury[1] is asking with much urgency for Brother H. de Syreford to give him the help he much needs, as I hear, in his episcopal duties; the brother is, as you know better than I, an ardent spirit, with a keen intellect, ready speech, and suitable, I think, for office, as one who has neither been convicted of any admitted transgression or thought to be charged with any such thing, although tongues may wag as they please. How will it be if your prudent holiness considers granting the said brother to the lord bishop, either to stay with him according to the form of his request, or on the other hand to have the brother stay at a suitable place to be assigned by you, from which he will come to the bishop as affairs require it and when called upon to do so by his lordship?[2] As I see it, that is at present an arrangement in this case with which in my small way I do not disagree, when the brother has been admonished by your fatherly persuasion regarding the maturity of his way of living and governing his speech.

May the Lord keep you in health, etc.

privilege *Petitionibus vestris* of Innocent IV forbidding prelates to maintain friars in their households and employ them for business purposes; see Letter 168 n. 2.

208

To William of Nottingham, provincial minister

(1254)

Reuerendissimo in Christo patri, Fratri Willelmo, Fratrum Minorum in Anglia ministro, Frater Ada, que desursum est sapientiam, 'attingentem a fine usque ad finem fortiter et disponentem omnia suauiter'.[1]

Per quam, oro, longe fiat ab animabus sanctis in quas Ipse se transfert, amicos Dei et prophetas constituens, longe fiat, inquam, rigoris sacrilegi mentita magnanimitas, que nonnunquam, pro nefas, et diuine dispensationis moderamina perturbat et irritat spiramina Spiritus Sancti. Igitur per altissimam Sancte Trinitatis maiestatem, per adorandum uiuifice crucis patibulum, per emulandam beatissime Virginis uenerationem, per formidandum districtionis eterne iudicium inuito, suadeo, obsecro, adiuro, ut nulla conditione sub celo declinare presumatis beatum operande salutis officium, quod uobis iterato imponere curauit occulto consilii sui decreto per tam numerosam saluifici assensus electionem[2] Is, qui non tam apostolis quam apostolicos labores secundum secularem successionem introeuntibus, sub patrocinii celestis immutabili sponsione promittit, dicens 'ecce ego uobiscum sum usque ad consummationem seculi'.[3]

Continere calamum nequiui quin per priuatam litteram id agerem quod actum est in communi. Letificet uos letitia sempiterna. Letificauit me littera uestra michi a Lugduno transmissa. Sit uobis in omnibus et industria infallibilis, et inuincibilis constantia, et temperantia inuiolabilis, et incorruptibilis innocentia, in Christo Iesu semper et beatissima Virgine. Salutat uos uester Laurentius dictus frater.

---

208   [1] Wisd. 8: 1. Adam's use of one of his favourite quotations as an unusual form of address was prompted by the fact that William of Nottingham was away attending the general chapter of the order at Metz: Eccleston, p. 42 and note.

  [2] Adam here refers to William's re-election in his absence by the provincial chapter to the office of provincial minister. Adam and the rest were unaware that William had already been absolved from office by the general chapter of Metz. From Metz he was dispatched to

208

To William of Nottingham, provincial minister

(1254)

Brother Adam to the most reverend father in Christ, William, minister of the Friars Minor in England, the wisdom that is from above 'which reaches from end to end mightily and ordereth all things sweetly'.[1]

Through it I pray that the false magnanimity of a sacrilegious severity may be far removed from the souls of the saints, in whom He makes his dwelling, making them friends of God and prophets, a severity which sometimes—alas—disturbs the ruling of divine dispensation and nullifies the inspirations of the Holy Spirit. Therefore, by the most high majesty of the Holy Trinity, by the adorable gibbet of the life-giving cross, by the zealous veneration of the Blessed Virgin, by the stern and fearsome eternal judgement, I entreat you, I urge you, I beg you, I adjure you not under any circumstance under heaven to presume to decline the blessed office of working for salvation, which has once more been laid upon you through an election in which so many concurred,[2] by the hidden decree of Him who solemnly promises not only to the apostles, but also to those entering into the labours of the apostles in succession age after age under the unchanging protection of heaven, saying 'lo, I am with you even unto the end of the world'.[3]

I could not restrain my pen from signifying by personal letter what has been done in community. May our joy give you joy for ever. I was delighted by the letter you sent me from Lyons. May you have in everything an unerring zeal, an invincible constancy, and inviolable discretion and an incurruptible innocence, ever in Christ Jesus and the Blessed Virgin. Your Laurence, called brother, sends his greetings.

the pope, but died at Genoa on the way and was buried at Marseilles. The English friars, having received news of his resignation, but not of his death, convened a second chapter and elected him once more: Eccleston, pp. 43 and note, 100; Little, *Franciscan Papers, Lists and Documents*, p. 190. Cf. Letter 164.

[3] Matt. 28: 20.

209

To an unnamed provincial minister

(?1254)

Ministro Anglie Frater Ada salutem, et spiritum scientie salutaris cum spiritu propense pietatis.[1]

Hanc petitunculam, quam retraxit importunitatis formido, supplicantis improbitas animauit. Igitur sicut nouerit et uoluerit, cum portitore presentis carte rogo faciat circumspecte[a] sanctitatis ⟨uestre⟩ benigna consideratio. Quis nouit si hec sit anima quam alloquens districta misericordissime diuinitatis clementia, non premisit obiurgationis censuram, scilicet 'Quam uilis facta es, nimis iterans uias tuas, et ab Egypto confunderis',[2] nisi subiungeret gratiam reconciliationis, uidelicet 'Tu fornicata es cum amatoribus multis; tamen reuertere ad me et ego suscipiam te'?[3]

Quis negabit hunc esse filium qui non cum meretrice sed cum meretricibus deuorauit substantiam suam, apostatice uiuens in regione dissimilitudinis, et tamen non tam dudum reuersum, quam adhuc reuertentem paternorum uiscerum, que nunquam obliuiscitur misereri, benigna dilectio et pristine dignitati restituit et honore sublimiori cumulauit?[4]

Agendum in hiis puto cum deuota sedule deliberationis oratione, ne uel facilitas uenie prebeat incentiuum delinquendi, uel hominis seueritas abigat quem adigit diuina propitiatio.

Valeat paternitatis uestre clemens incolumitas, etc.

210

To an unnamed minister of the English province

Ministro Anglie[1] Frater Ada ⟨salutem⟩ et subiectam salutaris obedientie promptitudinem.

Licet nuper desiderabili uestre suauitatis colloquio fruitus fuerim

---

209 *a* circumspectem *MS.*

---

209 [1] The omission of the provincial minister's name suggests the letter was written in an interregnum such as must have followed the mistaken re-election of William of Nottingham in 1254; cf. Letter 208 and n. 2.

[2] Jer. 2: 36.   [3] Ibid. 3: 1.

209

To an unnamed provincial minister

(?1254)

Brother Adam to the minister of England,[1] greetings and a spirit of knowledge and kindly piety.

Fear of its impropriety withdrew this little petition, which was inspired by the depravity of the petitioner. As you know, therefore, and wish, I ask your prudent holiness to give kind consideration to the bearer of this letter. Who knows whether this is not a soul whom the divine and most merciful clemency is addressing and rebuking in advance, that is saying 'How vile thou art made, wandering too much in thy ways, and from Egypt thou shalt be confounded'[2]? unless He offers the grace of reconciliation, namely: 'thou hast prostituted thyself to many lovers; nevertheless, return to me and I will receive thee'.[3]

Who will deny that this is a son who has wasted his substance, not with a whore, but with many whores, living as an apostate in a far country, and nevertheless who is not long since returned and is still returning, on whom the loving kindness of his father's heart, which never forgets pity, has both restored him to his early privileges and heaped still higher honours upon him?[4]

In these cases one must, I think, act with careful deliberation and prayer, lest an easy pardon should provide encouragement to sin or the severity of man should drive away one whom divine forgiveness brings back.

Wishing you good health, kind father, etc.

210

To an unnamed minister of the English province

Brother Adam to the minister of England,[1] greetings with prompt and humble obedience.

Although I recently enjoyed a longed-for conversation with you in

[4] Cf. the Prodigal Son, Luke 15: 11–24.

210 [1] The minister's name is omitted. Possibly the recipient was the successor of William of Nottingham; cf. Letter 209 and n. 1.

in Domino, ne non interueniente cursore per salutationem litteralem paternitatem uestram filialis famulatus ueneraretur, ut dignum est, humilitatis qualiscunque, presentem cartulam uobis transmisi. Nempe temporis angustia et occupationum uarietas, agonia studii et inquietationum turbamina, prolixos litterarum tractus excludunt. Copia quoque scribendorum scribendi cogit inopiam.

Etenim si ⟨non⟩ uacaret, quis inter tanta salutis discrimina, inter tot uiolentias rebellium, in tantis moliminibus insidiantium, in tam salutarem et omnibus seculis spectabilem coniuratus professionem, quantum diuinitus permitteretur, rebus non consuleret per sollicitam epistolarum frequentiam, ubi uiuas uocis energias conserere non permittit locorum distantia? Sed, proth dolor, in causis salutaribus hodie epistole torpent et silent uoces—ad ineptias perditionum diuisarum mentium tota preceps ruit intentio. Quid igitur nobis poterit esse consilii nisi ut nequaquam infimis hereamus infirmiter et in altissima conscendamus alacriter in Ipsum uiuendi, qui ait (Io. 15), 'Hec locutus sum uobis | ut pacem in me habeatis. In mundo pressuram habebitis; sed confidite, quia ego uici mundum.'[2]

f. 70ᵛ

Conseruetur uobis, oro, et uirtus et prudentia det emulatio in Christo semper et beatissima Virgine.

Audiui aliquid quod nolui, lingua enim coniecturam prestat de corde.

211

To William of Nottingham, provincial minister

(January 1245)

Reuerendo patri in Christo, Fratri Willelmo, Fratrum Minorum in Anglia ministro, Frater Ada salutem in Domino.

Nouerit paternitatis uestre pia discretio dominum Lyncolniense[1] cum suis, ut uisum est solito ualidiorem, benedictus Deus, in crastino Epiphanie[2] Lugdunum intrasse, ubi a domino papa[3] et cardinalibus in gratia specialis honorificentie est susceptus. Promisit autem ei dominus pontifex post aliquot dies, quod in breui expediret eum in causa contra capitulum, quam speramus diuinitate propitia, fine laudabili terminandam, nisi ipsam, quod absit, peccata prepediant.[4] Mortalibus

the Lord, lest, for lack of a courier, my filial service should not be respectfully conveyed to your fatherly person, as is proper, by a letter of greeting, I have passed this letter on to you. To be sure, pressure of time, my various employment, the struggle of learning, and a whirl of troubles make extended letters impossible. Also the multitude of things that have to be written compels me to write sparingly.

Who, even if he lacked leisure, when vowed to the most beautiful religious profession of all time, and surrounded by threats to salvation, the violence of insurgents, and such exertions of evil plotters, would not, so far as God allowed, advise on matters by solicitously and constantly writing letters, where distance prevents us from joining our efforts by the spoken word? But, alas, today in questions of salvation letters are idle and voices are mute; the whole tendency of distracted minds is to fall headlong into folly and ruin. What therefore can we advise except not to cling in weakness to things that are base and to rise fast to the heights of living in Him who says, 'These things I have spoken unto you, that in me ye might have peace. In the world ye shall have tribulation: but be of good cheer; I have overcome the world.'[2]

May your virtue, prudence, and zeal be ever maintained in Christ and the blessed Virgin.

I have heard something I did not wish to hear, for the tongue vouches for the heart.

211

To William of Nottingham, provincial minister

(January 1245)

Brother Adam to the reverend father in Christ, Brother William, minister of the Friars Minor in England, greetings in the Lord.

I wish you to know, prudent father, that the lord bishop of Lincoln,[1] seeming in better health than usual—blessed be God— entered Lyons with his party on the morrow of the Epiphany,[2] where he was graciously received with special honour by the lord pope[3] and cardinals. Some days later the lord pope promised that he would expedite the bishop's case against the chapter, and we are hoping with God's favour for a laudable conclusion to it[4] unless, which heaven

---

[4] Grosseteste's long-standing dispute with the Lincoln chapter over his visitation rights was settled by a judgement of Innocent IV dated 25 Mar. 1245: *CPL* i. 219; cf. Letter 41.

tamen dubius est euentus belli. Non enim cessat impietas macinationum, diffugia tergiuersationum, calliditates cauillationum, dilationes exceptionum processui salutis obluctari.

Ceterum, proponit episcopus concilio interesse, quod papa celebrare concedit ad festum Sancti Iohannis Baptiste,[5] et in aliquo loco opportuno extra Curiam usque ad illud tempus expectare, ignorans tamen adhuc penitus quando se poterit a Curia transferre. Scripsit dominus papa ministro generali[6] secundum formam quam scribit aliis prelatis, ut accedat ad concilium.

Iterum proponit dominus papa mittere Fratres Minores electos in instanti passagio ueris ad gentes que destruxerunt, ut dicitur, Terram Sanctam, Chorasmenos[7] scilicet, et ad Tartaros[8] et ad Saracenos, qui perferant mandata apostolica ad illos;[9] et eorum responsa, si Dominus fuerit propitius, ad dominum papam referant. Inter fratres autem mittendos designati sunt duo Anglici, scilicet Frater Iohannes de Stanford[10] et Frater Abraham de Lard'. Bene formidant sapientes in Curia de formidando statu mundi.

Receperunt me et Fratrem Iohannem, karissimus pater, Frater Desiderius, minister Burgundie, et Frater Gabriel, uicarius ministri generalis, ceterique fratres in Curia et in conuentu Lugduni commorantes sui gratia cum magna caritate. Putant fratres discreti quod multa et grauia attemptabuntur contra fratres in instanti concilio per prelatos diuersarum partium orbis Christiani. Longe facti sunt fratres a fauore Curie in suis petitionibus stultam sapientiam mundi sapientibus; unde plurimum gaudendum uidetur in Domino.

Mitto uobis duas bullas de facto Fratrum Predicatorum et Minorum, pro quibus Frater Petrus de Theokesbury moratus est post solutum capitulum generale,[11] quia non constitit michi an illas hactenus receperitis, quas reliquit Frater Petrus cum in Angliam rediret.

---

[5] 24 June. The First Council of Lyons opened on 26 June 1245: *Conciliorum oecumenicorum generaliumque decreta: editio critica*, ed. G. Alberigo et al. (CC; Turnhout, 2006–), i. 273–301.

[6] Crescentius of Jesi, Minister General 1244–7.

[7] The peoples of central Asia settled around the Aral Sea (Chorasmias lacus), now Turkestan; see Graesse, Benedict, Plechl, *Orbis Latinus* (1971).

[8] Tartars, the name of a particular tribe, was used by Western writers to describe the Mongols in general.

[9] Pope Innocent's letters to the rulers of the Mongols were sent in an effort to ward off a repetition of the great Mongol invasion of central Europe in 1241. His letter to the Great Khan was dated 5 Mar. 1245: Berger, nos. 1364–5.

forbid, it is held up by sin. But the outcome of war is uncertain for mortal men. For the process of salvation is unceasingly resisted by impious knavery, the subterfuge of changing direction, cunning sophistry, and pleas for delay.

Well, the bishop intends to be present at the council, which the pope agrees to celebrate on the feast of St John the Baptist;[5] and he proposes to wait until that time in some suitable place outside the Curia, but still totally unknowing when he will be able to move out of the Curia. The lord pope has written to our minister general[6] in the same form with which he is writing to the other prelates with a request to attend the council.

Further, the lord pope proposes to send chosen Friars Minor in the coming spring to the peoples who, as it is said, have destroyed the Holy Land, that is the Chorasmians,[7] and to the Tartars[8] and the Saracens, to take them the papal mandates[9] and, if the Lord is favourable, to bring back their replies to the lord pope. Among those to be sent two Englishmen have been designated, namely Brother John of Stamford[10] and Brother Abraham de Lard'. Wise people at the Curia are very fearful about the state of the world.

Our dearest father, Brother Desiderius, the minister of Burgundy, and Brother Gabriel, the vicar of the Minister General, and the rest of the brothers at the Curia and those resident at the Lyons convent have received me and Brother John for their part with great charity. Discerning brothers think that many serious attacks will be mounted against the friars at the coming council by prelates from several parts of the Christian world. The friars have been much alienated from favour at the Curia by their petitions, which smack of the foolish wisdom of the world, regarding which, it seems, we should much rejoice in the Lord.

I am sending you the two bulls relating to the Friars Preachers and the Minors, for which Brother Peter of Tewkesbury stayed on after the closure of the general chapter,[11] as I was uncertain whether you had yet received them; Brother Peter left them behind when he returned to England.

---

[10] John of Stamford was custodian of Oxford in 1253 and provincial minister *c*.1257–64; cf. Letters 123, 168, 186, 218.

[11] Peter of Tewkesbury was custodian of Oxford 1236–*c*.1248, minister of Cologne, provincial of England, 1254–*c*.1257: Eccleston, p. 91 and n.; Little, *The Greyfriars in Oxford*, p. 127. The general chapter referred to was that of 1244. The bulls for which Peter waited were *Non solum* dated 17 June 1244 and *Meminimus* dated 24 June 1244: Sbaralea, i. 342–3, 345–6.

LETTERS OF ADAM MARSH

Recommendationes dominis cardinalibus et fratribus faciendas, secundum quod iniunxistis, ante confectionem presentium, illis quos in Curia inueni feceram preterquam domino Egidio. Dominus Hostiensis,[12] dominus S. de Comite, dominus Reiuerius, dominus Ricardus Hamb', nondum uenerunt citra montes.[13] Coniicio quod per ministrum generalem uocabuntur ad concilium aliqui fratres discretiores de singulis prouinciis, super quo audiui fieri sermonem. Vnde uidetur michi quod bonum erit, ut uos cum fratribus sapientioribus conferatis super eis que iudicaueritis petenda et proponenda in tempore concilii, si quos oporteat mittere.

Rogo quatinus, si placet, faciatis michi transmitti per clericum domini episcopi, quem dominus Iohannes de Crachal[14] mittet ad eum Moralia Beati Gregorii, que relicta fuerunt apud Rading', et Rabanum de Natura Rerum, et capitula Philosophie Prime,[15] que habuit karissimus frater in Christo Thomas de Eboraco. Per prefatum clericum, si uobis non displiceat, desidero uestram michi signari uoluntatem. Dominus papa mutauit consilium de mittendis Fratribus Minoribus ad gentes supranominatas, unde nullus de prouincia Anglie hac uice mittetur.

Valeat paternitatis uestre benignitas in Christo semper et beatissima Virgine. Rogo salutari obsequio meo karissimos patres, Fratres Ricardum de Wauz, Iohannem de Stanford, reliquosque fratres socios, scilicet et filios uestros; in quorum, si placet, sanctis recordationibus me et Fratrem Iohannem renouare uelitis in Domino. Scripsi plura de hiis seorsum Fratri Petro, custodi Oxoniensi, et Fratri Andree de Lexinton'. Salutat uos Frater Iohannes multum, qui paternitati uestre insufficientiam suam recommendat. Bene, si placet, faciatis componi libros prenominatos ablatis asseribus in panno cerato. Frater Gabriel uicarius est ministri in Curia. Frater N. de Marnio et Frater Boiolus, propinquus domini pape, stant cum ipso satis ei familiares.[a]

211   [a] *This letter is followed by a blank half page.*

Before composing this letter, I had, as you enjoined, given your greetings to those of the lord cardinals and brothers whom I found at the Curia, except for the lord Giles. The lord Hostiensis,[12] the lord Reiuerius, and Sir Richard Hamb' had not yet come to this side of the mountains.[13] My guess is that some more discerning friars from separate provinces will be summoned to the council by the Minister General, about which I have heard talk. As regards this, it seems to me it would be a good thing for you to confer with wiser brethren about things that you judge should be sought for and proposed at the time of the council, if it should be proper to send any of them.

I ask you, if you please, to have sent me by the clerk of the lord bishop, whom Sir John Crakehall[14] will send to him, the *Moralia* of St Gregory, which was left at Reading, and Hrabanus's *De Natura Rerum*, and the chapters of the *First Philosophy*,[15] which was in the possession of our very dear brother in Christ, Thomas of York. I wish, if you would not mind, that you would indicate what are your wishes through the aforesaid clerk. The lord pope has changed his mind about the Friars Minor to be sent to the aforesaid peoples; so no one will be sent from the English province this time.

Farewell, kind father, ever in Christ and the Blessed Virgin. I ask my greetings and duty to be conveyed to our very dear fathers, Brothers Richard de Wauz, John of Stamford, and the rest of the brothers—that is to your associates and sons. Please commend the recollection of me and Brother John to their holy memory. I have written a lot about the matters above to Brother Peter, the custodian of Oxford, and to Brother Andrew of Lexington. Brother John sends you many greetings, father, and commends his inadequte self to you. Please have the books I have mentioned above well packed with the boards removed in a waxed sack. Brother Gabriel is the vicar of the minister at the Curia. Brothers N. de Marmo and Boiolus, a relative of the lord pope, are quite closely associated with him.

---

[12] Henry of Segusia, the famous canonist, who resided in England and served on the king's council 1236–44, subsequently cardinal of S. Sabina 1262–71.

[13] *Citra montes* an expression commonly applied at the Curia for those resident in Italy.

[14] Grosseteste's steward; see Letter 21 n. 1.

[15] The *Liber de Philosophia Prima* was the title of the Metaphysics of Avicenna in Latin translation: *Avicenna Latinus, Liber de Philosophia Prima*, ed. S. van Riet (Louvain, 1977).

212

To Geoffrey de Brie, minister provincial of France

f. 71 Desideratissimo sibi in Christo patri, ministro Francie,[1] Frater Ada
salutem et deuotum debite dilectionis famulatum.

Pro sedulis inolite benignitatis officiis ab ingenua mente mee
modicitati per liberalem suauitatem impensis, etsi non ut uellem,
tamen ut ualeo, pie paternitati suppliciter assurgo cum gratiarum
actionibus. Certe letificat quod occasione reperta rationabili, quod in
persona non sufficio, per litteram sanctitatis uestre desiderabilem
adire presentiam, quam et uirtus ualida et industria subtilis et feruens
emulatio, ad gloriam sui nominis et salutem sue plebis superb-
enedictam Dei clementia multipliciter insigniuit. Liberet[a] profecto
in tractum prolixiorem presentis allocutionis seriem deducere, sed
cohibeo calamum, putans hac uice sufficere si amantissimos sinus lati
cordis repleuerim[b] per obsequialis scripture breuitatem officiosam
mee paupertatis recordationem.

Ceterum cum karissimo Fratre N. de Anilers,[c] iuuene moris
honesti et spei laudabilis, docilis ingenii et competentis litterature,
quem reuerendissimus pater minister generalis uestre discipline filiis
aggregandum designauit,[2] piam beneuolentiam uestre discretionis
humiliter rogo, supplicans obnixius quatinus ei deuotissimo uestro
licentiam concedere uelitis gratiosam, ut in administratione Anglie
solito sollicius per instantis anni spatium diuinorum studii ualeat
inuigilare. Nempe memoratus frater in hac parte consiliis spirituali-
bus acquiescens, pro eo quod alibi quam in Anglia ad profectum
studii litteralis nequaquam ei putantur in presentiarum accessura, que
requiruntur, tam opportune subsidia, una mecum presentem consensit benigne paternitate uestre dirigere petitionem; ut diuinitate
propitia, quem ad tempus abesse concesseritis, iterum promptius
aptatum ad ministerium diuinum pro tempore recipiatis.

Concedat, oro, mi benigne, uobis superessentialis purgatio, super-
affectualis illuminatio, supereffectualis perfectio, ut anime uobis
commisse, diuinitus per uos purgate, illuminate, et perfecte,

---

212   [a] Liberet *inserted in margin by corrector.*   [b] repleuerim *inserted in margin by*
corrector.   [c] *Possibly* Anibers.

---

212   [1] Geoffrey de Brie, minister provincial of France 1243–57: A. Callebaut, 'Les
Provinciaux', *AFH* x (1917), 315.

212

To Geoffrey de Brie, minister provincial of France

Brother Adam to the most dear father in Christ, the minister of France,[1] greetings and devoted and due service.

As far as I am able, not as far as I would wish, I humbly thank your fatherly goodness for the thoughtful favours bestowed on my poor self by your generous kindness. Truly it gives me joy that a reasonable occasion has been found for me to approach your holiness by letter, which I could not do by my personal presence. For by the clemency of God you are in many ways distinguished by your mighty virtues, the fineness of your labours, and your fervent zeal, to the glory of His name and the blessed salvation of His people. It would be pleasant to prolong this address with a lengthier discourse, but I am restraining my pen, thinking it enough this time to have filled your generous and loving heart with the assurance of my duty by writing humbly but briefly as a respectful remembrance of my poor self.

For the rest, I am writing together with our dear Brother N. de Anilers, a young man of honourable behaviour, praiseworthy hopes, teachable talent, and well-equipped in letters, whom the most reverend minister general has designated to join the sons of your school.[2] I humbly ask of your benevolence and prudence with a pressing request to grant him, your most devoted servant, a gracious licence to enable him to study theology with added intensity in the English province for the period of the coming year. Truly, the said brother accepting spiritual counsel in this matter, has agreed with me to send your kind fatherhood this petition, for the reason that such suitable aids to advancing the study of letters are not thought to be available to him elsewhere than in England. This is in the hope that him to whom you have given leave of absence for a time, you will receive back again for that time more equipped for the sacred ministry.

May you be granted, my kind friend, a superessential purification, a suprasensible illumination, and a super-effectual perfection, that the souls committed to you, being divinely purified, illumined, and perfected by you, may reform the kingdom of God in purity,

[2] The choice of friars to be sent to study at a studium generale of the order was a prerogative of the Minister General; in this instance the school must have been Paris.

regnum Dei purum, clarum et sanctum ad supersublimem puritatem,
superdecoram claritatem, superiocundam sanctitatem reforment,
secundum cogentissimam altissime professionis exigentiam.

Valeat uestre suauitatis incolumitas in Christo.

213

To Geoffrey de Brie, provincial minister of France

Desideratissimo patri in Christo, Fratri G⟨alfrido⟩, Fratrum Minorum Francie ministro,[1] Frater Ada salutem et eternalis brauii
premium post exercitium cursus temporalis.

Vestra meminit benigna paternitas, ut arbitror, quod circumspectionis uestre sollers consideratio, iam emenso unius anni et mensium
aliquot spatio, ad mee modicitatis instantiam concesseritis, ut karissimus Frater N. de Aynelers sub ministro Anglie ad tempus moram
traheret[a] iuxta quod profectus sui ob certas circumstantias requirebat
opportunitas. Proinde quum, ut uideo, utile foret[b] memorato fratri
usque ad festum Pentecoste proximo futurum in prouincia Anglie
causis quibusdam sibi necessariis et nequaquam citra tempus prefatum expediendis, si uestre pietatis beneplacito sederit, insistere,
presentem paternitati uestre petitionem censui destinandam, rogans
attentius quatinus in hac parte, perpensis rerum exigentiis, dicto filio
uestro sic paterna uelit prouidere sedulitas, ut eidem optata proue-
niant commoda et rationis requisita non ledantur.

Concedat uobis, oro, in scala Iacob uices ascendendi et descendendi
frequentare cum angelis Dominus innixus scale, ut pro temporum
moderamine sanctos ascensus contemplande ueritatis et iustos des-
census impendende caritatis sibi inuicem indefessa succedant uigilantia, ut ex illo iste iugiter animetur, et augeatur incessanter ille per
istum, in Christo semper et beatissima Virgine.

---

213   [a] trahere *MS.*   [b] fore *MS.*

beauty, and holiness to make it one that is supersublime in purity, supremely beautiful in renown, supremely joyful in sanctity, in accordance with exacting demands of our very high profession.

Wishing your charming person health in Christ.

213

To Geoffrey de Brie, provincial minister of France

Brother Adam to the most dear father in Christ, Brother Geoffrey, minister of the Friars Minor in France,[1] greetings and the prize of eternal reward after the trials of time.

As I think you remember, father, a year and some months ago now, with your circumspect sagacity, you granted, at the suggestion of my poor self, that our very dear Brother N. de Aynelers should stay for a time under the minister of England, according as certain circumstances offered an opportunity for his progress. Since, as I see it, it would be useful to the said brother to stay in the English province until next Whitsun, to devote himself, if it please you, to matters necessary to him which are in no way to be resolved within the time previously said, I have thought it good to send you this petition with a pressing request that in this matter, having considered the requirements of the situation, you would out of solicitude provide for your said son so that he may obtain the desired advantage, without damage to what reason requires.

May the Lord grant you, I pray, in turn to ascend and descend frequently supported with the angels upon Jacob's ladder, so that for the management of time your untiring vigils may in succession experience holy ascents to contemplate truth and just descents to bestow charity, so that the latter may be perpetually inspired by the former, and the former may be ceaselessly increased by the latter, ever in Christ and the Blessed virgin.

213   [1] Geoffrey de Brie; cf. Letter 212.

214

To the minister of the Trinitarian Friars at Paris

(1249)

Honorabili uiro et amicissimo in Christo patri et domino S. ministro Ordinis Fratrum Sancte Trinititis Parisius, Frater Ada salutem et post pacem temporis gloriam eternitatis.

De consueta uestre benignitatis sedulitate confisus, quanta possum affectione suppliciter rogo quatinus per strenuam religiose pietatis interuentionem, quam, sicut multiplicibus comprobatur experimentis, ad causas salutares expediendas indefesse geritis efficacem,[a] apud dominam Blancam,[1] excellentissimam reginam Francorum, secundum modum quem insinuauerit propitia diuinitas, satagere uelitis, ut inter illustres uiros comites Tolose[2] et Leycestriensem[3] desideranda pacis reformatio proueniat per serenissimam eiusdem regine clementiam, que dudum sui gratia etiam mee modicitati in hac parte sue uoluntatis manifestauit promptitudinem.

Inueni quoque comitis Tolose ad pacem memoratam secundum cor meum mentem inclinatam. Comes uero Leycestriensis ad beneuolum dicte pacis consensum sufficienter est persuasum. Quid ergo restat quam ut intuitu Illius qui pacificos Dei filiatione beatificat,[4] concordes affectus diuinitus conceptos ad pacatam perducat unanimitatem uestre sanctitatis placida discretio, tanto propensioris diligentie sollicitudinem adhibendo quanto presens negotium propter gloriam diuini honoris uniuersis amplius fore cognoscitur emulandum?

Valeat sanctitatis uestre pia paternitas in Christo semper et beatissima Virgine.

Scripsissem super hiis prenominate domine regine, sed celsitudo maiestatis exilitatem meam a scribendo reuocauit. Necesse autem erit ut, si placet, mi pater amicissime, sub ea que conuenienter fieri poterit acceleratione, hoc etenim res requirit, ad interpellandum procedere curetis. Iterum in eternum valete.[b]

---

214 [a] efficaciam MS.   [b] *The reverse of the folio containing this letter has another letter, lacking any clause of address, written in a different hand, which Brewer printed in his edition, but which is in fact a letter of Grosseteste addressed to the archdeacon of Canterbury: see Grosseteste Epistolae, no. 128, pp. 432 ff.*

214

To the minister of the Trinitarian Friars at Paris

(1249)

Brother Adam to the honourable and most dear father in Christ and lord S. minister of the Order of Friars of the Holy Trinity at Paris, greetings, and after peace in time the glory of eternity.

Trusting in your customary zeal and kindness, as it is shown by numerous instances that you act with tireless efficacy in furthering salutary causes, I beg you with all possible affection to intervene with your forceful goodness to act upon Lady Blanche, the most excellent queen of the French,[1] in a manner suggested to you by divine inspiration, so that a desirable peace may be restored between the illustrious counts of Toulouse[2] and Leicester,[3] through the serene clemency of the said queen. A short time ago, she graciously disclosed her clear will in this matter even to my humble self.

I felt in my heart that the mind of the said Count of Toulouse was inclined to such a peace. Really the earl of Leicester is sufficiently persuaded to agree to the said peace with good will. So what remains, having in view Him who blessed peacekeepers as sons of God,[4] except for the quiet discretion of your holiness to lead these divinely inspired sentiments of concord to a peaceful unanimity, applying diligence and solicitude to the negotiation all the more readily as it is recognized by all to be desirable for the glory and honour of God?

Farewell, your holiness and good father ever in Christ and the Blessed Virgin.

I would have written about this to the aforesaid lady queen, but the highness of her majesty discouraged my miserable self from writing. But it will be necessary, if you please, my dearest father, to be active and proceed with your appeal with all possible speed, for the matter undoubtedly requires it. Again, farewell for ever.

---

214   [1] Blanche of Castile, who died in Dec. 1252.
    [2] Raymond VII, Count of Toulouse, who died in 1249. On his conflict with Montfort see Matthew Paris, *Chron. Maj.* iv. 228–9, 231.
    [3] Simon de Montfort.
    [4] Cf. Matt. 5: 9.

215

To Brother John, papal nuncio

Fratri Iohanni, domini pape nuntio,[1] Frater Ada salutem et deuotum debite dilectionis famulatum.

Pro uiro uenerabili, magisto Henrico de Bathonia,[2] quem et excellens morum honestas et eminentia scientie spectabilis ad opinionem celebrem titulis illustrant clarioribus, inolite circumspecte discretionis benignitati, quam multiplicia pii pectoris argumenta apud sedulitatis uestre diligentiam feruere comprobant indesinenter, supplico obsecrans attentius quatinus dicto magistro Henrico in sue necessitatis urgentiis deliberationis consilium et adiutorium executionis, prout uestra secundum Deum censuerit industria, perhibere non ducatis indignum.

Valeat uestre dilectionis suauitas, etc.

216

To Brother John, papal nuncio

Desideratissimo patri, Fratri Iohanni, domini pape nuntio, Frater Ada salutem in Domino.

Pro domino abbate de Oseneye,[1] eiusdemque loci conuentu, per presentem litteram circumspectam paternitatis uestre discretionem interpellare consensi, rogans attentius quatinus procuratori eorumdem ad Curiam Romanam pro quibusdam negotiorum suorum urgentiis profiscenti, efficacis adiutorii subuentionem et directionem consilii salutaris secundum rerum requisita exhibere non ducatis indignum. Quibus ad causarum suarum importunitates maxime puto fore consultum ut, si quo modo fieri poterit, per honestam pacis formam litium instantia conquiescat.

Valeat incolumitatis uestre benigna suauitas in Christo Iesu semper et beatissima Virgine.

Exponet uobis prefatus procurator, si placet, uiua uoce factorum circumstantias, ut inde deliberatius mentis uestre sententiam, ut noueritis et uolueritis, aperire ualeatis.

In eternum ualete.

215 [1] Brother John of Kent, papal nuncio; cf. Letters 94, 171 and n. 3.
[2] Master Henry of Bath was a canonist, DCL and papal judge-delegate in 1254: *BRUO* i. 130.

215

To Brother John, papal nuncio

Brother Adam to Brother John, nuncio of the lord pope,[1] greetings with loving and devoted obedience.

On behalf of the venerable Master Henry of Bath,[2] whose outstanding integrity and notable eminence in learning distinguish him with eminently clear entitlement to his widespread reputation, I beseech the native kindness and discriminating judgement, which the manifold proofs of your pious breast show to be constantly burning in the care and diligence you exercise, begging you very earnestly that you would deign to offer the said Master Henry your considered advice and practical help in his pressing needs, as according to God you consider appropriate.

Farewell, beloved.

216

To Brother John, papal nuncio

Brother Adam to the most dear father, Brother John, nuncio of the lord pope, greetings in the Lord.

I have agreed to appeal to your fatherly discretion on behalf of the lord abbot of Oseney[1] and the community of that place, with a pressing request that you would be so good as to provide their proctor, who is setting off for the Roman Curia on some pressing business of theirs, with your efficacious help and the guidance of your salutary counsel, as the business demands. I think that, given the awkward nature of their case, it will be most advisable to settle the litigation by means of an honourable form of peace, if it can in any way be done.

Wishing your kind person good health ever in Christ and the blessed Virgin.

The said proctor will explain to you by word of mouth, if you please, the circumstances of the matter, so that you may be able to disclose your decision on it with more deliberation, as you will know and desire.

For the last time farewell.

216 [1] Adam de Berners, abbot of Oseney 1249–54.

217

To Brother John, papal nuncio

Honorabili uiro et patri amantissimo, Fratri Iohanni, domini pape nuncio, Frater Ada salutem et post cursum temporis brauium eternitatis.

Mi desideratissime, quod locutione non ualeo, suppleo non sicut uolo, uidelicet amabilem benignitatis uestre presentiam adeo ⟨per litteram⟩, quod ne faciam personaliter ecce coram inuiolabilis amicitie fideli constantia uel inuitum arcent importune caduce conditionis urgentie. Ceterum suauissime circumspectionis amabili beneuolentie supplico, sollicius rogans quatinus cum opportunitas non defuerit, si fieri possit, circa instantem Assumptionem beatissime Virginis[1] accedere uelitis ad uenerabilem dominum Lyncolniensem super causis non mediocriter festinandis, iuxta suum desiderium et mei interuentum cum eodem salutares in Domino tractatus habituri. Et utinam inde recedere non disponat uestra suadibilis ut res expostulat dilectio quousque, diuinitate propitia, me contingat uobis ibidem occurrere.

Valeat gratissima uestre paternitatis incolumitas, etc.

218

To Brother John of Stamford, custodian of Oxford

(September–October 1253)

Desideratissimo patri in Christo, Fratri Iohanni,[1] custodi Oxoniensi, Frater Ada salutem in Domino.

Consoletur uos supermundani Spiraminis infusio. Consolatorium attulit meste menti remedium amicissime fidei fida sinceritas, quam preferebat admodum optata uestre manus epistola. Cui licet succincta breuitas fecisset angustiam, eidem tamen lati cordis gratiosa suauitas, uirtutis, ueritatis, pietatis ministrauit affluentiam. Molestat ergo nimirum dilata uestre uiue uocis expectatio, cui prestitam esse gratulamur energiam confirmandis uacillantibus, plurimis edocendis,

217 ¹ 15 Aug.

218 ¹ John of Stamford was custodian of Oxford until *c.*1258, when he succeeded Peter of Tewkesbury as provincial minister; cf. Letters 34, 219, 220; Little, *The Greyfriars of Oxford*, p. 128.

217

To Brother John, papal nuncio

Brother Adam to the honourable and most loving father, Brother John, nuncio of the lord pope, greetings and after time has run its course, the prize of eternity.

My dearly beloved, what I cannot do by word of mouth I am making good, not in the way I wish, that is gaining access to your kind presence by a letter. The importunate pressure of my frail condition prevents me, however unwilling, from doing this in person in the presence of your faithful and unbreakable friendship. I humbly supplicate your prudence and loving kindness with an earnest request that, if opportunity arises, you would, if it can be done, go to our venerable lord the bishop of Lincoln around the time of the feast of the Assumption of the Blessed Virgin[1] that is soon to be upon us, to deal with cases that greatly need to be hastened and to have discourse with him on matters of salvation in the Lord, in accordance with his wishes and my intercession. And I would that your amiable self may be open to persuasion and, as the matter demands, not arrange your departure until, God willing, I may be in a position to meet you there.

With best wishes, gracious father, for your health.

218

To Brother John of Stamford, custodian of Oxford

(Sept.–Oct. 1253)

Brother Adam to our dearest father in Christ, Brother John,[1] custodian of Oxford, greetings in the Lord.

May you be consoled by the outpouring of the Holy Spirit. The sincerity of your faithful friendship had brought my sad mind consolation, a remedy that was exceedingly enhanced by the letter from your hand. Although its succinct brevity shortened the relief, the gracious sweetness of your generous heart ministered to my pain with an abundance of strength, truth, and goodness. It is troubling to wait excessively long for your living voice. We are thankful for the efficacy given it to strengthen the wavering, to instruct many, to

trementibus animandis 'a Patre luminum',² per Illum qui 'uiuus est
sermo Domini et efficax, et penetrabilior omni gladio ancipiti';³ qui
non cesset, oro, per salutare sollicitudinis uestre ministerium et
seuientium uiolentias, et seducentium fallacias, et blandientium
petulantias potenter edomare, et prudenter explicare, et diligenter
eliminare in regno Dei perpeti perseuerantia.

Eadem die qua recepi litteras paternitatis uestre michi uestri gratia
transmissas,ᵃ feria quinta post octauam Pasche,⁴ porrecta est michi
etiam littera reuerendissimi patris ministri nostri, in eadem signantis
ut per meritum salutaris obedientie me transferrem Rading' circa
quindenam Pasche inde, si res hoc expostulat, ad partes London'
profecturum propter summi discriminis negotia sceptrumᵇ regni
contingentia.⁵ Hoc autem mandauit memoratus pater, sicut ipse
insinuauit, superatus instantia maiestatum, quibus hoc negare
nequiuit.

Quid portendatᶜ quod tanta difficultatum uexamina ignaram mee
modicitatis ignauiam indesinenter non tam affligunt quam obruunt,
cum inexplicabili pacis pariter et salutis, ut uereor, detrimento, nisi
affuerit superclemens diuinitatis propitiatio? Rogo sagaci mente
pertractate propter Altissimi considerationem, non tam suppliciter
orantes quam satagentes uigilanter formidanda portenta diuinitus in
bonum convertantur.ᵈ Vt quid supplicationum suadelis insisterem,
sciens in hac parte quod celitus sit sedulitati supplici potissime
persuasum? Maturate, obsecro, si fieri potest, etiam priusquam
scripsistis, uel saltem tunc, uestre paternitatis exhibere presentiam
suspense deuotorum expectationi. Sit benedictio diuino nomini super
profectum Fratris Gregorii de Bosellis cuius in littera meministis ad
fratrum et aliorum edificationem.⁶ Intimaui gardiano nostro Oxoniensi quod et iussistis.

Valete in Christo Iesu semper et beatissima Virgine.

218   ᵃ transmissam MS.   ᵇ septrum MS.   ᶜ protendat MS.   ᵈ conuerti MS.

invigorate the fearful, derived 'from the Father of lights',[2] through Him who is 'the word of God living and effectual and more piercing than any two-edged sword'.[3] May it not cease, I pray, through the solicitude of your saving ministry with everlasting perseverance powerfully to subdue, prudently to unravel, and assiduously to expel the fury of the deluded, the deceitfulness of seducers, and the viciousness of flatterers from the kingdom of God.

The same day that I received the fatherly letter you were so good as to send me, Thursday after the octave of Easter,[4] I was presented with a letter from the most reverend father, our minister, in which he signifies that I should under saving obedience transfer myself to Reading, in readiness to set out thence for the London region within fifteen days from Easter, if the matter requires it, on account of business of the utmost danger touching the governance of the kingdom.[5] The said father has commanded this, as he himself indicates, being prevailed upon by the insistence of their majesties, to whom he could not refuse it.

What does it mean that such great and difficult vexations should ceaselessly not merely afflict but overwhelm my ignorant and pusillanimous self, with inescapable harm to my peace and, I fear, to my salvation, unless the supreme mercy of God comes to my help? I beg you, think hard with the sagacity of your mind through regard for the Most High, not so much humbly begging as striving with vigilance that the fearful omens may with God's help be turned to good. I ask what supplications I, as a petitioner, should press for, knowing in this case that persuasion is granted by heaven above all to perseverance in supplication. Make haste, I beg you, if possible before you write, or at least then, to manifest your fatherly presence in response to the delayed hopes of those devoted to you. Blessed be the divine name for the advancement of Brother Gregory de Bosellis which you mention in your letter, to the edification of the brethren and others.[6] I have intimated to our guardian at Oxford what was also your command.

Farewell in Christ Jesus and the blessed Virgin.

---

[2] James 1: 17.   [3] Hebr. 4: 12.   [4] 1 May 1253.
[5] The king had summoned a parliament at London for the quindene of Easter (4 May 1253): *Chron. Maj.* v. 373; *Councils & Synods*, ii/1, pp. 474–6.
[6] Perhaps referring to Gregory's appointment as vicar to the provincial minister; see Eccleston, p. 101.

219

To Brother John of Stamford, custodian of Oxford

Desideratissimo patri, Fratri Iohanni, custodi Oxoniensi, Frater Ada salutem et post uirtutum uictoriam coronam beatitudinum.

Pauperi scolari Radulfo de Multon, moris honesti, spei laudabilis, litterature competentis, quem michi meriti specialis familiare copulauit contubernium, cui quoque diutine ualetudinis grauis importunitas erumnosos cruciatus inflixit, interiori cordis affectione compatiens, uestre paternitatis inolite liberalitati suppliciter obsecro, rogans obnixius quatinus fraterne salutis negotium salutari suscipientes pietate, propter solum Saluatoris intuitum permittere uelitis, ut memoratus scolaris ad dictum Fratrem Adam de Bechesoueres,[1] quem sibi, ut dicit, non mediocriter profuisse sentit, ad remedium personaliter accedens, per diuinitatis gratiam ab eodem Fratre Ada inchoatum medele solatium propensiore percipere ualeat officio.

Locutus sum Oxonie cum uenerabili patre domino Norwicensi[2] a peregrinatione sua reuerso, in crastino solempnitatis beate Marie Magdalene.[3] In cuius spiritu, sicut uideo, dispensatio diuina, sit benedictio Dei Filio, emulationi uestre magnum aperuit ostium ad ingerendum diuinitus Altissime Maiestatis timorem pariter et amorem. | Non pigritetur, obsecro, fidelis amicitie necessitudo, prout celitus prestabitur opportunitas, impletis dispensationis superne sudoribus, desiderabilem reditus nobis uestri maturare letitiam.

f. 72ᵛ

Valeat uestre dilectionis incolumitas optabilis in Christo, etc. Non pigeat facte preci precem inculcare, ut in causa pietatis piam litteram prefato Fratri Ade scribere dignemini, per quam ad benignam sedulitatis opem excitetur.

219

To Brother John of Stamford, custodian of Oxford

Brother Adam to our dearest father, Brother John, custodian of Oxford, greetings and after the triumph of virtue a crown of beatitude.

Our poor scholar Ralph of Multon, a man of honourable conduct, praiseworthy hope, and qualified in letters, whose particular merit has made him a close companion of mine, has suffered serious distress from a long illness, which has inflicted wretched torments on him. Out of my heartfelt sympathy and affection for him, I humbly appeal to your constant generosity, father, with a pressing request to undertake the matter of the brother's health and ask that you would, out of sole regard for our Saviour, allow the said brother to go in person for a remedy to the said Brother Adam de Bechesoveres,[1] who he feels, as he says, has been of considerable help to him, so that he may, by the grace of God, receive the comfort of the medical treatment begun by the said Brother Adam with more effective application.

On the morrow of the solemnity of blessed Mary Magdalen[3] I spoke to our venerable father, the lord bishop of Norwich,[2] now returned from his pilgrimage. I see that in his spirit divine providence has, blessed be the Son of God, opened a great gate to your zealous ministry, by which to instil both the fear and the love of the Most High Majesty. I beg you, let not the need of faithful friendship be slow, as heaven grants opportunity, to hasten our joy for your much-desired return to us, once your labours for heaven have been completed.

Wishing you health in Christ, etc. Do not be ashamed to press one petition after another, and be so kind as to write a good letter to the said Brother Adam in a good cause, so as to arouse him to give his kind efforts.

---

219 [1] Adam's medical skill was also invoked for another person in Letter 238.

[2] Walter Suffield, bishop of Norwich 1244–57.

[3] 23 July.

220

To Brother John of Stamford, custodian of Oxford

Amantissimo patri, Fratri Iohanni de Stanford, custodi Oxoniensi, Frater Ada caritatis impendende uitam cum uita contemplande ueritatis.

Libet littera, quod loquela non licet, paterne pietati paruitatem filialem qualicunque famulatiue deuotionis affectu presentare. Igitur fere interceptum spiritum aneli pectoris sub importabili sarcina sollicitudinum opprimentium, quia non ualeo, patefacio. Porro cordi toties transuerberato affert non modicum leuaminis remedium insinuasse silentio quod eloquio non sufficio, grassantes importuni-tatum uehementias, nimirum uite tedium inferentes, nec amicitiam non molestare nequiuit cruciantis angustie uehementia. Inter scri-bendum calamus herebit cum ad attonite mentis afflictiones manus stupida lacesseret.ᵃ

Succingo igitur sermonem, rogans ⟨ut⟩ faciatis quod scio prohibiti faceretis, uidelicet ut uobis dabit diuine propitiationis superexuberans affluentia ualere, uidere, uelle, michi ad salutem subuenire propter uulnera Saluatoris non cunctemini. Ceterum, si fieri potest, desider-atam persone uestre presentiam deuotis uestris maturius consolandis per benignum patrocinium et consilium prouisiuum nullatenus exhibere pigritemini.

Quod michi tanta sedulitate suasistis et constanter per fratrem secretarium mandastis, uidelicet ut me Rading' transferam desider-atissime quietis gratia ibidem quantum expedire uidebitur mora-turum, si Deus uoluerit, complere propono, si adhuc michi beneplacitum uestrum, quod citius fieri uellem, super hoc insinuare curaueritis.

Valeat paternitatis uestre sospes integritas in Christo Iesu semper et beastissime Virgine.

220   ᵃ lacesceret MS.

220

To Brother John of Stamford, custodian of Oxford

Brother Adam to the most loving father, Brother John of Stamford, custodian of Oxford, a life bestowing charity with a life of contemplating truth.

It gladdens my filial modesty to address your fatherly goodness with my affection and devoted service by a letter, as word of mouth does not allow. I disclose to you that the breath is almost torn from my gasping breast under the insupportable burden of the concerns that weigh upon me, for I am not well. It brings some relief to my so often pierced heart to have suggested by silence what I cannot express by speech: the severity of the problems make my life weary; yet I could not refrain from troubling a friend with my difficulties and torments. My pen will stick as I write when my senseless hand would give pain to your astonished mind.

I am cutting short my words, asking you to do what I know you would do, even if forbidden, that is, as the superabundance of the divine mercy will grant you the strength, to see, to wish, that for the wounds of the Saviour you would not be slow to come to my aid for my salvation. So, if it can be, do not hesitate at all to come sooner in person to your devoted servants, to console them with your kind protection and perceptive advice.

I propose to carry out what you have so assiduously urged on me and constantly commanded me through my brother secretary, that is to transfer myself to Reading for the sake of most desired peace, and to stay there as long as it seems expedient, if it is God's will, if you are still good enough to indicate to me your good pleasure on the subject, which I would wish to be done quickly.

Wishing you sound health, father, ever in Christ and the blessed Virgin.

221

To Robert of Thornham, custodian of Cambridge

Fratri Roberto, custodi Cantabrigiensi,[1] Frater Ada meritorum gratiam et gloriam premiorum.

Pro beneuola sedulitatis uestre diligentia, quam licet nullatenus meritam circa meam modicitatem lati cordis et affectus letior et liberalior effectus cumulare non desistit, quod insufficientie mee nequit erumpnosa pauperies uobis, oro, satisfaciat superne largitionis supersufficiens affluentia. Sicut ex prouisiua discretionis uestre benigna circumspectione signastis, erga fratres Oxonie studentes, Domino dante, fiet sine more dispendio. Satis michi molestum fuit quod karissimus noster frater Vr.,[2] cuius in littera meministis, cui et cunctis amabilem benignitatis uestre suauitatem contingentibus uotiua prompte uoluntatis officia impendere, nec immerito, ut ualet, mea cupit exilitas, proficiscendi, sicut intellexi necessitate compulsus, priusquam eidem communicassem optata mutue agnitionis officia,[3] repentinum profectionis sue regressum accelerauit.

Opportuno tempore post instans Pascha desidero, ut ualueritis, uideritis, uolueritis, de membrana uitulina necessitati nostre per uestre sollicitudinis industriam, quoad fieri ualuerit sine fratrum grauamine prouideri. Parcat, precor, amicitia fidelis improbitati, quam iugiter animat, non tam desperatio displicendi quam impetrandi confidentia, quam[a] uestri gratia prestare satagitis per continua experientie multiplicioris argumenta.

Valeat dilectionis uestre sospes incolumitas, etc.

Karissimam animam Fratris Iohannis de Bannebyr', michi a puero specialissimi filiorum uestrorum, fratrum nostrorum piis memoriis speciali deuotione rogo uelitis recommendare ob intuitum Saluatoris.

In eternum, etc.

---

221   [a] quod MS

---

221   [1] Robert of Thornham was first warden of Lynn and then from c.1232 custodian of Cambridge until c.1250, when according to Eccleston he formed a resolution to go to the Holy Land: Eccleston, p. 89 and n. Moorman, *The Grey Friars in Cambridge*, p. 143.

221

To Robert of Thornham, custodian of Cambridge

Brother Adam to Brother Robert, custodian of Cambridge,[1] merited grace and glorious rewards.

I pray that the superabundance of heaven's largesse may make up the thanks that my miserable poverty cannot suffice to render you for the caring kindness with which your generous heart and glad affection ceaselessly heap generous gifts upon my humble and most undeserving self. As to what you indicated regarding the brothers studying at Oxford with your provident discretion and kind prudence, as the Lord grants, let it be done without delay. It rather disturbed me that our dearest Brother Vr.,[2] whom you mentioned in your letter, for whom, and for all who chance to come in contact with the loving kindness of your goodwill, my poor self rightly desires to carry out the services requested with a ready will so far as it can, when he was compelled, as I understand it, by the obligation to set out, before I had communicated to him the desired service of mutual recognition,[3] he suddenly hastened to turn back from his departure.

At a suitable time after the coming Easter I desire, as you are able, see fit, and wish for our needs to be supplied through your active care with the skin of a calf, so long as it can be done without burdening the brethren. I pray your loyal friendship may pardon my impudence, which is constantly encouraged, not so much by despair of displeasing you as by confidence in gaining my requests, of which you give us experience by graciously supplying us with manifold proofs.

Best wishes for your health, etc.

I ask you, if you would, out of regard for our Saviour, to commend the very dear soul of Brother John of Banbury to the pious commemoration of our brethren. To me he was from boyhood a most particular friend among your sons.

For ever, farewell, etc.

---

[2] The copyist's abbreviation is ambiguous. Possibly the reference is to Brother Vincent of Coventry, who was the first lector to the Franciscans at Cambridge; see Little, *Franciscan Papers, Lists and Documents*, pp. 132–4; Moorman, *The Grey Friars in Cambridge*, p. 143.

[3] Meaning possibly recognition of the academic qualifications obtained by the brother in Cambridge. The passage is obscure: does the brother's obligation 'to set out' refer to a physical journey or to his academic progress?

222

To John, guardian of Hereford

Desideratissimo patri, Fratri I(ohanni),[1] gardiano Herfordensi, Frater Ada salutem et post cursum temporis gloriam eternitatis.

Litteras inolite benignitatis uestre non tam circumspectionis industriam quam gratiam sedulitatis preferentes, leta suscepi deuotione, officiose caritatis mansuetiori beneuolentie, quantum ualet exilis amici qualiscunque conatus, referens gratiarum actiones. Licet optabilis persone uestre presentia plurimum apud nos afforet opportuna, tamen propter indefessam operam de salutis diligentia, quam et uigenter et uigilanter et uiuaciter, sicut audio, multimodam fraterne necessitatis subuentionem iugiter exhibere studetis, sit diuino nomini superexaltata benedictio, corporalem absentiam, que spiritualem unitatem non disiungit, longanimi tolerantia in Christo dinoscitur esse perferenda.

Succingo sermonem, sciens quia persuasionibus sit supersedendum ad flagrantiorem prompte pietatis uoluntatem. Concedat igitur, oro, Dei uirtus, Dei sapientia, Dei sanctificatio, ut in omnibus, quod prudenter discernitis geritis fortiter, temperanter cohibetis, distribuitis equaliter, ad illum finem referatis cum effectu saluifico ubi est Deus omnia in omnibus, eternitate certa et pace perfecta.[2]

Exultationis iocunditatem amicissimus in Domino Frater Walterus de Rauenigham[3] animabus gloriam diuinitatis emulantibus ⟨prebet⟩, qui sicut nuntiat frequens testimonii credibilis assertio, quoniam ualide ad ueritatem ambulat in ministerio uerbi salutaris, et docet acutius et delectabilius tenet, flectit uehementius, et felicius promouet tam clerum quam populum ad uisionem ueritatis et caritatis communionem iugi animans efficacia. Quem nimirum in qualiquali tamen cordis domicilio collocaui.

222

To John, guardian of Hereford

Brother Adam to the dearest father, Brother John,[1] guardian of Hereford, after time has run its course, eternal glory.

I was glad to receive your kind letter bearing the marks of your attentive circumspection and gracious concern, and I thank you for your gentle benevolence and thoughtful charity, so far as the efforts of any poor friend can say. Although your longed-for presence would be exceedingly welcome to us here, yet by reason of your untiring labour in the cause of salvation by which you are continually zealous, as I hear, to offer manifold assistance to the needs of the brethren— blessed and highly exalted be the divine name—we know that we must bear with long suffering in Christ your bodily absence, which does not separate us spiritually, who are one.

I cut short my words in the knowledge that persuasion must give way to a will burning to be available to piety. May therefore the power of God, the wisdom of God, the sanctifying force of God grant that in all things what you discern with prudence, perform with resolution, govern with moderation, apportion with equity, you may with efficacy direct to that end where God is all in all, assuredly in eternity and perfect peace.[2]

Our most devoted brother in the Lord, Walter of Ravenham,[3] is a source of delighted rejoicing to souls who are zealous for the glory of God, as is frequently declared by credible testimony, for he lives as a powerful advocate of truth in his ministry of the word of salvation, he teaches acutely and holds attention with the pleasure of his discourse, persuades with the force of his arguments, and happily leads both clergy and people on to the vision of truth and a communion of charity. I have without any reservation taken him to my heart such as it is.

---

222 [1] Not identified. The extension of the name is hypothetical.
 [2] This valedictory admonition is from Augustine, *De civitate Dei*, xix. 20; *CSEL* xl, ii. 407. Adam also uses it in Letters 8, 73, 77, and 90.
 [3] Brother Walter of Ravenham was, according to a 14th-c. list inserted in Eccleston's chronicle, the tenth lector to the friars at Cambridge: Eccleston, p. 58; Little, *Franciscan Papers, Lists and Documents*, pp. 132–3.

223

To Thomas of York

Eximio Fratri Thome de Eboraco,[1] Frater Ada exilis salutem.

Si acerrimarum inuectionum cause uehementiores fores effregerint, putabimus soporatam letargici corporis socordiam excitare ualebunt? Verendum reor ne carnosi cadaueris moles emortua languidam spiritus tepidi scintillam, piget non dixisse fauillam, suffocare contingat. Arrogantiam execrabimus an accusabimus negligentiam? Vtramque longissime relegat fides amicitie. Sed quorsum hec? Non unius tamen sed et similium transgressionem sceleris dampnare compellor. Quod nunc loquor est tabula Trinitatis[2] toties prompte sepe promissa, nec exhibita saltem tardius. Faciem muto, quod compellit amor. Nuper michi de Curia Romana allatum est Apostolice Sedis priuilegium, pro quo laborare sui gratia uoluit amantissimus Frater Iohannes, domini papa nuntius,[3] quem rogo, si placet, ex intimis affectualium uiscerum medullis obsequio mei salutetis. Salutetis etiam ex nomine quos salutandos iudicaueritis uestros in Christo secretarios, eorundem orationibus meam recommendantes insufficientiam.

224

To Thomas of York

f. 73 Patri Thome de Eboraco Frater Ada ⟨salutem⟩

Propter sancta uulnera Dei et propter pium cruorem Filii Dei, illa tolerata, hunc effusum a Filio Dei liberandis animabus, regni[a] Dei suscipite causam, ut ualueritis et uideritis, contra tam diram immanitatem satellitum Diaboli laturi presidium, prout diuinitus concedetur, uiro commendabili, domino Willelmo presbitero, latori presentium, qui est unus de presentatis domine regine ad ecclesias de quibus audistis, et ad eius presentationem in ipsa, ad quam presentatus est ecclesia per dominum Elyensem[1] institutus.

224 ᵃ regnum MS.

223 [1] On Thomas of York see Letters 69 and n., 186, and 190.
[2] The work referred to is uncertain. Possibly the reference is to the first book of Thomas's great treatise on metaphysics, as yet unedited, which was uncompleted at the date of his death in 1260: Little, *Franciscan Papers, Lists and Documents*, p. 68.
[3] On Brother John of Kent see Letters 94 n. 3, 171, 215–17.

223

To Thomas of York

The lowly Brother Adam to the distinguished Brother Thomas of York,[1] greetings.

If there are cogent reasons for breaking into bitterest reproaches, shall we suppose that they will avail to stir the drowsy body from its sleepy negligence? I think the fear is that the dead lump of your fleshly corpse may end in suffocating a faint spark, I regret not to have said the ashes of your lukewarm spirit. Shall we execrate your arrogance or blame you for your negligence? Loyal friendship would utterly banish either suggestion. But what is this about? I am forced to condemn the sin not of one but of similar transgressions. What I am speaking about is the tabula of The Trinity,[2] so many times ready and so often promised, but not shown, even belatedly. I am changing my guise, as love compels me. I was recently brought from the Roman Curia a privilege of the Apostolic See, for which our most loving Brother John, the nuncio of the lord pope,[3] was graciously willing to labour. I ask you, please, to greet him with my warmest affection and service. Greet those of your secretaries in Christ by name to whom you consider it appropriate, and commend my inadequate self to their prayers.

224

To Thomas of York

Brother Adam to Brother Thomas of York (greetings).

For the sacred wounds of God, for the holy blood of the Son of God, the first endured, the second poured out by the Son of God for the deliverance of souls, take up the cause of the kingdom of God, as you are able and see fit, against the grim and monstrous acts of the Devil's satellites, as God will grant, to offer protection to the commendable Sir William, a priest, the bearer of this letter. He is one of those presented by the lady queen to the churches of which you have heard, and has on her presentation been instituted by the lord bishop of Ely[1] in that church to which he has been presented.

224   [1] Hugh of Northwold, bishop of Ely 1229–54.

Bene fecistis, sit benignitati uestre boni Dei benedicta retributio, qui pro patre secundum carnem dilecti Fratris Iohannis de Beuerlaco[2] in negotio sue salutis tam consultum uigilantie fidelis adiutorium, necnon et in ceteris presertim ad salutem animarum pertinentibus tam exquisita circumspectione exhibere uoluistis.

Etsi incliti comitis Leycestriensis[3] cause graues, propter tam uaria tantarum malignitatum molimina, inter formidandorum discriminum ancipites euentus pendere uideantur, tamen indubitatam fiduciam prestat superna clementia, de qua secundum Scripturam 'qui sperant habebunt fortitudinem, assument pennas ut aquile, current et non laborabunt, ambulabunt et non deficient'.[4] Quod desiderabilem grandium difficultatum exitum ad sui nominis gloriam et letitiam fidelium suorum propensius exhibebit, saltem illum quem pia uestre discretionis industria in littera michi nuper transmissa commemorauit. Satis argumentose tam domine regine quam comitisse Leycestriensis indefessa sollicitudo benedicta satagit,[b] sollicitudine operam impendere mitigandis motibus regie maiestatis, qui seuere nimis sunt concitati occasione supramemorate presentationis, licet hactenus, ut audio, profecerunt exiliter ad rediuiuam irritate celsitudinis indignationem. Orandum igitur est, ut imperet uentis et mari Is in cuius manu cor regis est, sicut dominationes aquarum, ut post tempestatem tam letiferam salutiferam faciat tranquillitatem. Numquid, nisi apud stultissimorum iniquitatem, res omnium grauissima leuiter pensanda est? Absit in eternum a sancta sapientum equitate.

225

To Thomas of York

Desideratissimo patri in Christo, Fratri Thome de Eboraco, Frater Ada salutem in Domino.

Validam uigilantiam, fulgidam industriam, feruidam emulationem, constantem perseuerantiam amabilis animi uestri in hiis que ad honorem Domini seculorum et salutem regni Dei cedere cognoscuntur, non sine gratiarum actione letus ex innumeris colligo experimentis. Excellenti uiro magistro Eustachio,[1] domini Cantuariensis

---

[b] satagunt MS.

---

[2] Cf. Letter 174.　　　　[3] Simon de Montfort.　　　　[4] Isa. 40: 31.

225　[1] Eustace of Lynn, archbishop's Official 1251–8; cf. Letter 26 and n.

You did well—may the good God reward your kindness—in being so good as to provide such carefully considered help and faithful watchfulness for the natural father of dear Brother John of Beverley[2] in the matter of his salvation, acting with such carefully considered prudence also in other things, especially those relating to the salvation of souls.

Though the grave position of the noble earl of Leicester[3] seems to hang upon the uncertain outcome of a fearfully perilous situation because of such great and various machinations by evil forces, yet the mercy from above gives us certain confidence, by which according to Scripture 'they that hope in the Lord shall renew their strength. They shall take wings as eagles; they shall run and not be weary; they shall walk and not faint.'[4] He will present us with the desired outcome from these great difficulties, to the glory of his name and the joy of his loyal people, at any rate that which you refer to with your pious discernment in the letter recently sent me. Both the queen and the countess of Leicester are making efforts with blessed and tireless solicitude to appease the wrath of his royal majesty, seriously aroused by reason of the presentation referred to above, though up until now they have made poor progress, as I hear, with assuaging his highness's renewed displeasure. So we must pray that He in whose hand is the heart of the king, just like the control of the waters, may command the winds and the sea, so as to make a saving calm after such a deadly storm. Is the most serious thing of all to be treated lightly except by the wickedness of the most foolish? May that ever be absent from the holy peace of the wise.

225

To Thomas of York

Brother Adam to our very dear father, Brother Thomas of York, greetings in the Lord.

With thanksgiving and joy I gather from innumerable proofs the news of your steady vigilance, your shining industry, fervent zeal, and constant perseverance of your lovely mind in those things that are known to redound to the honour of the Lord and the saving condition of the kingdom of God. Please take care to convey our most devoted thanks in place of our Saviour and from my duty to the excellent Master Eustace,[1] the Official of the lord of Canterbury, for not

Officiali, uice Saluatoris et mei officio grates rogo referre curetis deuotissimas, qui peruasurum Dei sanctuarium fauore prosequi non consensit. Cuius meminerit in bonum qui solus bonus est, quia a sanctuario repulit sacrilegum.² Multum, mi karissime, in hac parte recommendari uobis opto causam Filii Dei, quem tam unice diligitis. Non uideo aliud hac uice signandum domino Officiali.

In facto domini comitis Simonis, licet ingratissima malignitas debita responsa detrectet, spero respondebit prospera supergratiosa benignitas. Illa sui militis sudores despiciet; ista sui supplicis obsequia respiciet. Molestiosa scandalorum perturbamina, licet agi non sinam silentio pacis cunctis optate mortalibus, necesse est ut ueniant secundum ueritatis assertionem, ut domus Dei unde impingitur ut corruat, inde stabiliatur ut persistat, et electorum anime unde concutiuntur ne quiescant inde exerceantur ne fatiscant.ª Prestitit super hac re occasionem longi sermonis et interpretabilis, quod in epistole uestre calce apposuistis; sed succinxit eum et mea insufficientia et uite tedium inferens importunissima occupationum angustia. Etiam loquendi seriem intercepit irruentium improbitas.

Vtinam, si comes fuerit uita, propter urgentissima salutis discrimina concedatur diuinitus nobis uiue uocis inuicem frui colloquio circa instans festum Pasche. Comiti Simoni, precor, ob contemplationem Altissimi in uerbis uite consiliorum directiones impendere studeatis.

Valete in Christo Iesu semper et beatissima Virgine. Salutetis, obsecro, obsequio mei specialissimos patres, Fratrem Andream de Lexinton, Fratrem Ricardum de Walda, Fratrem Willelmum de Basinges, Fratrem Thomam de Hales, et alios michi deuotos. Mittit uobis Frater Laurentius quaternos matris prophetice³ pro quibus misistis. Capitula summas libri distinguentia, ut reor, non mediocriter ad eius intellectum utilia, Domino dante, alias habebitis. Specialiter presentate, peto, qualemcunque mee gratitudinis affectionem uenerandi patris, Fratris A. gardiani Londonensis latiori liberalitati.

225   ª lacescant *MS.*

consenting to confer his favour upon the devastation of God's sanctuary.[2] He who alone is good will remember to reward him because he has repelled a profane person from the sanctuary. In this respect I very much wish to commend to you, my dearest friend, the cause of the Son of God, whom you love so single-mindedly. I do not see that we need indicate anything else on this occasion to the lord Official.

In the matter of the lord earl Simon, although ungraciousness and ill-will refuse a due reply, I hope a kind and superlatively gracious reply in the affirmative will be given. The former will display contempt for the efforts of his knight; the latter will consider indulgence for the supplicant. Although I would not suffer troublesome scandals to be passed over in silence of the peace that all mortals desire, they must needs come, as the Truth declares, so that the things whereby the house of God is assaulted to bring it down are those that make it steadfast to continue; and the things whereby the souls of the saints are afflicted lest they should relax are those that exercise them lest they should faint. What you added on this subject at the foot of your letter warranted a long discourse worthy of comment; but it has been cut short by my inadequacy and the very grievous constraints of business which make life weary. The wretched onrush of demands interrupts even continuous speech.

I would that, if I am still alive, God would grant us the enjoyment of a talk together around the coming Easter, in view of the very urgent dangers to safety. I pray you, out of consideration of the Most High, take care to provide earl Simon with the words of life through counsel and direction.

Farewell ever in Christ and the Blessed Virgin. Give my greetings, I beg you, to our particular fathers, Brothers Andrew of Lexington, Richard of Walda, William of Basing, Thomas of Hales, and the others dear to me. Brother Laurence is sending you the quires of the prophetic mother,[3] for which you sent. You will have at another time, by gift of the Lord, the headings distinguishing the *summas* of the book, which are not a little useful, I think, to understanding it. In particular convey my affectionate gratitude to the open generosity of the venerable Father, Brother A. warden of London.

---

[2] Possibly a reference to Eustace's conflict with Bishop Aymer de Valence over patronage resulting in his violent abduction; cf. Letter 56 n. 2.

[3] The reference is obscure; possibly it is to the prophetic writings of St Hildegard of Bingen, as Brewer suggested.

226

To William Bellun

Fratri Willelmo Bellun[1] Frater Ada (salutem) et sincerum debite dilectionis affectum

De uobis innate benignitatis amicitia fideli, quamuis hoc meritorum meorum tenuitas non requirat, ex efficacibus argumentis experientie multiplicis uestri gratia plenam in Domino reportans fiduciam, discretionis uestre supplico sedulitati quatinus karissimum michi in Christo Thomam, latorem presentium, de consueta pietatis beneuolentia in negotio suo, quod ipse uobis, si placet, uiua uoce est expositurus, quatenus inheretur misericordie et iustitie deseruitur, intuitu Saluatoris salutari consilio iuuare uelitis.

Valeat caritatis uestre communicatio in Christo semper et beatissima Virgine.

227

To William Bellun

Predilecto Fratri Willelmo Bellun Frater Ada gratiam in presenti et gloriam in futuro.

Eadmundum, latorem presentium, quem michi dudum specialior in Domino coniunxit familiaritas, obnixius rogo quatinus, quatenus secundum Dominum fieri poterit, ob contemplationem diuinitatis in hiis que uobis, si placet, plenius est expositurus uel expressurus, per propensioris gratie fauorem non ducatis indignum.

Valeat uestre pietatis affectio in Christo, etc. Parcat michi, oro, suauitatis uestre tolerantia super hoc, quod compulsus necessariorum instantiis benignitatem uestram uelud importuna pulso frequentia. Iterum in eternum ualete.

226

To William Bellun

Brother Adam to Brother William Bellun,[1] greetings and a debt of true affection.

Having in the Lord gained full confidence in your faithful friendship and natural kindness, experienced from numerous and effectual demonstrations which I do not deserve, I am imposing upon your discretion and zeal with a request that, out of regard for the Saviour, you would be so good as to assist Thomas, the bearer of this letter, who is very dear to me in Christ, with sound advice in his business, which he will, if you please, explain to you by word of mouth, so long as mercy is embraced and justice is served.

Farewell, reciprocating your charity ever in Christ and the Blessed Virgin.

227

To William Bellun

Brother Adam to the specially beloved Brother William Bellun, grace in the present time and glory to come.

I fervently ask you that, so far as it can be done in accord with the will of the Lord, you would deign as a very gracious favour to help Edmund, the bearer of this letter, who has long been joined to me in the Lord in a close association, in those matters which, if you please, he will explain or represent to you more fully.

May your piety and affection flourish in Christ, etc. I pray you will with your sweet tolerance forgive me for so frequently imposing upon your kindness, driven as I am by pressing needs.

---

226 [1] From Letters 234 and 235 it is evident that William Bellun was a friar resident at court, with access to King Henry; cf. Introduction, pp. xxxvii–xxxviii.

228

To William Bellun

f. 73ᵛ Desideratissimo patri, Fratri Willelmo Bellun, Frater Ada salutem et post merita temporis premia felicitatis.

Pro karissimo michi in Christo magistro Randulfo de Hukelbi, uiro probate conuersationis et eminentis litterature, michi quoque in Christo predilecto, ad supplicem ipsius instantiam benignitatis uestre discretioni petitionis huius cartulam destinaui, rogans attentius quatinus eidem in necessitatis articulo, quem ipse, si placet, uobis uiua uoce est expositurus, sedulitatis consuete consilium fauorabiliter exhibere uelitis, quatenus clementie consentitur nec obuenitur innocentie.

Valeat dilectionis uestre suauitas, etc.

229

To William Bellun

Fratri Willelmo Bellun Frater Ada salutem.

Fateor, mi karissime frater, quod uariis sedulitatis occupationibus, sub quibus uestram supra modum conspicio iugiter laborare sollicitudinem, ingerere uereor importunas intercessionis multiplicate petitiones. Verum cum Thome Cornuwario, latore presentium, qui lapsus facultatibus angustioris fortune et propter debitorum grauamina constringitur indigentiis, compassionis affectum negare nequiui. Benignitati uestre, quam in causis pietatis rediuiuam indesinenter exhibere cognoui diligentiam, presentem direxi petitiunculam, rogans obnixius quatinus iuxta quod sue necessitatis articulus uobis, si placet, uiua uoce exponendus requirit,ᵃ eidem secundum Deum propensiori fauore uelitis suffragare.

Valeat dilectionis uestre sinceritas, etc.

---

229 ᵃ requirit *added by a corrector in the margin.*

228

To William Bellun

Brother Adam to the dearest father, Brother William Bellun, greetings and after the merits won in time the rewards of happiness.

I have directed the document containing this petition to your kind
attention on behalf of Master Randulf Hukelby, who is very dear to
me in Christ, a man of proven good life and outstanding learning,
who is also specially dear to me in Christ, at his humble insistence,
with a pressing request for you to favour him with counsel with your
customary concern in a matter of necessity which he will, if you
please, explain to you by word of mouth, so far as it accords with
mercy and does not hinder innocence.

Farewell, dear and gentle brother.

229

To William Bellun

Brother Adam to Brother William Bellun, greetings.

I confess, my dearest brother, that I fear imposing unwelcome and
multiplied requests for help upon the various and excessive preoccupations under which I see you constantly labouring so con-
scientiously. But I could not deny my compassion for Thomas of
Cornwall, the bearer of this letter, who, having lost his means of
support by harsh ill-fortune, is in the grip of indigence on account of
the burden of his debts. I have directed this little petition to your kind
self, knowing what lively concern you ceaselessly devote to good
causes, with a pressing request that you would support him with your
ready favour, as God wills, according to what is required by the
particulars of his need, which he will, if you please, explain to you by
word of mouth.

Farewell, true beloved, etc.

230

To William Bellun

Dilectissimo patri, Fratri Willelmo Bellun, Frater Ada salutem ex spiritu scientie cum spiritu pietatis.

Cum dominam Julianam uiduam, quam, sicut laudabile uulgauit testimonium, et in Deum deuotio et in pauperes liberalitas et honestas conuersationis et suauitas mansuetudinis plurimum reddunt commendabilem, sicut intellexi, uiolata lege publice rectitudinis, peruiolente potestatis grauis oppressio deseuiat, et non sit huiusmodi[a] personis in hiis et similibus importunitatum angustiis ad regalis clementie protectionem presidialem defensionis refugium;[1] memorate uidue lacrimosa me compulit obsecratio presentem deprecatoriam uestre caritati destinare, suppliciter obsecrans ut, ob contemplationem Illius qui precipue potentatibus per Scripturam suam clamat, dicens, 'Non despiciet Dominus preces pupilli',[2] etc.[b]

231

To William Bellun

Desideratissimo patri in Christo, Fratri Willelmo Bellun, Frater Ada salutem et de innumeris ingenue mentis munificentiis plusquam obsequiales perpetis amicitie gratiarum actiones.

Scio quoniam sufficit benigne strenuitati desiderium insinuasse fraternum propter quod, licet mea frequentius deuotionem uestram precibus improbitas onerauerit, tamen rogo, mi amantissime, quatinus pro Thoma de Marisco, uobis uestri gratia non incognito et michi sanguine coniuncto,[1] cum ipsius negotium per latorem presentium uobis uiua uoce fuerit insinuatum, illud secundum quod res requisierit et uestra melius nouerit industria, prosequi uelitis efficaci benignitatis diligentia.

Valeat dilectionis uestre probata suauitas in Christo semper et beatissima Virgine.

---

230   [a] huius *MS*.   [b] *The text thus breaks off incomplete.*

230   [1] Meaning that her case does not qualify her for a common law defence of possession such as one concluded by a royal writ of right.
   [2] Ecclus. 35: 17.

230

To William Bellun

Brother Adam to the dearest father, Brother William Bellun, greetings from the spirit of knowledge and the spirit of piety.

Since the Lady Juliana, a widow, who, as her excellent and
widespread reputation bears witness, is recommended both by her
devotion to God and her generosity to the poor, and the integrity of
her life and sweet clemency, is, as I understand, the object of serious
oppression by a violent exercise of power in breach of the law of
public justice; and persons of this sort do not enjoy the governmental
protection of the royal clemency[1] as a defence and refuge in these and
similar distressing straits; the tearful entreaty of this widow has
driven me to send this appeal to your charity with a humble request
that you would, out of regard for Him who cries aloud through his
Scriptures, especially to those in power, saying 'The Lord will not
despise the prayer of the orphan',[2] etc.

231

To William Bellun

Brother Adam to the most dear father, Brother William Bellun,
greetings and thanksgiving for the innumerable gifts of his noble
mind and still more for his perpetual friendship.

I know that it is enough to have suggested a brother's wish to your
kindness and energy and on this account, although so frequently I
have wickedly imposed upon your devotion with my requests, I
nevertheless ask you, my beloved, on behalf of Thomas Marsh,
thanks to you not unknown to you and related to me by blood,[1]
that when his business has been indicated to you by the bearer of this
letter by word of mouth, if you please, you would be kind enough to
favour it with your assistance, as the matter requires and you know
best.

Farewell beloved, and your proven gentleness ever in Christ and
the Blessed Virgin.

231 [1] Thomas Marsh; see Introduction, p. xix. Cf. Letters 12, 110, 111.

232

To William Bellun

Desideratissimo patri, Fratri Willelmo Bellun, Frater Ada salutem et obsequialem affectus deuoti promptitudinem.

Tanto confidentius pro hiis qui familiari contubernio michi sunt coniuncti, uestram petitoriis benignitatem interpellare consentio, quanto sedulam inolite benignitatis diligentiam apud uestre discretionis industriam erga meam modicitatem plurimis, licet non meruerim, argumentorum experimentis probaui fuisse liberaliorem. Quocirca pro karissimo michi in Christo domino Willelmo de Radenore, rectore ecclesie Christi de Clopham,[1] uestre supplico dilectioni, rogans attentius quatinus eidem in negotio quod ipse, si placet, uobis uiua uoce est expositurus, quoad fieri poterit ueritate preuia et inoffensa iustitia, salutaris consilii et efficacis adiutorii iuxta caritatis uestre circumspectionem uelitis impendere.

Valeat uestra benignitas in Christo semper et beatissima Virgine. Reuerendissimum patrem, dominum Nicolaum,[2] ecclesie Christi Cantuariensis priorem, filiosque uestros obsequio mei rogo salutetis, insufficientiam meam piis ipsorum orationibus recommendantes.

233

To William Bellun

Fratri Willelmo Bellun Frater Ada.

Letificauit me leta littera latioris animi. Letificet uos letitia sempiterna latitudinis immense. Magnificentie reginalis liberali gratie mensuram supereffluentem inexhausta largitio rependat, oro, pro indeficienti fontalium beneficiorum affluentia. Indefessam sedulitatis uestre strenuitatem clementi semper dignatione respiciens, pro eo quod insufficientiam meam apud inclitum comitem Cornubiensem[1] efficaci diligentia excusare studuistis, dignas[a] dilectionis uestre fidei, quantas ualeo, refero gratiarum actiones. Cum quo uobiscum, sicut insinuastis, non mediocriter gauderem habere colloquium, si loci

233   [a] dignum MS.   [b] auerto MS.

---

232   [1] Clapcot (Berkshire) or possibly Clopton (Northamptonshire).
   [2] Nicholas of Sandwich, prior 1244–58.

232

To William Bellun

Brother Adam to the most dear father, Brother William Bellun, greetings with humble affection and ready devotion.

I agree to impose upon your kindness with petitions on behalf of those connected with me in a household association, all the more confidently as I have tested by very many proofs the great extent of your inborn kindness and discreet labour on behalf of my humble self, though I did not deserve it. For this reason I am supplicating you on behalf of Sir William Radnor, rector of the church of Christ of Clopham,[1] who is very dear to me in Christ, with a pressing request that with your charity and prudence you would be so kind as to give him salutary counsel and efficacious help over the business that he will himself explain to you, if you please, by word of mouth, so long as it can be done while adhering to truth and without compromising justice.

Farewell, kind brother, ever in Christ and the Blessed Virgin. I ask you to greet for me the lord Nicholas, the prior of Christ Church Canterbury,[2] and your sons, commending my inadequate self to their pious prayers.

233

To William Bellun

Brother Adam to Brother William Bellun.

I was gladdened by the joyful letter from your capacious mind. May you rejoice in the eternal joy that is boundless. I pray a boundless generosity may superabundantly repay the generous grace of the queen's magnanimity for the unfailing flow from the fountain of her benefactions. Looking at your tireless energy and conscientious effort marked by fitting kindness, I offer you all the thanks I can for your loyalty and love and for your effective efforts to excuse my inadequate self from attending the noble earl of Cornwall.[1] It would give me no small pleasure to have a conversation with him and you, if an opportune place and time and other circumstances were

233   [1] Richard, earl of Cornwall, 1209–72; cf. Letter 30 n. 6.

et temporis et aliarum circumstantiarum optabilis interueniret opportunitas, quam ad presens apparentem non aduerto;[b] presertim cum
memorati domini comitis statum, quem prosperum faciat diuinitas
propitia, magnorum euentuum multa uarietas mutationibus improui-
sis de facili ualeat hiis diebus uariare.[2] Michi quoque incumbat circa
instantem Dominicam in Ramis Palmarum uersus dominum Lyncolniensem, iuxta urgens ipsius mandatum, propter discriminosa causarum grauium molestamina iter arripere.

Valeat amicitie uestre benigna suauitas in Christo, etc. Obsequio
mei salutari peto karissimum patrem, Fratrem W. etc.

234

To William Bellun

(1249)

Desideratissimo patri, Fratri Willelmo Bellun, Frater Ada salutem et
inuiolabilem debite dilectionis necessitudinem.

Mi karissime, super quod ualeo memor amicitie benigne sedulitati
referre cupio gratiarum actiones, nec immerito, quia erga meam
humilitatem affectio rediuiua uestre benignitatis ⟨auxilium⟩ uicibus
frequentatis[a] satagit ostendere. Ceterum strenuam caritatis uestre
promptitudinem in causarum salutarium promotione sepius compro-
batam, ob intuitum Saluatoris suppliciter obsecro quatinus reuerendi
Patris Aniani, electi de Sancto Asaph,[1] pium negotium apud regalem
clementiam ad ecclesiastice salutis incrementum, sub eterne retribu-
tionis expectatione, secundum quod uestre discretioni diuinitus fuerit
inspiratus, diligenter uelitis adiuuare.

Valeat uestre dilectionis suauitas, etc.

235

To William Bellun

f. 74 Desideratissimo patri, Fratri Willelmo Bellun, Frater Ada salutem,
pacem in terris et gloriam in excelsis.

Cum preter yemales elementorum iniurias, preter prolixas uiarum

---

234   [a] sequentatis *MS.*

to be found, which I think are not at present in evidence; especially since the status of the said lord earl—which may God's favour prosper—may easily be subject to change these days by the unforeseeable changes of great events.[2] Also I myself am obliged to set off around the coming Palm Sunday to see the lord bishop of Lincoln, in response to his urgent command on account of dangerous troubles arising from grave matters.

Farewell, kind and gentle friend in Christ, etc. For my service I ask our dearest father, Brother W., to be given my greetings.

234

To William Bellun

(1249)

Brother Adam to the very dear father, Brother William Bellun, greetings with the inviolable love that is due.

My dearest brother, mindful of your friendship, I rightly desire to render thanks more than I am able to express for your sedulous kindness by which you repeatedly proffer assistance to my humble self. Now I am humbly appealing to the energy and promptitude of your charity, so often proved in promoting religious causes, and out of regard for our Saviour I beg you to be so good as to give your care and help to the holy business of the reverend father Anian, bishop elect of St Asaph,[1] in his dealings with the royal clemency, for the increase of salvation in the Church in expectation of an eternal reward, according as your discretion is inspired by God.

Farewell, gentle beloved.

235

To William Bellun

Brother Adam to the very dear father, Brother William Bellun, greetings, peace on earth, and glory in the highest.

Since beside the harm of the winter weather, the extensive problem

---

[2] The reference is to Earl Richard's bid for headship of the Roman Empire, in pursuance of which he was elected King of the Romans in 1257.

234   [1] Anian I, consecrated bishop of St Asaph in Nov. 1249.

difficultates, preter importuni temporis angustias, preter uexati uigoris fatigationes, etiam inualide ualetudinis grauitas obsistat, quominus iuxta regalis excellentie iussionem, ad instans festum Sancti Eadwardi[1] personaliter accedere sufficiam, suppliciter obsecro ut sicut potuerit, nouerit, uoluerit benigni cordis diserta strenuitas apud regie maiestatis celsitudinem urgentes prompte deuotionis detinentias, si tamen id opportunum fore censueritis, uigilanti uelit excusare diligentia; tanto propensiori petitionem presentem prose-quentes[a] sedulitate, quanto mentem sauciam dolor anxius ex memor-atis obsistentiis acrius affligit.

Valeat amabilis dilectionis uestre sinceritas in Christo semper et beatissima Virgine.

236

To Brother Ralph called Monk

Fratri R⟨adulpho⟩ dicto Monacho Frater Ada salutem

Amatum clericum, ut puto, mansueto more honestatum, re famil-iari attenuatum, atroces iniurias perpessum, ob diuine miserationis intuitum estimo plurimum esse compatiendum cum effectu, cum Is qui ait, 'Estote misericordes, sicut et Pater uester misericors est',[1] etiam quinto loco beatificans misericordes, 'Beati' inquiens 'miser-icordes, quoniam ipsi misericordiam consequentur'.[2] Rogo igitur benignam interuentionis uestre strenuitatem, ut eundem clericum Magistro Roberto de Sancta Agatha[3] uel Magistro Rogero,[4] uel Magistro Nicholao,[5] uel quibusdam eorum uel omnibus, uice uestri et mei recommendare uelitis in Domino, uel alicui alio,[a] sicut expedire censueritis, ut in negotiis suis expediendis in curia domini Lyncolniensis beneuoli fauoris opportunitas secundum Dominum et in Deo maturius exhibeatur, etiam pro ipso apud dominum inter-uenientes ut aliquam elemosine sue portiunculam pauperrimus percipiat, licet alias idem dominus sui gratia de memorata elemosina sua illi fecerit subuenire.

235 ᵃ MS adds admittentes
236 ᵃ alii MS.

235 ¹ 13 Oct., an occasion often celebrated by King Henry with a banquet and meeting of a great council or 'parliamentary' assembly.

236 ¹ Luke 6: 36.　　　　　　　　　² Matt. 5: 7.

of the roads, the hardships of the inconvenient season, the weariness of my jolted strength, the burden of my failing health is also an obstacle to my being personally present, as bidden by the king's excellency, at the coming feast of St Edward,[1] I humbly beg you, as you can and know how, to be good enough with the energy of your kind heart to excuse my absence to his majesty's highness, with care and caution pleading the pressing obstacles detaining me from my prompt devotion—if however, you judge that would be opportune; pursuing this petition so much more forcefully as my mind is grievously afflicted by sorrow and anxiety on account of the obstacles I have mentioned.

Farewell, true beloved, ever in Christ and the Blessed Virgin.

236

To Brother Ralph called Monk

Brother Adam to Brother Ralph called Monk, greetings.

I consider a beloved clerk who, as I think, is graced by his gentle manners, his depleted family means, and has suffered terrible wrongs, should receive much effective sympathy, out of regard for the divine pity, since He who says 'Be merciful, as your Father is merciful'[1] even gives mercy the fifth place in the beatitudes, crying 'Blessed are the merciful, for they shall obtain mercy'.[2] Therefore I ask for your kind and vigorous intervention, that you would be good enough to recommend this clerk to Master Robert of St Agatha[3] or to Master Roger,[4] or to Master Nicholas,[5] or to some or all of them or to someone else, as you judge it expedient, so that while expediting his business at the court of the lord bishop of Lincoln, he may sooner be favoured with the chance of a benevolence, also appealing for him to the lord bishop that the very poor man may receive some little part of the bishop's alms, though otherwise his lordship may of his own accord cause him to receive support from the said alms.

---

[3] Master Robert of St Agatha was an officer, possibly chancellor, of Oxford University: see Letter 22 n. 1; cf. Letter 127.

[4] Possibly Master Roger de Burewardiscote, a member of Grosseteste's familia, with possessions in Oxford: *BRUO* i. 322; Major, 'The familia of Grosseteste', pp. 222–3.

[5] Possibly Master Nicholas Grecus, a member of Grosseteste's familia; Major, ibid. p. 229.

237

To Brother Ralph called Monk

(1251–2)

Desideratissimo patri, Fratri Radulpho dicto Monacho, Frater Ada
salutem.

Pro domina priorissa de Beletun[1] et eiusdem loci uenerabili collegio
uirginum, memini me nuper scripsisse domino Lyncolniensi et
domino archidiacono Oxoniensi[2] et domino archidiacono Leycestriensi[3] et uobis, mi karissime. Memorate autem moniales interpositas
a me pro ipsis huiuscemodi petitiones, per suam simplicitatem ut
reor, secundum rationabilem rerum necessariarum requisitionem
nequaquam ut oportuit sunt prosecute. Proinde non piget iterato
earundem causas uobis, si placet, uiua uoce exponendas, circumspecte
uestre strenuitatis industrie in Christo recommendare, pro quibus sub
quanto possum affectione instanter rogo, supplicans attentius quatinus ob benedicti Saluatoris intuitum eisdem de consueta sedulitatis
benigne uigilantia in hiis que ad prefate domus spectare cognoscuntur
pacem pariter et salutem apud memoratas dominas[a] consilium et
auxilium impartiri studeatis sagacitate beneuola.

Suasoriis supersedendum putaui ad eum cui persuasit inspiratio
diuina gratie sue dona non deserere, pro quibus laborosas operas
impendere non negastis. Anxie dolendum et stupendum apprime
puto quod pestis illa, per quam tante religiose conuersationis
corruptele supradicto conuentui, ut dicitur,[b] sunt ingeste, ut audio,
sub falso magistri nomine perdendis tam rebus quam moribus
perniciosius incumbit.[4] Torporis in hac parte fomitem subministrant,
ut astruitur, apud reuerentissimum pontificem quidam pestilentes, ad
instar scorpionum blandimento capitis caude percussionem[c] obte-
gentes. Vtinam abscindantur qui pii presulis prouisiuam clementiam
uicibus frequentatis que sua sunt, non que Iesu Christi querentes,
iugiter conturbare moliuntur.

Valeat dilectionis uestre, etc.

237　　[a] memoratos dominos *MS.*　　　[b] di *MS.*　　　[c] percussionem *added in margin,
partly obliterated.*

237　　[1] Grace Dieu priory; see Letter 26 and n. 8.
　　[2] Richard Gravesend, archdeacon of Oxford 1249–54.

237

To Brother Ralph called Monk

(1251–2)

Brother Adam to the very dear father, Brother Ralph called Monk, greetings.

I recall that I recently wrote to the lord bishop of Lincoln, and the lord archdeacon of Oxford,[2] and the lord archdeacon of Leicester,[3] and to you, my dearest brother, on behalf of the lady prioress of Belton[1] and the venerable college of virgins of that place. But the aforementioned nuns completely failed, through their simplicity as I think, to pursue the petitions of the kind interposed by me on their behalf with a reasonable request, as was fitting, for the things needed. Hence I have no qualms in repeating my words and commending to you for your prudent and vigorous action in Christ the nuns' cause, which they will explain to you by word of mouth, if you please. I ask you at once with all fervour I can, out of regard for our blessed Saviour, with your customary and kind concern, to act and offer the aforesaid ladies your counsel and sagacious help in these matters that are recognized as pertaining to the peace and likewise the safety of the said house.

I thought I should refrain from arguments addressed to one whom divine inspiration has persuaded to hold fast the gifts of divine grace for which you have not refused to perform laborious works. It is a matter for anxiety and sorrow, not to say astonishment, that the pest by whom so much corruption was introduced into the religious life of the said convent, as is said, is still destructively at work, masquerading under the name of their master, to the ruin of both property and conduct.[4] Certain pestilent persons are helping to encourage inactivity in this matter on the part of the most reverend bishop, like scorpions covering up an assault by the tail by flattery of the head. Would that those people could be cut off, who repeatedly strive to confuse the foresight and clemency of our good chief, seeking their own gain and not that of Jesus Christ.

Farewell, dear brother.

[3] John of Basingstoke, archdeacon of Leicester 1235–52.
[4] Cf. Letters 27, 69, 79.

238

To Brother Adam de Bechesoveres

Fratri Ade de Bechesoueres[1] Frater Ada ⟨salutem⟩

Totiens experta obsequialis benignitatis uestre liberalitas modicitati mee, licet immerite, precum inculcandi frequentiam in causis pietatis uestri gratia fiduciam administrat. Eapropter pro dilecto michi in Christo Rogero de Kirkeby, fratris nostri Ricardi de Kirkeby conuentus de Stanford germano, iuuene iuxta testimonii credibilis assertionem honeste conuersationis et spei laudabilis, sedulitatis uestre beneuoli discretioni presentem dirigo petitionem, rogans attentius quatinus eidem, secundum periculose ualetudinis requisitionem necessariam, quantum fuerit propitia diuinitas, subuentionis manum adhibere non ducatis indignum.

Valeat beneuolentie uestre gratia suauitas, etc.

239

To Brother Adam de Bechesoveres

Predilecto sibi in Christo patri, Fratri Ade de Bechesoueres, Frater Ada salutem in Domino.

Benignam sedulitatis uestre dilectionem rogo suppliciter, quatinus honorabilem uirum Walterun de Mertun[1] ad presentiam domini Lyncolniensis accedentem, ut per manuum suarum impositionem ordinem subdiaconatus, propitia diuinitate, suscipiat, propensioris officii liberali diligentia cum ad uos uenerit, iuxta quod requirit tanti amici digna familiaritas, prosequi curetis in Domino.

Valete.

---

238 [1] Adam de Bechesoveres, who was at some time stationed at the Oxford friary, received several requests for his medical help; cf. Letters 176, 184, 219, 239.

238

To Brother Adam de Bechesoveres

Brother Adam to Brother Adam de Bechesoveres (greetings).

Your kind generosity and compliance that I have so many times experienced towards my humble but undeserving self give me confidence, thanks to you, to impose frequent requests on you in good causes. On this account I am directing this petition to your kind discretion on behalf of my beloved in Christ Roger de Kirkby, brother of our Brother Richard de Kirkby of the Stamford convent, who according to the statements of credible witnesses is a young man of upright life and praiseworthy hope, with an earnest request for you to be so good as to extend to him your helping hand as is, so far as God favours it, necessary and demanded by his dangerous illness.

Farewell, kind and gracious brother.

239

To Brother Adam de Bechesoveres

Brother Adam to the very dear father in Christ, Brother Adam de Bechesoveres, greetings in the Lord.

The honourable Walter de Merton[1] is coming into the presence of the lord bishop of Lincoln to receive, by God's favour, the order of the subdiaconate through the laying on of his hands. I humbly beg you of your loving kindness and zeal to take care to honour him in the Lord with all alacrity by generous and attentive service, as is required and fitting for the familiar association of so great a friend.

Farewell.

---

239 [1] Walter de Merton took his name from the canons of Merton Priory, who were his patrons. He was a royal clerk by 1240, had custody of the Great Seal in 1258, and served as royal chancellor 1261–3 and 1272–4. He was Bishop of Rochester 1274–7. In 1264 he provided an endowment to support twenty scholars at the University of Oxford who constituted the nucleus of Merton College: *ODNB* xxxvii. 931–3.

240

To Brother Andrew of Lexington

Desideratissimo patri, Fratri Andree de Lexinton', ministri Anglie uicario,[1] Frater Ada salutem et deuotam in Domino subiecti famulatus obedientiam.

Quidni interioris cordis uerecundia exteriori faciem rubore suffunderet, cum mestus animus indubitanter attenderet, quanta sit ei defectionis difformitas ad desiderabilem illius hominis uirtutem, quem politus tenor dulcis epistole michi uestri gratia transmisse tam insigniter uenustauit. Sed concepte molestie hoc unum occurrit remedium, quod secundum philosophicam traditionem unumquodque est in recipiente per modum recipientis et non per modum recepti. Ex quo ueraciter collegi quod cuius in exordio littere meministis fidelis amicitie pia presumptio, non qualem habuit sed qualem amauit secundum inolitam sancte affectionis legem sibi formauit amicum. In quo ergo michi poterit esse consultum, nisi ut qualibuscunque uiribus nitar, si tamen diuinitus detur eniti, ad illud attingere quod michi affectat paternitatis uestre pia sedulitas, ut saltem per moris assimilationem uestre caritatis amplexibus arctius astringar, cuius sancto patrocinante suffragio illuc, diuinitate propitia, quo per se nullatenus sufficit pertingere, imbecillitatis mee | sustollatur defectio?

f. 74ᵛ

Hanc etiam solam nobis in mutue presentie desiderio, puto, conspicimus adesse consolationem: quod cum uerissime simus ubi uiuimus, in illo uiuere uelimus amore qui solus ueram concilians amicitiam tam presentes eos inuicem exhibet, quos disiungit locorum distantia, quam in se adunatos sibi absentes esse non permittit, cuius omnibus locis est indeficiens indiuisibilis essentia. Sed de hiis hactenus.

Ceterum de negotio fratrum de Scardeburg',[2] si illud irritat hominum peruicacia quod approbauit Dei iudicium, quid fieri ualebit nisi ut sapientie que desursum est adherentes, eis qui seculariter sapiunt quoad fieri potest per Christum resistatur, aut si possibilitas non suppetit, in ipso longanimiter perferantur? Denique quia incer-

---

240   [1] On Andrew of Lexington cf. Letters 176, 206.

   [2] The Franciscans settled in Scarborough in c.1239, but encountered opposition from the Cistercians, who had acquired by royal grant the church of Scarborough and the fisheries of Dogger Bank, and obtained a papal mandate ordering the building of the friars

240

To Brother Andrew of Lexington

Brother Adam to the most dear father, Brother Andrew of Lexington, vicar of the minister of England,[1] greetings with devoted and humble service in the Lord.

What am I to say? The blushing face without reveals the shame of the heart within, when my grieving spirit realizes with certainty how much it fails to match up to and how it falls short of the enviable virtue of the man of whom the polished style of the kind letter you sent me painted such a beautiful picture. But the one remedy for my troubled feelings is this: as the traditional philosophy has it, whatever is in the mind of the recipient is according to the mode of the recipient, and not according to the mode of what is received. From this I truly conclude that out of the faithful friendship which you mention at the beginning of your letter, your pious presumption has formed for itself not such a friend as it had, but one such as has been formed by love according to the rule of holy affection. In this, therefore, it shall be my resolve, depending not upon any strength but only upon the gift of God, to strive to attain what your fatherly care desires for me, so that at least by assimilating your manners I may be more closely clasped in the embrace of your charity, your holy patronage helping me to the point, with the favour of God, which of itself my inadequacy and weakness could in no way attain.

In our desire to be in each other's presence we perceive, I think, only this consolation: that since we are really living where we are, we should wish to live in that love which alone unites us in true friendship, making present to one another those separated by the distance of their location, as if it does not allow those united in spirit to be absent from each other. Its unfailing and indivisible essence is in every place. So much for this.

As regards the business of the friars of Scarborough,[2] if the obstinacy of men disturbs what the judgement of God has approved, what can be done except to cling to the wisdom that is from above, and so far as is possible, through Christ to resist those who judge by worldly standards or, if the possibility is not available, to bear it with

to be demolished. The Franciscan representative offered to withdraw rather than offend the monks; see Grosseteste, *Epistolae*, p. 321. For the course of the dispute see C. H. Talbot, 'Citeaux and Scarborough', *Studia Monastica* ii (1960).

tum est de mora mea apud Rading' post expleta negotia quorum meministis, puto fore consultum quod, nisi hoc itineris requirat commoditas, contemplatione mei Rading' hac uice transitum non faciatis, cum in capitulo instanti, si Deus uoluerit, de mutuo colloquio simus in Christo gauisuri.

Valeat benigne paternitatis uestre serenitas in Christo, etc.

241

To Gregory de Bosellis

Fratri Gregorio[1] Frater Ada salutem in Domino et sempiternam sincere dilectionis affectionem.

Coarctauit spiritum cordis mei anxia sollicitudo super facto ecclesie de Kemesyng'.[2] Cum enim occurrat orbis plenus sacerdotibus, uix inuenitur aliquis qui uel tolerabiliter ydoneus censeri ualeat ad agendum officium sacerdotis.[3] Tanta siquidem est moles malorum nouissimorum dierum periculosissimis temporibus et inexplicabilis defectuum uarietas, quibus hinc obsistunt sanctiones euangelice, illinc contrariantur canonice traditiones. Subsistit tamen mee cogitationis disquisitio in duabus personis, quarum une dicitur Magister * * *,[a] laudabiliter fungens sacerdotio et multiplicibus sufficientiarum titulis insignitus; alter[b] uero est Magister * * *[a] uobis non incognitus; de quo, si ad gradum sacerdotii fuisset promotus, quantum ad regimen animarum preteritorum experientia fidem faciat futurorum.

Valeat amicitie uestre fidelitas in Christo, etc.

242

To Brother Warin of Ashwell

Fratri Warin de Aswell[1] Frater Ada salutem.

Letificaret me, mi dilecte, de statu uestro letus auditus, quem, oro, promoueat superna manductio de uirtute in uirtutem quousque

---

241   [a] *Names left blank in the MS.*   [b] *altera MS.*

241   [1] *Sic* in the MS, but the tone and business of the letter indicate that the recipient was Gregory de Bosellis, who was acting as vicar for William of Nottingham during the latter's absence at the Chapter of Metz in 1254: Eccleston, p. 101.
   [2] Kemsing (Kent).

patience? Finally, as my stay at Reading is uncertain after the negotiations you mention are finished, I think it will not be advisable for you to pass through Reading this time unless required to do so by the convenience of your journey, since we are going to enjoy in Christ a conversation together in the coming chapter, God willing.

Farewell, kind and serene father.

241

To Gregory de Bosellis

Brother Adam to Brother Gregory,[1] greetings in the Lord with sincere and endless love.

My spirit and heart have been in the grip of anxious concern over the business of the church of Kemsing.[2] For when the world presents itself to us as full of priests, scarcely anyone is found who can be judged as suitable to perform a priest's office;[3] so great is the mass of bad people in these very perilous times of the last days, and such is the irremediable variety of failings to which the rules of the Gospel constitute obstacles or canonical tradition presents impediments. However, my thoughts and inquiries settle upon two people, one of whom called Master * * *, who carries out his duties as a priest in a praiseworthy fashion and who is distinguished by numerous claims to be adequately equipped; the other one is Master * * *, who is not unknown to you. If he is advanced to the order of priesthood, experience of his past work would make one confident in his future performance in governing souls.

Farewell, faithful friend in Christ, etc.

242

To Brother Warin of Ashwell

Brother Adam to Brother Warin of Ashwell,[1] greetings.

I should be delighted, dear brother, to hear how it is with you, praying that the hand of heaven may lead you on from strength to

---

[3] Cf. the wording of Adam's strictures on the secular clergy in Letter 40.

242   [1] Warin de Assewelle was listed by Eccleston as the 11th lector to the Franciscans at Cambridge: Eccleston, pp. 59, 98; cf. Little, *Franciscan Papers, Lists and Documents*, pp. 132–3.

uideatur Deus deorum in Sion. Quid, rogo, faciet ingenue mentis deuotio, quam commendat insigniter et uigoris efficacia et industria sensus et zeli uiuacitas, si non iugi satagat uigilantia beatam illam in quam coniurauit professionem, cum animabus, quas celeste feruefecit desiderium, et puram et claram et sanctam ad deiformem originem reformare? Vt quid conarer persuasoriis ad persuasum diuinitus affectum? Sufficiat nunc prestitisse peritie pietatis occasionem.

Valeat benignitatis uestre dilectio, etc.

Carum michi foret, karissime, si expositiunculam summariam 〈donares〉 quam, me tum presente, tabulari memorie commisistis tempore capituli London' celebrati, scripture illius *Noua lux Iudeis uisa est* secundum quod accipitur de natiuitate Beate Marie Virginis. Si non displiceat, peto illam per latorem presentium michi mitti in cartula.

Cum semotus a desiderabilium fratrum frequentia, uaste solitudinis salsuginem ingrederer amaricatem, dolor anxius, utpote inter spem et desperationem detrusum*a* 〈me〉 totaliter occupauit. Quis, oro, locus erit letitie ubi totam affectionem meror afficit intolerabilis, totam rationem totus horror occupat, totam mentem coangustat stupor pauidus? Nempe regnum cupiditatis effrenatissima rabie debaccari et captiuari luctuosissima calamitate regnum caritatis ille solus lacrimabili non plangit consideratione, quem*b* aut excecauit deus huius seculi, aut 〈qui ut〉 Balaam, arioli socius,[2] cadit apertos habens oculos;[3] iam oculis solis huius expositum est, proth dolor, dirum inauditum facinoris spectaculum. Etenim honorem puritatis atrox opprimit uiolentia, decorem claritatis fictio fantasmalis obnubilat, amorem sanctitatis conculcat uoluptatis affectatio.

Quid ergo? Numquid non expectatur trucidatum iri uniuersum celestis aule tyrocinium, cum gloriosa professio, quam ad subueniendum ecclesiastice depopulationi nouissimorum dierum periculosissimis temporibus non sine stupore totius mundi tam potenter excitauit, tam sapienter illustrauit, tam salubriter ampliauit 〈Deus〉[4] ut per singularem humilitatis mansuetudinem per spiritualem paupertatis exquisitionem, per prerogatiuam castitatis districtionem, 'contra

242 *a* detrusam *MS.* *b* quam *MS.*

[2] But Balaam was the son, not the companion, of the soothsayer: Num. 22: 5.
[3] Cf. Num. 24: 4.
[4] Here Adam appears to share the views of those Franciscans who identified the friars

strength until the God of gods may be seen in Sion. What, I ask you, will the devotion of your noble mind, distinguished by its energy and effectiveness, its application and intelligence and its lively zeal, do if it is not for ever actively engaged and vigilant in restoring to its godlike origin that blessed profession, pure, shining holy, to which it made the collective vow in the company of souls stirred to fervour by heavenly desire? Why should I attempt to persuade one persuaded by God? Let it suffice for now to have pointed out an opportunity to a person of experienced piety.

Farewell, beloved.

It would be a kindness to me, dearest brother, if you would let me have the concise exposition of that treatise *A new light has appeared to the Jews*, according to which this text is understood to refer to the nativity of the Blessed Virgin Mary, which you committed to written memory when I was present at the time of the chapter at London. If you would not mind, I beg you to send it in a folder by the carrier of this letter.

Since being separated from the company of the dear brethren, I have entered a bitter salt marsh of vast solitude, and I have been totally consumed by sorrow and anxiety, downcast, that is, between hope and despair. What place will there be for joy, I pray, where all feelings are affected by grief, reason is swamped by dread, and the whole mind is convulsed by fear and amazement? Surely only one blinded by the gods of this world, or who, like Balaam, the soothsayer's companion,[2] falls with open eyes,[3] will fail to lament at seeing the wild gloating of the kingdom of cupidity and the kingdom of charity made captive by a grievous calamity. Alas, the dire unheard-of spectacle of the wickedness is now disclosed to his eyes alone. For a horrible violence smothers the honour of purity, a spectral pretence darkens the beauty of reputation, a hunger for pleasure tramples underfoot the love of holiness.

What then? Are we not waiting for all the recruits to the court of heaven to be slaughtered, when the glorious profession which, to the astonishment of the whole world, God so powerfully raised up, so wisely illumined and profitably enlarged to come to the help of the Church laid waste in the perilous times of the last days,[4] that by gentleness and humility, by a spiritual quest for poverty, and by its pre-eminent observance of chastity, it might direct triumphant

with the spiritual people raised up by God in the last days of the world to succour the faithful according to the prophecies of Joachim of Fiore; cf. Letter 43 and n.

principatus et potestates, contra mundi rectores tenebrarum harum, contra spirituales nequitias in celestibus',[5] quasi iam soluto Sathana, stragem animarum exercentes, et triumphalia castra moueret, et expeditas acies instrueret et densos congressus constiparet; cum hec, inquam, professio uel inuita compellitur et caducis honoribus ambitiosius inhiare, mobilibus affluentiis curiosius inseruire, et fedis uoluptatibus deformius inherere, nonne ruina presens ut salua loquar, heu, heu, quorundam in manibus nephariorum principum conspicitur et 'ingredientium pompatice domum Domini, et confidentium in monte Samarie, et incubantium fictionibus lasciuientium, propter quod migrabunt nunc in capite transmigrantium, secundum quod tam terribiliter iurauit in animam suam Dominus Deus exercituum?'[6]

Sed quid unquam tristius cogitari poterit quam quod qui hec gratulabunda laudatione non prosequitur, aut seuientium concutitur cruciatibus aut insultantium uexatur contumeliis aut subsannantium deridetur despectionibus. O Altissime Maiestatis iniuriam! O inscrutabilis sapientie contradictionem! O inestimabilem clementie contemptum! 'Numquid qui plantauit aurem non audiet, aut qui finxit oculum non considerat?'[7] Absit. Propterea speluncam latronum constat quia non tardabit discutere Deus ultionis.ᶜ An putamus quod auris celi, que audit omnia, non attendit uoces clamantium sub altare Dei 'Vindica sanguinem nostrum, Deus noster'?[8] An credimus quod Is, in cuius conspectu non est aliqua creatura inuisibilis, uidens uideat afflictionem Egyptiacam et non descendit liberare populum suum? Sed quorsum ista? Vt quid flamantissimis feruoribus torpor tepidus insudaret? Igitur cohibeo calamum, quem lacrimosi cordis liquor cruentus intinxit.

Deliberauit nuper in publico ex uoce confusa facies an se iterum per scripturam uestris presentaret aspectibus. Siquidem hesitaui mecum deliberans an scriberem. Ignorauit enim | perturbate mentis mestitia quid scriberet. Scripsi tamen quoniam ad scribendum impulit exagitati spiritus nescio qualis impatientia, quam proferunt presentis carte caracteres, qui qualecunque remedium desperationis in facto Dei, quos indigni sermonis imperiti fragminibus emulatione qualiscunque prologuor, michi attulerunt, pro eo quod spiritualem inter mortales concepi fiduciam de uestrum inuicta uirtute, de

f. 75

ᶜ ultionem *MS.*

[5] Eph. 6: 12.   [6] Cf. Amos 6: 1, 7–8.
[7] Ps. 93: 9.   [8] Cf. Rev. 6: 10.

warfare against 'principalities and powers, against the rulers of the
darkness of this world, against spiritual wickedness in high places[5]—
working the slaughter of souls, as if Satan was unloosed—and draw
up lines in readiness for battle, and gather the people into close-knit
associations; when, I say, this profession of ours is driven, albeit
unwillingly, to yearn with ambition for transient honours and eagerly
concern itself with worldly goods, and is disfigured by its attachment
to detestable pleasures, is not its ruin evident to be seen, alas—to
speak the saving truth—at the hands of certain princes and of 'those
who go with state into the house of the Lord and have confidence in
the mountain of Samaria, and of the luxurious ones in their faction,
on account of which they shall go captive at the head of them that go
into captivity, according to what the Lord, the God of hosts, hath so
dreadfully sworn by his own soul'?[6]

But whatever can be thought sadder than the fact that he who does
not pursue these things, winning praise and congratulation, is either
afflicted with torments by enraged people or harassed by insults or is
derided by contemptuous scoffers. O what an insult to the majesty of
the Most High! O what a denial of the inscrutable wisdom! O what
immeasurable contempt of His mercy! 'He that hath planted the ear,
shall he not hear, or He that formed the eye, doth He not consider?'[7]
Heaven forbid. On that account it is certain that the God of
vengeance will not be slow to destroy a den of robbers, or do we
think that the ear of heaven, that hears all things, does not listen to
the voices crying under the altar of God 'Avenge our blood, O our
God'?[8] Or do we believe that He, in whose sight no creature is
invisible, does not perceive the affliction in Egypt and does not come
down to deliver his people? But where does this lead us? Why should
sloth and timidity labour to kindle a burning fervour? So I will
restrain my pen, dipped in the blood of my weeping heart.

After confused statements at our public meeting, I recently debated
whether I should show you my face again in writing. In fact, I
hesitated, debating with myself whether to write, for in the sadness of
my troubled mind, I did not know what to write. I have written,
however, because I was impelled to do so by a kind of impatience in
my troubled spirit, which is evidenced by the handwriting of this
letter, which has brought me some kind of remedy for my despair in
the action of God; I somehow articulate this in broken snatches of
unsuitable and clumsy speech in a desire for action of some sort, for
the reason that I have gained in my mind a spiritual trust in the

uestrum circumspecta industria, de uestrum feruida emulatione ad consummationem salutis operandam.

Propterea cum indubitanter acceperim quod piissimas animas fratrum nostrorum Londini commorantium Spiritus Sanctus ardenter professe perfectionis desiderio uehementer inflammauerit, sit Dei Filio perhenniter superexaltata benedictio, uestre beatitudinis caritatem per uestre salutis contemplationem exoro, per honorem beatissime Virginis inuito, per rubricatum pio cruore uiuifice crucis patibulum adiuro, quatinus apud piissimum patrem ministrum nostrum, ex Dei patrocinio, per angelorum subsidium in electorum suffragio, per omnem modum infatigabili laboretis diligentia, ut ad gloriam diuini nominis, ad nostre salutis reparationem, ad edificationem totius orbis, nullatenus differre consentiat illam desiderabilem uiuendi formam, que toties auribus ipsius per simplicissimas obsecrationes est inculcata, memoratis fratribus instituere diuinitus deinceps obseruandam.

Valeat desideratissima uestre dilectionis fides in Christo, etc.

243

To some brother Franciscans

Fratribus N. et N.[1] salutem.

Non sine gratiarum actione fulgide caritatis uestre efficacem epistolam consolatoriam preferre disertitudinem auidis consideraui luminibus. Cuius tamen series nequaquam risum miscuit dolori; sed multiplici proportione contra sententiam diuinitatis mixtionis legem excedens, illum in istius transtulit dominationem ut uehementius extrema gaudii luctus occuparet.[2]

Inseruistis pio sermoni exhortationem de non diffidendo, quia 'non est manus ⟨Domini⟩ abbreuiata ut saluare nequeat'.[3] Omnimodis benefecistis. Quis enim locus erit diffidentie cum dicat Dei uirtus, Dei sapientia, 'Confidite, quia ego uici mundum'?[4] Vere quidem sic est sicut scripsistis. Sed numquid hoc absterget omnem lacrimam ab oculis uirorum gementium et dolentium super abhominationibus que fuerint in medio Ierusalem? De quorum numero efficiat nos Ille, qui secundum tenorem excellentissime professionis nostre iuratam Spiritui Sancto, ante terrificum tribunal formidandissime Maiestatis

---

243 [1] Names omitted in MS.   [2] Cf. Prov. 14: 13.
[3] Isa. 59: 1.   [4] John 16: 33.

undefeated virtue of you among mortals, in your prudence and industry, in your fervent zeal to work for the ends of salvation.

On this account, as I have heard without question that the Holy Spirit has vehemently fired the pious souls of our brethren residing at London with a burning desire for the perfection of our observance—blessed and ever exalted be the Son of God—I beg your beatitude out of your charity and out of regard for your salvation, for the honour of the Blessed Virgin I invite you, by the life-giving cross reddened by the holy blood I adjure you, to labour with the good father, our minister, in every way with untiring effort, with the patronage of God and with the help of the angels as the voice of the elect, to persuade him that he should not, for the glory of the divine name, for the repair of our salvation, for the edification of the whole world, in any way consent to postpone instituting that desirable form of life for the said brothers, which has been urged upon him so many times with the most direct entreaties, for their observance hereafter.

Wishing you faith and love in Christ, etc.

243

To some brother Franciscans

To Brothers N.[1] and N., greetings.

Not ungratefully I have pondered with eager eyes over the shining charity and eloquence of your letter of consolation. Yet its contents in no way mixed laughter with sorrow, but by increasing the proportion of sorrow several times over, exceeding the rule of mixture contrary to what the Lord lays down, it makes the sorrow dominate the laughter, so that grief has fiercely taken over the place of joy to the greatest extent.[2]

You have inserted in your good words an exhortation not to lose faith, for 'the hand of the Lord is not shortened that it cannot save'.[3] You have done well in every way. For what place will there be for trust to fail, since the God of power, the God of wisdom, says 'Have confidence, for I have overcome the world'?[4] It is indeed so, as you have written. But will this wipe away every tear from the eyes of men who groan and lament over the abominations that are in the midst of Jerusalem? May He ensure that we are numbered among those who, according to the sense of our excellent profession that we have sworn to the Holy Spirit, summons us as his elect before the dread tribunal

electionem nostram in die ista uocat ad fletum et ad planctum et ad caluitium et ad cingulum sacci, et 'dignos nos faciens in partem sortis sanctorum in lumine, et eripiens nos de potestate tenebrarum et transferens in regnum Filii dilectionis sue'.[5]

Putandumne est quod omnipotentis sapientie benignitas, quam necesse est in uniuerso regno Dei perhenniter et bona probare et mala reprobare et uniuersa ordinare, aut nequeat aut nesciat aut nolit, et ruinas erigere et errores corrigere et praua dirigere? Numquid hoc et luctus prophetarum et patriarcharum lamentatio et fletus Vnigeniti et apostolorum ploratus et ultra lacrimosi sanctorum merores tam anxie prosequi temporum secularium diebus non desistunt? Absit hoc a mentibus fidelium. Siquidem non defuit perfidia que desperabiliter istud autumauerit, sed caritatis proscriptionem, sed exterminium fidei, sed confusionem[a] beate sanctificationis inexplicabili districtione comprehendat. Horum remedium 'qui respicit orationes humilium et non spernit preces eorum, audit gemitus compeditorum et soluit filios interemptorum, ut annuntient in Syon limpide contemplationis nomen Domini et laudem eius in Ierusalem'[6] tranquille conuersationis, solus nouit, ut uideo; contra quod quanquam speraui, ego penitus ignoro. Propter quod quid facto opus sit inuenire nullatenus sufficio, nisi deinceps ut indignus peccator uoces reprimat, exprimat lacrimas, et ad illud humiliato conetur silentio, per quod importunum attemptauit eloquium. Hoc michi plurimum fore lugendum conspicio, quod et ineptis litteris et lingua despicabili illa non sum expletus[b] presumere, a quo, heu michi, mea in me * * *[c] inconsideratio.

Vtinam amantissimis mentibus cordis ardor patesceret quoniam[d] quamuis cor littere uestre mitigarent,[e] ipsum tamen fortius amaricauit anxia caude percussio.

Valeat dilectionis uestre dulcedo in Christo, etc. Vereor quod fucorum fictiones in me etiam amicitiores mei suspicentur. Sed quid agam non inuenio. Ipse doceat quem non fallunt archana cogitationum. Breuiaui litteram que uestram, obsecro, prudentiam non fastidiat. Puto ⟨quod⟩ ante dies emensos in hac parte casso conatu per diuinitatem propitiam calamus fatuitatis mee uobis uel quibuscunque non erit importunus.

243   [a] confusibilem MS.   [b] tumulatus MS.   [c] There is a blank space at this point in the MS, leaving the sense uncertain.   [d] quem MS.   [e] mitigaret MS.

of his Majesty on that day, and calls us to weeping and lamentation, to shaven heads and girdles of sackcloth, making us worthy to share in the lot of the saints in light and 'delivering us from the power of darkness and translating us into the kingdom of his beloved Son'.[5]

Is it to be thought that the goodness of the Almighty Wisdom, which in the universal kingdom of God must perpetually approve the good, condemn evil, and direct all things, either cannot or knows not, or will not, raise up what is fallen, correct errors and rectify what is bad? Is not this the object so anxiously and ceaselessly pursued in the time of this world by the mourning of the prophets, the laments of the patriarchs, the tears of the Only-Begotten, the lamentation of the apostles, and still more by the tearful sorrow of the saints? Heaven forbid that the minds of the faithful should entertain such a thought. For there has been no lack of disbelief ready to assert this in despair, but it holds in its inextricable grip an opposition to virtue, contradiction of truth, a condemnation of charity, destruction of faith, and confusion of the blessed work of sanctification. As I see it, the remedy for these things is known only to Him who 'sees the prayers of the humble and does not despise their entreaties, who hears the groans of the prisoners and frees the sons of the slain, that they may proclaim the name of the Lord in the Sion of pure contemplation, and his praise in the Jerusalem of the peaceful life'.[6] Of this, contrary to my hopes, I have had no knowledge. For this reason I am in no way adequate to finding what needs to be done, except henceforth to suppress my voice as an unworthy sinner, to utter tears, and to try by humble silence to do what I have attempted through untimely speech. I see that I shall very much lament the fact that I did not accomplish it, with my unsuitable letters and contemptible speech, from which, alas, failing judgement * * *

I should hope that the warmth of my heart would be apparent to loving minds, for although your letter soothed the heart, the troublesome blow of its tail aroused in it strong feelings of bitterness.

Farewell, dear beloved in Christ, etc. I fear that even my closer friends will suspect me of colourful inventions. But I do not know what to do. Let Him who is not deceived by secret thoughts instruct you. I think that before long, through divine favour, my foolish pen will not trouble you or anyone else with my vain efforts.

[5] Col. 1: 12–13.   [6] Ps. 101: 18, 21–2 (Vulg.).

244

To a brother Franciscan

Fratri * * *[1] salutem et post temporis cursum brauium eternitatis.

Amabilissima caritatis uestre littera, quam nuper michi uestri gratia transmittere uoluistis, saucio cordi compassionis telum infixit. Sed quantacunque sit uis anxietatis, quia 'non contristamur sicut et ceteri qui spem non habent',[2] uim doloris mitigat diuine dispensationis pia consolatio, que flagellat omnem filium quem recipit. Propter quod indubitanter confido quod acerbior examinatio diuturne ualetudinis et expiauit ut sit pura, et illuminauit ut sit clara, et sublimauit ut sit sancta, piam animam, que non dudum flagrauit desiderio ad iocundas, ad luminosas, ad excelsas diuinitus suscipiendas mansiones.

Cum quanta exultatione quantumcunque temporaliter afflictis illud ad eternam occurrit consolationem quod scriptum est: 'Hoc autem pro certo habet omnis qui colit Te, quia uita eius, si in probatione fuerit, coronabitur, si autem in tribulatione fuerit, liberabitur, et si in correptione fuerit, ad misericordiam licebit uenire. Non enim delectaris in perditionibus nostris quia post tempestatem tranquillum facis, et post lacrimationem et fletum exultationem infundis. Sit nomen tuum, Deus Israel, benedictum in secula.'[3]

Absit a me ut erga suauissimum uestre benignitatis affectionem qualiscunque paruitatis mee deuotio, que uobis inter mortales nec immerito specialiter confitetur obnoxiam, aliquatenus aut minuat fidem amoris aut orationis affectum remittat. Numquid non illum cuius in littera meministis iustum formidandi examinis pauorem pium clementissime Virginis patrocinium absorbere debebit, ut multo amplius fidens conscientia letificet, quam tremens exultatio contristet? Scio quod hec superatur ab illa multum quidem per omnem modum, propter quod oro sit secure menti iuge conuiuium. Succingo sermonem, nolens erudite menti prolixitatis ingerere fastidium. Sufficiat sancto desiderio occasionem prestitisse.

Recommendationes quas michi iniunxistis pro uobis faciendas prompta uoluntate per Dei gratiam facere curabo. Si cogens hoc non excluderet necessitas, iocundissimum michi foret uobiscum uiue

---

244   [1] Name omitted in MS.
   [2] I Thes.: 4: 13.
   [3] Tobias 3: 21–3.

244

To a brother Franciscan

To Brother * * *[1] greetings and after time has run its course the prize of eternity.

Your most lovely letter of charity, which you were recently so good as to send me, has pierced my wounded heart with a shaft of sympathy. But however powerful the anxiety, the holy consolation dispensed by God, which scourges every son He accepts, mitigates the strength of our pain, for 'we should not be sorrowful, even as others who have no hope'.[2] On this account I have an undoubting confidence that the sharper trial of a long illness expiates for a devout soul to make it pure, and illuminates it to make it glorious, and elevates it to make it holy, when not long since it was burning with desire for pleasure, for enlightenment to occupy with divine help the highest dwellings.

Those afflicted for a time, however much, are struck with exultation to their eternal consolation by that passage that is written: 'Everyone who worships Thee holds this for certain, that if he be tested he will be crowned, but if he suffer tribulation, he will be delivered, and if he be corrected, he will be allowed mercy. For thou hast no pleasure in our ruin, who makest peace after the tempest, and after lamentation and weeping, thou dost pour out exultation upon us. Blessed be thy name for ever, God of Israel.'[3]

Far be it from me that the devotedness of my insignificant self to your very sweet and affectionate kindness, by which I confess I am particularly bound to you before all mortal men, should in any measure diminish my faithful love or slacken the devotion of my prayer. Ought not the patronage of the most gentle Virgin swallow up that just fear of the dread judgement that you mention in your letter, so that a faithful conscience may give much more joy than the sadness of a quaking exultation? I know that the latter is in every way surpassed by the former; on account of which I wish your untroubled mind a perpetual feast. I am cutting short my discourse, as I am unwilling to bore a learned mind with verbosity. Let it be enough to have opened an opportunity for holy desire.

I will take care, God willing, to carry out promptly the recommendations that you enjoined me to make on your account. If pressing necessity should not prevent it, I should very much enjoy

uocis habere colloquium; sed necesse est ut quod locorum excludit
distantia presentia suppleat spirituum in Christo, qui ait, 'Pater
sancte, serua eos in nomine tuo quos dedisti michi, ut sint unum
sicut et nos'.[4] Ad hec, licet super corporali incolumitate metum
incutiat anceps acerbe ualetudinis periculum, tamen securum pii
Saluatoris adiutorium prestat fiduciam. Nempe ipse est qui percutit
et sanat, uulnerat et medetur, castigat et morti non tradit. Ipsum
denique contra cuncta qualiumcunque cruciatuum discrimina benedictum summe salutis remedium diffinientem audiamus: 'In patientia
uestra',[5] etc.

245

To Sewal de Bovill, archbishop of York

(1256–7)

f. 80 **1.** Prima particula, epistolaris salutatio: | Reuerendissimo in Christo
patri et domino Sewal,[1] Dei gratia Eboracensi archiepiscopo, Frater
Ada dictus de Marisco, deuotissima subiecti famulatus obsequia cum
felici gloria et honore perhenni.

2. Secunda particula: *De prelati cui scribit et fratris qui scribit et per
consequens aliorum spirituali comitantia et presentia corporali disponendis
diuinitus ad profectum salutis.*[a]
Qui sublimitatem diuinam humane humilitati nexu copulauit indis-
solubili, et 'faciens concordiam in sublimibus suis'[b][2] (Iob xxv) in
nostris humilibus gratiam perficiens, sublimes humilibus coadunauit,
et tam illos quam istos 'eripiens de potestate tenebrarum transtulit in
regnum Filii dilectionis sue' (Col. i),[3] Ipse uestre sublimitatis ad
humilitatem meam, oro, necessitudinem conciliet inuiolabilem, quam
priore parte sui uestre disertitudinis epistola ex tam sublimi consideratione, ex[c] condescensione tam humili, tam sublimiter concepta,
tam amabiliter preferebat, sic, inquam, conciliet ut, licet interdum
pro absentia corporali homo doleat exterior, eo ipse iugiter amplius de
presentia spirituali homo gaudeat interior, in Eo qui 'exauditus pro

---

245 2 *a This heading omitted by B.*   *b add* prelatis B.   *c in* B.   *d* ego
omitted B.   *e* permanentur B.

---

[4] John 17: 11.   [5] Luke 21: 19.

245 [1] Sewal de Bovill, archbishop of York 1256–8.

having a face-to-face conversation with you, but as it is prevented by the distance between our locations, our mutual presence must needs be that of the spirit in Christ, who says, 'Holy Father, keep them in thy name whom thou hast given me, that they may be one as we also are'.[4] On this, although the dangerous uncertainty of illness strikes us with fear for our bodily condition, yet the sure help of our good Saviour induces confidence. To be sure, He it is who strikes down and heals, who wounds and cures, who chastizes, but not to death. Finally, let us hear Him designating the blessed remedy of our final salvation against all the crises and whatever torments: 'In your patience', etc.[5]

245

To Sewal de Bovill, archbishop of York

(1256–7)

1. The first part of the letter: the greeting: To the most reverend father in Christ and lord Sewal,[1] by the grace of God archbishop of York, devoted obedience and humble service from Brother Adam, called Marsh, with propitious glory and perpetual honour.

2a. *Concerning the spiritual company of the prelate to whom he is writing, and that of his brother who writes, and consequently of the others, and concerning his bodily presence, by God's help to be disposed to achieve the end of salvation.*

He who has joined together his divine sublimity to our humble humanity with an indissoluble bond, 'making peace in high places'[2] (Job 25) and bestowing grace on our humble condition, has united the sublime with the lowly, and has delivered both the former and the latter 'from the power of darkness and hath translated us into the kingdom of his beloved Son' (Col. 1),[3] I pray that He will bring together my humble self with the inviolable need of your sublime lordship, which your letter disclosed in the earlier part of your discourse with such sublime thought, out of such humble condescension and kindness. He will, I say, bring us together in such a way that although for the time being the outer man is saddened by bodily absence, by this very fact the inner man rejoices all the more in our

---

[2] Job 25: 2. Scriptural and patristic references, here shown in parenthesis, were written above the line in A, but more fully in the margins of the text by the copyist of B.
[3] Col. 1: 13.

sua reuerentia' (Heb v.)[4] semel, iterum, et tertio id ipsum orans, primitus ait (Ioh xvii) 'Pater sancte, serua eos in nomine tuo, quos dedisti michi, ut sint unum sicut et nos'; et rursum 'non pro eis rogo tantum, sed et pro eis quid credituri sunt per uerbum eorum in me; ut omnes unum sint sicut et tu, Pater, in me, et ego in te, et ipsi in nobis unum sint'; et adhuc, 'ego[d] claritatem quam dedisti michi, dedi eis, ut sint unum sicut et nos unum sumus. Ego in eis et tu in me, ut sint consummati in unum';[5] ut uidelicet ipsi sint unum secundum unanimam uoluntatis ordinate concordiam, sicut et nos unum sumus secundum eandem simplicitatis superunice substantiam inuicem, et in nobis consummati in unum.

Vbi etiam ita coniunctius uniendos, ut spiritu proficerent, deseruit corpore pro quibus exorauit, scilicet ne corporalibus hererent infirmiter, sed ex eis in spiritualia currerent alacriter. Qui propterea profectus nec locorum distantiis nec interuallis temporum aliquatenus impeditur, sed reuera nonnunquam adaugetur secundum illud (Ioh. xvi) 'Ego ueritatem dico uobis; expedit uobis ut ego uadam. Si enim non abiero, Paracletus non ueniet ad uos. Si autem abiero, mittam eum ad uos.'[6] Confido tamen, diuinitate propitia, quod ad accidentalem occasionem, licet non causam substantialem, proficiendi eminentius in Deum, anime mee desiderium quo spiritualiter inter presentia ferueo, tam de personali uisione quam de locutione uocali sanctitatis uestre opportunitate frequentiori replebitur in Domino; ita quidem quod, sicuti pretactum est, nequaquam in transeuntibus remaneatur[e] infirmiter, sed ex illis in permanentia transeatur alacriter.

3a. *De communi gaudio fidelium ex sublimatione domini Sewal archiepiscopi Eboracensis in dignitatem archiepiscopalem, cum causis generaliter eiusdem tam solempnis gaudii.*

O quam solempni gaudio sit altissimo Saluatori seculis omnibus superexaltata benedictio! Longe lateque passim audiuntur glorifica preconia dispensationis dominice, que per prouisiuam miserationis immense clementiam ad regitiuum Eboracensis metropolitane fastigium, maxime nouissimorum dierum temporibus periculosissimis, sublimauit archipresulem tam desiderabiliter[a] expectatum, tam salubriter obtentum, cuius in dies usquequaquam per effectuum euidentias uniuersis clarescunt illustrius et uirtus inuincibilis et

---

3a   [a] desiderantur B.

---

[4] Heb. 5: 7.   [5] John 17: 11, 20–3.   [6] John 16: 7.

spiritual presence in Him who 'was heard for his reverence' (Heb. 5).[4]
He prayed once, again, and a third time, saying the first time 'Holy
Father, keep them in thy name whom thou hast given me, that they
may become one, as we also are' (John 17), and again: 'Not for them
only do I pray, but for them also who through their word shall believe
in me, that they all may be one, as thou, Father, in me and I in thee;
that they all may be one in us' and further: 'The glory which thou
hast given me, I have given to them, that they may be one, as we also
are one, I in them and thou in me, that they may be made perfect in
one.'[5] That is to say, that they may be one in the unanimous concord
of an ordered will, just as we are one according to the same substance
of our transcendent simplicity, and they may be consummated in
unity.

There too he deserted in body those who were to be united more
closely in such a way that they might advance in spirit, for whom he
offered up prayers, meaning that they should not in their weakness
cling to the things of the body, but run swiftly to the things of the
spirit. Therefore this progress is not at all hindered by distance of
location or by the interval of time, but it is sometimes improved by
these circumstances, according to those words (John 16) 'I tell you the
truth; it is expedient to you that I go. For if I go not, the Paraclete will
not come to you; but if I go, I will send Him to you.'[6] I believe,
however, that by divine favour by an extraneous occurrence, though
not a substantial cause, for drawing closer to God, my soul's desire,
with which I am at present burning in spirit, will be fulfilled in the
Lord by a more frequent opportunity both of personally seeing your
holiness and of speaking with you; so indeed that, as said before, it
would not stay feebly entrapped in things that are transient, but
swiftly pass from them to things that are lastimg.

3a. *Concerning the general joy of the faithful at the elevation of the lord
Sewal, archbishop of York, to the archiepiscopal dignity, with the general
reasons for this solemn rejoicing.*
O with what great joy we should bless our most high Saviour for all
the ages. Everywhere far and wide is to be heard the glorious
proclamation of the Lord's dispensation, by which in his far-seeing
mercy He has in these last most perilous days raised to the
governance of the metropolitan see of York, an archprelate, awaited
with so much desire and so advantageously obtained. Daily he shines
more brightly upon us all, by the evidence of what he accomplishes

sensus infallibilis et zelus intemerabilis et actus infatigabilis[b] regno celorum, hoc est regimini ecclesiarum, et uiribus defendendo, et legibus emendando, et moribus adornando, et cultibus ampliando, contra seuientium uiolentias, contra seducentium fraudulentias, contra assentantium blanditias, contra perurgentium obstinatias.

4a. *De magnalibus sanctificationum que sperantur exhibenda fore iugiter ad principem, ad clerum, ad populum, per memoratum archipresulem, cum familiaribus ydoneis in sanctam cooperationem ab ipso prouidenter eligendis.*

Quem certe confidimus indeficienter exhibiturum ad principem inuiolate fidei prouisiuum adiutorium, ad episcopos patrocinium magnificentie, ad cleros doctrinam intelligentie, ad religiosos disciplinam sanctimonie, ad proceres presidium directionis, ad milites modestiam cohercionis, ad plebes clementiam subuentionis. In quibus euidentissime liquet quod necesse est ad familiare subsidium euocari auxiliarios efficaces, consiliarios eruditos, ministeriales accuratos, correctores exercitatos, et idcirco excellentes potestate, fulgentes ueritate, feruentes sanctitate, constantes stabilitate. Nempe necessario coram archipresule, istis salutari cooperatione assistentibus, princeps, episcopi, clerici, religiosi, proceres, milites, plebes totius prouincie assidue stare habent iudicandi; omnes etiam per archiepiscopi manuductionem et istorum diligentiam deducendi sunt per rectitudinem uie in lumine ueritatis ad patriam uite. Omnibus insuper per archipontificis illustrationem et horum prouisionem ratio salutaris reddenda est cuicunque poscenti de certitudine fidei, de dignitate morum, de pietate sacramentorum. Ex quibus etiam liquet quam prepollenter insigniri oportet uirtutum istarum apicibus eum qui, uice metropolitani in sede metropolitana, super omnes assmptus in omnibus habet adimplere.

5a. *Quam sit necessarium ut ad implendam regiminis sui magnificentiam |*
f. 80[v] *metropolitanus genere uiuendi composito ex sublimi contemplatione et salubri actione illustretur longe ceteris eminentius.*

Cum igitur tam euidenter hec sint que tenetur quisque metropolitanus in propria presertim exhibere prouincia, quis non uideat, nisi quem deus huius seculi penitus excecauit, quod ad implendum dignitatis sue ministerium necessarium sit ut habeat excellentius omnibus genus uiuendi compositum ex actuoso et otioso? Cum

---

[b] A *adds* et.

through his invincible courage, his unerring intelligence, his fearless
zeal, and his indefatigable action for the kingdom of heaven, that is,
for the governance of churches, both defending it with his powers and
reforming it with laws, and adorning it in its customs, and enlarging it
in its worship, against the savage violence of its enemies, its
fraudulent seducers, the allurement of flatterers and the obstinacy
of its oppressors.

4a. *Concerning the great works of sanctification which, it is hoped, the said
archbishop will manifest to the prince, the clergy, and the people, with the
suitable servants he will providentially choose to co-operate in his holy task.*
We have absolute confidence that he will unfailingly provide for the
prince the scrupulous help of his inviolable fealty, for the bishops his
great-hearted protection, for the clergy his learning and understanding, for the religious holy discipline, for the nobles his protection and
guidance, for the knights moderation in the use of force, for the
people gentle assistance. In all these it is most clearly apparent that
there is need to call to his help a company of effective assistants,
learned counsellors, caring ministers, and practised governors, who
are therefore tried in the exercise of power, of shining truthfulness, of
fervent holiness, and steadfast in their constancy. For indeed the
prince, the bishops, clergy and religious, the nobles, knights, and
people of the whole province have to stand before the judgement of
the archbishop and these assistants cooperating with him, to be led
through his leadership and the diligence of these helpers through the
uprightness of their lives, in the light of truth, to the homeland of the
living. Moreover, for all, through the archbishop's enlightened
instruction and the foresight of these his helpers, a saving account
must be rendered of whoever asks regarding certainty of faith, worthy
conduct or sacramental piety. From this it is apparent how exceedingly distinguished by pre-eminence in these virtues should be he
who in the place of a metropolitan is appointed in the metropolitan
see to exercise the metroplitan's office over everyone in all things.

5a. *How it is necessary for the metropolitan, in order to fulfil the magnificent
expectation of his regime, for him to be far more shining than others by his
kind of life, compounded of sublime contemplation and salvific action.*
Since these are the qualities that any metropolitan is bound to display,
especially in his own province, who would not see, unless utterly
blinded by the god of this world, that in order to fulfil the ministry of
his appointment it is necessary for him to have a kind of life more

quidem sint, sicut uestra melius nouit excellentia, tria genera uiuendi, secundum quod ex Scripturis eleganter ostendit Sanctus Augustinus, uidelicet genus uiuendi actuosum, genus uiuendi otiosum, et genus uiuendi compositum ex utroque.[7] Actuosum dicitur uita actiua, otiosum uita contemplatiua, compositum ex utraque temperatur ex duabus adunatis, scilicet uita actiua et uita contemplatiua; que proprie pertinet ad eos qui diuinitus assecuti sunt superiorem locum regiminis in ecclesia Dei. Quia enim necesse est ut, precipiente Domino, faciat omnia secundum exemplar quod sibi monstratur in monte, oportet ut cum Moyse nunc ascendat in montem, nunc descendat ad plebem, ut cum angelis in scala Iacob uices ascendendi ad celum et descendendi ad terram frequentet, quatinus uicissim se conferat modo ad otium amplexende diuinitatis, modo ad negotium impendende humanitatis: illuc superascendens per iuge desiderium, illuc[a] aliquando descendens per salutare ministerium.

Exercetur autem genus uiuendi actuosum in eloquiis ueritatis, in exemplis honestatis, in sacramentis pietatis. Perficitur genus uiuendi otiosum in purissimis orationibus, in clarissimis meditationibus, in sanctissimis contemplationibus. Etenim in illis tribus humanitati subuenitur, in istis tribus diuinitati coleretur. Quidni Reconciliator Dei et hominum, pastor scilicet animarum, et potissime Primas presulum et Rector pastorum, per hos quasi sex gradus throni Salomonis ab infimis[b] uelud senaria perfectione indesinenter sublimetur ad summa et, ut res expostulat, a summis nonnunquam deponatur ad infima; et carismata potentie, sapientie, clementie, permanentie, que percipit[c] a summis potenter, sapienter, clementer, permanenter communicet cum infimis.

6a. *Quod archipontifex cum familiaribus suis, quantecunque sint ille et iste precellentie, nullatenus sufficit ad ministerii sui complementum, nisi per prouinciam suam uigilantiori sollicitudine studeat eclesiis ubique pastores preficere sufficientes.*
Numquid ad tantam negotiorum celestium maiestatem archipontificis, cum familiari domesticorum suorum contubernio, sola sufficit quantacunque celica licet operatio, si non etiam adiungat[a] in id ipsum et ecclesiasticis prouincie sue ministeriis exquisita considerationis

5a   [a] istuc B.   [b] ab infimis *omitted* B.   [c] perficit A.
6a   [a] sibi adiunget B.

[7] Augustine, *De civitate Dei* xix. 2 (*CSEL* xl, ii. 368).

excellent than all others, compounded of action and leisurely contemplation? Since, as your excellency knows better than I, there are three kinds of living, according to what St Augustine elegantly shows us from the Scriptures,[7] namely the active kind of life, the leisured contemplative kind of life, and a kind of life consisting of both; one is called the active life, a leisured life is one of contemplation, the mixed life is one in which the two are mingled, that is both the active and contemplative life—which is appropriate to those who have by God's will been raised to a higher place of government in the Church of God. For as it is necessary, as the Lord commands, for him to do all things according to the example shown him on the mountain, with Moses he needs now to ascend the mountain, now to descend to the people, to associate with the angels on Jacob's ladder, in turn ascending to heaven and descending to the earth, in order that in turn he should now give himself the leisure to embrace the Godhead, and now to the business of his ministry to humanity. To the one he ascends above everything through perpetual desire, to the other he descends for his saving ministry.

The active kind of life is practised by uttering the words of truth, by exemplifying virtue, and by devotion to the sacraments; but the leisured kind of life is made perfect in purest prayer, the most lucid meditation, and the most holy contemplation. Really in the three former ways humanity is given support; in the latter three we consort with the Godhead. Is not He who reconciles God and man, who is the shepherd of souls and supremely the primate of rulers and governor of pastors, ceaselessly raised from the depths to the heights through these as it were six steps of the throne of Solomon, as by a sixfold perfection? And as circumstances demand, he is sometimes brought down to the depths, and by the charisma of power, wisdom, mercy, and endurance that he receives from the heights he will impart them powerfully, wisely, mercifully, and lastingly to the lowest.

6a. *That an archbishop with his associates, however excellent they may be, will in no way be adequate to fulfil his ministry unless he is solicitous and vigilant to appoint adequate pastors to churches everywhere throughout his province.*
Will the work of the archbishop with the company of his household associates, however celestial it may be, be alone sufficient for heavenly matters of such grandeur, if he does not also in addition, with a foresight born of prayerful consideration, distribute to the ecclesiastical

superne prouidentia distribuat procerum spiritualium sacerdotalem societatem, et procurande uitalium uirtutum ciuilitati et perturbande uitiorum letalium hostilitati, contemptis animo celesti quantiscunque persone, dignitatis, fame, facultatis quantumlibet terrificis[b] discriminibus?

7a. *De prerogatiua conditionum salutarium que de necessitate requiruntur in eis qui assumendi sunt ad regimen animarum.*

Itaque, sicut ex diuinitatis eloquio, prelatorum auribus simplicitas mea tam lingua quam calamo uelud assiduitate importuniori assolet inculcare, quoniam in memorato sempiterne salutis officio ad consummationem regni perhennis per ministerium pastorale prefici necesse est cure pastionis uiros excellentis glorie, ipsos definiens ait Dei sapientia (Deut. i): 'Date e uobis uiros sapientes et gnaros, quorum conuersatio sit probata in tribubus uestris, ut ponam[a] eos uobis principes.'[8]

'Viros' dixit, uirium uigore ualidos, quos nullatenus aut prosperitas emolliat aut frangat aduersitas. 'Sapientes' per quos sapienter doceatur et ueritas fidei[b] et morum honestas; 'gnaros', per quos prudenter dispensentur et celi carismata et compendia seculi. 'Quorum conuersatio sit probata in tribubus uestris'[c] quorum, inquam, conuersatio et honestioris prudentie, et discretioris industrie, et directioris innocentie, et stabilioris constantie, secundum humilem reuerentiam ad superiores, secundum mitem amicitiam ad compares, secundum sedulam miserationem ad inferiores, sit probata; hoc est, fideli probatioris experientie testimonio sit euidentius commendata. 'In tribubus uestris',[c] scilicet in legitimis graduum ecclesiasticorum distributionibus, que sunt spirituales uirorum ecclesiasticorum cognationes, ipsos uelud per tribus distinguentes. Illi quoque dumtaxat ad sanctum salutis operande principatum ex munere[d] Saluatoris saluandis animabus salubriter exhibentur, reliquis omnibus a Dei sanctuario terribiliter exterminatis, qui memoratis sanctionis diuine titulis celitus illustrantur, propter quod subiungit 'et ponam[e] uobis eos principes.'

---

[b] carnificis A.

7a [a] dabo B.   [b] uite A.   [c] suis B.   [d] dabo B.   [e] ponam: adhuc B.

ministries of his province a priestly society of spiritual leaders, both to procure a regime of living virtues and to throw into confusion the enemy, that is the deadly vices, despising with a heavenly spirit any kind of distinction, however formidable, of person, dignity, fame, or wealth?

7a. *Concerning the surpassing excellence of saving qualities that are necessarily required in those who are to be appointed to the government of souls.*

Therefore, as one drawing upon the word of God, my simple self is accustomed to impress upon the ears of prelates both by tongue and pen, as if with impertinent insistence, that in the aforesaid office of eternal salvation for the completion of the everlasting kingdom through the pastoral ministry it is necessary to place in charge of the pastoral care men of glorious excellence. The wisdom of God defines them, saying (Deut. 1) 'Let me have from among you wise and understanding men, and such whose conversation is approved among your tribes, that I may appoint them your rulers.'[8]

'Men', He has said, of assured strength, who are neither softened by prosperity or broken by adversity; 'wise men' through whom the truths of faith and integrity of conduct are wisely taught; 'understanding men', through whom the gifts of heaven and the profits of the world are wisely dispensed; 'whose conversation is approved among your tribes', whose life is one of integrity, prudence, discretion, and application, of uprightness and innocence, steadiness and constancy, accordingly showing humility and reverence towards superiors, kindness and friendliness towards equals, solicitude and compassion towards inferiors; 'let it be approved', that is, approved and recommended by the faithful testimony of proven experience; 'among your tribes', that is to say, in the lawful apportioning of ecclesiastical grades, which are the spiritual relationships of churchmen, sorting the relationships of churchmen, as it were by tribes. Only these, too, are wisely appointed to the holy office of working for the salvation of souls by the gift of our Saviour (all the others being dreadfully banished from God's sanctuary), upon whom the light of heaven shines with the said marks of divine approval, on account of which He adds 'and that I may appoint them your rulers'.

---

[8] Deut. 1: 13.

8a. *De sex salutaribus obseruantiis per omnem modum necessariis ad salutis operationem per pastores animarum.*

Qualiter autem ad beatitudinis perfectionem exequantur pastores animarum saluifice pastionis officium auctoritas edocet Euangelii, ineuitabili districtione precipiens ut is tantummodo pascendis ouibus dominicis presideat qui indeficienti pie sollicitudinis strenuitate, diuino per omnia fretus patrocinio, satagit, primitus ut pastor pascendis ouibus ouile dominicum non intret nisi per ostium (Ioh. x);[9] secundo, ut proprios uocet oues nominatim; tertio, ut emittat eas ad pascua; quarto, ut ante eas uadat; quinto, ut uocem eius audiri ab eis efficiat; sexto, ut animam suam pro illis ponat.

Quid est autem intrare per hostium nisi per Christum introire, ipso dicente, 'Ego sum ostium'?[10] Quod est in introitu Christo conformari in miti humilitate, in tenui paupertate, in salutari acerbitate. Quid uero est proprias oues uocare nominatim, nisi singulos subditorum per motus suarum affectionum, per studia suarum occupationum, per discrepantias suarum fortunarum, cum | benigno subuentionis desiderio distinctius designare? Quid etiam est eas emittere ad pascua, nisi de excessibus culpe, de erroribus ignorantie, de defectibus impotentie, ipsas per pie sollicitudinis adiutorium uitalibus reficiendas alimentis educere? Quid est insuper ante eas ire, nisi a posterioribus ad anteriora precedentem, sobrie et iuste et pie uiuendo, sobrie per pudiciorem munditiam, iuste per innocentiorem beneuolentiam, pie per deuotiorem sanctimoniam, ipsis se imitandum exhibere? Quid est autem[a] ut uocem eius audiant, nisi ad hoc idem et Dei patrocinium et angelorum presidium et sanctorum suffragium per indefessam orationis piissime iugitatem ipsis obtinere? Quid est denique animam suam pro illis ponere, nisi per carnis mortificationem, per spiritus contribulationem, per libidinum abdicationem presentis uite iocunditatem ipsis uiuificandis in se penitus interimere, sicque seipsum pro eisdem 'hostiam uiuam, sanctam, (Rom. xii) Deo placentem'[b][11] perseueranter immolare?

Quippe quod insuper incumbit pio rectori saluandis subditis et uitam temporalem incunctanter exponere, liquet ex Saluatoris sententia, qua dicitur, 'Bonus pastor animam suam dat pro ouibus suis' (Ioh. x).[12] Quo accedit euidenter sermo Sancti Iohannis Crisostomi

8a   [a] adhuc B.   [b] Deo placentem *omitted* B.

---

[9] John 10: 1.   [10] John 10: 7.
[11] Rom. 12: 1.   [12] John 10: 11.

8a. *Concerning six saving features in every way necessary for pastors of souls to perform the work of salvation.*

But how pastors of souls should perform the pastoral office for the attainment of beatitude is taught us by the authority of the Gospel, commanding us with inescapable sternness that only he may preside over the feeding of the Lord's sheep who, with untiring solicitude and relying in all things upon divine patronage, is zealous, first to ensure that the pastor to feed the sheep of the Lord's flock does not enter except through the door (John 10);[9] secondly, that he calls his own sheep by their names; thirdly, that he sends them out to pasture; fourthly, that he goes before them; fifthly, that he makes his voice heard by them; sixthly, that he may lay down his life for them.

But what is it to 'enter by the door' except to enter through Christ? as He himself says, 'I am the door';[10] which means when entering to be conformed to Christ in gentle humility, closely to Him in poverty and in saving severity. What is it to call one's own sheep by name except to single out each of one's subjects with a kind desire to support them through their active affections, their zealous concern for their employment, and through their changing fortunes? What is it to 'send them out to pasture' except to lead them away from their sins, from their errors and ignorance, from their helpless failings, and to restore them with life-giving nourishment by one's goodness and caring help? Again, what is it to 'go before them' except to proceed from their rear to their front and show oneself to them as a model to imitate by living soberly, justly and righteously—soberly through modesty and purity, justly through innocence and kindness, righteously through devotion and holiness? Yet what is it to make them 'hear one's voice' except to obtain for them the favour of God, the protection of the angels, and the intercession of the saints, by one's unwearying constancy in devout prayer? Lastly, what is it to 'lay down one's life for them' except, in order to give them life, to utterly destroy in oneself the pleasures of the present life by mortification of the flesh, the anguish of the spirit, the renunciation of lust, and thus to persevere in offering oneself for them as 'a victim holy and pleasing to God' (Rom. 12)?[11]

Indeed, that it is incumbent upon a good rector for the salvation of his subjects unhesitatingly to risk also his temporal life is apparent from the declaration of our Saviour, where He says 'the good shepherd giveth his life for his sheep' (John 10).[12] To this clearly relates the sermon of St John Chrysostom (John Chrysostom on

(Iohannnes Crisostomus in Luc. xxiii) alloquentis latronem beatum dicentem, 'Memento mei, Domine, cum^c ueneris in regnum tuum',[13] et introducentis responsionem eiusdem hoc modo: 'Dic michi, regnum commemorans, quid regni uides? Claui et crux est quod inspicis. Sed et ipsa crux', inquit, 'regnum est, et ideo eum regem nomino quia crucifixum inspicio. Imperatorum est pro omnibus mori, et regis optimi pro communi utilitate nunquam recusare supplicium. Ipse dixit, quia "pastor bonus animam suam ponit pro ouibus suis" et ideo imperator bonus animam suam pro hiis quos regit offerre festinat. Quoniam igitur animam suam pro nobis posuit, ideo eum imperatorem uoco.'[14]

9a. *Quod per uenerandos presules agendum est apud Saluatorem rogatu salutari saluifice orationis, ut exhibeat mittendos salutis operarios in messem hereditatis sue, scilicet pastores in plebem ecclesie sue.*
Cum autem apud uenerandos presules in supplicibus suasionum humilium obsecrationibus super memoratis salutarium dispensationum negotiis, aliquotiens agitur secundum urgentia causarum occurrentium requisita, nonnulli sepius respondere consuescunt, quomodo tales inueniri ualebunt saluificis regiminibus preficiendi quales ad hoc euocari diuina decernunt eloquia; quasi 'abbreuiata (Ys. 10) sit manus Domini ut saluare nequeat'.[15] Audiat, rogo, dispensatorum ecclesiasticorum fidelis obedientia quid in hoc dicat Altissimus Dominator omnium et animarum Amator piissimus apostolico culmini et ordini ecclesiastico (Mat. ix): 'Messis quidem multa, operarii autem pauci. Rogate ergo Dominum messis, ut mittat operarios in messem suam',[16] re uera per operarios rectores, per messem regendos in hereditate Domini signans.

Numquid incomparabilis misericordie ueritas incommutabilis, quod commendat rogandum, rogata denegabit? Numquid si iubet ut petatur, cum petitur non exaudiet? Absit. Absit procul^a ab animabus ortodoxis hec dementissima peruersitatis insane^b perfidia. Nempe uerissime constat quod quicquid precipit postulari postulanti prestabit, si fidelis Deus seipsum negare non potest potissime cum sincero feruore flagitatur pro quo dilectus Dei Filius placande Patris maiestati per altitudinem diuini consilii in ara crucis immolatur. Quid autem hoc est, nisi per ministros Dei in populo Dei operande salutis

^c dum A.

9a ^a procul *omitted* B.   ^b insanie B.

---

[13] Luke 23: 42.   [14] Chrysostom, *De Cruce et Latrone Homilia, PG* xlix. 445.

Luke 23), addressing the good thief, when he says 'Remember me, O Lord, when thou shalt come into thy kingdom',[13] introducing this answer in this way: 'Tell me, in referring to a kingdom, what kingdom do you see? What you see are nails and a cross. But the cross itself, he cries, is the kingdom, and therefore I call him a king because I see him crucified. It is the proper part of emperors to die for all people, and that of the best king never to refuse pain for the service of the community. He himself has said that "the good shepherd lays down his life for his sheep", and a good ruler hastens to offer his life for those whom he rules. So for the reason that He has laid down his life for us, we call Him our emperor.'[14]

9a. *That our venerable bishops should press our Saviour with saving requests and prayers to provide labourers of salvation to be sent into the harvest of his inheritance, that is, pastors for the people of his Church.*
When our venerable bishops are urged at various times with humble and persuasive entreaties regarding the business of making salutary arrangements to meet the pressing demands that occur, often some are wont to reply 'how will it be possible to appoint such men to the saving work of rectors as are perceived to be called to this role by the word of God, as if 'the hand of the Lord is shortened (Isa. 10) so that it cannot save'?[15] Let the faithful and obedient ministers of the Church hear, I beg you, what the Most High Lord of all and good lover of souls says in reply to this question to the apostolic head and order of the Church (Matt. 9): 'The harvest indeed is great, but the labourers are few. Pray ye therefore the Lord of the harvest that he will send forth labourers into his harvest',[16] by labourers signifying in truth rectors, and by the harvest those to be governed in the Lord's inheritance.

Will the changeless truth of incomparable mercy refuse us what He bids us to ask when he has been asked for it? If He commands us to make the request, will He not hear and answer when the request is made? Never. Far be such perverse and mad disbelief from the souls of orthodox believers. To be sure, it is an established truth that He will grant to a postulant whatever He commands him to ask, if God who is faithful cannot deny himself, above all when that is asked with sincerity and fervour, for which the beloved Son of God is offered upon the altar of the cross to appease the Father's majesty, through the depth of the divine wisdom. But what is this that is requested except the completion of the work of salvation for the people of God

[15] Isa. 59: 1.   [16] Matt. 9: 37–8.

salutaris adimpletio? 'Vnde uocabis', inquit, 'nomen eius Iesum. (Ma. i) Ipse enim saluum faciet populum suum a peccatis eorum.'[17] Quamobrem ait, 'Si quid petieritis Patrem in nomine meo, dabit uobis' (Ioh. xvi).[18] Quis autem est qui petit Patrem in Filii nomine, quod est 'Iesus' interpretatum 'salutaris', nisi qui ex salutari conceptu, per salutarem affectum, in salutari obtentu saluandis populis per salutaria ministeria, cum salutari Saluatoris reuerentia, clementiam Patris salutarem interpellat?

10a. *Quod nunc dicta rogatio pro mittendis a Saluatore salutis operariis fieri debeat sine omni hesitatione detestabilis diffidentie ubique et presertim in presenti rogatu condempnatissime.*

Permonetur autem ab Eius[a] apostolo Iacobo ut qui petit postulet in fide, nichil hesitans, alioquin non estimans quod accipiat aliquid a Domino.[19] Quis enim locus poterit esse apud eum qui rogat diffidentie, cum apud summum Saluatorem qui rogatur, et ut rogatur tam efficaciter inuitantem, nusquam locus esse poterit aut impotentie que nequeat, aut insipientie que nesciat, aut inuidentie que nolit, gratiam salutis saluifice prerogare? Quidni ueniat ira in filios diffidentie propter quam a Saluatore pigritantur rogare quod rogare precipiuntur per Saluatorem, uidelicet per ministros Saluatoris perfectam adimplende salutis operationem, ex Dei miseratione, in populo Dei? Nunquam[b] est hec dampnatissimi erroris diffidentia, nisi cum quis per execratissimam blasphemie peruicacis iniuriam apud Filium Dei, mundi Saluatorem, mendacissima delirationis amentia,[c] fingit pro perfectu[d] potentie defectum impotentie, pro perfectu sapientie defectum insipientie, pro perfectu beneuolentie defectum inuidentie; propter quod manifestissime nichil adeo contra deprecantis orationem indignationem Saluatoris prouocare comprobatur.

11a. *De quatuor primariis conditionibus orationis exaudiende cum Deus oratur ab homine, que sunt mortificatio amara, tribulatio[a] angusta, mansuetudo suauissima, humilitas lucidissima.*

Verum attendamus que sunt ea que ab homine oraturo orandus Deus exquirat. Scripturam audiamus frequentius adiungentem orationi[b] ieiunium et elemosynam. Unde est illud Tobie xii: 'Bona est oratio

10a   *a* Ipsius B.   *b* add enim B.   *c* A adds quam at this point, which B omits. *d* profecto A.

11a   *a* mortificationis tribulatio B.   *b* orationem B.

---

[17] Matt. 1: 21.   [18] John 16: 23.   [19] James 1: 6–7.

through God's ministers? Therefore He says 'thou shalt call his name Jesus (Matt. 1). For he shall save his people from their sins'.[17] On this account He says 'If ye seek anything from the Father in my name, he will give it to you' (John 16).[18] But who is it that petitions the Father in the name of the Son—who is Jesus, meaning salvation—except he who, out of his saving thoughts, through his saving love, with the saving intention of saving the people through his saving ministry, with the saving reverence of the Saviour appeals to the saving mercy of the Father?

10a. *That the said request for the Saviour to send labourers of salvation should be made without hesitation or a lack of faith contemptible everywhere but especially to be deplored in making this present request.*
We are advised by His apostle James that he who seeks should ask in faith, nothing doubting, otherwise not counting on receiving anything from the Lord.[19] For what place can there be for unbelief in someone making a request, when in the supreme Saviour, who is receiving the request and who so efficaciously invites us to make requests, there is no place for either impotence to deliver the salvific grace or want of wisdom which does not know it or malice that is unwilling to grant it? Would not the anger of God come upon the children of unbelief for the reason that they are slothful in asking from the Saviour what He bids them to ask, namely to complete the work of salvation in God's people by the mercy of God through the ministers of the Saviour? This damnable error of unbelief never exists unless someone, through a most dreadful insult offered by stiff-necked blasphemy to the Son of God, the Saviour of the world, in lying and senseless madness attributes to Him a defect of impotence instead of perfect power, a want of wisdom instead of perfect wisdom, a defect of malice instead of perfect benevolence. Nothing is so calculated to provoke the indignation of our Saviour against the prayer of a petitioner.

11a. *Of the four primary conditions for prayer to be heard when a man prays to God, which are harsh mortification, pressing distress, a sweet gentleness, and most transparent humility.*
Now let us consider what are the things God, to whom we should pray, seeks from a man who is going to pray. Let us listen to Scripture, which frequently associates prayer with fasting and almsgiving. On this there is that passage of Tobias: (Tob. 12) 'prayer is good with fasting and alms, more than to lay up treasures

f. 81ᵛ cum ieiunio et elemosyna | magis quam thesauros auri condere';[20]
insinuans per 'ieiunium' austeram carnis castigationem, per 'elemosynam' anxiam spiritus compunctionem. Et alibi Iudith ait (Iudith
ix): 'Humilium et mansuetorum semper tibi placuit deprecatio. Deus
celorum, Creator aquarum et Dominus totius creature, exaudi me
miseram deprecantem, et de tua misericordia presumentem.'[21] 'Mansuetorum', inquam, secundum placidam lenitatem mansuetudinis;
'humilium' quoque, secundum pauidam grauitatem humilitatis, ut
ueraciter ostenditur orationem non exaudiri nisi que transigitur in
austeriori seueritate mortificationis secundum carnem et in exactiori
anxietate compunctionis secundum spiritum, et in deuotissima
grauitate humilitatis in Deum, et in benignissima lenitate mansuetudinis in proximum, exclusa per mortificationem carnis omni con-
cupiscentia defedantis illecebre, per contritionem spiritus omni uitio
deprauantis nequitie, per suauitatem mansuetudinis omni affectione
humane uoluptatis, per deuotionem humilitatis omni ambitione
mundane uanitatis.

12a. *Qualiter quatuor karismata, scilicet castigatio et compunctio et
mansuetudo et humilitas, ex quibus sacra conficitur oratio, designantur
per quatuor aromata, scilicet stacten, onicam, galbanum, et thus, ex quibus
sacrum conficitur thimiama, sicut etiam sacra oratioᵃ signata in sancto
thimiamate.*
Opere pretium esse uidetur hic aduertere utrum iam dicta signarentur
per sermonem Domini ad legislatorem, ubi ait (Ex. xxx): 'Sume tibi
aromata, stacten et onicham et galbanum boni odoris et thus lucidissi-
mum; equalis ponderis erunt omnia; faciesque thimiama compositum
opere unguentarii mixtum diligenter et purum, sanctificatione dignissimum. Cumque in tenuissimum puluerem uniuersa contuderis,
pones ex eo in tabernaculo testimonii, in quo ⟨loco⟩ apparebo tibi.
Sanctum sanctorum erit uobis thimiama. Talem compositionem non
facietis in usus uestros, quia sanctum est Domino.'[22]
    Est igitur stacten, id est mirra purioris nature, custodiens contra
corruptelas etiam mortuorum corpora condita per ipsam conseruans;
onicha, id est ungula coclea ostri subtilioris facture caligines illumi-
nans; galbanum, succus ferule, letiferas ueneni pernicies exterminans;
thus, gummi perspicui candoris excellenter uirtutem uitalem con-
fortans. Potest ergo, sicut liquet studiosius consideranti spirituali
examinatione singulas presentium ⟨aromatum⟩ proprietates signari

12a   ᵃ oratione AB.

of gold',[20] implying by 'fasting' the stern castigation of the flesh, and by 'alms' an anxious compunction of the spirit. And elsewhere Judith says (Judith 9): 'The prayer of the humble and meek hath always pleased thee, O God of the heavens, creator of the waters and lord of the whole creation; hear me, a poor wretch, making supplication to thee, and presuming of thy mercy.'[21] 'of the meek' I say, according to the quiet gentleness of meekness; 'of the humble' also, with the trembling seriousness of humility. Thus it is truly shown that prayer is not heard unless it is performed in a state of severe morification of the flesh, and with an anxious compunction of spirit, and with a sincere and most devout humility towards God, and in a state of great goodwill and kindness toward one's neighbour, excluding all vile concupiscence by mortification of the flesh, all wicked vice by spiritual contrition, all love of human pleasure by meekness, all worldly ambition and vanity by devout humility.

12a. *How the four charisms out of which sacred prayer is composed, namely mortification, compunction, meekness, and humility are designated by four spices, that is myrrh, onycha, galbanum and frankincense, from which is composed thyme or incense, by which is signified holy prayer.*

It seems worth while here to consider whether the aforesaid things were indicated by the word of the Lord to the lawgiver where he says (Exod. 30) 'Take unto thee spices: stacte and onycha, galbanum of sweet savour, and clearest frankincense; all shall be of equal weight; and thou shalt make incense compounded by the work of the perfumer, well tempered together and most worthy of sanctification. And when thou hast beaten all into very small powder, thou shalt set part of it before the tabernacle of the testimony, in the place where I will appear to thee. Most holy shall this incense be unto you. You shall not make such a composition for your own uses, because it is holy to the Lord.'[22]

Stacte then is myrrh of a purer nature, a preservative against corruption, preserving even bodies of the dead when buried; onycha is an ointment of finer make from the shell of an oyster, illuminating darkness; galbanum the sap of the fennel, an antidote to the fatal effect of deadly poison; incense is a gum of conspicuous whiteness, admirably strengthening vitality. To one who studiously considers the particular properties of these aromas in their spiritual sense, it is

[20] Tob. 12: 8.   [21] Judith 9: 16–17.
[22] Exod. 30: 34–7.

per stacten austera maceratio castigationis secundum carnem; per onicham anxia contritio compunctionis secundum spiritum; per galbanum benigna suauitas mansuetudinis in proximum; per thus uotiua luciditas humilitatis in Deum; licet ista quatuor altioris misterii eminentiori notitia ualeant intelligi. Que quatuor omnia iuxta nunc dictum modum considerata, sunt quatuor aromata, uidelicet salutaria celestium appetituum spiramina. 'Et erunt equalis ponderis', librata scilicet equaliter pondere sanctuarii, quod est difinitiua sanctimonie affectualis inclinatio.

Ex quibus aromatibus fieri oportet thimiama, quod est sanctum salutaris orationis incensum, 'compositum opere unguentarii', scilicet Christi Domini, summi Saluatoris, qui ait (Joh. 14): 'Sine me nichil potestis facere',[23] qui quidem eo ipso uerissime dicitur unguentarius, quod per Ipsius dumtaxat operationem[b] ex supernis salutarium carismatum sanctimoniis saluificum sancte conuersationis conficitur unguentum, quo intellectualis creatura suo consecratur Auctori, a defectu ualetudinis sanata diuinitus; propter quod ad Ipsum ait (Cant. i): 'Trahe me post te; curremus in odorem unguentorum tuorum.'[24]

Mixtum est diligenter hoc thimiama cum presentium quatuor spiritualium superum affectus, uelud incorporantur omnium in singulis per studiosam diligentie sagacis sedulitatem; purum autem erit cum a terrene delectationis feculentia apud ipsum celica sinceritas fuerit expiata, et ita, quia ab infimis ad summa sublimatum, sanctificatione dignissimum, necesse est uniuersa in 'tenuissimum puluerem' contundi, id est in subtilissimas examinis considerationes discuti, ut efficaciter in salubrem misceantur redolentiam per exqui- situm sollertis industrie scrutinium, ut fiat thimiama salutifere orationis adolende coram Domino. Et 'ex eo thimiate ponendum est in tabernaculo testimonii' quia, quod ex orationis sancte salutari pietate conficitur, in intimo dilectionis celice domicilio, quod est tabernaculum testimonii, conseruandum oportet collocari, ubi testi- monium perhibens in diuine adoptionis (Est. i) hereditariam filiatio- nem,[25] et ideo est non tantum tabernaculum, sed tabernaculum testimonii.

Deus ipse nobis apparet seipsum manifestans secundum quod Ipse ait (Jo. xiv): 'Qui diligit me, diligetur a Patre meo, et ego diligam eum, et manifestabo ei meipsum.'[26] Erit autem hoc thimiama uidelicet et

---

[b] immoderata A

[23] John 15: 5.   [24] Song of Songs 1: 3.

therefore apparent that by stacte is signified the austerity of bodily
maceration; by onycha, contrition or anxious spiritual compunction;
by galbanum, kindness and gentleness to a neighbour; by incense,
transparency of prayerful humility towards God, although these four
can be understood by higher knowledge to signify a deeper mystery.
All of them, carefully regarded in the aforesaid manner are four
aromas, that is saving inspirations of eager heavenly desires, 'and they
shall be of equal weight', that is, weighed equally by the scales of the
sanctuary, which is a definite disposal towards holiness of the
affections.

From these aromas there must needs come thyme, which is the
sacred incense of saving prayer, compounded by the work of the
anointer, that is Christ the Lord, the supreme Saviour, who says
'Without me you can do nothing' (John 14).[23] He is for that very
reason most truly called the anointer, because through his working
the salvific ointment of holy life is constituted out of holy and
heavenly salvific charisms, by which the intellectual creature is
consecrated to its Author and divinely healed of its failing health.
On this account it says to Him, 'Draw me; we will run after thee to
the odour of thy anointments' (Song of Songs 1).[24]

This sacred thyme is compounded carefully when the present four
spirits of heavenly love are all as it were embodied in individuals by
zealous solicitude; but it shall be 'pure' when heavenly sincerity has
cleansed it from the infection of earthly pleasure; and thus, as it is
raised from the basest things to supreme heights and made 'worthy of
sanctification', it is necessary for it all 'to be beaten into very small
powder', that is, shaken apart into a mass of very fine reflections, so
that they may be effectively mixed into a salutary perfume with a
careful and skilful scrutiny, so that it may be an incense of saving
prayer to be offered before the Lord. And some of this incense 'shall
be set before the tabernacle of the testimony', for what is composed of
the saving piety of holy prayer should be placed for preservation in
the house of heavenly love, which is 'the tabernacle of the testimony',
where it bears witness to our hereditary sonship by divine adoption
(Esther 1),[25] and so it is not only a tabernacle, but 'a tabernacle of
testimony'.

God Himself appears to us, manifesting Himself, according to what
He Himself says: 'He that loveth me shall be loved of my Father; and I
will love him and will manifest myself to him' (John 14).[26] But this

[25] Cf. Exod. 30: 35–6.   [26] John 14: 21.

sacrosanctum salutifere orationis spiramentum, 'sanctum sanctorum';
hoc est, cetera sanctitatum dona sanctificans, et super ea spirituali
prerogatiua precipuum. Et ideo talis compositionis misticum thimiama tanta inhibetur districtione ne fiat in usus humanos peruersum
ad appetitiones temporalium, quod tanta diuinitatis diligentia con-
uersum est in desideria celestium, quia ipsum, sicut cernitur ex hiis
que nunc tacta sunt, tam celebri pietate diuinitus conscratum,
sanctum est Domino.

13a. *Que pura, que purior, que purissima est oratio.*
Hoc loco diligenter distinguendum esse cognoscitur de oratione que
pura, que purior, que purissima. Est autem oratio pura qua oratur pro
incommodis transitoriis propellendis uel temporalibus commodis
suscipiendis,[a] ut tranquilla sit deuotio corporalis conuersationis.
Oratio uero purior qua oratur pro expiatione uitiorum et institutione
uirtutum, ut moderata sit affectio naturalium passionum. Oratio
f. 82   insuper[b] purissima est qua oratur | non iam munera Sponsi, sed
ipse Sponsus per sincerum languentis anime desiderium suspiratur,
uidelicet ut beata sit consummatio perennium desideriorum, hoc est
quod sine fine uideatur, sine fastidio ametur, sine fatigatione laudetur.

      Pro incommodis transitoriis propellendis in Daniel ix: 'Propter
temetipsum inclina, Deus noster, aurem tuam et exaudi, aperi oculos
tuos et uide desolationem nostram, et ciuitatem super quam inuoca-
tum est nomen tuum';[27] in Act. xii: 'Et Petrus quidem seruabatur in
carcere; oratio autem fiebat sine intermissione ab ecclesia ad Deum
pro eo.'[28] Pro suscipiendis temporalibus commodis in Ier. xxix:
'Querite pacem ciuitatis, ad quam transmigrare uos feci, et orate
pro ea ad Dominum, quia in pace ipsius erit pax uestra.'[29] Ad i Tim.
ii: 'Obsecro primum omnium fieri obsecrationes, postulationes,
gratiarum actiones pro omnibus hominibus, pro regibus et omnibus
qui in sublimitate sunt constituti, ut quietam et tranquillam uitam
agamus in omni pietate et castitate.'[30] Pro utroque in ii Paral. xxxii:
'Manasses, postquam coangustatus est, orauit Dominum Deum
suum, et egit penitentiam ualde coram Deo patrum suorum. Depre-
catusque est eum et obsecrauit intente, et exaudiuit orationem eius et
reduxit eum in Ierusalem, in regnum suum.'[31] Et iterum Ro. xv:
'Obsecro igitur uos, fratres, per Dominum Iesum Christum et per
caritatem Spiritus Sancti, ut adiuuetis me in orationibus ad Deum, ut

13a   [a] uel incommodis transitoriis propellendis B.   [b] denique B.

---

[27] Dan. 9: 17–18.   [28] Acts 12: 5.   [29] Jer. 29: 7.

incense shall be also a holy inspiration of salvific prayer, a holy of holies, that is one that sanctifies the other gifts of sanctity, foremost among such spiritual privileges. Therefore the mystical thyme of this composition is reserved with such strictness lest that which has by God's great care been turned into a desire for the things of heaven be perverted to human use for seeking temporal advantages. For, as is clear from the things referred to, what has been divinely consecrated by such famous goodness is holy to the Lord.

13a. *Which prayer is pure, which is purer, and which the purest.*
Here we know we must distinguish between prayer that is pure, that which is purer, and that which is the purest. Now pure prayer is that by which we pray to ward off passing troubles or to obtain temporal advantages, that our bodily life may be one of tranquil devotion. Purer prayer is that by which we pray to expiate our vices and establish virtues, to restrain the feelings of our natural passions. Lastly, the purest prayer is that which does not ask gifts from the Spouse, but in which the Spouse Himself is longed for by the fainting soul with true desire, that He may be the blessed consummation of our eternal desires, that is, that He may be seen without end, loved without satiety, and praised untiringly.

'To ward off passing troubles' see in Daniel 9, 'Incline, O my God, thy ear and hear; open thy eyes and see our desolation and the city upon which thy name is called',[27] and in Acts 12, 'Peter therefore was kept in prison. But prayer was made without ceasing by the Church unto God for him.'[28] 'To obtain temporal advantages' see Jeremiah 29: 'Seek the peace of the city to which I have caused you to be carried away and pray to the Lord for it; for in the peace thereof shall be your peace.'[29] And at Timothy 2: 'I desire first of all that supplications, prayers, intercessions, and thanksgivings be made for all men, for kings and for all that are in high station, that we may lead a quiet and peaceable life in all piety and chastity.'[30] For both these advantages see 2 Chron. 32: 'Manasses, after he was in distress, prayed to the Lord his God, and did penance exceedingly before the God of his fathers. And he entreated Him and besought Him earnestly; and He heard his prayer and brought him again to Jerusalem into his kingdom.'[31] And again, see Romans 15: 'I beseech you, therefore, brethren, through our Lord Jesus Christ and by the charity of the Holy Ghost, that you help me in your prayers for me to God: that I may be delivered from the

---

[30] 1 Tim. 2: 1–2.   [31] 2 Chron. 33: 12–13.

liberer ab infidelibus qui sunt in Iudea, et obsequii mei oblatio accepta fiat in Ierusalem sanctis, ut ueniam ad uos in gaudio per uoluntatem Dei, et refrigerer uobiscum.'[32] Pro expiatione uitiorum in Eccl. xxiii: 'Domine Pater et Deus uite mee ne derelinquas me in cogitatu eorum, et extollentiam oculorum meorum ne dederis michi, et omne desiderium auerte a me. Aufer a me uentris concupiscentias et concubitus, ne apprehendant me.'[33] And in Iac. v: 'Infirmatur quis in uobis? Inducat presbiteros ecclesie et orent super eum, unguentes eum oleo sancto in nomine Domini; et oratio fidei saluabit infirmum, et alleuiabit eum Dominus, et si in peccatis sit, dimittentur ei.'[34] Pro institutione uirtutum in libro Macha. i: 'Beneficiat uobis Deus, et meminerit testamenti sui quod locutus est ad Abraham et Ysaac et Iacob, seruorum suorum fidelium[c] et det uobis cor omnibus ut colatis eum et faciatis eius uoluntatem corde perfecto et animo uolenti. Adaperiat cor uestrum in lege sua et in preceptis suis et faciat pacem.'[35] Et ad Phil. i: 'Et hoc oro, ut caritas uestra magis ac magis habundet in omni scientia et in omni sensu, ut probetis potiora, et sitis sinceri et sine offensa in diem Christi, repleti fructu iustitie, per Iesum Christum in gloriam Dei.'[36] Pro utroque in Psal. l: 'Auerte faciem tuam a peccatis meis et omnes iniquitates meas dele. Cor mundum crea in me, Deus, et spiritum rectum innoua in uisceribus meis.'[37] Et iterum ad Cor. 13: 'Oramus autem Deum, ut nichil mali faciatis, non ut nos probati pareamus, sed ut uos quod bonum est faciatis.'[38]

De claritate uisionis, Exo. xxxiii: 'Si ergo inueni gratiam in conspectu tuo, ostende michi faciem tuam.'[39] Et Io. xvii: 'Pater, quos dedisti michi, uolo ut ubi sum ego et illi sint mecum et uideant claritatem meam quam dedisti michi.'[40] De unitate dilectionis Can. i: 'Trahe me post te; curremus in odorem unguentorum tuorum.'[41] Et Io. xvii: 'Non pro hiis rogo tantum, sed pro eis qui credituri sunt, per uerbum eorum, in me; ut omnes unum sint, sicut et tu, Pater, in me et ego in te, ut et ipsi in nobis unum sint, ut credat mundus quia tu me misisti.'[42] De felicitate laudationis II Pali. xxxii:[43] 'Domine Deus omnipotens patrum nostrorum Abraham, Ysaac, et Iacob, ne simul perdas me cum iniquitatibus meis, neque in eternum reserues mala michi, quia indignum saluabis me secundum magnam misericordiam

[c] fidelium *omitted* A.

---

[32] Rom. 15: 30–2.
[33] Ecclus. 23: 4–6.
[34] James 5: 14–15.
[35] 2 Macc. 1: 2–4.
[36] Phil. 1: 9–11.
[37] Ps. 50: 11–12.
[38] 2 Cor. 13: 7.
[39] Exod. 33: 13.
[40] John 17: 24.

unbelievers that are in Judaea and that the oblation of my service may be acceptable in Jerusalem to the saints, that I may come to you with joy, for the will of God, and may be refreshed with you.'[32] For the expiation of vices, see Ecclus. 23: 'Lord, Father and God of my life, leave me not to their desires; Give me not haughtiness of my eyes, and turn away from me all coveting; take from me the greediness of the belly, and let not the lusts of the flesh take hold of me.'[33] And in James 5: 'Is any man sick among you? Let them bring in the priests of the Church and let them pray over him, anointing him with oil in the name of the Lord; and the prayer of faith shall save the sick man, and the Lord shall raise him up, and if he be in sins, they shall be forgiven him.'[34] For the establishment of virtues see in the book of Macc. 1: 'May God be gracious to you and remember his covenant that he made with Abraham and Isaac and Jacob, his faithful servants, and give you all a heart to worship and to do his will with a great heart and a willing mind. May he open your heart in his law and in his commandments and send you peace.'[35] And in Phil. 1: 'and this I pray: that your charity may more and more abound in knowledge and in all understanding, that you may approve the better things, that you may be sincere and without offence unto the day of Christ, filled with the fruit of justice, through Jesus Christ, unto the glory and praise of God.'[36] For both petitions see in Psalm 1: 'Turn away thy face from my sins, and blot out all my iniquities. Create a clean heart in me, O God, and renew a right spirit within my bowels.'[37] And again to Corinthians 13: 'Now we pray God that you may do no evil, not that we may appear approved, but that you may do that which is good.'[38]

Concerning clarity of vision see Exod. 33: 'If therefore I have found favour in thy sight, show me thy face'[39] and John 17: 'Father, I will that where I am, they also whom thou hast given me may be with me, that they may see my glory which thou hast given me.'[40] Concerning union of love, Song of Songs 1: 'Draw me; we will run after thee to the odour of thy ointments';[41] and John 17: 'Not for them only do I pray, but for them also who through their word shall believe in me; that they all may be one as thou, Father, in me and I in thee; that they also may be one in us, that the world may believe that thou hast sent me.'[42] Concerning the felicity of praise see 2 Chron. 36:[43] 'Lord God Almighty of our fathers Abraham, Isaac, and Jacob, destroy me not with my iniquities, nor save me evil for ever, for thou shalt save me

[41] Song of Songs 1: 3.   [42] John 17: 20–1.
[43] The prayer of Manasses: Vulgate, appendix 1; 2 Chron 33: 12 refers to the prayer.

tuam, et laudabo te semper omnibus diebus uite mee, quoniam te laudet omnis uirtus celorum, et tibi gloria in secula seculorum, Amen.' Et in Psalmo cv: 'Saluos nos fac, Domine Deus noster, et congrega nos de nationibus, ut confiteamur nomini sancto tuo et gloriemur in laude tua.'[44] Et iterum Hest. vi: 'Exaudi deprecationem meam, ut uiuentes laudemus nomen tuum, Domine, et non claudas ora canentium te'[45] et cetera. Que tria per prelibationem habentur in uia per saturitatem in patria.

14a. *Qualiter oratio fieri habeatur in lingua et in spiritu et in mente; uidelicet, et in uita sensus, et in uita spiritus, et in uita intellectus, ut fructum salutis optineat.*

Oportet insuper quod oratio, cum ipsa sit intente requisitionis intellectuale desiderium ascendens in Deum, impetrandi gratia, non solum lingua, nec solum lingua et[a] spiritu, sed omnino mente peragatur, secundum apostolum dicentem (1 Cor. xiv): 'Si orem lingua, spiritus meus orat, mens autem mea sine fructu est. Quid ergo est? Orabo spiritu, orabo et mente, psallam spiritu', etc.,[b][46] ut in oratione apex affectualis nullatenus subsistat quousque super linguam et spiritum in mentem conscendat, id est, super uitam sensualem et uitam spiritualem in uitam intellectualem exsurgat. Consistit autem integraliter homo uiuens in hiis tribus uite differentiis, uidelicet uita sensus, uita spiritus, uita intellectus, secundum illud Gen. ii: 'Formauit Dominus Deus hominem de limo terre, et inspirauit in faciem eius spiraculum uite, et factus est homo in animum uiuentem.'[47]

Agitur autem uita sensus in susceptione specierum sensibilium, uita spiritus in effigiatione figurarum ymaginabilium, uita intellectus in apprehensione formarum intelligibilium, ut cum lego solitarius in codice (Luc. x): 'Diliges proximum tuum sicut teipsum',[48] scripturam presentem sensu percipio per speciem sensibilem; proximum absentem effigio per figuram ymaginabilem, dilectionem ipsam nec sensu susceptibilem nec spiritu effigiabilem intellectu apprehendo, nec per speciem sensibilem nec per figuram ymaginabilem,[c] sed per formam intelligibilem. Ergo si oretur lingua solum in uita sensuali, uel oretur spiritu in uita spirituali, uel oretur lingua et spiritu in uita sensuali et

---

14a   [a] lingua et *omitted* A.   [b] psallam spiritu etc. *omitted* A.   [c] dilectionem ipsam . . . ymaginabilem B *omitted by* A.

[44] Ps. 105: 47.   [45] Esther 13: 17.
[46] 1 Cor. 14: 14–15.   [47] Gen. 2: 7.

according to thy great mercy, and I shall praise thee always all the days of my life, because all the might of heaven praises thee, and to thee be glory for ever and ever, Amen.' And in Psalm 105: 'Save us, O Lord our God, and gather us from among the heathen, to give thanks unto thy holy name, and to triumph in thy praise.'[44] And again (Esther 6) 'Hear my supplication, that we may live and praise thy name, Lord, and shut not the mouths of them that sing to thee, etc.'[45] These three are had by way of a foretaste on our journey to satiety in our homeland.

14a. *How prayer must needs be with the tongue and also in spirit and mind, that is in the life of the senses, and also in the life of the spirit and in the life of the intelligence, to obtain the fruit of salvation.*
Moreover prayer, as it is a desire of the mind searching and rising to God to make a request, must be performed not only by the tongue, nor by the spirit alone, but with the whole mind, following the Apostle in saying (1 Cor. 14): 'For if I pray in a tongue, my spirit prayeth, but my understanding is without fruit. What is it then? I will pray with the spirit; I will pray also with the understanding; I will sing with the spirit, etc.',[46] so that the apex of love is not reached in prayer until it rises above language and spirit to understanding, that is, above the life of sense and the life of spirit, to the life of the intellect. Now the whole man lives in these three distinct modes of life, that of the senses, that of the spirit, and that of the intellect, as that text of Genesis 2 has it: 'The Lord God formed man of the slime of the earth, and breathed into his face the breath of life, and man became a living soul.'[47]

The life of the senses acts in receiving the data of sense objects; the life of the spirit in forming images, the life of the intellect in the apprehension of intelligible forms, so that when I on my own read in the book (Luke 10) 'Thou shalt love thy neighbour as thyself',[48] I perceive this writing with my senses; with my spirit I form an imaginary image of my absent neighbour, but the love of him, which can neither be received by the senses nor formed as an image by the spirit, I apprehend with my intellect neither by sense reception nor by a figure of the imagination, but by an intelligible form. So if my prayer is only by my tongue and a product of my sense life, or if it is only a product of my spirit, or if it is a product of both my sense and spiritual life, unless it is also with understanding and a

[48] Luke 10: 27.

spirituali, nisi oretur in mente in uita intellectuali, orationi fructus salutis nequaquam adquiritur. Igitur nec tantum oratio uocalis sine

f. 82ᵛ sensuali, nec tantum oratio | ymaginabilis sine spirituali, nec simul oratio utraque, uocalis siue sensualis et ymaginabilis siue spiritualis, sine rationali siue intellectuali, fructum salutis obtinet a Saluatore. Sed tertia per seipsum, uel cum alterutra duarum uel cum ipsarum utraque, plene sufficit ad salutem.

Tres etenim, scilicet uita sensus, uita spiritus, uita intellectus, secundum Beatum Augustinum, tres sunt celi,[49] quos insinuans apostolus (Cor. xii): 'Scio', inquit, 'hominem in Christo ante annos quattuordecim, siue in corpore, siue extra corpus nescio, Deus scit, raptum huiusmodi usque ad tertium celum.'[50] Ergo cum cor sit originale uite domicilium, secundum illud Prou. x: 'Omni custodia custodi cor tuum, quoniam ex ipso uita procedit'[51] nullus, quod fieri necesse est, orat Deum toto corde, nisi per celeste desiderium celum uite sensualis superet, celum uite spiritualis transeat, celum uite intellectualis ascendat, et sic ad Deum Saluatorem, celi intellectualis saluificum habitatorem, in oratione salutari perueniat, intrans in cubiculum suum ibidem, iuxta uerbum Filii, orantis Patrem suum in abscondito. Quod nullatenus fieri ualet, nisi per superintellectualem summe diuinitatis operationem. Nunquam enim creatura, cum sit uirtus finita, ad creatorem, qui est uirtus infinita, pertingere ualet, nisi superseculariter agatur ad hoc illius finiti defectio per Istius infiniti perfectionem: propter quod ait Io. vi: 'Nemo uenit ad me, nisi Pater qui misit me traxerit eum.'[52]

15a. *De profectu orationis cum ipsi adsunt uniuersa superscripta et de defectu ipsius cum eidem abest aliquid de suprascriptis uniuersis.*

Que profecto si assunt suprascripta uniuersa, secundum iam insinuatam prouisiue diuinitatis institutionem ad orationis pie complementum, necesse est ex diuina promissione nullatenus negari quod oratione sic perfecta supplicatur optimum.ᵃ Quod si quid eorum que prescripta sunt in oratione petituro defuerit, quia diuinis obueniendo mandatis per preuaricationem legis sue Deum inhonorat, (Rom. ii) comprobatur omnino nequaquam misericordie dignationem impetrare, sed prouocare indignationem iracundie. Vnde est illud apostoli (Iac. v): 'Petitis et non accipitis, eo quod male petitis.'[53] Quoniam

15a ᵃ optineri A.

---

[49] *De civitate Dei*, xix. 2 (*CSEL* xl, ii, 368).   [50] 2 Cor. 12: 2.
[51] Prov. 4: 23.   [52] John 6: 44.   [53] James 4: 3.

product of my intellectual life, it in no way acquires the fruit of salvation. Therefore neither vocal prayer without the sense aspect, nor imaging prayer without the spiritual aspect, nor vocal prayer of the senses and imaging prayer of the spirit together, without rational or intellectual input, obtain the fruit of salvation from the Saviour. But prayer of the third kind, by itself or with either or both of the others, is fully sufficient for salvation.

Indeed the three lives, that of the senses, that of the spirit, and that of the intellect, are according to St Augustine three heavens,[49] to which the apostle (Cor. 12) refers: 'I know a man in Christ', he says, 'above fourteen years ago (whether in the body I know not, or out of the body I know not, God knoweth), such a one caught up to the third heaven.'[50] Therefore since the heart is the original domicile of life, according to that text of Proverbs 10: 'with watchfulness keep thy heart, because life issueth out of it',[51] no one prays God with the whole heart, as needs to be done, unless through heavenly desire he surmounts the heaven of sense life, passes through the heaven of the spiritual life, and ascends the heaven of the intellectual life, and thus, entering his bedchamber there and following the words of the Son praying his Father in secret, he reaches God our Saviour, the saving dweller in the intellectual heaven. This cannot be done in any way except by the supra-intellectual working of the supreme Godhead. For a creature, since he is of finite strength, can never attain the Creator, who is infinite power, unless it is worked for him in a way transcending this world through the perfecting of his finite weakness by Him who is infinite. On account of this He says (John 6) 'No man can come to me except the Father, who hath sent me, draw him.'[52]

15a. *Of the progress in prayer when all the things written above are present in it, and of its failure when any of the things written above are wanting.*
If all the above written conditions for progress to fulfil devout prayer are present in it, according to what has been established as indicated above, by the foresight of God, the best that can be asked for by a prayer thus perfected cannot, by the divine promise, ever be refused. But if anything that has been described above is lacking in the prayer of a petitioner, because it dishonours God by violating his law (Rom. 2), it is proved to be wholly unable to gain the condescension of divine mercy, but rather to provoke divine displeasure and wrath; on which there are those words of the apostle James (James 5): 'You ask and receive not, because you ask amiss.'[53] Because evil is the

enim malum est priuatio boni, erit orantis mala petitio cum priuata fuerit aliquo bonorum substantialium orationis orationem essentialiter constituentium, et tunc prorsus istius orationis mortua petitio non est petitio, sicut mortuus homo non est homo. Sed erit orantis bona petitio cum priuata non fuerit aliquo bonorum substantialium orationis orationem essentialiter constituentium, et tunc profecto illius orationis uiua petitio est petitio, sicut homo uiuus est homo. Vnde liquet quod non abhorret a doctrina uiuifici Saluatoris, ubi ait 'Petite et accipietis',[54] sententia sui apostoli, 'Petitis et non accipitis'.

16a. *Quod omnis pontifex cum prefatis orationis diuine conditionibus orans saluatorem, ut mittat operarios in messem suam, sicut predictum est, indubitanter exauditur.*

Quapropter 'omnis pontifex ex hominibus assumptus (Heb. iv), pro hominibus constitutus',[55] quandocunque cum prefatis orationis diuine conditionibus rogat Dominum messis ut mittat operarios in messem suam, hoc est, saluificum dominatorem ecclesie exorans interpellat, ut mittendo prouideat rectores idoneos ecclesie sue in salutis operatione preficiendos et, si oporteret, 'de lapidibus istis suscitare filios Abrahe',[56] beatus Saluator, cui nichil est impossibile (Luc. xix) ad saluationis officium indubitanter exhibebit quotquot habet necessarios.

17a. *Quid oranti prelato sit consultum, cum non adhuc diuinitus exhibetur rector ydoneus qui per eum preficiatur animabus.*

Quod si propter peccatorum obsistentias iustus Saluator salubriter interpellatus adhuc differat exhibere operarium salutis operande ydoneum, numquid licet in euentum quemcunque aliquatenus intrudere pro pastore deuoratorem, pro dispensatore dissipatorem, pro uificatore mortificatorem, pro sanctificatore profanatorem? Quis hoc ferat, nisi quem furie demonialis dira rabies occupauit? Cum enim secundum apostolum (Ro. 3): non sunt facienda mala ut ueniant bona,[57] putabiturne quacunque conditione hec facienda fore mala, ex quibus uere nulla sunt que ueniant bona, sed certe nulla sunt que non ueniant mala? Hic amplexetur inseparabiliter ueri Saluatoris diffinita promissio, pollicentis infallibiliter quod indeficiens oratio cum expectatione longanimi, quamuis non ad uotum semper, semper tamen exauditur ad salutem.

---

[54] John 16: 24. [55] Heb. 5: 1.
[56] Luke 3: 8. [57] Cf. Rom. 3: 8.

deprivation of good, the petition of one who prays will be bad when deprived of one of the substantial goods that are essential constituents of prayer, and then the dead petition of that prayer is not a petition at all, just as a dead man is not a man. But the petition of one who prays will be good when it is not deprived of any of the substantial goods that are its essential constituents, and then straight away the petition of that prayer is alive, just as a living man is a man. So it is clear that the statement 'You ask and do not receive' by the Lord's apostle is not contrary to the teaching of our life-giving Saviour when he says 'Ask and you shall receive'.[54]

16a. *That every bishop who prays the Saviour under the aforesaid conditions of divine prayer to send labourers of salvation into his harvest, is, as has been said before, undoubtedly answered.*
On this account, every high priest taken from among men (Heb. 4)[55] and appointed on behalf of men, whenever he asks the Lord of the harvest, observing the said conditions of godly prayer, to send labourers into his harvest, that is, prayerfully calls on the saving Lord of the Church to provide suitable rectors for his Church to be set over the work of salvation, and, if necessary, 'to raise up sons to Abraham from these stones',[56] the blessed Saviour, to whom nothing is impossible (Luke 19), will undoubtedly provide as many as He considers necessary.

17a. *What is advisable to a prelate who prays, when a suitable rector for him to appoint over souls has not yet been divinely provided.*
But if, on account of the hindrance of sin, our just Saviour when properly appealed to, still defers providing a labourer for salvation suitable for the task, is it permissible for whatever outcome to intrude in place of a shepherd one who devours, in place of a dispenser one who dissipates, in place of a life-giver a killer, in place of a sanctifier, one who profanes? Who would support this except someone possessed by demonic madness? For as according to the Apostle (Rom. 3), evil is not to be done that there may come good,[57] will it be thought in any circumstances whatever that this evil should be done, from which truly no good can come, but from which there are certainly no evils that may not result? Here let us firmly embrace the promise of our true Saviour, who infallibly promises that unfailing prayer with patient hope is always answered for our salvation, though not always as we wish.

18a. *Quam pernecabili rabie contra sanctiones euangelicas hiis diebus prelati maiores et per se et per suos inductos ecclesiam Dei dissipare non cessant, animas exponendo sempiterne condempnationis precipitationibus immanissimis.*

Ista igitur sacrosancta euangelice sanctionis decreta, quia dira rabies demonialis perfidie apud sublimes ecclesiarum principes hiis dampnatissimis diebus execrabiliter—pro nefas—conculcare non formidat, qui certe tam per seipsos quam per suos inductos in ecclesiis Altissimi nichil aliud peruicacissima canine uoracitatis impudentia consectantur quam caducam fastuum arrogantiam, quam mobilem questuum affluentiam, quam sordidam luxuum petulantiam, auctoritatem summe saluationis in perditionis eterne crudelitatem deprauantes, cernimus usquequaquam quasi solutum Sathanam effrenata^a tyrannide beatam hereditatem benedicti Dei immanissime depopulari et— proth dolor—animas sanguine testamenti redemptas exponi atrocissime 'deuorationi bestiarum agri' (Ese. xxxviii)[58] necnon in gehennalem flagitiorum omnium et cunctorum facinorum uoraginem passim, absque ulla miseratione precipitari. Propter quod, inter innumerabilia animaduersionis diuine fulmina^b de Scripturis Sanctis, omnipotens sapientia contra regitiuos culminis ecclesiasticici prepositos, tam preficientes quam prefectos, qui huiusmodi sunt capitales scelestissimarum immanitatum auctores, exhorrendissimam sententie tonantis addictionem contorquet dicens (Sap. vi): 'Audite reges, et intelligite; f. 83 discite, iudices finium terre, prebete aures, uos qui | continetis multitudinem, et placetis uobis in turbis nationum. Quoniam data est a Domino potestas uobis et uirtus ab Altissimo, qui interrogabit opera uestra et cogitationes scrutabitur; quoniam, cum essetis ministri regni illius, non recte iudicastis, neque custodistis legem iustitie, neque secundum uoluntatem Dei ambulastis. Horrende et cito apparebit uobis quoniam iudicium durissimum in hiis qui presunt, fiet. Potentes enim potenter tormenta patientur, fortibus autem fortior instat cruciatus.'[59]

19a. *Quanta necessitate Deo constringitur sepe dictus archiepiscopus et animabus liberandis secundum ea que predicta sunt, et arcendis proditoribus ab animarum peruasionibus.*

Quamobrem tante metropolis tantus antistes propter Eum qui amat animas, animarum amore^a quibus saluandis tam solempni sponsione

18a ^{a} efferata B. ^{b} sublimia A.

19a ^{a} morte A.

18a. *How lethal is the madness with which major prelates these days incessantly scatter the Church of God contrary to the decrees of the Gospel, both by themselves and through those they have installed, exposing souls to a headlong fall into eternal condemnation.*

Because the highest governors of the Church are possesed of a grim demonic madness, they have no fear in these most damned days to trample underfoot—for shame—the most holy decrees of the Gospel, and both through themselves and through those they have installed in the churches of the Most High they clearly pursue with the perverse and shameless greed of dogs nothing but the fleeting arrogance of pride, the profits of affluence, and the foul viciousness of their lusts. We see them perverting the high authority of salvation into the cruelty of eternal perdition, all the while as if Satan were let loose to lay waste the blessed inheritance of our blessed God with monstrous and rabid tyranny, and we see the souls redeemed by the blood of the covenant exposed to the atrocity of being devoured by the beasts of the field (Ezek. 38),[58] and everywhere without compassion plunged headlong into the hellish whirlpool of every sin and shame! On this account, among the numberless thunderbolts of divine punishment in the Holy Scriptures the almighty Wisdom hurls the most thunderous and fearful judgement against the ruling heads of the Church, both those appointing them and those appointed, who are the capital authors of the most sinful atrocities, saying (Wisd. 5), 'Hear, therefore, ye kings and understand; learn ye that are judges of the ends of the earth. Give ear you that rule the people and that please yourselves in multitudes of nations. For your power is given to you by the Lord and strength by the Most High, who will examine your works and search out your thoughts; because being ministers of his kingdom, you have not judged rightly, nor walked according to the will of God. Horribly and speedily will he appear to you, for a most severe judgement shall be for them that bear rule. For the mighty shall be mightily tormented, but a greater torment is ready for the more mighty'.[59]

19a. *How necessarily the said archbishop is obliged by God both to deliver souls, as has been said before, and to repel perverters and betrayers of souls.*
Wherefore, for the sake of Him who is the lover of souls, so great an archbishop of such a great metropolis, for the love of the souls to

[58] Ezek. 34: 5 and 8.   [59] Wisd. 6: 2–9.

tam districte professionis coram tam pauendo tribunali tam tremendi Iudicis animam suam defixit, apud tantum animarum redemptarum Vindicatorem, sub tanta iuratissime firmitatis obligatione, infatigabiliter necesse est inuigilet, secundum ea que predicta sunt, liberandis animabus propter quas redimendas benedictus Dei Filius, sub diro mortis supplicio, sacrum crucis patibulum ex pia cruoris affluentia irrigare decreuit habundantius; necnon semper a Dei sanctuario arcendis 'canibus impudentissimis nescientibus saturitatem' (Ys. lvi);[60] pestes nepharias demonialium nequitiarum loquor, uidelicet ouilium dominicorum peruicacissimos inuasores, quos—pro nefas—hiis diebus pessimis ubique conspicimus inexplebili rabie et seuitias et astutias et malitias et pertinacias sacrilegissimi furoris ecclesiarum[b] omnium assiduis urgere peruasionibus, ut earum lac comedentes et lanis opperti, crudelissima depopulatione ipsas—proth dolor—passim exponant deuorationi bestiarum agri, que sua sunt querentes, non que Iesu Christi.

20a. *Quod nulli possunt cogitari tam peruicaces inimici Dei, sicut qui, cum uiuificandis eternaliter animabus officium susceperunt animas perpetualiter occidere non exhorrent inaudito genere proditionis.*

Nunquam enim cogitari poterunt in prophanissimo regno cupiditatis diabolice tam peruicaciter inimicantes sanctissimo regno caritatis dominice, sicut hii tales, qui per usurpata saluificarum prelationum officia animas humanas per diuinitatem Altissimi formatas ad superclaram ymaginem Dei, et ad Ipsius supersanctam similitudinem reformatas per sanguinem testamenti (Zac. ix),[61] quibus eternaliter uiuificandis est occisus amator uite Filius Dei, perpetualiter occidere non exhorrent impernecabili fidei uiolate[a] proditione. Annon inauditum genus proditionis est populis Dei[b] perdendis insistere, quibus saluandis tam celebriter iuratum est coram senatu celi Regi seculorum? Annon adhuc inauditum genus proditionis est de stipendiis clementissimi regis uiuere, sed domini sui temerata fidelitate contra ipsum, cum inestimabili dampno desudantis exercitus, in castris hostilibus sub immanissimo tyranno militare?

21a. *Quod occisores animarum maxime sunt expertes caritatis.*

Ad hec, si occisores corporum nepharios affirmamus recte caritatis expertes, numquid non expertes caritatis uere iudicabimus perfidos animarum occisores?

[b] ecclesiasticorum AB.

20a [a] uiolata B. [b] Dei *omitted* A.

whose salvation he pledged his own soul with such a solemn promise, a sworn obligation so strictly professed in the tribunal of so dread a judge, under so great an obligation of sworn constancy before the mighty defender of the redeemed, must, as has been said before, be vigilant to deliver souls, for whose redemption the blessed Son of God in the dire torment of death determined to moisten the sacred gibbet of the cross with a copious outpouring of his holy blood. Also he must be vigilant to repel from God's sanctuary the shameless dogs who are insatiable (Isa. 56);[60] I speak of the pests of diabolical wickedness, that is, the very obstinate invaders of the Lord's flocks, whom we see everywhere—for shame—in these most evil days with insatiable fury and obstinate malice savagely and cunningly forcing themselves upon all churches, consuming their milk entirely and waiting for their wool, everywhere exposing those they ravage with great cruelty to being devoured by the beasts of the field; they who seek their own possessions, not those of Jesus Christ.

20a. *That no one can conceive such stubborn enemies of God as those who, when they have undertaken the office of giving eternal life to souls, have no fear in slaying them for ever with an unheard-of kind of treachery.*
For never could anyone have conceived of the enemies in the profane kingdom of the devil's cupidity who so stubbornly attack the most holy kingdom of the Lord's love, such as those who, by usurping the office of prelacy, display the deadly treachery of breaking their vows, and have no fear in slaying for ever the human souls formed in the supraglorious image of God and reformed to His most holy likeness through the blood of the covenant (Zech. 9),[61] who are to be made everlastingly alive by the slain Author of life, the Son of God. Is it not an unheard-of kind of treachery to work for the perdition of the people of God, for whose salvation one has so publicly sworn an oath before the senate of heaven to the King of the ages? Is it not a yet unheard-of kind of treachery to live on the wages of the most merciful King, but in defiance of fealty to the Lord, to fight against Him in enemy armies under a monstrous tyrant, with incalculable harm to the toiling army?

21a. *That the slayers of souls are supremely lacking in charity.*
On this, if we rightly assert that the wicked killers of bodies lack charity, shall we not truly judge the faithless killers of souls to be lacking in charity?

[60] Isa. 56: 11.   [61] Zech. 9: 11.

22a. *Quod rectores animarum uniuersas animas atrociter occidisse con-uincuntur, quibus ne occiderentur noscuntur nequaquam efficaciter inuigi-lasse.*

Sed certissime secundum immutabilem ueritatis eterne diffinitionem, cuncti curam uitalem regendis animabus assecuti animas uniuersas atroci nequitia perhenniter occidisse conuincuntur, quibus ne occi-derentur fideli prudentia dignoscuntur nequaquam iugiter inuigilasse, clamante Scriptura singulis familie dominice custodibus (Ege. 33): 'Virum hunc custodi, qui si lapsus fuerit, erit anima tua pro anima illius.'[62] Et iterum: 'Si speculator uiderit gladium uenientem et non insonuerit buccina' uidelicet, uiderit gladium mortifere preuaricatio-nis uenientem, et non insonuerit buccina euangelice predicationis 'et populus se non custodierit, ueneritque gladius et tulerit de eis animam, et ille quidem in iniquitate sua captus est; sanguinem autem eius de manu speculatoris requiram.'[63] Et alibi, propter preuaricationem populi Dominus ad Moysen (Num. xxv): 'Tolle', inquit, 'cunctos principes populi, et suspende eos contra solem in patibulis, ut auertatur furor meus ab Israel.'[64] In quibus omnibus non commissa sed omissa prelatorum addictione terrifica condempnantur.

23a. *Quod cuncti qui, suscepto animarum regimine, saluandis animabus perpeti caritate non inuigilant, propter occisionem animarum sunt caritatis penitus exsortes et rectissime condempnantur quantumlibet aliis glorientur excellentiis.*

Quamobrem quantumlibet quantumque talium sibi blandientes uelud securi glorientur uel de locutionum prerogatiua, uel de presagio prophetali, uel de ratione scientiali, uel de intelligentia misteriorum, uel de fide miraculorum, uel de humanitate operationum, uel de longanimitate passionum, ut sit summatim dicere, uel de loquele uel de notitie uel de constantie uel de patientie quantalibet eminentia, nisi saluandis subditis secundum sacrosanctas institutiones perpeti dili-gentia continue caritatis efficacius insudauerint, audiant contra se 'nichil altum sapiant' (Rom. xi)[65] sed timeant illum districtionis apostolice sententiam (Cor. 13): 'Si linguis hominum loquar et angelorum, caritatem autem non habeam, factus sum uelud es sonans aut cymbalum tinniens. Et si habuero prophetiam et nouerim misteria omnia et omnem scientiam, et habuero omnem fidem ita ut montes transferam, caritatem autem non habuero, nichil prodest; et si

---

[62] 3 Kgs. (1 Kgs.) 20: 39. [63] Ezek. 33: 6.
[64] Num. 25: 4. [65] Cf. Rom. 11: 20.

22a. *That the rectors of souls are convicted of a dreadful slaughter of all souls to whom they are known to have failed to give effective care to prevent their slaughter.*

But most assuredly, according to the immutable statement of truth, all those appointed to the vital care of governing souls are convicted of slaying them perpetually with dreadful wickedness, when they are known to have constantly failed to watch over them with faithful care to prevent their slaughter, as Scripture cries out to the individual guardians of the Lord's household: 'Keep this man; and if he shall slip away, thy life shall be for his life' (Ezek. 33),[62] and again, 'If the watchman see the sword coming and sound not the trumpet', that is, sees the sword of deadly prevarication coming, and does not sound the trumpet of evangelical preaching, 'and the people look not to themselves, and a sword come and cut off a soul from among them, he indeed is taken away in his iniquity, but I will require his blood at the hand of the watchman';[63] and elsewhere, He says to Moses (Num. 25) on account of the transgressions of the people: 'Take all the princes of the people, and hang them up on the gibbets against the sun, that my fury may be turned away from Israel.'[64] In all of which a fearful judgement condemns not the faults committed by prelates, but their omissions.

23a. *That all those who have assumed the government of souls and are not vigilant to save souls with constant charity, are utterly devoid of charity and are most rightly condemned, however much they boast of their other excellent achievements.*

On this account, however great such men are, and however much they flatter themselves and boast confidently of their gift of eloquence, or their prophetic wisdom, or their learning in argument, or their understanding of mysteries, or their trust in miracles, or their works of humanity, or their patience in suffering, to sum up, however great their eminence in speech, knowledge, constancy, or suffering, unless they labour effectively with constant diligence and charity in accord with the holy commandments for the salvation of their subjects, let them hear against them the words 'Be not high-minded' (Rom. 11)[65] and let them fear that severe judgement of the Apostle (Cor. 13): 'If I speak with the tongue of men or angels, but have not charity, I am like a sounding brass or a tinkling symbol. And if I have prophecy and know all mysteries and all knowledge and have all faith, so that I may move mountains, but have not charity, it avails

distribuero in cibos pauperum omnes facultates meas, et si tradidero corpus meum ita ut ardeam, caritatem autem non habuero, nichil michi prodest.'[a] [66]

f. 83[v] **24a.** *Quod potissime pro ista iustitia secundum predicta preficiendi pastores gregibus dominicis et arcendi latrones ab eisdem quanticunque terribilium martyriorum agones sunt, et constanter sustinendi et audacter prouocandi pro ista, inquam, iustitia tam inestimabilis excellentie.*

Denique super illam que nunc dicta est iustitia preficiendi ⟨sunt⟩ pastores gregibus dominicis et latrones arcendi ab eisdem secundum modus supradictos, qualiter unquam sublimes animi quantumcunque uel traditionibus canonicis uel euangelicis sanctionibus uel inspirationibus celicis uel lucidis reuelationibus illuminati, poterunt intelligere iustitiam aliquam beatioris glorie, pro qua amplius teneantur ecclesiarum prelati, omnibus omnino nichil impensis, que unquam ualet uel prosperitas leta conferre, uel inferre tristis aduersitas, omnimodis triumphalium martyriorum agonias non tantum in se ipsis tolerare longanimiter, sed uiriliter contra se prouocare, ut non tantum propter istam iustitiam persecutionem in se sustineant, 'ludibria et uerbera experti, lapidati, secti, in occisione gladii mortui, circumeuntes in melotis, in pellibus caprinis, egentes, angustiati et afflicti, quibus dignus non est mundus',[67] sed insuper propter istam iustitiam persecutionem contra seipsos exsuscitent, 'exultantes audacter, in occursum pergentes armatis, contempnentes pauorem nec cedentes gladio, feruendo et fremendo sorbentes terram, nec reputantes tube sonare clangorem, procul odorantes bellum, exhortationem ducum et ululatum exercitus'.[68]

Quis est qui ista perspicaciter non aspiciat, nisi quem premit cordis caligo formidolosa? Nempe cum diffiniatur iustitia, quod sit amor rectus seruatus propter ipsam rectitudinem qua tribuatur unicuique quod suum est, patenter hec quam nunc loquor[a] iustitia, gloriosam gratiose iustitie nuncupationem speciali priuilegio iustissime rationis sibi uindicare comprobatur, per inuincibles homines[b] principatus ecclesiastici iugitate infatigabili protegenda, per quam potissime et regnum uite restauratur et exterminatur mortis imperium, ueritas catholica confirmatur et confutatur heretica falsitas, mundo corruenti

23a   [a] et si distribuero . . . prodest *omitted by* A.

24a   [a] loquor B *omitted* A.   [b] heroes B.

---

[66] I Cor. 13: 1–3.   [67] Heb. 11: 36–8.   [68] Job 39: 21–5.

me nothing, and though I bestow all my goods to feed the poor, and though I give my body to be burned, and have not charity, it profiteth me nothing.'[66]

24a. *That pastors are to be placed over the Lord's flocks above all for this righteousness according to the things aforesaid, and thieves are to be repelled from them, however great are the struggles of martyrdom that must be endured and boldly invited for the sake, I say, of this righteousness of such incalculable excellence.*

Finally, regarding what is now called righteousness, pastors are to be set over the Lord's flocks, and thieves to be kept away from the same, in the ways described above; however, high minds, enlightened to whatever extent by canonical tradition or the commands of the Gospel or heavenly inspiration or shining revelations, have been able to understand some righteousness more blessed and glorious. For the sake of this the prelates of churches, counting as nothing whatever joy prosperity can confer or adversity inflict, are bound not only to endure with patience in every way the struggle of triumphant martyrdom, but vigorously to invite it against themselves, so that they not only endure persecution on account of that righteousness, but 'have trials of mockeries and stripes, are stoned, cut asunder, are put to death by the sword, wandering about in sheepskins, in goatskins, being in want, distressed and afflicted, of whom the world was not worthy',[67] but over and above this, they arouse persecution against themselves for the sake of this righteousness, 'they prance boldly, they go forward to meet armed men, they despise fear, nor turn their backs to the sword, chasing and raging they swallow the ground, neither do they make account when the noise of the trumpet soundeth, they smell the battle afar off, the encouraging of the captains and the shouting of the army'.[68]

Who fails to see this clearly except one who is oppressed by the darkness of his timorous heart? To be sure, since justice is defined as being a right love preserved on account of its rightness, by which each is accorded what is his own, this justice of which I am now speaking is evidently proved to justify the glorious appelation of gracious righteousness by a special privilege of most just reason, to be perpetually and tirelessly protected through the invincible heroes of the Church's leadership, through which above all both the kingdom of life is restored and the empire of death banished, catholic truth is affirmed and heretical untruth refuted, the falling world is rescued and the

obuenitur, et subuenitur ecclesie periclitanti; qua qui diligit legem, impleuit; per quam ideo fidelium sanctificatio 'potest comprehendere cum omnibus sanctis que sit latitudo, longitudo, et sublimitas et profundum',[69] uidelicet sublimitas maiestatis, profundum ueritatis, latitudo iocunditatis, longitudo eternitatis secundum presentem pregustationem,[c] et secundum satietatem futuram in seculi Saluatore, Filio Dei, qui est benedictus in secula. Amen.

25a. *Submissa uenie petitio*
Quamquam in presentiarum opus esset sermo longus et interpretabilis, tamen sufficiat simplici occasionem prestitisse sapienti, compesco calamum sub humili recognitione, uenia petita super eo quod de rebus predignis ad[a] predignum presulem indigna serie pauper indignus dicere temptaui, ut timeo, tante puritatis, tante claritatis, tante pietatis, tante firmitatis inuoluens sententias sermonibus imperitis.

26a. *De precellenti gloria qua sancte recordationis dominus Robertus, quondam Lyncolniensis episcopus,[70] diuinitus esse creditur illustratus propter uigorem amoris insuperabilem et inuincibilem[a] zeli feruorem, quibus iugiter aspirabat saluandis animabus secundum formas superius insinuatas.*
Quid est quod piissime recordationis dominum Robertum quondam Lyncolniensem episcopum, qui dum uelocia mortalitatis humane transigeret uolumina, spirituali affectionis[b] sancte prerogatiua salutarem sinceritatis uestre pietatem inter cunctos in carne uiuentes uisceralis affectus sacro complexu continebat in incommutabili uite perhennalis Auctore; quid, inquam, ⟨est⟩ quod ipsum per diuinam miserationem, secundum quod fideliter asseuerat deuotio fidelium, tam glorifice et coronauit in excelsis[71] et in terris mirificauit, nisi quod ex inuincibili serenissime fidei firmitudine—apud illum 'fortis ut mors dilectio, et dura ut infernus emulatio'[72]—in spiritu et uirtute Helie, secundum ea que predicta sunt, sanctitatis impauide perseuerantia uigilantius aspirabat ad Dei honorem et hominum salutem?

---

[c] degustationem B.
25a [a] apud B.
26a [a] irremissibilem B.   [b] dilectionis B.

[69] Eph. 3: 18.   [70] Grosseteste died 9 Oct. 1253.

imperilled Church is reinforced, and the glorious felicity of saving charity is exalted. By this he who loves has fulfilled the law. Through this the sanctified faithful are 'able to comprehend, with all the saints, what is the breadth and length and height and depth',[69] that is, the height of the majesty, the depth of the truth, the breadth of the joy, the length of eternity, according to the foretaste and future fulfilment in the Saviour of the world, the Son of God, who is blessed for ever. Amen.

25a. *A petition for pardon submitted*
Although there was need of the present long explanatory discourse, since it is enough for a simple man to have offered an opportunity to one who is plainly wise, I am restraining my pen in humble acknowl-edgement, and beg pardon for the fact that I, a poor unworthy man, have essayed to speak out of turn to a most worthy prelate about matters of very great worth, involving, as I fear, judgements of so great a purity, clarity, piety, and certainty expressed in my untutored words.

26a. *Concerning the pre-eminent glory by which the lord Robert, formerly bishop of Lincoln, of holy memory,[70] is thought to have been divinely inspired, on account of the insuperable strength of his love and the fervour of his zeal with which he constantly strove for the salvation of souls, in the ways indicated above.*
Why is it that the lord Robert of most holy memory, formerly bishop of Lincoln, who while passing through the swift changes of this mortal life, embraced your devoted person with a special affection, in the Author of eternal life, among others living in the flesh? Why is it, I say, that, according to what the devotion of the faithful faithfully asserted, by the divine mercy He crowned him so gloriously in heaven and made him wonderful on earth,[71] unless because he strove with the perseverance of a fearless sanctity for the honour of God and the salvation of men with the invincible strength of his most serene faith in the spirit and power of Elijah, according to what has already been said. With him 'love was as strong as death and zeal as hard as hell'.[72]

---

[71] Adam's belief in Grosseteate's sanctity was widely shared by the chroniclers. Matthew Paris reported miracles at his tomb: *Chron. Maj.* v. 407, 419. Shortly after his death the Lincoln chapter sent Master Nicholas Grecus to Rome to postulate his canonization: Eric Kemp, 'The attempted canonization of Robert Grosseteste', in Callus, *Robert Grosseteste*, pp. 241–6.
[72] S. of S. 6: 6.

27a. *Quod ab eximio archipresule frater exiguus[a] super insuetis ecclesie tribulationibus requisitus, illi ueritus est respondere.*

Distinctio secunda

Ubi aspiciebam quod prelatus a priuato, doctus ab indocto, expertus ab inexperto, preclarus ab obscuro, super uexationibus ecclesiasticam dignitatem pregrauantibus rescripta requirebat, iuxta quod in sui parte posteriori continebat uestre dominationis epistola, uerebatur nec immerito uestre magnitudini modicitas mea respondere.

28a. *Quam necessaria dispensationis diuine prouidentia ecclesiam sanctam semper exercent tribulantia persecutionum affligentium uexamina.*

Verum si Scripturarum testimoniis, si sanctorum exemplis, si rationum efficaciis, si modernorum experientiis fideliter adquiescitur, agnoscitur infallibiliter tribulationum grassantium uehementias immaniores sanctam ecclesie catholice beatitudinem et excellentius erigere et erudire luculentius, et salubrius animare et solidare constantius, ut celestis regni predestinata felicitas non tam in bono glorificetur proprio quam ex malo magnificetur alieno. Propter quod et ait Rex seculorum Dei regnum reformaturus (Mth. v): 'Si quis te percusserit in unam maxillam, prebe ei et alteram; et ei qui uult tecum in iudicio contendere et tunicam tuam tollere, dimitte ei et pallium; et quicunque angariauerit te mille passus, uade cum eo alia duo',[73] et per apostolum (Cor. iv): 'Maledicimur et benedicimus; persecutionem patimur, et sustinemus; blasphemamur, et obsecramus;'[74] magis et in concussionibus, et in calumpniis, et in angariis, et in contumeliis tolerantiam passionum saluificam beatificans, quam commendans magnificam actionum resistentiam.

29a. *Quod infelicius nequit accidere ecclesie nostri temporis quam ut tam inermiter[a] uiuens sub pace transitoria feliciter agat.*

Reuera, mi domine, secundum quod perspicue cernit clarissima uestre sinceritatis industria, nunquam infelicius accidere poterit nostre dierum presentium ecclesie quam ut feliciter nepharia tempora

f. 84 transigat, tam enormiter uiuens, mortua tam horribiliter, | remotis molestantium tribulationum asperitatibus, per reprobantem diuinitatis prouocate iracundiam.

Second Part

27a. *That when a distinguished archbishop asked a little friar about the unaccustomed tribulations of the Church, he feared to reply to him.*

When I perceived that a prelate was asking for a written reply from a private individual, a scholar from one unlearned, a proven champion from a novice, a distinguished person from one who is obscure, about the grave troubles afflicting the dignity of the Church, according to the matters contained in the latter part of your lordship's letter, my humble self was not without reason frightened to reply to your eminence.

28a. *That it is by the necessary providence of God's dispensation that the vexations of persecution always afflict Holy Church.*

Truly, if the witness of Scripture, the examples of the saints, the effective arguments of reason, and the experience of modern times are accepted, we recognize unerringly that immense and violent tribulations raise the Catholic Church to greater heights of blessedness, instruct it with greater clarity, increase the health of its life, and establish it more firmly, so that the felicity of the heavenly kingdom to which it is predestined may be not so much glorified by its own goodness as magnified by the evil outside it. On this account, the King of the ages, when about to restore the kingdom of God, says (Matt. 5) 'If one strike thee on the right cheek, turn to him also the other; and whosoever will force thee one mile, go with him other two';[73] and through the Apostle (Cor. 4): 'We are reviled and we bless. We are persecuted and we suffer it. We are blasphemed, and we entreat',[74] more blessed by blows, calumnies, exactions, and affronts, and the saving endurance of suffering, than by recommending magnificent acts of resistance.

29a. *That nothing more unfortunate can happen to the Church of our time than that it should happily go on so defenceless living in a transitory peace.*

Truly, my lord, as your noble zeal clearly perceives, never can anything more unfortunate happen to our Church in these days than that it should pass happily through evil times so defenceless, living so outrageously yet terribly dead, having avoided the bitterness of tribulation, through the condemnation and wrath of a deity it has provoked.

[73] Matt. 5: 39–41.   [74] 1 Cor. 4: 12–13.

30a. *Quod cuncti fere hiis diebus ecclesie rectores ad hoc inhiant ut per ecclesiasticam auctoritatem defensi, quiete libidinibus suis inseruiant.*

Ad quid^a inhiare conspiciuntur passim hodie periclitantis ecclesie speculatores impiissimi, nisi ut sub autentica protectione celsitudinis ecclesiastice et aduersus concussiones, et aduersus calumnias, et aduersus angarias, et aduersus contumelias propensiori uigilantia uigentius defensati, et libidinibus dominandi, et libidinibus possidendi, et libidinibus delectandi, et libidinibus habundandi, nunquam licet adimplendis, adimplendis tamen semper inseruiant, nullatenus—proh nefas—estimantes feliciter agere ciuitatem ecclesie nisi late licentie libidinum letalium stantibus menibus sue dignitatis, et ruentibus moribus sue sanctitatis, ubique debaccando peruagentur infelicius? Contra quos etiam uitiis suis ecclesiasticam defensionem affectantes,^b tam terribiliter prophetale fulminans eloquium (Ys. lvi): 'Omnes', inquit, 'bestie agri, uenite ad deuorandum, uniuerse bestie saltus, speculatores eius ceci omnes, nescierunt uniuersi; canes muti, non ualentes latrare, uidentes uana, dormientes et amantes sompnia. Et canes impudentissimi nescierunt saturitatem. Ipsi pastores ignorauerunt intelligentiam. 'Omnes in uiam suam declinauerunt, unusquisque ad auaritiam suam a summo usque ad nouissimum. Venite, sumamus uinum et impleamur ebrietate, et erit sicut hodie, sic et cras, et multo amplius.'⁷⁵

Quid enim hiis diebus manifestius, heu, heu, heu, Domine Deus, quam quod 'omnes bestie', hoc est omnes uastitates nequitiarum demonialium 'agri' apertius seuientium, et 'saltus', occultius insidiantium, siue 'omnes bestie agri', carnalium spurcitiarum, 'uniuerse bestie saltus', spiritualium uersutiarum, uelud uocate uehementius uenerunt ad deuorandum, scilicet in sui malignas pernicies uoraciter trahiciendum redemptas animas, quibus sibi adunandis in indiuiduum beate uite consortium tam amara morte mortuus est auctor uite Filius Dei? Causa quoque tantarum perditionum, quo nichil est euidentius, subiungitur istud: 'Speculatores eius ceci omnes' etc.^c Factio lasciuientium insinuatur inuicem se inuitantium ad hauriendum uinum mundane^d iocunditatis usque ad ebriosam alienationem de die in diem adaugendam, maxime sub protectionis ecclesiastice pacifica defensione.

30a ^a quid *add* enim B.   ^b uitiis . . . affectantes *omitted* A.   ^c *Here A repeats the entire quotation from Isaiah* 56: 9–12, *above.*   ^d mundane *omitted* A.

⁷⁵ Isa. 56: 9–11.

30a. *What almost all rectors of churches hunger for these days is this: that being protected by ecclesiastical authority, they may serve their lustful desires in peace.*

What are the irreligious watchmen of the imperilled Church seen everywhere today to be hankering for with open mouths except— while they are under the genuine protection of high ecclesiastical authority being defended with calculated and vigorous vigilance against assaults, against calumny, against enforced services and abuse—that they may for ever work to fulfil their lust for domination, their lust for possession, their lust for pleasure, and their lust to accumulate plenty, which are never satisfied, in no way—for shame!—considering the city of the Church fortunate in its acts unless, while the ramparts of its dignity remain standing and the sanctity of its conduct is in ruins, licences for deadly lusts are spread far and wide in general dissolution? Against them, eager for the defence of the Church even in their vices, thunders the utterance of the prophet so fearfully (Isa. 56): 'All ye beasts of the field', he says, 'come to devour, all ye beasts of the forest. His watchmen are all blind. They are all ignorant: dumb dogs not able to bark, seeing vain things, sleeping and loving dreams, and most impudent dogs they never had enough; the shepherds themselves knew no understanding. All have turned aside into their own way, everyone after his own gain, from the first to the last. Come, let us take wine and be filled with durnkenness; and it shall be as today, so also tomorrow, and much more.'[75]

O Lord God, what is more manifest in these days, alas, alas, than that 'all the beasts' that is, all the wastes of diabolical wickedness, 'of the field', of those in the open, and 'of the forest', of those secretly lying in wait, or 'all the beasts of the field', meaning those in carnal filth, 'all the beasts of the forest', meaning those of spiritual deceitfulness, as if they had been urgently called, have come to devour, that is voraciously to cast into their own malignant ruin the souls of the redeemed, for whom the Author of life, the Son of God, died such a bitter death to unite them to Himself to share individually in the life of the blessed? Also nothing is more obvious than the cause of such a great ruin, which is supplied thus: 'His watchmen are blind', etc. The company of the lascivious is indicated by those inviting each other to drink the wine of worldly joy to the point of losing themselves in drunkenness, to increase it from day to day, above all under the peaceful protection of the Church.

31a. *Quod iam dicti tam pestilentes impii sibi tam nephariorum scelerum promittunt impunitatem, licet tamen inaniter.*

Verumptamen in tam nephariis dampnatissimorum scelerum erroribus uecordi pertinacia quietius immorantes contra indeclinabiles ultionis diuine districtiones sibi blandiuntur, confidentes in uerbis mendacii, secundum illud prophetici sermonis directi ad principes domus Iacob et iudices domus Israel, scilicet actiue luctationi et speculatiue uisioni in ecclesia prepositos et prelatos, qui ad immunitatem uite sue tam perditricis, tam flagitiose, tam facinorose, propheticum illud inculcant (Ier. iv): 'Templum Domini' etcetera, 'confidentes', inquam, 'in uerbis mendacii'[76] secundum illud (Mich. iii): 'et requiescebant super Dominum, dicentes, "Numquid non Dominus in medio nostrum? non uenient super nos mala."'[77] Sed contra nequissimam mendacium assertionum confidentiam sequitur Mich. iii: 'Propter hoc, causa uestri, Syon quasi ager arabitur, et Ierusalem quasi aceruus lapidum erit, et mons Templi in excelsa siluarum.'[78] Numquid prophanantes Templum Domini proteget contra iustissimas uindictas ultionis[a] diuine, quin uigilet Dominus super uerbum suum, ut faciat illud[b] in fulmineo 'splendore fulgurantis haste sue',[79] reddens[c] ultionem istis hostibus peruicacissimis, et hiis qui atrocissime oderunt Eum, retribuat, inebrietque sagittas suas in sanguine et gladius suus deuoret carnes[80] carnis curam perficere semper satagentium in desideriis?

32a. *Quam rationabili diuine dispensationis moderantia per prelatos et principes pax ecclesie temporalis continue conseruari debeat.*

Num ista dixerim ut suadere uelim ne rectores ecclesiarum se accingere debeant contra tribulationes pacem ecclesiasticam perturbantes? Nequaquam. Etenim postquam Rex regum et Dominus dominantium, per supremum sui omnipotentatus arbitrium, et curuauit imperia mundi et mundi regna inclinauit, et humiliauit potentiam mundi et mundi gloriam prostrauit, sub precelsa ecclesie sue sanctitate condita sunt iura tam canonica quam ciuilia ex eternalibus decretis Altissimi, per ora prelatorum et principum diuinitus promulgata, cohercendis pacis ecclesiastice persecutoribus, immutabiliter statuendo ut in uniuersis omnium ecclesiarum ordinibus iugiter conseruetur sospitas quantum ad personas, utilitas

---

31a [a] afflictionis B.   [b] ut faciat illud *omitted* A.   [c] et reddat B.

[76] Jer. 7: 4.   [77] Mic. 3: 11.   [78] Ibid. 3: 12.

31a. *That the said impious pests promise themselves to escape punishment for their wicked offences, though in vain.*

Quietly staying in their wicked errors and lamentable sins, however, they flatter themselves in the face of the inescapable severity of divine vengeance, putting their trust in words of untruth, according to those prophetic words addressed to the princes of the house of Jacob and the judges of the house of Israel, that is to the heads and prelates in charge of the struggle of the active life and the contemplative life in the Church, who for the sake of the immunity of their ruinous shameful and sinful life despise that prophecy of Jeremiah 4: 'The Temple of the Lord', etc. 'Trust not in lying words', etc.[76] on which there is that text of Micah 3: 'They leaned upon the Lord, saying: "is not the Lord in the midst of us? No evil shall come upon us".'[77] But contrary to their wicked confidence in lying assertions there follows 'Therefore, because of you, Sion shall be ploughed as a field, and Jerusalem shall be as a heap of stones, and the mountain of the Temple as the high places of the forests.'[78] Shall the Lord protect those who profane the Temple of the Lord from the just punishment of divine vengeance, and shall He not watch over his word, rendering vengeance on these stubborn enemies with the flashing lightning of His spear?[79] To do it He will repay them that monstrously hate Him, and will 'make his arrows drunk with blood, and His sword shall devour the flesh'[80] of those who are always busy fulfilling the desires of the flesh.

32a. *How reasonable is the governance of divine dispensation by which the temporal peace of the Church ought constantly to be preserved by prelates and princes.*

Have I said this with a wish to persuade rectors of churches not to arm themselves against tribulations that disturb the peace of the Church? By no means. For after the King of kings and Lord of lords had by the supreme judgement of his omnipotence humbled the empires of the world and made kingdoms fall, had humbled worldly power and cast down worldly glory, under the pre-eminent holiness of his Church both canon and civil laws were established based upon the eternal decrees of the Most High, and were promulgated by the mouths of prelates and princes. To restrain disturbers of the peace of the Church, they laid down that the welfare of all orders of the Church should be perpetually maintained, as regards the safety of their persons, their comfort as regards their possessions, their

[79] Hab. 3: 11.   [80] Cf. Deut. 32: 41–2.

quantum ad substantias, immunitas quantum ad operas, unanimitas quantum ad concordias. In hiis enim, sicut liquet euidentius, contra concussiones, contra calumpnias, contra angarias, contra contumelias dumtaxat ecclesie sancte prouidetur et dignitati et libertati et tranquillitati et securitati protegendis indeficienter per patrocinia sacerdotum et imperatorum adiutoria, ut ecclesia Dei placida suauitate salubriter uiuat, secundum mandata, iudicia, ceremonias, et promissa Dei, amplectendo felicius mandata per formam bene uiuendi, iudicia per censuram recte iudicandi, ceremonias per ritum pie colendi, promissa per profectum digne gloriandi. Quo fiat ut rete apostolicum magnos et paruos capiat, militia Christiana fortes et debiles colligat, familia dominica precipuos et pusillos contineat, ecclesia sancta suprapositos et submissos comprehendat, ad beatam

f. 84ᵛ regni Dei consumationem | sub protectione Altissimi optabili pace pie conseruando, licet paucitatem maiorum semper examinet, minorum*ᵃ* multitudinem sepe confringat persecutionum grassantium laxata uexatio. Quapropter quantum teneantur sacerdotes patrocinio, imperatores adiutorio pacis ecclesiastice beatificam dispensationem infatigabili stabilire uigilantia liquere poterit consideranti pretaxatas eloquiorum diuinorum sanctiones.

33a. *De pernecessaria discretione habenda pro propellendis ab ecclesia persequentium*ᵃ *iniuriis.*

Discerni tamen summopere oportet ab inuicem*ᵇ* in propulsandis iniuriis magnificentias sollicitudinum. Etenim, sicut claret, et in mente cecutientibus, prorsus secernende sunt persecutionum iniurie que directe uergunt in detrimentum eternale, ab illis que qualitercunque cedunt in preiudicium temporale. Pro illis enim est anima feruentius exponenda; in istis uero est anima moderantius exercenda, cum tamen ex salubri discretione illud oporteat facere, istud uero non omittere.

34a. *Quod temporibus modernis pene rectores ecclesiarum uniuersi eternalium incrementis omnino seipsos subtrahunt, sed compendiis temporalibus ampliandis seipsos penitus impendunt.*

Quamquam hiis diebus—proh dolor—fere cernamus nostri temporis uniuersos ducatus ecclesiastici moderatores commodis eternalibus adaugendis omnino seipsos subtrahere, sed compendiis temporalibus

32a   ᵃ maiorum B.

33a   ᵃ persecutionum B.   ᵇ ab inuicem *omitted* A.

immunity as regards their work, and their unanimity in concord. For in these things, as is very apparent, provision is made for the holy Church against attacks, calumny, violent oppression, and abuse; and for unfailingly protecting its dignity, liberty, peace, and security through the patronage of priests and the help of emperors; so that the Church of God may live in health and sweet peace, in accordance with the commands, judgements, liturgies, and promises of God, most happily embracing his commandments through a form of good living, justice through right judgements, the ceremonies of divine worship, and the promises of deserving glory through its progress. By this let it come to pass that the apostolic net catches great and small, the Christian militia gathers the strong and the weak, the Lord's household contains the distinguished and the little ones, and Holy Church includes superiors and subjects, to the blessed consummation of the kingdom of God, under the protection of the Most High living in a wished-for peace which must be devoutly preserved, even though the loosing of a harsh persecution always tests a few of the great, and often breaks the multitude of lesser folk. On this account, it can be clear to one who considers the said divine utterances how much priests are bound to maintain the blessed dispensation of the Church's peace by their protection, and emperors to help maintain it with untiring vigilance.

33a. *Of the discrimination very necessary in warding off from the Church the harm done by those persecuting it.*
It is supremely important in warding off injuries and vexations to distinguish between different magnitudes of concern. For, as is obvious even to those who are mentally blinded, injuries inflicted by persecution which tend immediately to eternal loss should be distinguished from those that lead to some kind of temporal harm. In response to the former one must react with fervour of spirit; in response to the latter, the spirit should react with greater moderation. Yet, the former must be acted upon with a salutary discretion, while the latter must not be neglected.

34a. *That in modern times almost all the rectors of churches deprive themselves entirely of eternal rewards, but apply all their efforts to increasing their own temporal gains.*
We observe almost all the holders of positions of ecclesiastical leadership these days completely withdrawing themselves—for shame—from adding to their eternal rewards, and exerting all their efforts to

ampliandis penitus seipsos impendere, ob id tam despicabiliter
designatos per uaccas Samarie apud illud propheticum (Amos iv):
'Audite uerbum hoc, uacce pingues, que estis in monte Samarie, que
calumpniam facitis egenis et confringitis pauperes',[81] uaccas eos
uocans, uelud in posterioribus erectos, depressos in anterioribus;
uaccas quoque pingues feminei sexus et carnee crassitudinis, osten-
dens per femineum sexum ad omnia ualida fructuum spiritualium
effeminatos; per carneam crassitudinem, ad omnia uilia carnalium
operum dilatatos. 'Que estis', scilicet per amoris affectum mansiue
uiuentes 'in monte Samarie', id est in elatiori opulentia pastoralis
custodie. Nomen namque Samarie sonat interpretatum custodiam.

   Cum ergo egenus sit qui non habet quod sibi sufficiat, pauper uero
qui non habet quod alteri communicet, illum calumpniantur quem
duris exactionibus spoliando attenuant; istum confringunt quem seuis
defraudationibus amaricando mortificant. Audiant calumpniantes
egenum et pauperem (Prou. xxii): 'Qui calumpniatur pauperem et
egenum ut augeat diuitias suas, dabit ipse ditiori et egebit.'[82] Audiant
confringentes pauperem (Eccl. xxxiv): 'Panis egentium uita pauperum
est; qui defraudat illum, homo sanguinis est.'[83] Etenim ista nomina
pauper et egenus sepe pro se inuicem accipiuntur, sicut nomina
sapientie et scientie secundum Sanctum Augustinum. Sic ergo per
tam duras exactiones indebita sibi congerentes, et per tam seuas
defraudationes aliis deputata sibi retinentes, uiuendo tam nepharie
prouentus ecclesie, quod est patrimonium Christi, Christi sanguinem
egenis et pauperibus comparatum transuertere non formidant, et per
urgentis[a] auaritie scelestissimam cupidinem, quod perceperunt[b] de
manu Domini sub tanta reddende rationis districtione, ad subleuan-
dam dumtaxat per fidelis prudentie dispensationem fidelium suorum
inopiam, secundum illud Saluatoris ad pastores ecclesie (Math. xxiv):
'Quis putas esse fidelis seruus et prudens, quem constituet Dominus
super familiam suam, ut det illis cibum in tempore?'[84] cibum certe tam
temporalem quam eternalem quorum facinorose neutrum dispensant,
pascentes semetipsos, sicque famulos Domini utrobique tam crudeliter
interimunt, quibus saluandis per uigilem sedulitatis prouide custodiam
tam cogenti sponsione Domino iurauerunt.

   O nefas! O scelus! O flagitium! O piaculum cunctis uiuentibus

34a [a] purgeatis B.   [b] susceperunt B.

[81] Amos 4: 1.   [82] Prov. 22: 16.
[83] Ecclus. 34: 25.   [84] Matt: 24: 45.

enlarging their temporal gains; on account of which they are con-
temptuously described as the cattle of Samaria in that prophetic
passage (Amos 4): 'Hear this word, ye fat kine that are in the mountains
of Samaria, you that oppress the needy and crush the poor',[81] calling
them kine as being high up in their posteriors and low down at front;
also fat kine of the feminine sex and fat in their flesh, indicating by
feminine sex their womanish attitudes to all true fruits of the spirit, by
the fatness of the flesh their enlarged capacity for all the vile works of
the flesh; 'that are in the mountains of Samaria', that is, living and
dwelling for love of it in the exalted opulence of the pastoral care; for
the name Samaria, when interpreted, signifies care.

Since then he is needy who does not possess enough for his needs,
and a poor man is one who does not possess anything to give to
another, they falsely calumniate the former, whom they impoverish
with harsh exactions; the latter they reduce to nothing and kill with
bitterness by their beastly fraudulence. Let the oppressors of the
needy and the poor listen to the words (Prov. 22) 'He that oppresseth
the poor to increase his own riches, shall himself give to one that is
richer, and shall be in need'.[82] Let those who reduce a poor man to
nothing hear the words (Ecclus. 34) 'The bread of the needy is the life
of the poor; he that defraudeth them thereof is a man of blood'.[83] For
these names 'poor man' and 'needy' are often taken for each other, as
are the names 'wisdom' and 'knowledge', according to St Augustine.
Thus by harsh exactions amassing for themselves things not due to
them, and by cruelty and fraud retaining for themselves things
destined for others, living thus wickedly they have no fear in
misappropriating the income of the Church, which is the patrimony
of Christ obtained by his blood for the needy and poor. With the
sinful cupidity of their avarice, they take what they have received
from the Lord with a strict demand to render account, to relieve the
poverty of his faithful people through their faithful and prudent
dispensation according to that statement of our Saviour addressed to
the pastors of the Church (Matt. 24), 'Who thinkest thou is the
faithful and wise servant, whom his lord setteth over his family, to
give them their measure of food in due season?',[84] namely the
temporal as well as eternal food, of which they so sinfully dispense
neither, feeding themselves, and thus they cruelly slaughter the
servants of the Lord on either count, for whose salvation they have
sworn to the Lord with such a binding promise of vigilant care.

O what an abomination, what a crime, what a disgraceful sin! a

exhorrendum! Attendendum est hic illud apostoli (1 Cor. iv): 'Sic nos
existimet homo ut ministros Christi et dispensatores misteriorum
Dei. Hic iam queritur inter dispensatores ut fidelis quis inueniatur.'[85]
'Dispensatores' ait, non dominos. Non enim, secundum quod nunc
insinuatum est, memoratum Christi patrimonium, in tam pios usus
tam districta lege deputatum diuinitus, aliquo modo transferri ualet in
dispensatorum dominium, nisi usurpatiuo non[c] tam furti quam
latrocinii sacrilegio. Qui tamen dispensatores, dummodo si seminant
spiritualia, legitime metent carnalia, ut ex eis habentes alimenta et
quibus tegantur, hiis contenti sint. 'Qui uero non uult operari non
manducet',[86] 'dignus est enim solus mercede sua operarius'.[87] Patet
ergo quam conuenienter contra istos directus est sermo prophetalis:
'Audite hoc, uacce pingues que estis in monte Samarie, que calumpniam facitis egenis, et confringitis pauperes.'

Hiis adiungendum putaui quod de talibus nominis usurpati
pastoribus ille tantus euangelice pastionis emulator loquens ait
Bernardus super Cantica sermo x: 'Quanti hodie secus, scilicet
quam pastoribus ecclesie conueniat, affectos se ostendunt; de hiis
dico, qui animas regere susceperunt. Quod enim sine miserabili
gemitu dicendum non est, Christi opprobria, spute, flagella, clauos,
lanceam et crucem et mortem, hec omnia fornace auaritie conflant et
profligant in adquisitionem turpis questus; et patrimonium uniuersitatis suis marsupiis includere festinant, hoc solo sane a Iuda Scariothis
differentes, quod ille omne horum emolumentum denariorum
numero compensauit, isti uoraciori ingluuie lucrorum infinitas exi-
gunt pecunias; hiis insatiabili desiderio inhiant; pro hiis ne amittant
timent, et cum amittunt dolent; harum in amore quiescunt, quantum
dumtaxat liberum est eis aceruandi uel augmentandi curam animarum, nec casus reputatur nec salus. Non sunt profecto matres, qui
cum sint de Crucifixi patrimonio nimium incrassati, impinguati,
dilatati, non compatiuntur "super contritione Ioseph".[88] Que mater
est non dissimulat: prebet ubera et non uacua. "Gaudere cum
gaudentibus, flere cum flentibus"[89] nouit. Non cessat exprimere
quidem de ubere congratulationis,[d] lac exhortationis, de ubere uero
compassionis lac consolationis.'[90]

[c] non *omitted* B.   [d] *MS A ends here uncompleted.*

[85] 1 Cor. 4: 1–2.   [86] 2 Thess. 3: 10.
[87] Luke 10: 7.   [88] Amos 6: 6.   [89] Rom. 12: 15.
[90] St Bernard, *Sermones super Cantica*, ed. J. Leclercq, C. H. Talbot, and H. M. Rochais (Rome, 1957), pp. 49–50.

wickedness to make all the living shudder! Here we must take notice of that passage of the apostle (1 Cor. 4): 'Let a man so account of us as of the ministers of Christ and the dispensers of the mysteries of God. Now it is required among the dispensers that a man be found faithful.'[85] 'Dispensers' he says, not lords. For according to what is here indicated, the said patrimony of Christ, divinely assigned by strict law to such pious uses, cannot in any way be transferred to the possession of the dispensers, except by a sacrilegious usurpation and theft, with a proviso that if they sow a spiritual harvest, they may lawfully reap carnal goods, so that having from these food and shelter, they may be satisfied. 'If any man will not work, neither let him eat';[86] 'for only the labourer is worthy of his hire'.[87] It is evident, therefore, how appropriately the words of the prophet are directed against these people: 'Hear this word, ye fat kine, that are in the mountains of Samaria, you that oppress the needy and crush the poor.'

I thought it appropriate to add to these words what was said about such pastors, who usurp the name, by that great evangelical champion of the pastoral office, Bernard, in his tenth sermon on the Song of Songs, saying 'How many today show themselves to be of a disposition other than is fitting to pastors of the Church. I am speaking of those who have undertaken the government of souls. For what cannot be said without a groan of misery, is that they bring together the reproach of Christ, the spitting, the scourging, the nails, the lance, and his cross and death, and squander it in the acquisition of filthy gain, and they hasten to put the patrimony of the whole Church into their purses, differing from Judas Iscariot only in this, that he assessed all his pay for these things at a fixed number of pennies; they in their voracious greed for gain extort unbounded money. They pant for this with an insatiable desire, fearing to lose it, and when they do lose it, they grieve. They rest quietly in their love of this, so long, that is, as they are free to acquire and multiply cures of souls, and neither their fall or salvation is taken into account. Surely these are no mothers, though excessively fattened and swollen from the patrimony of Christ, who have no compassion for "the grief of Joseph".[88] One who is a mother does not dissemble: she offers her teats, and they are not empty. She knows how "to rejoice with the joyful and to weep with those who weep".[89] Indeed she does not cease to press from the breast of joy the milk of exhortation, and truly from the breast of compassion the milk of consolation.'[90]

Quis procurat uestimentum et corpus non curatur? Quis componit escam et animam exponit? Quis unquam cultorum materiam edificat et uineam contempnit? Quis unquam ducum uallum erigit et negligit exercitum? Rogo, separemus pretiosum a uili, propter eum qui presertim ad ecclesiasticos ait (Jer. xv): 'Si separaueris a uili, quasi os meum eris.'[91]

35a. *Recitatio persecutionum ecclesiam nunc temporis tribulantium, cum petitione rescripti super eisdem.*

Post alia scripsit michi uestra dominatio subiunctam seriem. Inter cetera grauamina que uobis ab hominibus inferuntur, illa uos grauius affligunt que per potestatis terrene ministerium sponsam Christi ancillare nituntur et eius subuertere libertates:

'Recipimus namque pluries mandata regis, quod iuxta dudum inolitam corruptelam clericos et ministros ecclesie tribunali regio sistamus super personalibus actionibus et plerisque criminibus et aliis, iuxta corruptelam huiusmodi responsuros. Nuper etiam inconsuete forte litteram domini regis recepimus, cuius tenorem uobis transmittimus, qui talis est:

"H. Dei gratia rex Anglie, dominus Ybernie, dux Normannie, Aquitanie, et comes Andegaue, uenerabili in Christo patri S., eadem gratia Eboracensi archiepiscopo, salutem. Cum omnis pecunia ex quacunque, tam Terre Sancte subsidio deputata, nobis sit pro excusatione[a] uoti nostri ab Apostolico Sede concessa,[92] et quidam clerici et laici uestre dyocesis conuicti sint coram executoribus dicti negotii ab eadem Sede de nostro consilio deputatis, ipsos nobis debere denarios subscriptos; ecclesiasticam uolentes libertatem quam in nobis est per omnia illesam conseruare, uobis mandamus quatenus sine dilatione habeatis per aliquem de uestris apud Nouum Templum Londonie in octaua Sancti Hillarii predictos denarios soluendos executoribus predictis."

'et quibusdam interpositis adiungit:

"Tantum facientes quod non oporteat nos ad baroniam uestram capere, nec ad ea que ad ecclesiam pertinent, propter defectum

---

35a *a possibly* executione.

[91] Jer. 15: 19.
[92] King Henry took the crusader's vow on 6 Mar. 1250, and Pope Innocent IV agreed to levy a subsidy of one tenth on the English clergy to be paid to the king for this purpose. But subsequently Henry accepted the papal offer of the crown of Sicily for his son Edmund, and in May 1255 Pope Alexander IV authorized the commutation of the king's vow and the

Who buys a garment, and gives no care to the body? Who puts a meal together, and throws away his life? Who ever builds up the materials for cultivation, and despises his vineyard? What leader ever erects a rampart, and neglects his army? I ask you, let us separate the precious from the vile, for the sake of Him who says, especially to ecclesiastics, 'If thou wilt separate the precious from the vile (Jer. 15), thou shalt be as my mouth.[91]

35a. *A recitation of persecutions troubling the Church now at this time, with a request for a rescript on the same.*
After other matters, your lordship wrote to me the following, which I add below. Among the other troubles inflicted upon you by men, you are more seriously afflicted by those that endeavour to enslave the Spouse of Christ and to undermine her liberties through the ministry of earthly power:

'For we have frequently received royal mandates to the effect that, following a corrupt practice lately introduced, we should cause clerks and ministers of the Church to stand before royal courts to answer in personal actions and to many criminal charges and others in accordance with a corrupt practice of this kind. Recently we have even received, perhaps unusually, a letter of the lord king, the message of which I am transmitting to you; it is as follows:

"Henry, by the grace of God King of England, Lord of Ireland, Duke of Normandy and Aquitaine, Count of Anjou, to the venerable father in Christ S., by the same grace Archbishop of York, greetings. Whereas all money, from whatever source, designated for the relief of the Holy Land has been granted us by the Apostolic See for the implentation of our vow,[92] and certain clerks and laymen of your diocese have been proved before the executors of the said transaction deputed by the same see on our advice to owe us the monies listed below; wishing in all things to preserve the liberty of the Church which is in our keeping, we command you to produce without delay through someone of your ministers the said monies to be paid to the said executors at the New Temple of London on the octave of St Hilary."

'And with some other insertions, it adds:
"Doing so much that we are not obliged to seize your barony or to extend the arm of secular power to those things that pertain to the

diversion of the subsidy to the conquest of Sicily; see Lunt, *Financial Relations of the Papacy*, pp. 265–6.

uestrum, manum extendere secularem; et habeatis ibi hoc breue.
Teste meipso. Apud Vyntoniam xx die Nouembris, anno regni nostri
xli. Per magistros W. de Lichefeld, Nicholaum de Plumton; Philippum Luuel, Edward' de Westmonasterio, et alios barones de
scaccario.''⁹³

Interpositis igitur pluribus euidentium rationum efficaciis, ostendentibus quod in hac parte domini regis mandato non uideri esse
parendum, nouissime idem subiunxit uestra excellentia: 'Verum
igitur statum et beneplacitum, et quid tam in primo quam in secundo
articulo facere expediat, nobis petimus rescribatis. Prelati namque
alii, sicut audiuimus, a domino rege mandatum consimile receperunt.
Valete feliciter.'

36a. *Quod prefate tribulationes, licet recte ingerant compassionem, tamen*
dignius exultationem inducunt.

Quamuis ergo hec excogitata temptationum tribulantium uexamina
nec immerito anxiam ingerant compassionem, tamen multo iustius
eximiam inducunt exultationem, dicente Scriptura inter innumerabilia in id ipsum testimonia (Hebr. x): 'Rememoramini pristinos dies
in quibus illuminati magnum certamen sustinuistis passionum; in
altero quidem opprobriis et tribulationibus spectaculum facti, altero
autem socii taliter conuersantium effecti. Nam et uinctis compassi
estis, et rapinam bonorum uestrorum cum gaudio suscepistis,
cognoscentes uos habere meliorem et manentem substantiam.'⁹⁴ Et
illud (i Pet. i): 'Benedictus Deus et Pater domini nostri Iesu Christi,
qui secundum magnam misericordiam suam regenerauit nos in spem
uiuam', et infra, 'in quo exultabitis modicum nunc, si oportet
contristari in uariis temptationibus, ut probatio fidei uestre multo
pretiosior sit auro, quod per ignem probatur'.⁹⁵ Huc quoque accedunt
que subiungo testimonia, uidelicet illud (i Cor. iv): 'Id quod in
presenti est momentaneum et leue tribulationis nostre supra modum
in sublimitate eternum glorie pondus operabitur in nobis.'⁹⁶ Et
illud (Hebr. xii): 'Flagellat Deus omnem filium quem recipit.'⁹⁷ Et
illud (Ys. xxviii): 'Per omne flagellum erudieris, tu Israel.'⁹⁸ Et illud
(ii Cor. i): 'Sola uexatio dabit intellectum auditui.'⁹⁹ Licet ergo
tribulationum uexamina turbando contristent, tamen per Eum, 'qui
consolatur nos in omni tribulatione nostra'¹⁰⁰ letificant secundum

⁹³ Walter Suffield, bishop of Norwich, was designated Collector of the subsidy for the whole province of York: *CPR 1247–58*, p. 370.
⁹⁴ Heb. 10: 32–4.   ⁹⁵ 1 Pet. 1: 3, 6–7.   ⁹⁶ 2 Cor. 4: 17.
⁹⁷ Cf. Heb. 12: 6.   ⁹⁸ Isa. 28: 18.   ⁹⁹ Ibid. 28: 19.

Church on account of your default. And have this writ at that place. Witness myself, at Winchester, the 20th day of November and the forty-first year of our reign. By Masters W. de Lichfield, Nicholas of Plumpton, Philip Luvel, Edward of Westminster, and other barons of the Exchequer.'''[93]

Inserting, therefore, many effective arguments to show that in this case the king's mandate should not really be obeyed, your excellency added this last of all: 'So truly, we beg you to write back as to your condition and pleasure, and regarding both the first and second items as to what it is expedient to do. For, as we have heard, other prelates have received a similar mandate from the lord king. Happily farewell.'

36a. *That although the aforesaid tribulations rightly excite sympathy, they more fittingly induce feelings of exaltation.*

Although, then, these considered vexations and troublesome tribulations deservedly induce sympathy and anxiety, they more rightly arouse feelings of high exaltation, as Scripture says, among innumerable evidences for the same (Hebr. 10): 'Call to mind the former days, wherein, being illuminated, you endured a great fight of afflictions and on the other hand indeed, by reproaches and tribulations, were made a gazingstock; and on the other, became companions of them that were used in such sort. For you both had compassion on them that were in bands, and took with joy the being stripped of your own goods, knowing that you have a better and a lasting substance.'[94] And in that passage (1 Pet. 1); 'Blessed be the God and Father of our Lord Jesus Christ, who according to his great mercy hath regenerated us unto a lively hope', and lower down, 'wherein you shall greatly rejoice, if now you must be for a little time made sorrowful in divers temptations, that the trial of your faith is much more precious than gold which is tried by the fire.'[95] This is supported by these testimonies which I add, namely that of 1 Cor. 4: 'For that which is at present momentary and light of our tribulation, worketh for us above measure exceedingly an eternal weight of glory';[96] and that text (Heb. 12): 'God scourgeth every son whom He receiveth'[97] and that text (Isa. 28): 'By every scourging thou, Israel, will be instructed.'[98] And (2 Cor. 1) 'Only vexation will give the hearer understanding'.[99] Therefore, although tribulations and vexations disturb us and make us sad, yet they give us joy through Him 'who consoles us in all our tribulation',[100] according to the Scriptures, by hugely strengthening

[100] 2 Cor. 1: 4.

Scripturas, et roborando ingentius et ueracius erudiendo et expiando
sincerius et stabilius confirmando. Nempe commutabilium amorem
ab ipsis auertendo mortificant et uiuificant conuertendo ad ipsum
amorem incommutabilium, non^a secus quam amara superlinita uber-
ibus ablactandos auertunt a lactis suauitate et ad soliditatem panis
conuertunt.

37a. *Quod in dictis tribulationibus commemoratum archipresulem oporteat
ante omnia Saluatoris amplecti uestigia.*

Quid igitur primitus in hiis consultum poterit esse pro archipresule,
pietatis apostolice successore, nisi ut illud inseparabiliter amplectatur
imitandum infatigabiliter quod ipsorum Auctor apostolis omnibus et
cunctis apostolicis ait (Ioh. xvii): 'Hec locutus sum uobis, ut in me
pacem habeatis. In mundo pressuram habebitis, sed confidite, quia
ego uici mundum';[101] sicut etenim omnia poterit in Eo, qui eum
confortat Christus.[102]

38a. *Quod inter omnia fidelibus securiorem prestat fiduciam per prefatum
archipresulem archipresulatus officium glorifice fore complendum. Hoc
quidem ipsum dispensatio diuina in presentia tribulationum succrescentium
sanctis suis associauit.*

Si quid ecclesie coram sanctitatis uestre dignissima prelatione
letificam expectationis secure fiduciam, per Iesum Christum Saluatorem nostrum, potissime prestat fidelium emulatio, quod ad
honorem Dei, ad hominis salutem, ad liberationem ecclesiarum et
uestri coronam sacrosanctam, archipresulatus uestri ministerium,
Diuinate propitia, per successum salutarem ad felicem exitum
inspectabili gloria perducetur. Huius, inquam, tam gloriose glorie
precipue securam prestat fiduciam quod superclemens predestina-
tionis Altissimi^a dignatio inuictis ecclesie sue propugnatoribus, per
uaria succrescentium persecutionum molimina, triumphalem uestri
certaminis agoniam associare decreuit, quorum unus ille principum
inuictissimus, 'Si consistent, inquit, 'aduersum me castra, non
timebit cor meum. Si exsurgat aduersum me prelium, in hoc ego
sperabo.'[103] De quibus etiam scriptum est (Iudith viii): 'Memores
esse debent quomodo pater noster Abraham temptatus est, et per
multas temptationes probatus, amicus Dei effectus est.'[104] Sic Ysaac,
sic Iacob, sic Moyses, et omnes qui placuerunt Deo, per multas

36a   ^a hec B.
38a   ^a Altissime *MS.*

us and truly instructing us, by wholly expiating us and establishing us more firmly. For truly they mortify our love of transitory things by averting our eyes from them, and give us life by converting us to the love of things that are unchanging, in the same way that bitter things smeared on the breasts convert those to be weaned from the sweetness of milk and convert them to solid bread.

37a. *That in the said tribulations the archbishop should before all else cling to the footprints of the Saviour.*
What, therefore, can the archbishop, successor to apostolic holiness, be advised to do in the first place except to embrace inseparably and untiringly imitate what their Author says to all the apostles and to the rest of their successors (John 17): 'These things I have spoken unto you, that in me you might have peace. In the world ye shall have tribulations, but be of good cheer; I have overcome the world';[101] as he can do all things in Him, Christ who strengthens him.[102]

38a. *That among all things he should give the faithful confidence that amidst all this the archiepiscopal office will be gloriously performed through the said archbishop. Indeed in this the divine dispensation associates him with his saints in these growing tribulations of the present time.*
If the zeal of the Church, and above all that of the faithful, exhibits joyful trust and certain hope, through Jesus Christ our Saviour in the most worthy prelacy of your holiness, that your archiepiscopal ministry will be guided by God's mercy through a saving procedure to a happy outcome with reflected glory to the honour of God, the salvation of men, the liberation of the churches and your most holy crown; a sure guarantee of that glorious glory is provided, I say, by the fact that a most merciful predestination of the Most High has, through various exertions and growing persecutions, decreed to associate your triumphant struggle with that of the unconquered champions of the Church, of whom that one most unvanquished of leaders said 'If armies in camp should stand against me, my heart shall not fear. If a battle should rise up against me, in this will I be confident.'[103] Regarding which it is also written (Judith 8) 'They must remember how our father Abraham was tempted, and being proved by many tribulations, was made the friend of God'.[104] So Isaac, so Jacob, so Moses, and all that have pleased God, passed through many

---

[101] John 16: 33.   [102] Cf. Phil. 4: 13.
[103] Ps. 26: 3.   [104] Judith 8: 22.

tribulationes transierunt fideles, ipsius perpetim disponente clementia, cui dictum est (Thob. iii): 'Hoc autem pro certo habet omnis qui colit Te, quia uita eius si in probatione fuerit ⟨coronabitur; et si in correptione fuerit⟩ ad misericordiam tuam uenire licebit. Non enim delectaris in perditionibus nostris; quia post tempestatem tranquillum facis, et post lacrimationem et fletum exultationem infundis. Sit nomen Dei Israel benedictum in secula.'[105] De quo apostolus (Rom. xvi): 'Deus', inquit, 'pacis conteret Sathanam sub pedibus uestris uelociter.'[106] Quia enim, 'Ecce', inquit, 'ego uobiscum sum omnibus diebus usque ad consummationem seculi'.[107]

39a. *Oratur ut archiepiscopali requisitioni diuinitus salutaria respondeantur.*

Verum ad ea super quibus excellentia uestra meam requirere uoluit

f. 99 exilitatem, sine me respondeat, oro, uobis salutaria Saluatoris | sapientia, qui tam uobis quam illis in quorum locum successistis, ait (Luc. xxi): 'Ego dabo uobis os et sapientiam, cui non poterunt resistere et contradicere omnes aduersarii uestri';[108] et alibi (Math. x): 'Ad reges et presides ducemini propter me, in testimonium illis et gentibus. Cum autem tradent uos, nolite cogitare quomodo aut quid loquamini; dabitur enim uobis in illa hora quid loquamini.'[109] Vbi certe prohibetur sensus humani sollicitudo, non affectus diuini meditatio, tamenque quicquid respondeatur non cogitetur humanitus, sed diuinitus affectetur. Subiungit enim, 'Non', inquiens, 'uos estis qui loquimini, sed Spiritus Patris uestri qui loquitur in uobis'.[110] Et alibi (Iac i): 'Si quis autem uestrum indiget sapientia, postulet a Deo, qui dat omnibus affluenter, et non improperat, et dabitur ei. Postulet autem in fide, nichil hesitans.'[111]

40a. *De uehementiore persecutionis afflictione hiis diebus contra ecclesiam seuiente propter duos gladios, spiritualem et materialem, ad nocendum adunatos.*

Vehementius uero exaggerat hiis diebus contra ecclesiam tribulationum pericula ut multum persecutio moderna, duos gladios, de quibus senatus apostolorum (Luc. xxii): 'Ecce duo gladii hic',[112] copulans insimul ut noceat efficacius. Quorum uterque quidem est ecclesie, spiritualis scilicet et materialis. Propter quod spiritualis quidem

---

[105] Tobias 3: 21–3.
[108] Luke 21: 15.
[111] James 1: 5–6.

[106] Rom. 16: 20.
[109] Matt. 10: 18–19.

[107] Matt. 28: 20.
[110] Matt. 10: 20.
[112] Luke 22: 38.

tribulations, remaining faithful, through the perpetual mercy of His dispensation, of whom it is said (Tobias 3): 'But this everyone is sure of that worshipeth thee, that his life, if it be under trial, shall be crowned; and if it be under tribulation, it shall be delivered; and [if it be under correction,] it shall be allowed to come to thy mercy. For thou art not delighted in our being lost, because after a storm thou makest a calm, and after tears and weeping thou pourest in joyfulness. Be thy name, O God of Israel, blessed for ever.'[105] Of whom the Apostle cries (Rom. 16): 'The God of peace shall crush Satan under your feet speedily.'[106] For 'behold', He says, 'I am with you all days, even to the consummation of the world.'[107]

39a. *A prayer that the archbishop may receive from God a saving answer to his request.*

Truly, concerning the matters about which your excellency wished to ask my poor self, allow me, I pray, to answer you with the saving wisdom of our Saviour, who says both to you and to those to whose place you have succeeded (Luke 21): 'I will give you a mouth and wisdom, which all your adversaries shall not be able to resist and gainsay',[108] and in another place (Matt. 10), 'you shall be brought before governors and before kings for my sake, for a testimony to them and to the Gentiles. But when they shall deliver you up, take no thought how or what to speak, for it shall be given you in that hour what to speak.'[109] Here certainly anxiety about human understanding is forbidden, but not so meditation on the divine love, yet let it not be thought what human answer should be given, but let a divine one sought. For He adds: 'For it is not you that speak, but the Spirit of your Father that speaketh in you.'[110] And elsewhere (James 1): 'If any of you want wisdom, let him ask of God who giveth to all men abundantly and upbraideth not, and it shall be given him. But let him ask in faith, nothing wavering.'[111]

40a. *Concerning the affliction of the persecution raging against the Church in these days on account of the two swords, the spiritual and the material, united to do harm.*

Truly, modern persecution much increases the dangers and tribulations for the Church these days, joining together the two swords, of which the apostolic senate says (Luke 22): 'Behold here are two swords'[112] to harm more effectively; each of which belongs to the Church, namely the spiritual and the material one. On account of this indeed the most diligent spiritual investigator of salvific

causarum spiritualium diligentissimus inuestigator[113] ad summum
pontificem de gladio materiali (Bernard ad Eugenium, libro iiii°);
'quid', inquit, 'denuo usurpare temptes, quem semel iussus es reponere
in uaginam? Quem tamen qui tuum negat non satis michi uidetur
attendere uerbum Domini dicentis sic: "Conuerte gladium tuum in
uaginam." Tuus ergo, et ipse tuo forsitan nutu, etsi non tua manu,
euaginandus. Alioquin si ad te nullo modo pertineret, et hiis dicentibus
apostolis "Ecce gladii duo hic", non respondisset Dominus "satis est",
sed "nimis est" (Luc. xxii), uterque ergo ecclesie et spiritualis gladius et
materialis; sed is quidem pro ecclesia, ille uero etiam ab ecclesia
exserendus; ille sacerdotis, hic militis manu, sed sane ad nutum etiam
sacerdotis et iussum imperatoris.'[114]

Horum ergo utrumque gladium exercet in ecclesiam Dei contra
leges diuinas uexatio periculosior, quos hiis diebus ad hoc simul
adunauit astutia callidior uulpium demolentium uineam Domini, de
qua per prophetam (Ys. v): 'Vinea Domini exercituum domus Israel
est' et adiungit 'et uir Iuda desiderabile germen eius.'[115] Et quid est
domus Iuda nisi ecclesia Domini, et quid uir Iuda nisi Christus
Dominus? Igitur aduersus ecclesiam Domini et aduersus Christum
eius moderna persecutio solito uehementior efferari conspicitur in
duobus gladiis, materiali scilicet et spirituali, uulpium caliditate
coniunctis, uidelicet astutorum Sathane satellitum, clericatum arro-
ganter profitentium, et clerum immaniter persequentium, iugiter
quos conatu callido machinantium imperialem seducere celsitudinem,
et sanctitatem circumuenire sacerdotalem. Proinde quis poterit
estimare discrimen in eo, quod una cum proprio dirus hostis ciuem
modestum in gladio extorto per hostilem manum de manu ciuili
letaliter inuadere non desistit? Et quid si celestem potentiam gladii
spiritualis solum impugnaret gladii materialis potentia secularis, que
ratio posset esse formidandi?

41a. *Qualiter gloria triumphi de iam dicta persecutione quamlibet
uehementi diuinitus obtinetur.*
Verum cum publice potestati potestas ecclesiastica presidio existit ad
confligendum, quis belli pondus sustinebit, nisi quem firmat et dirigit

---

[113] i.e. St Bernard.
[114] *De Consideratione*, in *S. Bernardi Opera*, iii. 454.
[115] Isa. 5: 7.

causes[113] addresses the supreme pontiff (Bernard to Eugenius, Book 4) concerning the material sword, saying 'Why will you endeavour to usurp that sword which you have once been commanded to replace in its sheath? He who denies, however, that it is yours seems to me not sufficiently heeding the word of the Lord, saying "Put up thy sword again into its place". It is yours, therefore, and to be drawn at your signal perhaps, but not by your hand. Otherwise, if it in no way belonged to you and to the apostles, when saying the words "Behold here are two swords", the Lord would not have responded (Luke 22) "It is enough", but "It is too much". Each, therefore, the spiritual and the material sword, belong to the Church; but the latter, to be sure, to be drawn on behalf of the Church, the former also by the Church; the former by the hand of the priest, the latter by that of the warrior, but rightly at the signal of the priest and that of the emperor.'[114]

Dangerous assailants are using both of these swords against the Church contrary to divine law; these swords have been joined together in these days for that purpose by the cunning of wolves bent on destroying the vineyard of the Lord, of which it is said by the prophet (Isa. 5): 'The vineyard of the Lord of hosts is the house of Israel', adding 'and the man Juda, his pleasant plant.'[115] And what is the house of Juda except the Church of the Lord, and what is the man Juda except Christ the Lord? We see the modern persecution, therefore, raging more fiercely than usual against the Church of the Lord and against its Christ using two swords, the material and the spiritual, joined with the cunning of wolves, that is of the clever satellites of Satan, of those who arrogantly profess clerical status and monstrously persecute the clergy, constantly seeking with a rash attempt to lead astray the imperial highness and to circumvent the holiness of the priesthood. Who then can calculate the danger in the fact that the grim foe does not desist from assaulting the quiet citizen with his own sword, together with an unsheathed sword taken by hostile hand from the hand of the citizen? And what if the secular power of the material sword alone were to assault the heavenly power of the spiritual sword? What reason could there be to fear?

41a. *How with God's help a glorious victory will be gained over the said persecution, however fierce it may be.*
Truly when the ecclesiastical power steps out to assist the power of the state in a conflict, who will be able to support the oppression of war except he who is strengthened and directed by Christ, the power

Christus, Dei uirtus et Dei sapientia (I Cor. i),[116] 'saliens corde et fortis robore' (Iob ix)?[117] Porro quanto difficilius est certamen prelii,

f. 90ᵛ tanto pretiosior est | laura triumphi. Et quis est locus hesitandi de triumpho, ubi 'qui habitat in adiutorio Altissimi'[118] perseuerantia finali legitimi certaminis Ipsum ueraciter audit annuntiantem (Iac. i): 'Beatus uir qui suffert temptationem: quoniam cum probatus fuerit, accipiet coronam uite, quam repromisit Deus diligentibus se'?[119]

42a. *Abbreuiata recitatio persecutionum moderni temporis ecclesiam contra sacros canones pregrauantium cum allegationibus persequentium pro sua parte.*

Demumne per pontifices ad mandatum regium tribunali regio sistantur clerici super personalibus actionibus et plerisque criminibus iuxta presumptam dierum aliquot corruptelam responsuri, ut melius nouit pietatis uestre sollertia? Venerande sacrorum canonum traditiones omnimodis obsistere non dubitantur. Super hiis autem abusionibus, quia segnius actum est per prelatos quamdiu in Ecclesia Anglicana, profecto difficilius corrigentur. Allegat enim in hac parte importunus dominus rex cum consiliariis suis pro se diuturnam consuetudinem, a qua si recederetur et dignitati regie et totali regno fieret enorme preiudicium, quam, ut aiunt, nec debet Ecclesia Romana nec Ecclesia Anglicana aliquatenus immutare.

Littera etiam domini regis a uobis nuper recepta tenoris inconsueti pro pecunia domino regi ab Apostolica Sede concessa, ut eam certis die et loco habeatis per aliquem de uestris soluendam executoribus dicte concessionis, continere uidetur, etiam iuxta rationum efficacias in scriptura uestra michi destinata expressas, manifestas institutionum canonicarum iniurias, quamuis, sicut reor, dominus rex, cum illis quorum nititur consiliis, asserat se in causis huiusmodi potestatem regiam accommodare ordinationibus apostolicis adimplendis, et sic in nihilo ecclesiastica iura per eum uiolari, cum per ecclesiasticam auctoritatem satagat ex deuotione regia ut iussiones apostolice peragantur, secundum quod ipsum executores a domino papa delegati uice eiusdem super hoc interpellant diligentius et requirunt.

---

[116] 1 Cor. 1: 24.   [117] Job 9: 4.
[118] Ps. 90: 1.   [119] James 1: 12.

of God and the wisdom of God (1 Cor. 1),[116] 'wise in heart and mighty in strength'?[117] (Job 9). To be sure, the harder the battle, the more precious is the laurel of victory; and what place is there for doubt about victory, where 'he who dwells in the help of the Most High',[118] persevering to the end of his lawful struggle, truly hears Him declaring (James 1): 'Blessed be the man that endures temptation, for when he hath been proved, he shall receive the crown of life which God hath promised to them that love him.'[119]

42a. *A summary recitation of the persecutions afflicting the Church in modern times against the sacred canons, with the allegations of the persecutors on their behalf.*
Is it not through bishops that, at the royal command, clerks are brought before the royal court to answer in personal actions and to many criminal charges in accordance with a corrupt ordinance enacted some days before, as your reverence knows better than I? There is no doubt that the venerable traditions of the sacred canons are in every way opposed to this. It will be more difficult to correct these abuses now, as for some time the prelates of the English Church have been slow to act in these matters. For in this question the lord king with his councillors is pressingly alleging on his behalf a long custom, the abandonment of which would be highly prejudicial to the royal dignity and the whole kingdom, a custom which, as they say, neither the Roman Church nor the English Church ought to change in any respect.

The lord king's letter of an uncustomary tenor that you have received regarding the money granted the lord king by the Apostolic See, to the effect that you should have the money on a fixed day and at a fixed place to be paid by one of your executors of the said grant, seems to involve manifest detriment to canon law, according indeed to the effective arguments set out in your letters that were sent to me. Although the lord king, as I think, with those on whose counsel he relies, asserts that in these cases he accomodates the royal power to fulfil the papal ordinances, and that thus the laws of the Church are in no way being violated by him since, on ecclesiastical authority and out of his royal devotion, he is actively working for the implementation of the apostolic commands in accordance with what the executors delegated by the lord pope diligently claim in this case and ask.

43a. *Quod pii presules contra temporalia modernarum tribulationum uexamina sic studeant adhibere remedia, ne per eorum remedialem uigilantiam ecclesie Dei eternalium perditionum incurrant detrimenta.*

Verum cum ex hiis que superius et modo dicta sunt, ecclesie uideantur intolerabilia imminere grauamina, necesse est ut pii presules, zelo domus dominice fruentes, contra tanta discrimina opportuna studeant adhibere remedia, precedentium patrum in omnibus sequendo uestigia. Cauendum tamen potissimum esse cognoscitur (Math. xiii) 'ne forte colligentes zizania, eradicent simul cum eis et triticum',[120] neque 'decimantes mentam et anetum et ciminum, relinquant que grauiora sint legis et iudicium, misericordiam et fidem', sed nec excollantes culicem, camelum autem glutiant.[121] Absit. Hic illud quidem insequitur scilicet sermo sancti sapientis (B. ad Eugenium iiii to): 'Vides omnem ecclesiasticum zelum feruere sola pro dignitate tuenda. Honori totum datur, sanctitati nichil aut paruum; de placito Dei ultima mentio est. Pro iactura salutis nulla cunctatio, nisi quod sublime est, hoc salutare dicamus, et quod gloriam redolet, id iustum.'[122]

Sic igitur hic agendum ne, dum modica defenduntur, amittantur maxima, ne dum corporibus momentanee prouidetur, animabus perpetue noceatur. Non desunt uiri gloriosi utriusque Testamenti tam ad regem quam ad sacerdotium pertinentes, diuinitus in hoc ad f. 100 imitandum propositi, | qui secundum dispensationem salutarem interdum tolerarent hostes ne ciues trucidarent. Nam sicut iam insinuata dierum istorum pericula, quid hodie dignius expauescitur quam si sacri pontifices aggressu precipiti configere temptauerint contra prefatas uite temporalis inquietationes, quod imperiali gladio seuienti sacerdotalis gladius afferat adiutorium in suspensionum et excommunicationum, priuationum et depositionum seuerissimis additionibus, et sic contrito castrorum celestium propugnatore, furentissimo sacrilegio sacratissimum sanctuarium contingat irrumpere instar leonum truculentissimos, instar luporum rapacissimos, instar serpentum callidissimos, instar demonum malignissimos, truculentia leonina, rapacitate lupina, calliditate serpentina malignitate demonica destructuros ciuitates sanctorum, predaturos patrimonia

---

[120] Matt. 13: 29.
[121] Matt. 23: 24.
[122] St Bernard *De Consideratione*; see above, n. 114.

43a. *That good prelates should be zealous to apply remedies for the temporal vexations and present-day tribulations in such a way that the Church of God should not incur the damage of eternal loss through their watchful remedies.*

Truly, since from what has been said and is said now, intolerable oppression seems to be threatening the Church, it is necessary for good prelates, enjoying the zeal of the Lord's house, to be active in applying opportune remedies against such great dangers by following in all things in the footsteps of the fathers who were their predecessors. But we know that care must be taken above all (Matt. 13) lest, when 'gathering the tares, they should uproot the wheat',[120] or while 'you tithe the mint and anise and cummin, they have left the weightier things of the law: judgement and mercy and faith, or while straining out a gnat they do not swallow a camel'.[121] Heaven forbid! Here is apposite that discourse of the wise saint (Bernard to Eugenius, Book 4): 'One sees all the zeal of the Church fervently devoted only to protecting dignity; everything is given to honour, little or nothing to holiness; pleasing God is the last thing to be mentioned. There is no hesitation in casting away salvation, unless we call that of saving worth which is the most lofty, and that just which emits a perfume of glory.'[122]

Thus action must be taken so that, whilst things of moderate importance are defended, the greatest things are not lost; so that whilst the short-term interests of the body are provided for, perpetual damage is not done to souls. In each Testament there is no lack of glorious men, pertaining both to the king and the priesthood, divinely set before us for our imitation, who in accordance with a saving dispensation tolerated enemies for a time lest they should slay citizens. For like the creeping perils of those days, what is more properly to be feared today than, if sacred bishops attempt by precipitate aggression to strike against the aforementioned disturbances of their temporal life, that the sword of the priest should bring help to the furious sword of the ruler with the stern addition of suspensions, excommunications, deprivations, and depositions, and thus, when the champion of the heavenly host has been crushed, the most holy sanctuary may be broken into with furious sacrilege by those in the likeness of ferocious lions, in the likeness of ravenous wolves, in the likeness of cunning serpents, the likeness of most malignant demons, with leonine ferocity, wolfish rapacity, serpentine cunning, and devilish malice to destroy the cities of the saints, to

iustorum, perdituros corpora fidelium, perempturos animas pauperum; latrones loquor immitissimos, sub usurpato nomine pastorum, et dignitates et prebendas et parochias et monasteria
uastitate hostili in hunc euentum peruasuros. Itaque cum horrore
summe lamentabili frustratur et uictoria belli et pro quo bellum
initur, salus populi. Queso cernatur si alioquin hic intercidit ambi-
gendi possibilitas

44a. *Quod duces ecclesie hostibus ecclesie continue repugnent, tamen melius
sub moderamine posthac adiuncto, certe seipsos impensuri pro animabus
incunctanter, quotiens ab animarum peremptoribus animabus perimendis
instituitur.*
Num ista idcirco scripserim ut persuadeam ecclesie propugnatoribus
mentium quamlibet diffidentia uel desperatione pusillanimi dextras
dare persecutoribus ecclesie? Absit a me in sempiternum tam
detestabilis insania. Est namque necessitas ineuitabilis ut ecclesie
duces hostibus ecclesie uirtute potenti patentis controuersie continue
resistendo contradicant, et contradicendo resistant. Sed melius nonnunquam hoc fiet, ut uideo, sub dispensatiuo moderamine, quod in
simplicitate mea, sicut estimo, ex Scripture tam doctrinis quam
exemplis ad uestram iussionem ausus sum annectare. Suprascriptis
sane perpetim intellectis[a] quidem ad indefessam strenuitatem opportune promptitudinis Redemptori animarum, animarum rectores
obligatissime constringuntur, ut liberandis animabus proprias
animas mortalis uite quibuscunque discriminibus incunctata solllici-
tudine festinent exponere, quotiens intemptores animarum animarum
peruasionibus comperiuntur imminere.

45a. *De quadripartito moderamine diligentie uigilantioris adhibenda per
sepe dictum archipresulem contra supradicta modernarum tribulationum
turbamina pro periclitantis ecclesie liberatione.*
Hiis igitur ab insufficientia mea, ut fieri ualet, sollicite propositis,
consultum michi fore uidetur, in tanto tali quam ancipiti causarum
inestimabilium certamine, ut ante omnia per prouisiuam sanctitatis
uestre uigilantiam recurratur ad efficacissime continuarum orationum
presidia, secundum illud prophete (Ioel i): 'accingite uos, et plangite,
sacerdotes; ululate, ministri altaris; ingredimini, cubate in sacco,
ministri Dei mei; quoniam interiit de domo Dei uestri sacrificium
et libatio. Sanctificate ieiunium, uocate cetum, congregate senes et

44a   *a* intellecto *MS.*

plunder the patrimony of the just, to destroy the bodies of the faithful and carry off the souls of the poor. I am speaking of pitiless thieves who, under the usurped name of pastors, will invade dignities and prebends, parishes and monasteries, with hostile devastation in this event. Therefore with dread and great lamentation both victory in the war is rendered vain and also the salvation of the people, for whom the war was begun. I beg, let inquiry be made as to whether there is a possibility here of settling this matter in some other way.

44a. *That the leaders of the Church should continually oppose the enemies of the Church, but preferably by the method enjoined below, surely spending themselves without hesitation for souls as often as the slayers of souls are determined to slay them.*

Have I written this in order to persuade the champions of the Chuch to encourage its persecutors by any want of mental confidence or pusillanimous despair? Heaven save me from such contemptible madness! For it is an inescapable necessity for leaders of the Church to withstand its enemies strongly in open dispute, contradicting them by their resistance, and resisting them by contradiction. But this may sometimes be better done, as I see it, with an economical moderation, which I in my simplicity have ventured to add at your command, excerpted, as I reckon, from both the teaching and the examples in the Scriptures. If the things written above are always properly understood, the rectors of souls are bound to the Redeemer of souls by a very strong obligation to work with tireless energy and readiness to hasten to offer their own mortal lives to whatever dangers with unhesitating solicitude for the liberation of souls, as often as the tempters of souls are found to be threatening to invade them.

45a. *Of the fourfold managerial steps to be taken with diligence and greater vigilance by the aforesaid archbishop against the said disturbances and present-day tribulations for the liberation of the Church in peril.*

As my inadequate self has made these proposals for its accomplishment, in such a doubtful conflict with incalculable risks it seems to me that it will be advisable for your watchful holiness to have recourse before all things to the most efficacious assistance of continual prayer, according to that call of the prophet (Joel 1): 'Gird yourselves and lament, O ye priests, howl, ye ministers of the altars; go in, lie in sackcloth, ye minsters of my God; because sacrifice and libation is cut off from the house of your God. Sanctify a fast, call an assembly, gather together the ancients, all the inhabitants of the land into the

omnes habitatores terre in domum Dei nostri, et clamate ad Dominum. A, a, a, diei! quia prope est dies Domini, et quasi uastitas a
potente ueniet.'[123] Nonne orante Moyse per uirtutem diuinam
deuictus est Amalech ab Israele? (Exod. xvii).[124] Nonne orante
Ezechia per angelicum presidium percussis de Assiriorum exercitu
.clxxxv. millia, Senacherib a Iudea exterminatus est? (Yse. xxxvii).[125]

Deinde ut modis congruentibus per insignem pietatis uestre
prudentiam excitetur dominus Cantuariensis cum suis suffraganeis,
quos opprimunt, assidue gementes et plangentes indesinenter, prefata
molestium uexationum pondera. Si forte constipatis bellicarum
acierum agminibus, iuxta quod gloriosius inchoatum est, cum
adhuc in carne uiueret, ad hoc salutari uigilantia laborans sancte
recordationis dominus Robertus, quondam Lyncolniensis episcopus,
corde uno et anima una, sub concordi uincendi fiducia una uobiscum
prelientur prelia Domini.

Annon Abram cesurus quatuor reges impios, ad roborandum
expeditionem accepit in socios Aner, Escol et Mambre? (Gen.
xiv).[126] Annon rex Israel per Dei uoluntatem expugnaturus Moab
inimicantem Deo, sibi in adiutorium associauit regem Iuda et regem
Edom? (iv Reg. iii).[127]

Postea ut apud regiam maiestatem de communis assensus unanimi
diligentia, premissis et admonitionibus et eruditionibus et obsecrationibus satagatur etiam prestationibus, si forte ad clementie mansuetudinem inclinetur per diuinam Illius operationem de quo dicitur
(Prou. xxi): 'Sicut ductiones aquarum, ita cor regis in manu Domini;
quocunque uoluerit inclinabit illud.'[128]

Rex euangelicus iturus committere bellum aduersus alium regem,
priusquam procedat ad confligendum securus cogitat quid facto opus
sit; et si euidenter emineat de bellico conflictu periculosior euentus,
rogat ea que pacis sunt (Luc. xiv).[129] Numquid non patriarcha Iacob,
reuersus in patriam, Esau fratris seuitiam decreuit copiosis muneribus
esse placandam? (Gen. xxxii).[130] Numquid non rex Iuda et de templo
et de palatio amplis preciosorum munerum largitionibus regem Syrie
auertit ab oppugnatione Ierusalem? (iv Reg. xii).[131]

Denique licet uenerandus cetus cardinalium prelatorum Anglie nec
immerito redarguat[a] ecclesie predicta grauamina et alia nonnulla

---

45a [a] *MS adds* ecclesia.

[123] Joel 1: 13–15.   [124] Exod. 17: 8–13.   [125] Isa. 37: 15, 36–7.
[126] Gen. 14: 13–16.   [127] 4 Kgs. (2 Kgs.) 3: 6–10.   [128] Prov. 21: 1.

house of your God; and cry ye to the Lord: Ah, ah, ah, for the day,
because the day of the Lord is at hand, and it shall come like
destruction from the mighty.'[123] Was not Amalek defeated by Israel
by the power of God at the prayer of Moses? (Exod. 17)[124] By the
prayer of Hesekiah (Isa. 37) were not a hundred and eighty five
thousand of the Assyrian army slain by the guardian angels, and was
not Sennacherib driven from Judaea?[125]

Then in appropriate ways the lord archbishop of Canterbury may
be stirred to act by the noble prudence of your piety, with his
suffragans, whom they are oppressing with weighty trouble and
vexations, as they ceaselessly groan and lament. Perhaps with their
ranks gathered together in battle lines, as was gloriously begun when
the lord Robert of holy memory, formerly bishop of Lincoln, was still
living in the flesh, toiling for this with his salutary watchfulness, they
may with one heart and mind in a common confidence of victory,
together with you fight the battles of the Lord.

Did not Abraham, when he was going to strike four profane kings,
take Aner, Escol, and Membre as companions to strengthen his
expedition? (Gen. 14)[126] Did not the king of Israel, setting out by
the will of God to fight Moab, the enemy of God, associate with him
as helpers the king of Juda and the king of Edom? (4 Kgs. 3)[127]

Afterwards, by common agreement and with unanimous effort, let
the king's majesty be actively pressed with the aforesaid admonitions,
instructions, and pleas, even with payments, if by chance he is disposed
to gentleness and mercy through the divine working of Him of whom it
is said (Prov. 21): 'At the division of the waters, so the heart of the king
is in the hand of the Lord; whithersoever he will, he shall turn it.'[128]

A king ruled by the Gospel, when setting out to make war against
another king, thinks carefully before proceeding to fight what needs
to be done, and if a more dangerous outcome may emerge from the
conflict of war, he asks for terms of peace (Luke 14).[129] Did not the
patriarch Jacob, when returning to his homeland, decide that the
wildness of his brother Esau should be tamed by copious gifts? (Gen.
32).[130] Did not the king of Juda, by the bestowal of many precious
gifts from his palace, deflect the king of Syria from attacking
Jerusalem? (4 Kgs. 12).[131]

Finally, although the venerable company of the cardinal prelates of
England not undeservedly rebukes the said oppressions of the Church

[129] Luke 14: 31-2.   [130] Gen. 32: 13-20.   [131] 4 Kgs. (2 Kgs.) 12: 17-19.

conniuentia,*b* immo desidia, modis omnibus expedire uidetur, secundum quod congruere iudicabitur, per nuntios ad hoc sufficientia
instructos affluenti summam Apostolice Sedis auctoritatem interpellare sine more dispendio, sicut alioquin licet adhuc minus
efficaciter factum est, ut per sanctissime papalis excellentie prouidentiam contra iam induratas horribilium errorum afflictiones quamuis dudum statuta denuo iura statuat, et per apostolicam
protectionem in idipsum manus prelatorum roborare dignetur.
Stupendus est admodum si quis in tanto gemine dilectionis erga
diuinam maiestatem et ecclesiasticam necessitatem negotio, quam-
cunque licet ubicunque prosequendo causetur uel laborum difficulta-
tem uel nimietatem sumptuum, dicente Domino (Ap. i), qui dilexit
nos et lauit nos a peccatis nostris in sanguine suo (Matt. xi), 'Venite
ad me omnes, qui laboratis et onerati estis, et ego reficiam uos'.[132] Et
iterum (Cant. ult.) 'Si dederit homo omnem substantiam domus sue,
pro dilectione quasi nichil despiciet eam'.[133]

46a. *Qualiter agere incumbit sepe scripto archiepiscopo si deficiat omnis
humane considerationis secundum formas iam dictas sancta moderatio.*
Quod si deficiat omnino ecclesie Dei reformande secundum formas
nunc dictas prouide superspectionis sancta sollicitudo, quid nunc
restare dignoscitur, nisi ut omnipotenti Sapientie, superclementi
prouidentie, committendo que tam beatifici amoris tam sollicito
amore tam condigne formidantur, sub patrocinio diuino, per angelicum presidium cum sanctorum adiutorio, in suffragio sacramentorum, archipresulis uestri, quantum ad mortalium societatem uirtus
solitaria contra diros hostes ecclesie dura subeat certamina per
patientie longaminis indefessam*a* constantiam. Solus Saluator |
principatum huius mundi superatum exterminauit, per quem solum
Saluatorem solus Helyas Samariam, solus Elisius Syriam, solus
Petrus circumcisionem, solus Paulus preputium[134] (Gal. ii), solus
Thomas Angliam, et sic ceteri innumerabiles celestis regni propugna-
tores soli, scilicet sine collegis certaminum, immanissimas seculi
tyrannides nonnunquam triumphaliter oppugnasse cognoscuntur.

f. 101

b coniuentia *MS.*

46a *a* indefensam *MS.*

and some other cases, it seems that their connivance, nay, their sloth is absolutely expedient, and in accordance with this it will be judged best to appeal without delay to the supreme authority of the Apostolic See through envoys, abundantly equipped for this, as has been done in other cases, though yet less effectively; so that through the pope's most holy providence he may re-establish laws (which have been enacted long since) against the afflictions and horrible errors of long duration, and that he may through his apostolic protection deign to strengthen the hands of prelates for this purpose. It is a wonderful thing when a man engaged in so great a matter from his twofold love of the divine majesty and of the Church-in-need should in pursuit of this contend with labour and difficulty or excessive expense whatever or wheresoever; as the Lord (Rev. 1), who has loved us and washed us from our sins in His blood (Matt. 11), says, 'Come unto me all you that labour and are burdened, and I will refresh you';[132] and again (Song of Songs last): 'If a man should give all the substance of his house for love, he shall despise it as nothing.'[133]

46a. *How it is incumbent upon the oft-named archbishop to act if holy restraint according to the forms aforesaid fails to win any human consideration*

But if a holy solicitude and prudent oversight in the forms now stated should wholly fail to produce the reform of the Church of God, what, do we know, remains except that, committing to the Almighty Wisdom, to the most merciful providence the things that are rightly feared, with so solicitous a love for a love so beatific, under the divine patronage, through the protection of the saints and the assistance of the sacraments, the virtue of our archbishop, alone so far as mortals are concerned, should undergo a hard struggle against the dread enemies of the Church with the tireless constancy of his long-suffering patience. The Saviour alone overcame and drove out the principality of this world; through the Saviour alone Elyas conquered Samaria; Elisius alone conquered Syria; Peter alone overcame the circumcision; Paul alone the foreskin (Gal. 2);[134] Thomas alone conquered England; and thus the rest of the innumerable champions of the kingdom of heaven alone, that is without comrades in their struggle, are known to have at times fought triumphantly against the most monstrous tyrannies of the world.

---

[132] Matt. 11: 28. [133] Song of Songs 8: 7. [134] Cf. Gal. 2: 3–7.

47a. *Finalis terminus epistole*

Consideret, obsecro, dignitatis uestre sublimis intelligentia, priusquam aut admittantur aut abiciantur, utrum hec uerba hoc loco referri debeant uel ad lacessentem ignauiam uel ad industriam prospicientem. Propter semetipsum doceat nos de omnibus Dei Filius magister omnium, unus Christus, per Spiritum Sanctum suum docens omnem ueritatem (Ioh. xvi),[135] ut ambulantes in lumine Ipsius (Ys. ix), per uite presentis caliginem[136] perseuerenter in omnibus prudenter discernendo, agendo fortiter, temperanter cohibendo, distribuendo equaliter, omnia perpetue referatis ad illum finem ubi est Deus omnia in omnibus, eternitate certa et pace perfecta,[137] per cuius altissimam miserationem conseruetur ecclesie sue per tempora diuturna desiderandissima sanctitatis uestre sospitas in Christo Iesu semper et beatissima Virgine. Amen.

47a. *The final end of the letter*

I beg your lordship with your high understanding to consider whether these words, before they are either accepted or rejected, ought in this place to lead to arousing people from idleness or to a prospect of action. For his own sake may the Son of God, the master of all, teach us all truth through his Holy Spirit (John 16),[135] that walking in his light (Isa. 9) through the dark mist of the present life,[136] making prudent distinctions and persevering in everything, acting steadfastly, governing with moderation, and apportioning with equity, you may perpetually refer all things to that end, where God is all in all, assuredly in eternity and perfect peace.[137] By his most high mercy may the most desired health of your holiness be preserved for his Church for a long time to come, ever in Christ Jesus and the Blessed Virgin. Amen.

[135] John 16: 13.   [136] Isa. 60: 19.
[137] Augustine, *De civitate Dei*, xix. 20; *CSEL* xl, ii. 407, a valediction used by Adam in several letters.

INDEX OF QUOTATIONS AND ALLUSIONS

A. THE BIBLE

Old Testament

Genesis
1: 26 — 6
2: 7 — 598
2: 18 — 379
3: 14 — 233
14: 13–16 — 642
25: 22 — 209
27: 12–44 — 101
28: 12 — 22, 193, 482
32: 13–20 — 642
Exodus
17: 8–13 — 642
23: 8 — 196
23: 20–3 — 342
23: 27, 29–30 — 342
23: 29–30 — 344
25: 40 — 278
30: 34–7 — 591
30: 35–6 — 593
31: 7–11, 18 — 194
32: 6 — 142
32: 32 — 406
33: 13 — 596
Leviticus
19: 18 — 199
19: 15 — 196, 203
Numbers
6: 14, 17 — 142
22: 5 — 564
24: 4 — 564
25: 4 — 608
27: 16–17 — 5, 7
Deuteronomy
1: 13 — 22, 27, 100, 155, 180, 186, 363, 583
7: 11–24 — 342
7: 22 — 344
27: 19 — 196, 203
27: 25 — 203
28: 28–9 — 231
32: 4 — 492

32: 10 — 126
32: 41–2 — 619
Joshua
7: 8 — 111
1 Kings (1 Samuel)
2: 25 — 131
3 Kings (1 Kings AV)
8: 51 — 101
18: 21 — 89
19: 18 — 60
20: 39 — 223, 410, 608
4 Kings (2 Kings AV)
1: 9–12 — 325
3: 6–10 — 642
6: 16 — 42
6: 17 — 42
9: 16–26 — 355
12: 17–19 — 643
17: 33 — 189
19: 3 — 229
2 Chronicles
29: 13–16 — 217
33: 12–13 — 595
33: 12 — 597
Tobias
3: 21–3 — 258, 572, 632
3: 22 — 270
12: 8 — 591
Judith
8: 22 — 631
9: 1, 18–19 — 102
9: 16–17 — 591
13: 17 — 88
Esther
13: 2 — 356
13: 17 — 598
14: 2–3 — 102
Job
4: 2 — 3
4: 18 — 307
5: 2 — 379

Job (*cont.*)
6: 12	113, 433, 479
9: 4	636
9: 28, 30	305
10: 1	74
12: 4–5	145
13: 15	472
15: 15	307
20: 15	34
25: 2	575
31: 28	338
38: 10–11	462
39: 19–22	504
39: 19, 21–2, 25	42, 122
39: 19, 22, 25	112, 212
39: 21–5	610
39: 21–2	430
40: 18	34
40: 24	59

Psalms
3: 7	504
17: 14	130
26: 3	504, 631
26: 14	330
33: 8	325
50: 11–12	596
63: 8	107
76: 10	260
90: 1	636
93: 9	566
101: 18, 21–2	571
105: 47	598
106: 16	60
113: 1	203
115: 15	350
121: 6	229
147: 15	452

Proverbs
4: 23	600
8: 14–17	335
9: 7	426
9: 9	363
14: 13	459, 568
16: 7	361
16: 18	359
16: 32	258, 329
18: 6	117
20: 8	325
20: 9	305
21: 1	330, 642
22: 10	426
22: 16	622
28: 1	42, 346

28: 14	305
29: 11	348

Ecclesiastes
31: 28	109

Song of Songs
1: 3	592, 596
2: 15	235
6: 6	613
8: 7	645

Wisdom
2: 9	229
6: 2–9	605
6: 13	61
7: 26	110
7: 27	74
7: 30	41
8: 1	68, 107, 130, 143, 191, 212, 346, 472, 508
11: 24–5	454
11: 24–5, 27	268
11: 24, 27	387
11: 27–12: 1–2	454
11: 27	307
12: 18	41, 196, 200, 361
18: 14–19	131

Ecclesiasticus
7: 37–8	216, 301
11: 27	268
20: 7	348
21: 29	348
23: 4–6	596
27: 12	415
34: 25	622
35: 17	548

Isaiah
1: 5–6	159
5: 7	634
27: 1	186, 233
28: 18	628
28: 19	628
29: 4	229
37: 15, 36–7	642
40: 4	60
40: 31	156, 540
49: 15	268
53: 3	107, 260
53: 5, 7	107
56: 9–12	5, 20, 36, 179
56: 9–11	616
56: 10	179
56: 11	607
57: 18	268
58: 7–8	103

59: 1   568, 587

60: 19   647

64: 6   304

64: 1   131

65: 25   233

Jeremiah

2: 13   237

2: 36   264, 510

3: 1–4   265

3: 1   172, 510

7: 4   618

9: 1   34, 462

12: 7   474

15: 19   626

17: 18   196

29: 7   594

Lamentations

1: 6   111

1: 10   188

Ezechiel

33: 6   132, 221, 608

34: 2–6   9

34: 2–5   296

34: 5, 8   605

Daniel

7: 10   74

9: 17–18   594

Joel

1: 13–15   642

Amos

4: 1   622

6: 1, 7–8   566

6: 6   624

9: 9   209

Obadiah

3–4   231

Micah

3: 11–12   296

3: 11   618

3: 12   618

3: 9–12   20

6: 8   335

Habakkuk

3: 11   131, 619

Zechariah

9: 11   107, 607

Malachi

2: 1–3   265

1 Maccabees

1: 2–4   596

1: 4   237

2 Maccabees

10: 38   356

New Testament

Matthew

1: 21   588

3: 9   382

5: 7   554

5: 9   116, 523

5: 10–12   42

5: 39–41   615

5: 40   117

6: 24   189

6: 33   368

7: 8   474

8: 24–6   459

9: 37–8   587

9: 38   114

10: 16   307

10: 18–19   632

10: 19–20   145

10: 20   632

10: 25   145

11: 28   223, 645

12: 30   189

13: 29   638

14: 14   329

17: 2–4   194

23: 24   638

24: 15   126

24: 21   126

24: 28   74

24: 45   622

25: 21   114

26: 75   473

28: 18   151

28: 20   69, 151, 509, 632

Mark

4: 37–9   69

4: 38–9   459

9: 1–4   194

Luke

1: 77   476

1: 78   476

3: 8   382, 602

6: 36   554

8: 23–4   303

10: 2   114

Luke (*cont.*)

10: 7	624
10: 27	599
10: 42	406
14: 31–2	643
15: 10	454
15: 11–24	511
15: 13–24	172, 456
16: 10	186
16: 19, 22	109
21: 15	632
21: 19	259, 574
21: 28	120, 333
22: 31–2	211
22: 38	632
22: 62	473
23: 42	586

John

6: 37	333, 387, 442
6: 44	600
10: 1	584
10: 2–4	179
10: 7	179, 584
10: 11	211, 584
10: 12	118, 135
11: 3	163
13: 1	163
14: 6	128
14: 21	593
14: 27	227
15: 5	156, 406, 592
15: 13	173
15: 15	392
16: 7	392, 576
16: 13	647
16: 23	588
16: 24	602
16: 33	42, 118, 134, 151, 211, 224, 254, 406, 512, 568, 631
17: 11, 20–3	576
17:11	74, 574
17: 20–1	597
17: 22, 24	74
17: 24	596
21: 15–16	194
21: 17	254

Acts

12: 5	594

Romans

3: 8	602
5: 20	270
8: 8	474
8: 31	134, 151, 325

11: 20	608
12: 1	9, 142, 179, 584
12: 15	624
12: 18	225
13: 8	210, 367
13: 13–14	235
15: 4	32
15: 30–2	596
16: 20	34, 632

1 Corinthians

1: 20	248
1: 24	636
1: 27	59
3: 3	235
3: 6–7	66
3: 7	171
4: 1–2	624
4: 3	305
4: 5	376
4: 12–13	615
6: 1–7	117, 235
6: 7	235
12: 31–13: 1	425
13: 1–3	610
14: 14–15	598

2 Corinthians

1: 3	387
1: 4	629
4: 4	277
4: 17	628
5: 16	392
11: 20	50
11: 29	172
12: 2	600
13: 7	596

Galatians

2: 3–7	645
5: 15	235

Ephesians

3: 18	612
5: 16	209
6: 12	133, 189, 566

Philippians

1: 9–11	596
1: 23	260
4: 7	118, 381
4: 13	156, 631

Colossians

1: 12–13	571
1: 13	34, 36, 236, 575
1: 20	13, 155
3: 12–13	225

1 Thessalonians
  4: 13   527
2 Thessalonians
  3: 10   221, 624
1 Timothy
  2: 1–2   595
  2: 4   167
  2: 9–10   381
  3: 15, 16   239
  5: 23   113
  5: 8   103
  5: 17   196
2 Timothy
  2: 24   117, 225, 235
  4: 2   158
  4: 5   194, 217, 270, 277
Hebrews
  4: 12   529
  5: 1   602
  5: 4   252
  5: 7   576
  9: 11   177
  10: 28–9   20, 265
  10: 29   180
  10: 32–4   628
  11: 36–8   610
  12: 6   628
James
  1: 4   259

  1: 5–6   632
  1: 6–7   588
  1: 12   636
  1: 17   189, 397, 529
  3: 14–16   236
  3: 15   229
  3: 17   236
  4: 3   600
  5: 14–15   596
1 Peter
  1: 3, 6–7   628
  1: 25   452
  2: 11–12   267
  2: 25   442
  3: 1–4   381
  5: 6–7   330
1 John
  3: 7   210
  5: 4   60
Revelation
  3: 15–16   189
  6: 10   566
  9: 10   212
  12: 4   229
  12: 12   47
  14: 4   475
Pr. of Man.   597

B. NON-BIBLICAL SOURCES

Avicenna, *Liber de philosophia prima*
                                516–17
Aristotle, *Nicomachean Ethics*, viii. 5
                                392–3
Augustine, *De civitate Dei*:
  i. 30–1   344–5
  i. 30   344–5
  i. 31   344–5
  xix. 2   191–2, 580–1, 600–1
  xix. 19   254–5
  xix. 20   24–5, 176–7, 196–7, 240–1,
          314–15, 320–1, 356–7, 363–4,
                446–7, 536–7, 646–7
Bernard:
De consideratione ad Eugenium Papam,
  iv. 7   4–5, 634–5, 638–9

Sermones super Cantica 10   624–5
Chrysostom, John, *De cruce et latrone
  homilia*   586–7
Gregory the Great, *Moralia in Iob* 516–17
  x. c. 29   236–7, 334–5
Grosseteste, Robert, *De regno et
  tyrannide*   56–7
Jerome, *Epistolae* 48   106–7
Nova lux Iudeis visa est   564–5
Peter Lombard, *Sentences*   104–5, 464–5
Rhabanus Maurus, *De natura rerum*
                                516–17
Richard of St Victor, *De Trinitate* 484–5

INDEX

A. of Brangford, Brother, 488–9

A. of Hereford, Brother, Adam's socius, 412–13

Abingdon, *see* Edmund of; Robert of

Achab 132–3

Adam de Bechesoveres, physician, 420–3, 530–1, 558–9; letters to: nos. 238–9

Adam de Berners, abbot of Oseney, 14–15, 524–5

Adam of Buckfield, Master, 150–1 and n. 1

Adam of Hekeshovere, Brother, 102–3

Agnellus of Pisa, English provincial minister, xiii, xv

Aigueblanche, *see* Peter of

Albini, Isabella d', countess of Arundel, 440–1

Aldeham, *see* Peter of

Alexander III, king of Scotland (1249–86), 52 n. 3

Alexander IV, pope, xlii

Alexander of Hales, xvi

Alnwick, *see* Martin of

Amwell, *see* Henry of

Andrew of Lexington, Brother, reformer of Franciscan province of Ireland; vicar of the English provincial, 420–1, 502–3, 516–17, 542–3, 560–3; letter to: no. 240

Anian I (Einion), bishop of St Asaph's (1249–66), 312–13, 552–3

Anilers (Amilyers), *see* N. de

Anjou, *see* Henry of

Anstand, *see* Thomas of

Antioch, depopulation of, 348–9

Aristotle: *libri naturales*, 150 n. 1; translation of *Ethics*, 64–5, 392–3

Arius, 132–3

Arnold, Brother, 138–9

Arnulf, Brother, 138–9

Artaxerxes, 356 n. 3

Arundel, *see* William of

Ashwell, *see* Warin of

Atchirche, *see* John of

Athanasius the Alexandrian 132–3

Augustine of Hippo, St, 132–2, 426–7, 622–3; *De Doctrina Christiana*, used by Adam Marsh, xviii

Avicenna, 516–17

Aymer de Valence (Lusignan), bishop elect of Winchester (1250–60), 12 and n. 2, 13 and n. 1, 30–1, 44–5, 152 n. 1, 156–7 and n. 1, 166–9, 312–15, 447–8, 450–1, 543 n. 2; letter to: no. 124

Bacon, Brother Thomas, 470–1

Bacon, Roger, xviii n. 27, 304 n. 2

Balsham, *see* Hugh of

Banbury (Oxon), 52–5; *see also* John of

Barford St Michael (Oxon), 70–1 and n. 4

Barjols, Hugh de, *see* Hugh of Die

Bartholomew, rector of Reedwell, 306–9; letter to: no. 119

Basing, *see* William of

Basingstoke, *see* John of

Baskerville, Anora de, abbess of Elstow, 122–3 and n. 2

Basset, Fulk, bishop of London (1244–59), 92 n. 2, 146–7, 458–9; letter to: no. 74

Batale, Brother William, 374–5, 402–3

Bath, *see* Henry of; Reginald of

Bath and Wells, bishop of, *see* Giffard, Walter

Beauchamp, Ida, countess of, 390–1; letter to: no. 163

Beauchamp, William, sheriff of Worcester, 11 n. 1, 366–7, 390–1; letter to: no. 148

Bechesoveres, *see* Adam de

Bedford, archdeacon of, *see* John of Dyham

Bel, Robert le, *see* Robert le Bel

Bellun, Brother William, 544–55; letters to: nos. 226–35

Belton priory, *see* Grace Dieu

benefices, presentation to, 68–9, 104–5, 180–3, 540–1

Berions, Hugh de, *see* Hugh of Die

Bernard of Clairvaux, St, 4–5 and n. 5, 624–5

Berners, *see* Adam de

Beverley, *see* John of

Bishop Wearmouth, Northumberland, rector of, xiv and n. 9

Blanche of Castile, queen of France, 522–3

Bloxham (Oxon), vicarage of, 54–5, 64–5, 68–71

Bluet (Bloet), Emma, prioress of Godstow, 366–7; letter to: no. 149

Bonaventure, St, minister-general of the Friars Minor, 396–400; letters to: 166–7

Boniface of Savoy, archbishop of Canterbury (1241–70), xxvi, xli–xlii, xlvi, xlviii, 57 n. 1, 323 n. 1, 349 n. 15, 359 n. 7, 372 n. 2, 386 n. 2, 430 n. 9; excommunicates the bishop of London 146–7, 152–3; *familia* of, 104–5, 446–7, 458–9; leaves England for papal Curia, 92–3, 146–7; letters to: nos. 1–5; metropolitan visitations of, xvii, xxviii, 92–3, 146–7, 409 n. 1, 428–9, 434–5; official of, *see* Lynn, Mortimer; seeks Adam's assistance, 446–50, 458–9, 460–1

Bordeaux, commune of, 80–1

Bosellis, Gregory de, xxxviii, 1 and n. 2, 98–9, 104–5 and n. 9, 266–7, 340–1, 348–9 and n. 13, 352–3, 358–9, 376–7, 384–5, 400–1 n. 1, 408 n. 6, 436–7, 473, 500–1, 528–9, 562–3; letter to: no. 241

Boulogne, 448–9, 452–3

Bovill, Sewal de, archbishop of York (1256–8), 574–647; letter to: no. 245; royal mandate to 627–8

Bradley, *see* Walter de

Brangford, *see* A. of

Brie, *see* Geoffrey de

Bromhall Priory (Berks.), 128–9

Buckden (Huntingdon): bishop of Lincoln's manor of and palace, xix, xxix, xxxiii, 31 n. 4, 97–8, 100–1, 138–9, 308–11, 430–1, 434–5; bailiff of, *see* Marsh, William

Buckfield, *see* Adam of

Buckingham, archdeacon of, *see* Matthew de Stratton

Buoncompagno, *Antiqua Rhetorica* of, xlv–xlvi and n. 135

Burewardiscote, *see* Roger de

Cambridge, 410 n. 4, 416–17, 421 n. 1, 423 n. 1, 425 n., 430–3, 479 n. 3, 534–7, 563 n. 1

Canterbury: archbishops of, *see* Boniface; Edmund of Abingdon; archdeacon of, *see* Stephen of Vienne; Christ Church Priory of, 30 n. 1, 226–41; consistory court of, 72–3; Franciscans of, xiii, 226–7; official of, *see* Lynn, Mortimer; prior of, *see* Nicholas of Sandwich; synod of, 153 n. 2, 169 n. 3; *see also* Ralph of

Cantilupe, Walter, bishop of Worcester (1236–66), xlii, 10–11, 32–3, 78–9, 338–9, 352–3, 450–1; letters to: no. 70–1, 73

Carru (Carew), N. de, 148–9 and n.

Causton (Norfolk) 273 n. 1; *see also* Jerome/Jeremy de

Cauz, Geoffrey de (judge), 246–9; letter to: no. 95

Cauz, Geoffrey de (knight), 247 n. 1

Cerde, *see* William of

Chauverture, Walter de, prior of Newnham, 240 n. 1; letter to: no. 91

Chesterton (Cambs.), parish of, 221 n. 5

Chorasmians, 514–15 and n. 7

Chrysostom, St John, 586–7

Cirencester, *see* William of

Cistercian Order, runaway from, 170–1

clergy (secular): benefit of, 12 n. 2, 626–7; celibacy of, 22–3; criticism of, 114–15, 178–81, 382–3, 604–5, 620–1, 624–5; taxation of, 12 n. 2, 47 n. 4, 176 n. 1, 626–7

Cofle, oratory at, 148–9

Corbridge, *see* Ralph of

Corham, Henry, 243 n. 1

Cornwall: countess of, *see* Sancia of Provence; earl of, *see* Richard of Cornwall; *see also* Thomas of

Cote, Brother Hugh, 454–5, 464–5, 472–3, 474–5

Courçon, Cardinal Robert, xv

Crakehall, *see* John of

Crescentia, *see* Gregory de

Crescentius of Jesi, minister general of Friars Minor (1244–7), 320–1, 514–15

Crusade of St Louis: defeat of, 52–5, 352–5; preaching of, 404–5

Cuchur, Roger, 310–11

Curia, papal, xvi, xxi, xxix, 136–7, 146–7, 400–3, 408–9, 434 n. 2, 514–17, 524–5, 538–9

Darlington, *see* John of
Derby, *see* John of
Desiderius, Franciscan provincial of Burgundy, 514–15
Despencer, Geoffrey de, 164–5, 312–13, 364–5; letter to: no. 146
Die, *see* Hugh of
Dington, *see* John of
Dionysius Exiguus, *see* Pseudo-Dionysius
Docking, *see* Thomas of
Dorchester, abbot of, *see* Robert of Dorchester
Dover, *see* Simon of
Druel (Druer), S., knight, 366–7, 390–1
Durham, *see* William of; bishop of, *see* Marsh, Richard
Dyham, *see* John of

Easthall, *see* Robert of
Eccleston, *see* Thomas of
Edmund of Abingdon, St, archbishop of Canterbury (1234–40), 300–1
Edward of Westminster, keeper of the King's Works, rector of Milton Keynes, 40–1 and n. 8, 628–9
Eleanor of Provence, queen of England, xxxviii–xxxix, 42–5, 68–9, 98–9, 128–9, 275 n., 358–9, 362–3, 368–75, 386–7, 400–1, 404–9, 440–3, 448–9, 538–41, 502–3, 550–1; letters to: 150–3
Elias, Brother, Franciscan minister-general, xxxiv
Elstow Abbey: abbess of, *see* Baskerville; community of, 122–3
Ely, bishops of, *see* Hugh of Balsham; Hugh of Northwold
Erlandson, John, bishop of Roskilde (1249–53), 18–25; letter to: no. 8
Esrigge, Peter, 298–9
Essex, archdeacon of, *see* Hugh of St Edmund
Eugenius III, pope, 634–5
Eustace of Normanville, lector, chancellor of Oxford, 420–1, 424–5, 488–9
Eustache of Lynn, official of Archbishop Boniface, 64–5 and n. 6, 98–9, 152 n. 1, 244 n. 1, 300–1, 540–1; letters to: nos. 93, 115

Evesham, *see* Walter of

Faba, Guido, xlv–xlvi
Faversham, *see* Haymo of
Felda, *see* John de
Fingest (Bucks.), rector of, 160–1
Francis of Assisi, St, xiii
Franciscan brothers, 568–75; letters to: nos. 243–4
Friars Minor, Order of: general chapters of, xiii, xvii n. 24, xxxii–xxxiv, xxxvii, 24–5 and n. 13, 105 n. 9; ministers general of, *see* Bonaventure; Crescentius of Iesi; Elias; John of Parma; ministers of the English province, election of, 480–1; *see also* Haymo of Faversham; John of Stamford; Peter of Tewkesbury; William of Nottingham; privileges of, 400–1, 514–15, 538–9; reform of, xxxiv, 490–1; provision of lectors in, 482–4; at Oxford, xxxiv–xxxv, 416–17, 438–9, 494–5
Frille, *see* R. de
Fuldon, *see* Roger de

G. of St Edmund, Brother, 494–5
Gabriel, vicar of the minister general, 514–17
Gallus, Thomas, abbot of St Andrew's, Vercelli, xxiii–xxiv, 219 n. 1; letter to: no. 87
Gascony, duchy of, xxxix–xli, 79–91, 96–7, 326–7, 331 n., 348–9, 376–7, 378 n. 1, 383 n. 2, 384–5, 386 n. 3, 500–1
Geoffrey de Brie, minister of the French province, 518–21; letters to: no. 212–13
Geringes, Robert de, 214–15
Gien, S. (St Germans), Master, 260–1, 306–7; letter to: no. 101
Giffard, Walter, bishop of Bath and Wells (1264–6), 318–19 and n. 2
Godstow, abbey (Oxon), 36–7, 52–3, 54–5, 68–9, 76–7, 366–7; abbess of, *see* Bluet
Grace Dieu priory (Belton, Leics.), 66–7 and n. 8, 72–3, 90–1, 170–1, 204–5, 206–7
Gras, Master John le, 62–3 and n. 1

Gravesend, Richard, archdeacon of
   Oxford (1249–54), dean of Lincoln
   (1254–8), bishop of Lincoln
   (1258–79), transl. to London
   (1280–1303), xx, 58–9 and n. 5, 95
   n. 3, 248 n. 1; letters to: nos. 75, 96
Greece, minister general's visit to, 25
   n. 13, 134–5
Gregory de Crescentia, 150–1
Grimele, Master William, 166–7
Gros, Geoffrey le, rector of Ockendon,
   180–1 and n. 11
Grosseteste, Robert, bishop of Lincoln
   (1235–53): addresses Pope Innocent
   IV on abuses, xxviii, 130–9, 144–8;
   dispute with the Lincoln chapter,
   116–19; educates Montfort's
   children, 146–7, 336–7; *familia* of,
   32–3; *see also* John of Crakehall;
   Roger, steward of Bishop
   Grosseteste; Thomas of York;
   William of Lincoln; his funeral, 430
   n. 9; his Greek studies and
   translations, xxii–xxiii, 64–5; letters
   to: nos. 9–69; management of his
   estates, 70–1; opposes grant of
   ecclesiastical tenth to King, 47 n. 4;
   posthumous reports of sanctity,
   612–13; his relations with Adam
   Marsh, xviii–xxx; relations with
   monks of Canterbury, 226–41; his
   relations with University of Oxford,
   39–41, 50–1, 100–1; report on his
   health, 384–5; his sister Juetta, 32–3,
   148–9; visits Godstow abbey, 68–9;
   visits papal Curia, 144–7, 514–15;
   writings 56–7; his written works left
   to the Franciscans, 184–5
Guernsey, earthquake at, 126–7

H. of Syreford, Brother, 506–7
Hadley, *see* William of
Hailes Abbey (Glos.), 52–3
Hales, *see* Alexander of; Thomas of
Hampton, Sir William, 370–1
Haverin, *see* Richard of
Haye, Sir John de la, 336–7, 386–7
Haymo of Faversham, 472 n. 1
Hekeshovere, *see* Adam of
Hemingborough, *see* William of
Henry III, King of England (1216–72),
   313 n. 1, 318 n. 2, 320–1, 336–7,
   358–9, 364 n. 1, 370–1, 386–7,

400–3, 404–5, 408–9, 432–3, 446–7,
   449–52, 459–60, 554–5; is angered
   by Adam's preaching and debars
   him from court, 462–3, 548–9;
   assembly for feast of the Confessor,
   108 n.; commissions Simon de
   Montfort to govern Gascony, xxxix;
   commutes his crusading vow and
   obtains papal mandate to tax the
   clergy, 626–7; expedition to
   Gascony, 14–15 n. 2; orders arrest of
   the rebel shepherds in England,
   56–9; his patronage of the friars,
   xxxvii; his political ineptitude, xli;
   presides over trial of Montfort,
   xl–xlii, 78–91; spends Christmas at
   Winchester, 402–3; takes the Cross,
   404 n. 3, 626 n. 92; visits Oxford and
   is petitioned by the University, 66–7
Henry of Amwell, abbot of Waltham, 223
   n. 1; letter to: no. 88
Henry of Anjou, 314–15; letter to: no. 126
Henry of Bath, canonist, 524–5
Henry of Lexington, bishop of Lincoln
   (1253–8), 34 n. 1, 188 n. 10, 274–5,
   552–3
Henry of Segusia, *see* Hostiensis
Henry of Thorney, Master, 168–9
Hereford, *see* A. of; John, Brother of;
   bishop of, *see* Peter of Aigueblanche
Holy Cross, Robert of, 444–5
Holy Land, state of, 52–3, 66–7, 348–9,
   352–3, 432–3, 514–15, 626–7
Horningdun, Juliana de, 272–3
Hose, William de la, 386–7
Hostiensis, Cardinal Henry of Segusia,
   516–17 and n. 12
Hugh of Balsham, bishop of Ely
   (1256–86), xvii
Hugh of Die (de Barjols, de Berions),
   64–5 and n. 3, 138–9
Hugh of Lewknor, Brother, 482–3
Hugh of Lyndon, 488–9, 492–3
Hugh de Mandeville, 160–1
Hugh of Mistreton, Brother, OP,
   canonist, 466–7
Hugh of Northwold, bishop of Ely
   (1229–54), 538–9
Hugh of St Edmund, archdeacon of
   Essex, 215 n. 1; letter to: no. 85
Hukelby, Master Ralph, 546–7
Huntingdon, archdeacon of, *see* William of
   Arundel

Innocent IV, pope, 135 n. 15, 313 n. 2,
  400 n. 2, 408 n. 7, 430–1 n. 11, 447
  n. 5, 512–13, 626 n. 92; privilege
  Petitionibus vestris of, 400–1, 506
  n. 2, 512–15
Ireland, Franciscan province of, 420–1,
  502–5
Iver (Bucks.), church of, 150–1

Jean de la Rochelle, Master, xvi
Jerome, St, 106–7
Jerome/Jeremy de Causton, 272–3; letters
  to: nos. 105, 111
Joachim of Fiore, prophecies of, xxx,
  118–21
John of Atchirche 244–5
John of Banbury, Brother, 334–5
John of Basingstoke, archdeacon of
  Leicester, 216 n. 1; letter to: no. 85
John of Beverley, 540–1
John of Crakehall, archdeacon of Bedford,
  Grosseteste's steward, 48–9, 52–3,
  58–9, 70–1, 256–7, 276–9, 308–11,
  314–15 n. 3, 320–1, 516–17; letters
  to: nos. 94, 99, 109, 120–2, 130
John of Darlington, OP, xxxviii
John of Derby, Master, 186–7
John of Dington, Brother 444–5
John of Dyham, archdeacon of Bedford
  (*c*.1246–60), 96–7, 162–3
John de Felda, abbot of Gloucester, 448–9
John of Kemesing, Brother, 444–5
John of Kent, Brother, papal nuncio,
  246–7 and n. 3, 410–11 and n. 3,
  438–9, 524–7, 538–9; letters to:
  nos. 215–17
John of Leicester, 158–9
John of Lexington, royal judge, steward of
  the king's household, 364–5; letter
  to: no. 147
John of London 304–5 and n. 2
John of Parma, minister general of
  Franciscans (1247–57), 24–5 nn.
  12–13, 390–5, 476–7, 496–9; letters
  to: nos. 164–5
John of Reading, formerly abbot of
  Oseney 422–3 and n. 4
John of St Giles, archdeacon of Oxford,
  94–5, 162–3, 458–9; letters to:
  nos. 77, 198–201
John of Sharstead, Master, canon of
  Lincoln, rector of Pocklington, 26–7
  and n. 1, 100–1

John of Stamford, custodian of Oxford,
  Franciscan provincial of England
  (1258–*c*.1264), 100–1 and n. 13,
  312–13, 396–7 and n. 3, 402–3,
  420–1, 434–5 n. 15, 452–3, 460–5,
  468–9, 484–5, 514–15, 526–33;
  letters to: nos. 189, 218–20
John of Stockton, canon of Huntingdon,
  46–7
John de Stokes, Master, 304–5; letter to:
  no. 118
John of Uffington, canon of Wells and
  Lincoln, commissary to Oxford
  chancellor, papal chaplain,
  dispensation for illegitimacy, xlvii,
  262–73; letters to: nos. 102–4
John of Warwick, Brother, 484–5
John of Weston, Brother, 478–9
John, Brother, custodian of Worcester,
  474–7; letter to: no. 194
John, Brother, guardian of Hereford,
  536–7; letter to: no. 536
judges delegate, papal, 458–9
Juetta, sister of Robert Grosseteste, 32–3,
  148–9 and n.
Juliana, a widow, 548–9

Kemesing, *see* John of
Kent, *see* John of
Kirkby, *see* Richard of
Knights Hospitallers, Order of, 370–1;
  English master of, *see* Manneby
Konole, Brother Robert, 472–3
Kyllum, Peter de, rector of St Mary's
  Oxford, 26–7, 252 n. 1, 253 n. 3,
  320–1; letter to: no. 98

La Rochelle, *see* Jean de
Lambeth, manor of, 152–3 and n. 1, 450–1
Langford, prebend of, 188–9 and n. 10; *see
  also* Roger of
Lard', Brother Abraham de, 514–15
Lateran Council, the Fourth (1215), xviii,
  xxvi
Laurence of St Martin, bishop of
  Rochester (1251–74), 115 n. 1
Laurence of Sutton, Brother, sought by
  Adam as secretary, 414–15, 508–9
Lechlade, *see* William of
Leicester: archdeacon of, *see* John of
  Basingstoke; Solomon of Dover; earl
  of, *see* Montfort, Simon de; *see also*
  John of

Leighton Buzzard, prebend of, 95 n. 4
Lewknor, *see* Hugh of
Lexington, *see* Andrew of; Henry of; John of
Lichfield, *see* W. of
Lincoln: archdeacon of, *see* Gravesend, Richard; Lupus, William; Marsh, Robert; Thomas of Wales; bishops of, *see* Grosseteste, Robert; Henry of Lexington; chancellor of, *see* Nicholas of Wadingham; chapter of, 116–17, 428–9, 512–13; dean of, *see* Gravesend, Richard; Marsh, Robert; diocese of, 428–9; prebends of, 184–9; *see also* William of
Little Wymondley priory, 216–17
Lombard, Peter, *Sentences* of, xviii, 104–5 and n. 8, 438 n. 2, 464–5
London: bishop of, *see* Basset, Fulk; chapter of, 146–7; Franciscan school at, 416–17, 422–3; Friars Preachers at, 176–7; Great Council at, 108–9; New Temple at, 626–7; *see also* John of; Simon of
Louis IX, king of France (1226–70), xvii, xxxvii, xlii, 52–5, 352–5
Ludlow, *see* William of
Lupus, William, archdeacon of Lincoln (1248–54/5), letter to: no. 76
Lutterworth Hospital, 164–5, 310–11, 364–5
Luvel, Master Philip, 628–9
Lyndon, *see* Hugh of
Lynn, *see* Eustache of
Lyons: papal Curia at, xvi, 93 n. 3, 136 n. 1, 348–9 n. 15, 377 n. 2, 501 n. 1, 508–9, 513–14; First Council of (1245), xvi, 312 n. 4, 512–17

Maddely, Brother Walter de, 402–3, 477–9 and n. 1
Mandeville, *see* Hugh de
Manneby, Robert, master of Hospitallers in England, 370–1
Manners, Peter de, 468–9
Mansel, John, the elder, King's minister, provost of Beverley, 184–7, 292–3, 318–21; letters to: no. 110, 129
Margaret, daughter of King Henry III, 52–3 and n. 3
Marham Abbey, 440 n. 5

MARSH, ADAM (de Marisco)
accompanies the archbishop on his visitations, 92–3, 146–7, 428–9
accompanies Grosseteste to the papal Curia, 512–15
applauds Grosseteste's demarche at the papal Curia regarding abuses of power, 137–9, 146–7
appointed delegate on mission to France to negotiate peace treaty, xvii
approves Grosseteste's translation of Aristotle's *Ethics*, 64–5
attends parliaments and synods, 12–13, 46–7
counsellor to Eleanor de Montfort, 376–90
declines request of Archbishop Boniface to join his *familia*, 446–50
on ecclesiology: the two swords, 634–5
his family, xiv, xix
influenced by Joachim of Fiore, 118–21
his instructions to Archbishop Sewall on prayer, 591–601
his interest in Greek translation and Pseudo-Dionysius, xxii–xxiv, 220–1
letters:
  to abbots, *see* Henry, abbot of Waltham; Robert, abbot of Dorchester; Thomas, abbot of St Andrew's, Vercelli
  to archbishops, *see* Boniface to Savoy; Bovill, Sewal de; Rigaud, Odo
  to archdeacons, *see* Hugh of St Edmund; John of Basingstoke; John of St Giles; Lupus, William; Matthew de Stratton; Rufus, Giles; Solomon of Dover
  to bishops, *see* Aymer de Valence; Basset, Fulk; Cantilupe, Walter; Grosseteste, Robert; Erlandson, James; Richard de Wych
  to counts and countesses, *see* Montfort, Eleanor de; Peter of Savoy, Sanchia of Provence
  to deans, *see* Gravesend, Richard
  to earls, *see* Monfort, Simon de
  to kings and queens, *see* Eleanor of Provence
  to masters, *see* Eustace of Lynn; Geoffrey de Cauz; Gien, S.; Gravesend, Richard; Henry of Anjou; Hugh de Mortimer; John of

MARSH, ADAM (*cont.*)
  letters: to masters (*cont.*)
    Uffington; Ralph of Canterbury;
      Ralph of Sempringham; Reginald of
      Bath; Roger de Fuldon; William of
      Pocklington
    to ministers general, *see* Bonaventure,
      St; John of Parma, *and also* letter
      214
    to priors and prioresses, *see* Bluet,
      Emma; Nicholas, prior of Christ
      Church Canterbury; Walter de
      Chauverture
    to provincial ministers, *see* Geoffrey de
      Brie; William of Nottingham, *and
      also* letters 209–10
    to others, *see* Adam de Bechesoveres;
      Andrew of Lexington; Bartholomew,
      rector of Reedwell; Beauchamp, Ida;
      Bellun, William; Bosellis, Gregory
      de; Despencer, Geoffrey; hordarius
      of Winchester Cathedral Priory;
      Jerome/Jeremy de Causton; John,
      Brother; John, guardian of Hereford;
      John of Crakehall; John of
      Lexington; John de Stokes; John of
      Stamford; Mansel, John; Monk,
      Ralph called; Peter de Kyllum; Peter
      of Stamford; Robert of Easthall;
      Robert of St Agatha; Robert of
      Thornham; Simon de Walton;
      Thomas of Anstan; Thomas of York;
      W., Brother; Walter de Bradele;
      Warin of Ashwell; William of
      Beauchamp; William of
      Hemingborough
  meets councillors on royal business at
    Reading and Odiham, 128–9
  negotiates in dispute between Christ
    Church Canterbury and bishop of
    Lincoln, 227–41
  on persecution of the Church, 626–31
  his preaching angers the king and he is
    debarred from court, 348–9, 446–7
  his regency at Oxford in Theology,
    xv–xvii, 32–3, 258–9, 464–8
  his relationship with Queen Eleanor,
    xxxviii–xxxix, 128–9, 368–73, 400–1,
    406–7
  his relations with Grosseteste, xviii–xxx
  reports to Grosseteste on management
    of his estates, 53
  his secretaries, xliii and n. 126

  seeks escape from duties imposed on
    him by the minister general, 498–9
  his spiritual guidance of Simon de
    Montfort, 332–9
  a *Summa de Penitentia* attributed to him,
    xviii
  witnesses the trial of Montfort over
    Gascony, 78–91
Marsh, Richard, bishop of Durham
  (1217–26), royal chancellor, xiv,
  124–5 and n.
Marsh, Master Robert, archdeacon of
  Oxford, dean of Lincoln, xix–xx,
  38–9 and n. 2, 94–5, 98–9, 102–3,
  140–1
Marsh, Thomas, Adam's relative, xix,
  30–3, 246–7, 292–3, 364–5, 548–9
Marsh, William, Adam's brother, bailiff of
  Buckden, xix, 308–9, 310 n. 1
Martin, Brother, guardian of Oxford,
  416–17, 492–3
Martin of Alnwick, Brother, 417 n. 1, 613
  n. 71
Matthew Paris, xl–xli, 434 n. 3
Matthew de Stratton, archdeacon of
  Buckingham (1221–69), 218–19 n. 1;
  letter to: no. 86
Merton, *see* Walter de
Mistreton, *see* Hugh of
monastic life, admissions to, 76–7, 170–1,
  222–3, 370–1, 470–1
Mongols, papal mission to, 514–15
Monk, Ralph called, 58–9, 442–3, 554–5;
  letters to: nos. 236–7
Montfort, Countess Eleanor de: Adam's
  spiritual advice to and reproof of,
  378–83; in conference with Queen
  Eleanor, 371–3; letters to:
  nos. 155–62; her pregnancy at
  Kenilworth, 326–7, 376–7
Montfort, Henry de, earl Simon's son,
  58–9
Montfort, Peter de, a loyal follower of
  Earl Simon, to whom he was
  unrelated, 78–9 and n. 5.
Montfort, Simon de, earl of Leicester:
  Adam Marsh's spiritual guidance of,
  332–9; Adam asked to join him and
  his wife in Boulogne, to assist them
  in negotiations, 448–9; his
  commission to govern Gascony,
  xxxix; his friendship with
  Grosseteste, xxxix; letters to,

nos. 133–44; in negotiation with
Raymond VII of Toulouse, 522–3;
his project to rescue captives, 58–9;
receives subvention from king for his
work in Gascony, 336–7; his trial
coram rege re Gascony, xl–xli, 78–91
Mortimer, Master Hugh de, official of
Archbishop Boniface, 322–3, 386–7,
446–7; letter to: no. 131
Mount Grace, *see* Grace Dieu
Multon, *see* Ralph of
Munchensy, *see* Warin de

N. de Anilers (Anibers?) (Amilyers),
Brother, 414–15, 518–20
Newnham Priory (Beds.), 104–5, 120–1;
prior of, *see* Chauventure, Walter de
Nicholas, Master Grecus, 554–5 and n. 5
Nicholas of Plumpton, Master, 628–9
Nicholas of Sandwich, prior of Christ
Church Canterbury (1244–58),
386–7; letter to: no. 90
Nicholas of Wadingham, chancellor of
Lincoln, 166–7 and n. 1
Normanville, *see* Eustace of
Northampton: archdeacon of, *see* Rufus,
Giles; Franciscans of, 374–5
Northwold, *see* Hugh of
Norton, *see* Robert of
Norwich, bishop of, *see* Ralegh, William;
Suffield, Walter
Nottingham, *see* William of

Ockendon (Wiskendum, Essex), church
of, 180–1
Odiham, Montfort's castle of, 128–9,
326–7
Odo of Chateauroux, cardinal-bishop of
Tusculum (1244–73), letters
reporting disaster of King Louis's
crusade, 44–5 and n. 5, 52–3, 54–5
Offinton, *see* John of Uffington
Oliver of Lexington, *see* Sutton, Oliver
Oseney (Oxon), 14–15, 46–7; abbot of, *see*
Berners, Adam de; John of Reading;
canons of, 150–1
Oxford, archdeacon of, *see* Gravesend,
Richard; John of St Giles; Marsh,
Robert; vintner of, 320–1
Oxford, University of, 62–3, 300–3, 307
n. 8, 316–17, 318 n. 2, 374–5, 416–17,
422–3, 450–1, 555 n. 3; Adam Marsh
lectures at, 358–9; bursaries for poor

scholars at 100–1, 559 n. 1; chancellor
of, *see* Eustace of Normanville; Ralph
of Sempringham; congregation of,
38–41, 466–7; custodian of, *see* John
of Stamford; Peter of Tewkesbury;
disturbance at, 66–7, 300–5;
Dominican Friars at, xiii; Friars
Minor at, xiii, xv–xvii, 416–17, 438–9
and n. 2, 482–3, 486–90, 494–5, 497
nn. 2–3, 558 n. 1; inception
procedure at, 464–7; king and queen
at 66–7; petitions to Grosseteste on
government of, 38–41, 50–1;
privileges of, 66–7; requirements for
inception in theology, 464–70; St
Mary's Church of, 26–7, 252–3,
318–21; seal of, 40–1 and n. 4

P., scholar at Oxford, 316–17
P. of Worcester, Brother, 486–7
papal provisions to benefices, 448–9
Paris, Matthew, *see* Matthew Paris
Paris, University of, xv, 315 n. 1, 316 n. 3,
476–9, 484–5, 489 n. 3, 496–7, 519
n. 2, 522–3; Friars Minor at, 479
n. 3, 496–7
parliamentary assemblies, xvii, 46–7 and
n. 4, 176–7 and n. 1, 528–9 and n. 3
Parma, *see* John of
pastoral care, Adam's view of, 42–3,
158–9, 186–7, 252–7
Pastoureaux (Shepherds), revolt of in
France and England, xxxi, 56–7 and
n. 1, 76–7
Pateshull, *see* Richard de
Pathy, Philip, 298–9
Paulinus, Brother, 402–3
Pecham, John, scholar (future archbishop
of Canterbury, 1279–92), 314–15
Peter, Master, rector of Wimbledon,
physician to the Queen, 64–5
Peter of Aigueblanche, bishop of Hereford
(1240–68), 446–7
Peter of Aldeham, canon of Lincoln, 98–9
and n. 5
Peter of Pontoise (Pontissera), crusader,
18–19, 324–5
Peter of Savoy, count, earl of Richmond,
78–9 and n. 4, 128–9 and n. 8,
358–63; letter to: no. 145
Peter of Stamford, warden of Lutterworth
Hospital, 164–5, 310–11; letter to:
no. 123

Peter of Tewkesbury, custodian of
    Oxford, minister of Cologne,
    provincial minister of England
    (1254–8), 44–5, 402–3, 410–11,
    418–19, 514–15
Peter of Wileby, Master, 300–1
Petitionibus vestris, privilege of Innocent
    IV, 400–1 and n. 5, 506–7 n. 2
Pisa, *see* Agnellus of
Plumpton, *see* Nicholas of
Pocklington, *see* William of
Pontoise, *see* Peter of
popes, *see* Alexander IV; Gregory the
    Great; Innocent IV
Provence, *see* Eleanor of; Sanchia of
provincial ministers, unnamed, 510–13;
    letters to: nos. 209–10
Pseudo-Dionysius, mystical writings of,
    xxiii–xxiv, 220–1

R. de Frille, Brother, guardian of
    Stamford, 478–9
Ralegh, William, bishop of Norwich
    (1239–42), translated Winchester
    (1242–50), 30–1 n. 2
Ralph, *see* Monk, Ralph called
Ralph of Canterbury, Master, 250–3,
    350–1; letter to: no. 97
Ralph of Corbridge, xvi, 40–1 n. 7
Ralph of Multon, Brother, 530–1
Ralph of Sempringham, Master,
    chancellor of University of Oxford,
    xxxvii, 40–1 and n. 3, 300–3; letter
    to: no. 116
Ravenham, *see* Walter of
Raymond VII, count of Toulouse, 522–3
Reading, 322–3, 440–1, 469–70, 498–9,
    516–17; council at, 128–9, 561–3;
    Franciscan house at, 528–9, 532–3;
    see also John of
Reginald of Bath, Master, 76–7, 294–5;
    letter to: no. 112
Reginald de Stokes, Master, physician,
    regent at Oxford, 62–3, 128–9
Richard, earl of Cornwall (1225–72),
    younger brother to King Henry III,
    king of the Romans (1257–72), 48–9
    and n. 3, 80–1, 84–5, 136–7, 298–9,
    358–9, 360–1, 374–5, 450–1, 550–1
Richard of Cornwall, Master, not fluent in
    English, rector of Scremby (Lincs.),
    canon of Lincoln, 98–9 and n. 6

Richard (Rufus) of Cornwall, Brother,
    438–9, 470–1, 484–5, 488–9, 495–7
Richard of Havering (Averigus), steward
    of Simon de Montfort, 350 n. 18
Richard of Kirkby, Brother, 558–9
Richard de Pateshull, 168–9
Richard de Rupella, knight, 180–1
Richard of Walda, Brother, 542–3
Richard of Waltham, Brother, 420–1
Richard de Wauz, Brother, at the Curia,
    515–16
Richard de Wych, St, bishop of
    Chichester (1245–53), xlii, 174–5;
    letter to: no. 72
Rigaud, Odo, archbishop of Rouen
    (1248–75), 16–19; letters to: nos. 6–7
Risborough, church of, 300–1
Robert, abbot of Dorchester, 224–5 and
    n. 1, 278–9; letter to: no. 89
Robert, runaway Cistercian monk, 170–1
Robert of Abingdon, 300–1
Robert le Bel, canon of Oseney, 15 n. 2
Robert of Easthall (Esthall), bailiff of
    Grosseteste, 70–1 and n. 6, 298–9,
    302–3; letters to: no. 106, 114, 117
Robert of Norton, Master, 294–5
Robert of Rostun, Brother, 434–5
Robert of St Agatha, Master, official of
    the bishop of Lincoln, possibly
    Chancellor of Oxford, 50–1 and n. 1,
    302–3, 316–19, 554–5; letter to:
    no. 127
Robert of Thornham, Brother, custodian
    of Cambridge, 410–11, 422–5, 432–3
    and n. 6, 458–9, 534–5; letters to:
    nos. 177, 221
Robert de Wynkele, Master of Northern
    Nation, Oxford, 58–9 and n. 7
Roger, steward of Bishop Grosseteste
    (post 1249/50), 48–9
Roger de Burewardiscote, 555 n. 4
Roger de Fuldon, Master, 274–5 and n. 1;
    letter to: no. 107
Roger of Langford, 270–1
Roskilde: bishop of, *see* Erlandson, John;
    Franciscans at 22–5 n. 8
Rostun, *see* Robert of
Rufus, Giles, archdeacon of Northampton
    (1246–72), 200–3; letter to: no. 78
Rupella, *see* Richard de
rural chapters, 68–9

St Asaph's, bishop of, *see* Anian I

St David's, bishop of, *see* Thomas of
Wales (Wallensis)
St Germans (S. Gien), Master, 260–1,
306–7
Salimbene, xiv, 119 n. 1
Sanchia of Provence, countess of
Cornwall, 374–5; letter to: no. 154
Sandwich, *see* Nicholas of
Saracenus, John of, translator of Pseudo-
Dionysius, xxiii
Savoy, *see* Peter of Savoy
Scarborough, Franciscans at, 560–1
Sempringham, *see* Ralph of
Sharstead, *see* John of
Simon of London, Master, 184–5 and n. 5
Simon of Walton, 322–3; letter to: no. 132
Solomon of Dover, Master, archdeacon of
Leicester (1252–74), canon of
Lincoln and prebendary of Leicester
St Margaret (1252), 98–9 and n. 4,
204–5 and n. 1; letter to: no. 79
Stamford, *see* John of; Peter of
Standun, *see* William of
Stephen of Vienne, archdeacon of
Canterbury, 428–9 and n. 5
Stockton, *see* John of
Stokes, *see* John of; Reginald de
Stratton, *see* Matthew de
Suffield, Walter, bishop of Norwich
(1244–57), 450–1, 530–1
Sulby (Northants.), church of, 164–5,
312–13, 364–5
Sutton (Kent), 90–1, 148–9; *see also*
Laurence of
Sutton, Master Oliver (alias Lexington),
dean, then bishop of Lincoln
(1280–99), 34–7, 190–1 and n. 18
Syreford, *see* H. de

Taunton, *see* William of
Tewkesbury, *see* Peter of
Thame, prebend of, 184–91
Thomas of Anstan, 294–5; letter to:
no. 113
Thomas of Cornwall 546–7
Thomas of Docking 486–7
Thomas of Eccleston, chronicle of, xiii,
xvi
Thomas of Hales, Brother, 176–7, 542–3
Thomas of Verdon, Master, 72–3
Thomas of Wales (Wallensis, Waleys),
archdeacon of Lincoln, bishop of St

David's (1248–55), 124–5 and n. 4,
458–9
Thomas of Wicke, 470–1
Thomas of York, Brother, xxxvi, 22–5,
64–5, 170–1 and n. 1, 438–9, 450–1,
454–5, 465–70, 474–5, 482–3, 497
n. 2, 516–17, 538–43; letters to:
nos. 224–5; *Tabula Trinitatis* by,
538–9
Thorney, *see* Henry of
Thornham, *see* Robert of
Thornton Abbey (Lincs.), 124–5
Tihehurst, 468–9
Toseland, lady of, 432–3
Tracy, Eve de, 36–7 and n. 1
Travers, John, sheriff of London, xiii
Trinitarian Friars at Paris, 522–3; letter
to: no. 214
Trivet, Nicholas, Chronicle of, xliv
Tusculum, cardinal-bishop of, *see* Odo of
Chateauroux

Uffington, *see* John of

Valence, *see* Aymer de
Ver, Brother G. de, 434–5
Verdon, *see* Thomas of
Vienne, *see* Stephen of
Vincent, Master, 156–9

W., Brother, vicar of provincial minster in
England, 472–5; letter to: no. 193
W. of Lichfield, Master, 628–9
Wadingham, *see* Nicholas of
Walda, *see* Richard of
Wales, *see* Thomas of
Walter, prior of Newnham, *see*
Chauverture, Walter de
Walter de Bradley (Bradele), keeper of
Queen's Wardrobe, xxxviii, 274–75
n. 1, 368–9; letter to: no. 108
Walter of Evesham, Brother, sent to
improve the Irish province, 420–1
Walter de Merton, 558–9
Walter of Ravenham, lector at Cambridge,
536–7 and n. 3
Walter de Werth, canon of Oseney, 15
n. 2
Waltham, *see* Richard of
Walton, *see* Wimon of
Warin of Ashwell, 562–9; letter to: no. 242
Warin de Munchensy and his wife,
Denise, 60–1 and n. 15

Warner, vintner of Oxford 320–1

Warwick, *see* John of

Wauz, *see* Richard de

Werth, *see* Walter de

Westminster, *see* Edward of

Weston, *see* John of

Wicke, *see* Thomas of

Wileby, *see* Peter of

William, Master, clerk of Archbishop of Canterbury, 52–3

William of Arundel, archdeacon of Huntingdon, glossator, 216–17

William of Basing 542–3

William of Cerde, 214–15

William of Cirencester, 366–7

William of Durham, Master, 316–17 and n. 3

William of Hadley, Brother, 486–7

William of Hemingborough, 313–14; letter to: no. 125

William of Lechlade, deacon, 26–7

William of Lincoln, marshal of Grosseteste, 104–5

William of Ludlow, Master, 160–1 and n. 1

William of Nottingham, English provincial of the Friars Minor (1240–54), 314–15, 358–9, 394–5, 400–60, 464–73, 476–509, 512–19; letters to: nos. 168–76, 178–88, 190–2, 195–208, 211

William of Pocklington, Master, Adam's secretary, 44–5 and n. 4, 72–3, 96–7, 102–3, 256–7 n. 1; letter to: no. 100

William of Standun, Master, 294–5

William of Taunton, prior of St Swithin's, Winchester, 31

William of Worcester, Brother, 400–1

Winchester: bishops of, *see* Ralegh, William; Valence, Aymer de; prior of St Swithin's, *see* William of Taunton; royal palace at, 403 and n.; St Swithin's chapter of, 12–13; hordarius of cathedral priory, letter to: no. 92

Windsor, court at, 128–9

Worcester, *see* John, Brother of; P. of; William of; bishop of, *see* Cantilupe, Thomas; custodian of, 474–5

Wych, *see* Richard de

Wynkele, *see* Robert de

York, *see* Thomas of York; archbishop of, *see* Bovill, Sewal de